MEETING HOUSE

2 Litchfield Road
Londonderry, NH 03053
Meetinghouseofnhdems@gmail.com

Praise for *Mystery on the Isles of Shoals*

"Most New Englanders think they know all about the brutal Smuttynose Island ax murders. I know I did. But once I began Robinson's new book, I truly couldn't put it down. The massive amount of new details he has uncovered are not only wonderfully horrific but are skillfully woven into a fascinating look at that time in our history. This is a superb piece of work."

—Judson D. Hale, Sr., editor-in-chief, *Yankee Magazine*

"J. Dennis Robinson opens one of history's most compelling cold cases and solves it with aplomb. This a gripping page-turner that will keep you up nights—so vibrant you can smell the brine and the blood and see the island shores. Lizzie Borden's got nothing on Louis Wagner."

—Andrew Vietze, bestselling author of *Boon Island*

"J. Dennis Robinson unravels history and mystery into one of the most entertaining and informative books I've read in years."

—Ernest Hebert, professor of English, Dartmouth College, and author of the acclaimed Darby Chronicles

"Robinson's book is thoroughly captivating. Why, Robinson asks, can we not let stories about murder end? This question cuts to the heart of genre. His meticulous study of the Smuttynose murders is an exceptional entry in the canon of American true crime literature."

—Elizabeth Hewitt, associate professor of American literature and popular culture at The Ohio State University

"Robinson places the Smuttynose murders in a wide historical context, encompassing a time when small fishing villages gave way to summer resort hotels and when a national press reported and fed rampant rumors. In this telling, the author considers how fact informed rumor and gossip informed fact as the accused, local residents, the authorities, and the press created multiple narratives of this infamous crime."

—Elizabeth De Wolfe, professor of history, University of New England, and author of *The Murder of Mary Bean and Other Stories*

"Robinson's book has the scope and sweep of a great novel—except that every word is true."

—Rodman Philbrick, Newbery Honor–winning author

"Many authors have written about the infamous Smuttynose murders, but none has delved as deep as J. Dennis Robinson. The reader is transported to the rough side of Portsmouth in 1873 and learns how police work and justice were carried out. An impressive work!"

—Peter E. Randall, popular New England publisher, author, photographer, and filmmaker

"Case closed! J. Dennis Robinson's meticulously detailed account solves the famous Smuttynose murders once and for all. It is entertaining, fascinating, and horrifying, all at the same time."

—Emerson W. Baker, History Professor at Salem State University and author of *The Devil of Great Island* and *A Storm of Witchcraft*

"Enjoyed every page! This book is a reader's delight, combining the thrills of a murder mystery with the intrigue of a courtroom drama—all of it played out against a colorful backdrop of nineteenth-century New England fishing communities and island resort hotels."

—Carolyn Gage, award-winning Maine playwright

"For decades there have been many questions about the murderous events that took place on the historic Isles of Shoals back in 1873—taking the lives of two innocent women—but J. Dennis Robinson expertly and skillfully peels away the legends and myths to get to what really happened. Highly recommended."

—Brendan DuBois, award-winning mystery author of *Fatal Harbor*

"Spoiler Alert! 'This book is not a whodunit. We know who did it.' So says author J. Dennis Robinson, whose reexamination of the Smuttynose murders is a form of the finest forensic journalism. Much like Truman Capote, Vincent Bugliosi and Joe McGinniss, he elevates the true crime genre to the realm of literature."

—John Clayton, author of *You Know
You're in New Hampshire When . . .*

"Eighteenth-century history with twenty-first century cultural sensibility . . . a riveting tale told by a truly gifted and graceful teller of tales. I loved it!"

—Rebecca Rule, New Hampshire–based author

"An outstanding book. I predict this will become the gold standard for works about the historic Isles of Shoals."

—Jane E. Vallier, author of *Poet On Demand: The Life,
Letters and Works of Celia Thaxter*

"It's all here—stunning shoe-leather detective work, vivid depictions of character, a genuine feel for the historical Isles of Shoals landscape and period boats, and a compelling case that would make any prosecutor proud. Robinson looks evil in the eye and doesn't flinch."

—W. Jeffrey Bolster, Bancroft Prize–winning author of *The Mortal Sea:
Fishing the Atlantic in the Age of Sail*

Other Books by J. Dennis Robinson

UNDER THE ISLES OF SHOALS
Archaeology & Discovery on Smuttynose Island

AMERICA'S PRIVATEER
Lynx and the War of 1812

STRAWBERY BANKE
A Seaport Museum 400 Years in the Making

WENTWORTH BY THE SEA
The Life & Times of a Grand Hotel

History books for young readers

STRIKING BACK
The Fight to End Child Labor Exploitation

JESSE JAMES
Legendary Rebel and Outlaw

LORD BALTIMORE
Founder of Maryland

With Richard M. Candee
MARITIME PORTSMOUTH
The Sawtelle Collection

With Lynne Vachon
RICH WITH CHILDREN
An Italian Family Comes to America

MYSTERY

on the ISLES OF SHOALS

CLOSING THE CASE ON THE SMUTTYNOSE AX MURDERS OF 1873

J. DENNIS ROBINSON

Skyhorse Publishing

For my brother Jeff
who loves a good yarn

Skyhorse Publishing books may be purchased in bulk at special discounts for sales promotion, corporate gifts, fund-raising, or educational purposes. Special editions can also be created to specifications. For details, contact the Special Sales Department, Skyhorse Publishing, 307 West 36th Street, 11th Floor, New York, NY 10018 or info@ skyhorsepublishing.com.

Skyhorse® and Skyhorse Publishing® are registered trademarks of Skyhorse Publishing, Inc.®, a Delaware corporation.

Visit our website at www.skyhorsepublishing.com.

10 9 8 7 6 5 4 3 2 1

Library of Congress Cataloging-in-Publication Data
Robinson, J. Dennis.
   Mystery on the Isles of Shoals : closing the case on the Smuttynose ax murders of 1873 / J. Dennis Robinson.
        pages cm

    ISBN 978-1-62914-578-5 (hardback)
    1. Murder--Maine. 2. Maine--History--19th century. I. Title.
    HV6533.M2R63 2014
    364.152'30974195--dc23
                                                2014032738

Cover design by Brian Peterson
Cover photo by J. Dennis Robinson

Ebook ISBN: 978-1-63220-057-0

Printed in the United States of America

TABLE OF CONTENTS

CAPTURE

TRIAL

DEATH ROW

TABLE OF CONTENTS

AFTERMATH

ACKNOWLEDGMENTS

Three things made this project possible. First, I was suddenly given access to the collection of newspaper clippings and articles gathered by the late Dorothy and Dr. Robert "Bob" Tuttle, who had long hoped to write about the Louis Wagner case, but never got the chance. Second, my agent Jake Elwell of Harold Ober Associates said, "Hey, why don't you write a book about those murders on Smuttynose Island?" Third, I received financial encouragement from a wonderful group of sponsors including the Shoals Marine Lab on Appledore Island, the Star Island Corporation, the Isles of Shoals Steamship Company, the Isles of Shoals Historical and Research Association, and Portsmouth Harbor Cruises. It was primarily their support that allowed me to spend eighteen months digging into the facts and writing this book.

I would like to thank my expert readers of early drafts: Captain Sue Reynolds of the tour boat M/V *Uncle Oscar*; Thomas Hardiman, Keeper of the Portsmouth Athenaeum; attorney Thomas Watson; attorney John Perrault; David J. Murray of ClearEyePhoto.com; Isles of Shoals historian and Smuttynose Steward Ann Beattie; Professor C. Laurence Robertson; novelist Rodman Philbrick; former Portsmouth police chief Professor David "Lou" Ferland; Dan Chartrand of Water Street Books; Maryellen Burke of Discover Portsmouth; my editor, Nicole Frail; and my best friend and technology guru, William S. Roy; and Kathryn Cowdrey, for moral support during tough times.

My thanks as always to two local research teams including Nicole Cloutier, Mike Huxtable, and Richard E Winslow III of the Portsmouth Public Library, and to Carolyn, Robin, Ronan, James, Jim, Steve, and Courtney at the Portsmouth Athenaeum. I also received research assistance from Joyce Volk, Elizabeth Farish, Laurence Bussey, Jim Cerny, the Thomaston Historical Society, lighthouse expert Jeremy D'Entremont, playwright Carolyn Gage, Professor Nathan Hamilton, and from William David Barry at the Maine Historical Society, Wendy Pirsig at Old Berwick Historical Society, and Patricia Potter at the University of Southern Maine Library. A special tip of the hat to Maine lobsterman David Kaselauskas who piloted the chase boat as Dan O'Reilly proved how quickly one can row a wooden dory from Portsmouth to the Isles of Shoals. Thanks to Nate Hubbard and Marty Oberlander, the owners of Smuttynose Island, and to my fellow Smuttynose Stewards. And although I never met them, I am in debt to the Vesterheim Genealogical Center in Madison, Wisconsin, to Gloria Nielsen Echarte, and to Tormod Riise, who assisted Dot and Bob Tuttle in their genealogical studies. My thanks to all others who added support and encouragement or argued convincingly through thirty foggy years of pondering this case.

NOTES ON SPELLING AND
WORD CHOICE

With so many varied spellings of locations, Norwegian names, and nineteenth century New England words, to avoid confusion, I usually selected one spelling and stayed with it throughout. I prefer, for example, the modern spelling of the word "ax" instead of "axe," except where quoted by someone else. When it comes to names, Maren Hontvet, the surviving victim, was also called "Mary S" or "Marie" in some source material. The family name Hontvet is sometimes spelled "Hontvedt" and even misspelled "Huntress" in other texts. The spelling for the surnames "Christensen" and "Ingebretsen" are standardized here but appear in many forms. I went with "Ivan" Christensen, the husband of one of the murdered women, sometimes spelled "Evan" elsewhere. I chose "Jorges" Ingebretsen instead of "George" because it rings more Norwegian and distinguishes him from attorney George Yeaton and a host of other Georges who pop up in the story. Louis Wagner's first name is occasionally spelled "Lewis" in newspaper accounts. These variations on names may present problems for those doing genealogical research, but spelling was flexible in those days and even the trial transcriptionist, who took notes phonetically, made his share of spelling errors on words and names with which he was unfamiliar.

When it comes to place names, again, I simplified an array of terms to keep the general reader on track. I used the modern spelling for "Smuttynose" Island instead of "Smutty Nose" or the hyphenated version, except where quoted in an earlier work. "Hog Island" was renamed "Appledore Island" in 1848 and I use the version that is appropriate for the time being discussed. "Gosport" is the name of the New Hampshire town that existed on Star Island from the mid-1700s until soon after the building of the Oceanic Hotel when the town ceased to exist. These three islands are key to our story and are among the nine members of the Isles of Shoals (sometimes spelled "Isle of Shoals" in earlier accounts). You may find other texts that refer to the islands collectively as Gosport, or more accurately as "Gosport Harbor," a term I use to describe the ocean harbor inside the breakwater linking Star, Cedar, and Smuttynose Islands today.

The three key islands each had a major hotel at some point, the Appledore on Appledore Island, the Oceanic on Star Island, and the Mid-Ocean House (or Haley House) on Smuttynose. Only the newest hotel, the Oceanic, is still standing. The older of two surviving houses on Smuttynose Island today is the "Haley Cottage," a term I use to distinguish it from the much larger Haley Hotel that once stood next door. The duplex where the crime took place also burned long ago. It is traditionally known as the "Hontvet House" or the "Red House," while the newspapers sometimes dramatically called it the "Wagner House" or "Murder House" in later years.

While they differ slightly in design, I use the term "dory" and "wherry" interchangeably, but readers may simply imagine any traditional wooden rowboat. A "schooner" here is a much larger vessel with sails.

In its founding years, the city of Portsmouth, New Hampshire, where much of this story takes place, was called "Strawbery Banke." That name was discarded in 1653. Three centuries later, in the 1960s, Strawbery Banke Museum opened on the site of the original English settlement, sometimes also called "Puddle Dock." The ten-acre campus of historic houses, using the archaic spelling, is now one of the city's most popular tourist sites. The riverfront museum is located on Marcy Street, formerly Water Street, which is a key scene in this story.

And finally, any reference to the "Chronicle" here indicates the *Portsmouth Chronicle*, and the "Atlantic" is the *Atlantic Monthly*. For brevity, I often refer to the *Portsmouth Times* as the "Times," while any citation from the *New York Times* is fully spelled out. Hopefully the context will make these minor details transparent throughout.

INTRODUCTION

In March of 1873, a powerful young fisherman stole a wooden dory and cast off to commit the perfect robbery. He rowed ten miles from Portsmouth Harbor in the dark of winter to a tiny isolated island off the coasts of New Hampshire and Maine. He slipped silently into the only occupied house on barren Smuttynose Island. The thief knew the door would be unlocked. He knew the three fishermen who lived in the duplex would be gone all night and that the two women remaining on the island would be sleeping unprotected. He knew, or thought he knew, where six hundred dollars lay hidden in a wooden trunk.

But the robbery went horribly wrong. There was a third woman sleeping in the dark in the kitchen of the small apartment. She woke when the thief entered. She cried out, waking the other women. There was an ax leaning just outside the door—and the perfect robbery became a gruesome double homicide. One of the women, wearing only her nightclothes, escaped through a window onto the frigid rocky island. The killer searched for her in vain. Then, leaving two mangled bodies behind, he cast off into the dark sea, rowing desperately toward the mainland, racing the sunrise.

Two decades before Lizzie Borden was acquitted of hacking her parents to death with a hatchet in Massachusetts, America met Louis Wagner, the "Isles of Shoals murderer." Thousands tried to lynch him in the streets. Thousands more visited the handsome fisherman in his jail cell or read about him in the newspapers or bought his photograph for a quarter. Many were mesmerized by Wagner's charming blue-eyed gaze, his religious conversion, his detailed alibi, and his protestations of innocence.

In more than two years between his capture in Boston and his execution on the gallows in Maine, Louis Wagner became a darling of the Victorian media. His jailhouse antics, including a highly publicized prison break, were unprecedented. His lawyer's quirky legal attempts to keep Wagner from the gallows only added to his reputation. The newspapers called him "inexplicable" and "one of the most remarkable criminals the country has yet produced." On the day of his death, a reporter for the *New York Times* predicted that Wagner's case "may hereafter be quoted by students in psychology endeavoring to unravel the mystery of human crime."

So this book is not a whodunit. We know who did it, or at least, I know. Others disagree, sometimes wildly. I have been listening to conspiracy theories and tales of Wagner's innocence for decades. Almost a century and a half after the two innocent victims were buried, people along the Maine and New Hampshire coasts still get riled up over the details of the infamous "Smuttynose Murders." Teachers examine the trial transcript in their classrooms. Tourists hear the story on ferry boats that circle the Isles of Shoals, which comprises nine islands. The murders have been fictionalized in a bestselling novel, acted out in local theaters, choreographed into a ballet, examined on television documentaries, and released as a Hollywood movie. Everybody has an opinion, but few know the facts.

I first heard the story in a ballad by Maine poet and folksinger John Perrault, who was also a practicing criminal attorney. In "The Ballad of Louis Wagner," the poet confronts the ghostly figure of the murderer wandering the foggy waterfront of Portsmouth, New Hampshire. Perrault imagined Wagner, an impoverished and handsome Prussian immigrant, as a character straight out of the pages of Russian literature. Like the ax murderer Raskolnikov in the classic novel *Crime and Punishment*, Wagner seemed to operate within his own moral code. Wagner, however, remained unrepentant to the end.

John Perrault heard the story from Rosamond Thaxter, who summered in the two surviving houses on Smuttynose Island. Rosamond's grandmother, Celia Laighton Thaxter, lived on Smuttynose as a child in the 1840s. Celia's father, Thomas Laighton, built the large and successful Appledore Hotel at the Shoals, luring the wealthy, adventurous, and artistic folks of Boston and other cities to the romantic island resort. Celia's family rented the Red House on Smuttynose Island to a doomed Norwegian fishing family and employed Karen, one of the victims, as a hotel maid. Celia heard the gory details of the murders on the morning following the attack directly from the mouth of Maren Hontvet, the only survivor. An accomplished author in her own right, Celia Thaxter later reported her version of the bloody story in the prestigious *Atlantic Monthly*. Her often-anthologized 1875 article, "A Memorable Murder," has been hailed as one of the best essays in American literature and went a long way toward keeping the island tragedy in the public eye.

The horrific death of Karen and Anethe Christensen continues to be recycled in New England publications. Along the coast, according to one newspaper, it remains "the most remarkable of all stories in criminal history." But it was Harvard-educated librarian Edmund Pearson who reopened the case to a wider audience with his 1926 book *Murder at Smutty Nose and Other Murders*. Considered a father of "true crime" writing, Pearson crafted a detailed study and convinced many readers of Wagner's guilt. But his book also stirred the pot for a new generation of armchair detectives. Isles of Shoals historian Lyman Ruttledge left tantalizing room for doubt in his privately published booklet in 1958 titled "Moonlight Murder at Smuttynose," still in circulation today. A 1980 article in *Yankee Magazine* detailing Wagner's crime was followed in a later issue by a "shocking response" from a reader. Picking up on a century-old legend, the *Yankee* reader claimed that Maren Hontvet, the surviving victim, killed her sister and sister-in-law in a jealous rage. Novelist Anita Shreve took that theory and ran with it. Shreve, who says she was "haunted" by the infamous Shoals murders, fictionalized the historical events in her 1997 bestseller *The Weight of Water*. Drawing heavily on the actual transcripts of the 1873 Wagner trial, Shreve invented a deathbed confession letter from Maren, spawning yet another generation of conspiracy theorists. *The Weight of Water* was adapted into a film of the same name by Academy Award–winning director Kathryn Bigelow.

Every summer, I spend a week on Smuttynose Island. As a volunteer steward of the privately-owned island, I keep an eye on the tourists who sail, row, or motor into the tiny cove. I clear the walking trail to the back of the primitive island, now occupied almost exclusively by seagulls, muskrats, Norway rats, and green snakes. The rocks are streaked with white guano and rodent scat. The nettles, thistles, and poison ivy thrive among wildflowers, abandoned stone walls, and craggy sycamores.

There is no easy access to the island, never has been. The stone pier used by fishermen has long been abandoned. There is no dock and the cove drains completely with every tide leaving any boat high and dry. Visitors must clamber up over a large slippery boulder to reach the sloping lawn where the two houses stand. There are no permanent residents of the island today. There is no road, no electrical power, no plumbing, no public restroom, no snack bar or souvenir stand, not even a tree in sight. The island's fresh water cistern, ringed with large stones where the murderer washed up in the winter of 1873, went brackish decades ago. We stewards row across the harbor each day for fresh water and mow the lawn where the victims' lifeless bodies once lay.

Stewards spend a week living in the rustic 1770-era Haley Cottage that tourists often mistake for the site of the murder. I patiently explain to them that the Hontvet "murder house" burned long ago. I point out the loose rock foundation partially hidden in the tall grass where the building once stood. I carefully tick down the facts of the crime and the trial based on my many years of research. But all too often a visitor knows better. No one could row a wooden dory ten miles to the Shoals and back in a single winter's night, the visitor explains. It is just not possible. Besides, our guest has it on good authority that Louis Wagner was framed. His defense attorney was inept. The police conspired against him. An innocent man was hanged while the real killer escaped capture. The visitor learned the truth, I'm told, from a novel or saw it in a movie or read about it online. Sometimes I argue back. Sometimes I bite my lip until I can taste the blood.

The goal of this book is to set the record straight. Like Celia Thaxter, Anita Shreve, Edmund Pearson, and countless others, I have been haunted by this tale. It is time, once and for all, to ease the disquieted spirits of the victims, to restore the reputation of the surviving woman, and to send the killer back to hell. But to do so, I'm afraid, we must come to know Louis Wagner. Wagner not only robbed these women of their lives and property, but he also stole all the headlines. It is Wagner, complex as he may be, who is the most documented and best remembered character in this tale. And it is Wagner's own twisted words and actions that form the noose from which, should I succeed, he will be hanged again before your very eyes.

As an historian, I know full well that truth comes at a cost. By breaking open the Wagner case once more, this book will inevitably engender another wave of skeptics and naysayers ready to ignore the obvious and dispute the minutia. Wagner's picture will be more widely distributed, while the women who were killed, of whom no photographs are known to exist, will remain obscure. He will make his way onto more websites and show up on more Internet searches. An army of exploitative "ghost hunters" will comb the murder site with bogus electrical equipment to record imaginary hauntings. But as a history writer, if I just sit by, I become an accessory to murder. I cannot allow the fictions, rumors, and false theories to roam free when I possess the firepower to take them down.

On the surface *Mystery on the Isles of Shoals* is a shocking true crime story, gothic horror tale, and courtroom drama. But, for me, the real mystery of the Wagner case is why we so often tell the story wrong. Why can't we handle the truth? Why won't we let the story end? Why don't we trust that the police, the prosecuting attorneys, and dozens of witnesses got it right? And why, against all evidence and based solely on the killer's seductive words, do we continue to search for a reasonable doubt that will upend the jury's verdict?

There is much more worth uncovering here. The Isles of Shoals have many deep secrets to unpack. "New England was settled," according to popular historian Brian Fagan, "not by Pilgrims escaping persecution . . . but by roistering cod fishermen." Those earliest of European fishermen, our forgotten founders, staged their profitable operations right here, drying and salting their valuable cod on the same flat rocks of Smuttynose Island where Wagner felled his victims.

Karen and Anethe, like Wagner himself, were members of a dying breed. They belonged to a centuries-old tradition of fishing families who clung to the barren islands like barnacles. One or two seasonal lobster fishermen still work from the Isles of Shoals. But in the very year of the murders, the entire fishing village on nearby Star Island disappeared. In debt and unable to survive on dwindling fishing stocks, the last of the Shoalers sold their homes and moved permanently to the mainland. At the very hour when Maren Hontvet, bloodied and half frozen, was screaming for help, carpenters at Star Island nearby were tearing down the fishermen's huts and replacing them with a huge, gleaming, modern hotel. And even as Louis Wagner was standing trial for his crimes in the summer of 1873, a horde of Victorian tourists were swarming toward these little rocky islands. They came to escape the stench of their polluted industrial cities and to breathe in the fresh salt air. But they also smelled blood. The tourists arrived by the hundreds, by the thousands, dressed in their fine city fashions. Then they rowed, clumsily, or were ferried across the ocean harbor by the last of the island fishermen. The curious visitors crawled over the rocks in Smuttynose Cove and up the slope to a plain weather-beaten house. They stared, shocked but thrilled, upon the scene of what the newspapers were then calling "the crime of the century."

J. Dennis Robinson
Portsmouth, NH 2014

PROLOGUE

Evening, March 6, 1873

Smuttynose Island was dead quiet. The bodies of the two murdered women had been lying half clothed on the icy floor of the empty house for upward of seventeen hours. The killer had fled long ago and was still at large. Maren Hontvet, the surviving victim, had been rescued early that morning by a dory fisherman from a neighboring island at the rocky Isles of Shoals off the New England coast. Fragments of her horrific story had by now drifted back to the mainland and leaked into the late edition of the local newspaper, transforming the peaceful citizens of Portsmouth, New Hampshire, into a frenzied vengeful mob.

"The men who come from the Shoals are so excited that it is impossible to get many particulars from them," the *Portsmouth Daily Evening Times* admitted, "and this news reached us just as we go to press."

So the earliest printed reports were understandably flawed. The first victim identified was Karen Christensen, a Norwegian immigrant, not "Cornelia" as the newspapers called her. The second victim was her sister-in-law, Anethe Christensen, whom the report listed as "Annetta Lawson." The *New York Times* reported they were two German girls. The women had "quite a large sum of money, and that is now missing" the *Portsmouth Daily Chronicle* erroneously added. The thief, they would soon discover, had taken roughly sixteen dollars.

"They were killed with an axe by some person as yet unknown," the *Evening Times* continued, "although the people who live there have no doubt in regard to his identity.... The suspected man is a Mr. Lewis [sic] Wagner. He is said to be a desperate character."

It was early Thursday evening by the time the Portsmouth newsboys began shouting the headline "TERRIBLE TRAGEDY AT THE ISLES OF SHOALS." Demand for newspapers was so great that copies quickly ran out.

Directly across the deep swirling Piscataqua River, at the Portsmouth Naval Shipyard, a solemn group was filing onto a steam-powered tugboat to visit the murder scene. Despite its name, the historic Portsmouth Naval Shipyard, founded in 1800, is located in Kittery, Maine. The Piscataqua, one of the fastest-flowing rivers in the nation, divides New Hampshire from Maine. That invisible border extends three miles to the mouth of the river and another seven miles out to sea where it splits the nine tiny Isles of Shoals between the two states.

It was 6:45 p.m. by the time the coroner's jury began their grim mission. A team of at least fifteen men including doctors, reporters, law enforcement officers, and observers settled in for an hour-long ride inside the large heated cab of the USS *Mayflower*. The iron-hulled tug, designed during the recent Civil War, pulled slowly away from the dock and into icy waters. The trailing cloud of coal soot was all but invisible against the black sky and the black water. The 137-foot tug appeared in silhouette as it chugged past Portsmouth Harbor Light off the starboard bow and soon the glimmer of Whaleback Lighthouse on the port side. Here the surging Piscataqua River met the sea. Then the tug faded to a speck of gaslight against the open ocean.

Aboard the USS *Mayflower*, reporters representing six or seven newspapers, mostly from nearby Boston, clustered around one man. The *Evening Times* had mistakenly called him "Mr. Huntress," his nickname among the island fishermen, but his name was John C. Hontvet. A fair-haired Norwegian immigrant, he was captain of the fishing schooner *Clara Bella*. He was the man who rented the only house occupied year-round on Smuttynose Island. John's landlords, the Laighton family, owned the big tourist hotel on Appledore Island at the Isles of Shoals. It was John Hontvet's wife, Maren, who had survived the deadly attack and who had named Louis Wagner as the killer. And it was John, his brother, Matthew, and his brother-in-law, Ivan, who had first seen the bodies of the slaughtered women that same morning when they arrived home on Smuttynose Island from an overnight fishing trip.

Now, despite the darkness and the chill, the coroner's team was on a mission to gather the facts and uncover the truth. The *Mayflower* followed the route the suspected killer had taken the night before as he rowed mightily toward the few flickering lights at the Isles of Shoals, following the invisible ocean border separating New Hampshire from Maine. The steam engine slowed to a crawl as the tug rounded Appledore Island, home of the famous poet Celia Laighton Thaxter and her family's summer resort. The expansive wooden hotel was dark but there were lights visible in the poet's cottage. A few lamps also flickered on Star Island to the right on the New Hampshire side of the cluster of flat islands, little more than rocks sticking out of the sea. The flame at the top of the lighthouse tower on White Island, a mile further to the south, helped define Smuttynose Island, a gray shape floating like a drowned giant in the near blackness. At night and from this direction, the long black point of rock stretching to the southeast would not be visible. That is the smudged or "smutty" nose from which the island takes its curious name.

The captain of the *Mayflower*, a man named Baker, guided his ship into the rocky inlet below the darkened Appledore Hotel. The crew secured a mooring and the captain cut the engine. To the reporters and members of the coroner's jury—men familiar with the constant clanks, hisses, and squeals of Victorian city life—the silence of the Shoals must have been stunning. After a momentary sense of deafness, the human ear quickly tunes itself to subtler sounds. The murmur of a gull, the distant clang of a navigation buoy, and the slapping of water against the hull of a ship rushed in to fill the emptiness. One feels, in the silence of the islands, that it is possible to hear everything for miles in all directions.

It was now eight p.m. and, with the exception of the tugboat lamps, it was fully dark. The pale three-quarter moon had barely risen. One by one, the reporters, doctors, lawmen, and witnesses climbed awkwardly over the railing of the sturdy tug and down a cold ladder into a tiny fleet of fishing boats that bobbed in the waves below. It was only a short pull of the oars, no more than half a mile, around the tip of Appledore Island and across a fast-flowing channel to Gosport Harbor and into Smuttynose Cove. But for men unused to the sea at night, it could be a heart-stopping ride. With a fresh breeze and a now choppy sea, one group of nervous reporters almost capsized their launch, filling the boat halfway to the gunwales with numbingly cold salt water.

In the silence, the wooden boats screeched as the landing party hauled them across pebbles, fish bones, and broken seashells in the sandy cove. The men secured the boats against the dark stone pier slick with cold seaweed. No light shown from any of the dark ramshackle buildings encircling the cove. There was nothing here, at first, but a billion flickering stars and the stench of rotting fish.

Thrusting their glaring lanterns at arm's length, the coroner's team followed John Hontvet over the stone boulders and up the slippery incline toward a stark, scarlet-colored building. Shoalers called it the Red House, but at night the two-story duplex was as black as the other shadowy structures on the island. The snow was flattened all around by the footprints of those who had first visited the murder scene earlier that day.

An ax, a key piece of evidence, still lay in the snow by the front of the house, its handle broken and the blade thick with frozen gore. What had been gruesome by daylight had grown fearsome by night. A large flat rock not far from the corner of the house was coated with dark blood. A long streak of blood trailed from the rock to a door marked with a stained handprint. Mr. Hontvet ushered the first of the observers through the narrow doorway on the right side of the duplex, through a cramped entranceway hung with coats, and into the kitchen, lit now only by their sputtering lamps. Anethe Christensen's half-frozen body still laid face up in the center of the kitchen floor near the stove, her head toward the door. Her "lower extremities" were unclothed, according to Dr. Daniel W. Jones, one of six members of the coroner's jury. A cloth or napkin was tied tightly around her neck. One hand was clenched. Someone covered the woman's partially naked form with a stray garment.

The doctor and others on the team placed the bludgeoned corpse of the once-beautiful twenty-five-year-old Norwegian immigrant onto a wooden plank and lifted it onto the kitchen table for a hasty medical examination. They had to clear aside the blood-stained dishes where the killer had apparently eaten a meal of tea and cake before making his escape back to the sea. Anethe's face was savaged beyond recognition, her skull crushed by a powerful blow.

"The head was, as you might say, all battered to pieces," a member of the coroner's team later testified in court. Anethe's body, the witness said, was "covered with wounds, and in the vicinity of the right ear, two or three cuts broke through the skull so that the brains could be seen running through them."

As the doctors worked and the reporters scribbled in their notepads, the policemen searched the ransacked rooms by lamplight. The floors creaked eerily as they walked. In the other half of the duplex, the officers found Karen Christensen. Her body was partially naked and thrust under a bed. A scarf was wrapped so tightly around the woman's neck that her tongue protruded and her eyes bulged. The feet were straightened out "as if she had been in great agony."

It was past two a.m. Friday morning before the coroner's men reassembled aboard the USS *Mayflower* for the return to Portsmouth Harbor. It was breaking dawn before the Boston and New York reporters could telegraph the gory details to their editors. By Friday afternoon, readers up and down the Atlantic coast knew all about the bloody ax with the broken handle, the smashed furniture, the mangled bodies, and Maren Hontvet's miraculous escape from the Grim Reaper's blade. They were amazed by the news that a clock, apparently smashed during the island attack, had stopped precisely at 1:07 a.m., potentially fixing the time of the murders.

By the next morning, the narrow streets of the old seaport were thick with hundreds, eventually thousands, of shocked and angry citizens. The alleged killer, according to rumor, had already been apprehended in Boston and was headed back to Portsmouth by train under police guard. Armed with brickbats and snowballs, the mob gathered at the city's eastern railroad depot. They were determined to waylay Louis Wagner, a fisherman and the former employee of John Hontvet, as soon as the prisoner arrived. They chanted, "Lynch him! Kill him! String him up!"

But back on Smuttynose Island, it was a calm and peaceful day with spring not far off. Except for the distant tapping of carpenters, who were building a grand new tourist hotel on Star Island, there was only the familiar cry of gulls and the muffled splash of waves against the rocks. Anethe and Karen Christensen still occupied the silent house where the coroner's team had left them. They would lie there another full day, cold and mute, until the undertakers arrived from Portsmouth with their coffins.

I

BACKSTORY

"It is in rather ruinous condition, and only two houses on the island are inhabited. It once contained a population of 400 or 500 souls. This, however, was before the Revolution, and there are no signs of its former prosperity, a few hollows where cellars were once dug, and some moss-covered tombstones."

—Richard Henry Dana on Smuttynose Island, 1843

"It was on this island that one of the most sickening murders in the criminal history of our country was perpetrated....Few events of this kind have been more sensational, or sent such a thrill of horror through the country."

—George T. Ferris, writer, 1882

"Some of us live on Appledore, some of us live on Smuttynose. Some souls take the high way and some take the low."

—Carl Heath Kopf, Boston minister and radio preacher

Chapter 1

WAGNER'S DORY

The lure of the terrible event on Smuttynose is inescapable. The story paints its own picture. We can easily visualize, with the barest of description, a solitary figure rowing a tiny boat on a dark, vast sea. We imagine three women alone on a speck of land entirely surrounded by deep water.

At first glance, it is the man in the boat who is in danger. It is cold and he is tired and very far from land. The women are sleeping, warm and secure in their home. Suddenly the scene erupts to life in a furious collage of indistinct shapes. There are sharp cries and a flash of metal against a backdrop of black and gray. A voice cries out. A blade glints in the moonlight. More silence. At dawn, the scene could be the cover of a pulp detective paperback. We see blood on the snow and an ax by the door, its handle shattered. A woman in a white nightgown shivers in the shadow of a sharp rocky cave as the yellow sun rises.

The killing of Anethe and Karen Christensen, on the surface, is a story so simple and graphic that it cannot be ignored. Almost 150 years later, it is still told and told again. But there is a second tragedy here because, by its simplicity, the story risks becoming a cartoon. For generations, the 1873 murders at the Isles of Shoals have been stripped of their historic context, edited into newspaper columns and magazine features, cleansed of distracting facts, and boiled down to a palatable horror story for tourists. The result is a tale that everyone knows, but no one knows well.

Although it feels timeless, the Smuttynose tragedy is deeply anchored in 1873, a year still powered by horses and ruled by social convention, and yet on the brink of a recognizably "modern" age. Breakthrough communication technology that year included the first typewriter and the first US postcards. Showman P. T. Barnum opened his first circus and outlaw Jesse James robbed his first train. Ulysses S. Grant, a hard-drinking military hero of the Civil War, was beginning his second term as President of the United States, a term remembered for government corruption and a lengthy depression that began with the Financial Panic of 1873. The previous year, Susan B. Anthony had struck a blow for women's rights when she attempted to vote in a New York election. She was arrested and, after her trial in 1873, fined one hundred dollars, which she adamantly refused to pay.

Critics complain that there was only a single suspect in the crime that shocked New England. Louis Wagner, a fisherman recently emigrated from Prussia, was captured the same day as the ax murder of two Norwegian women on an island in Maine. Wagner had lived among the fishing family on Smuttynose, knew the women he killed, and believed that the family kept a significant amount of money in the house. Wagner protested his innocence from his arrest until minutes before he was hanged two years later. No one saw Wagner steal a dory in Portsmouth, New Hampshire, and row ten miles to the Isles of Shoals on March 5, 1873. Only the two victims saw the face of Louis Wagner. He was tried and convicted in a tightly constructed body of circumstantial evidence and hanged. Most who have truly researched the Wagner case agree with the verdict, yet the legends of Wagner's innocence live on.

The media coverage then, as now, was all over the field. A few journalists set out the facts of the Wagner case honestly as they evolved. Other newspapers played fast and loose, disseminating rumors, for example, of a broken love affair between Wagner and one of his victims, or declaring that the gentle and pious prisoner himself was the victim of false evidence planted by the local police. There were later rumors that Mary S. "Maren" Hontvet, the surviving Smuttynose Island victim, had confessed to the murders on her deathbed. But the greatest threat to the facts of the Wagner case must be human nature itself. Our natural curiosity, our desire to oversimplify, to connect the dots without facts, and to jump to conclusions, combined with a culture of cynicism and distrust of authority has turned every criminal case into an open-ended mystery. In a twenty-first-century world addicted to plot twists, double agents, alternate endings, hidden agendas, and conspiracy theories, Louis Wagner has much to offer. His ability to seduce, deceive, and obfuscate have kept his name alive and in the public debate while his victims are almost forgotten.

Even before this story begins, it is vital to put the most common misconception of the Wagner case to death. On a clear day, the Oceanic Hotel and the White Island lighthouse, both nineteenth-century structures, are visible to the naked eye from the coast of New Hampshire. They poke up like small white dots on the blue horizon. The nine small stone islands are so flat that they flicker in and out of view. Beyond them, there is nothing but ocean. It is a good six or seven miles from the nearest point on the Isles of Shoals to the mainland at Rye Harbor and another three or four miles down the wily Piscataqua River to downtown Portsmouth, the only seaport in the "Live Free or Die" state.

"That's impossible," people often say with certainty upon first hearing the story. "No one could row a boat that far and back in a single night." It is one of those spontaneous deductions that sounds obvious at first blush. But like so much of the Wagner story, there is more here than meets the eye.

Rowing to the Shoals is an adventurous, but certainly not a daunting journey for an experienced person powering a small boat under favorable conditions. In the 1800s, it was not uncommon for the fishermen of the Shoals to row their wooden boats to the mainland and back. John Hontvet, Maren's husband and Wagner's employer, testified that he had made the trip propelled by muscle and oars from Smuttynose Island to Portsmouth fifty or sixty times in the few years he lived at the Shoals. Another fisherman testified that he had made the entire distance rowing one way in ninety minutes. True crime writer Edmund Pearson, author of *Murder at Smutty*

Nose (1926), argued that Wagner's defense attorneys never once mentioned the act of rowing to the Shoals in their attempts to raise a reasonable doubt among the jurors. It was not an issue. For men living on the New England coast, this was an entirely familiar and believable feat, though only a desperate or foolhardy man would risk the trip alone on a winter's night.

The trip is not always safe and it is not always wise even in season. Uncounted victims have lost their lives over the centuries in the watery expanse along the Shoals. On a perfect summer afternoon in 1825, for example, seven men and boys returning to Portsmouth from a Sunday school outing were caught in a surprise squall. Not even their experienced captain could save the little pilot boat. Searchers found nothing but a hat belonging to one of the teachers floating placidly on the waves. In 1902 a boat carrying passengers, mostly waitresses from the Oceanic Hotel, capsized in a similar "evil wind" off the Shoals. "The squall took me entirely by surprise," the grief-stricken captain told reporters. "The boat turned bottom up like a flash." Fourteen passengers drowned. That record would stand until the submarine USS *Squalus* sank in 240 feet of water on a test dive off the Isles of Shoals in 1939. Thirty-three crewmen were rescued with a diving bell, but twenty-six sailors were lost.

Yet athletic rowers in fiberglass kayaks and ocean-going rowing shells make the trip every year, often stopping in the cove at Smuttynose Island to explore the flora, the fauna, and historic sites. Today the smart rowers tend to travel in pairs, wearing protective wetsuits and carrying emergency tracking devices. A few years ago, a solo kayaker got stranded on an uninhabited island at the Shoals in bad weather and died of exposure before he was discovered. But there was nothing startling about a dory fisherman rowing a considerable distance in 1873. The crossing—depending on the tide, the wind, the current, and the waves—could take two or three or four hours. We know the tides were favorable on the Piscataqua River on the night of the murder. By eight p.m., the estimated time of Wagner's departure in a stolen boat from Pickering's Dock in Portsmouth's South End, the first three miles' journey to the open ocean would be merely a matter of coasting in the swift outgoing tide with little muscle required.

Roughly eleven hours elapsed between the time Wagner was last seen in Portsmouth and when he was spotted by three witnesses arriving at Little Harbor in New Castle, New Hampshire, the following morning. There he abandoned his boat and made his way back into the city on foot. At a comfortable but unspectacular rowing speed of about three miles per hour, the roughly eighteen-mile round trip could have been completed in four, five, or six hours, leaving at least five hours unaccounted for while the killer was on the island.

Wooden boat builder Greg Hopkins laughs at the notion that rowing to the Shoals is anything special. He has built and sold seven "murder boats" based on what he considers the most likely design of the boat Wagner stole from a fisherman named David Burke. Hopkins works from a shop at his home in Portsmouth about two miles from where Burke's dory disappeared between seven-thirty and eight-thirty p.m. on March 5, 1873.

"My main interest in the murder story is the boat that Wagner rowed out to the Isles in," Hopkins says. "It was probably between sixteen to eighteen feet long. I fashioned my replicas after what locals call a 'wherry.' These were the standard of the region back then, sort of the taxicab of the Piscataqua, for running back and forth across the swift river."

Using an ancient Norse system of overlapping, or "lapstrake" planks, the Piscataqua builders were able to use thinner planks that, when attached to one another, were extremely solid, yet lightweight and cheap to build. The wherries that Hopkins builds today are based on an 1850s design and are trimmed in mahogany. They weigh about two hundred pounds. They are, he says, a bit sexier than other members of the flat-bottomed dory family but functionally the same. The elegant planking system gives the wherry a shapelier front, or "bow." The transom, the panel that forms the back or stern of the boat, is a little higher in the wherry to prevent waves from washing in. Designed to work along the inner two saltwater bays and many tributaries of the Piscataqua estuary, these handcrafted rowboats were incredibly seaworthy and surprisingly fast.

To underline his point, Hopkins brushes a fragrant stack of wood shavings from his work bench, pulls down a book, and points to a passage by Isles of Shoals writer Celia Thaxter. Thaxter's family owned Smuttynose Island and was renting the house to the Hontvets at the time of the tragedy. In her famous 1875 essay, "A Memorable Murder," Thaxter claimed to have seen Louis Wagner a year before the murders. He was fishing solo from a wherry off Star Island, Thaxter wrote, and not making much money.

Reproductions of the Piscataqua wherry are prized today among rowing purists. Two similar historical designs are known as the "Strawbery Banke" or the "Isles of Shoals" dory. The late Aubrey Marshall sparked a revival of these classic wooden boats in the 1970s at Strawbery Banke Museum, a campus of historic buildings on the Portsmouth waterfront. Marshall, whose career began in 1923 at the Lowell Boat Shop in Amesbury, Massachusetts, calculated that he worked on upwards of thirty thousand dories in his lifetime. During his years building boats at Strawbery Banke Museum, his shop was located only yards from the boarding house where Louis Wagner had lived a century before.

"The idea that it is too difficult to row from Portsmouth to the Shoals is silly," Greg Hopkins says, pointing to the skeleton of another boat in progress at his workshop. A sign above reads: PISCATAQUA WHERRY— SMUTTYNOSE MURDER BOAT?

"Making three miles an hour is very easy in one of these," Hopkins says. "Wagner had plenty of time with the tides and the weather in his favor."

Indeed, the eighteen-mile round trip from shore to Shoals and back pales in comparison to the 1,600-mile rowboat journey of Nathaniel Stone in his memoir *On the Water* (2000). Departing from the Brooklyn Bridge, Stone rowed solo from the Hudson River to the Great Lakes, down the Mississippi, along the Gulf Coast, and up the Atlantic seaboard to the Canadian border. While Stone traveled in fiberglass boats, one with a sliding seat powered by his legs and the other with a stationary seat propelled by arm muscles, his crafts were no larger than Wagner's dory. Once accustomed to the trancelike repetition of the oars, rowing one stroke per breath, Stone was able to increase his daily distance to twenty, thirty, even sixty miles per day.

Stone's trip was inspired, he writes, by the journey of Nova Scotia doryman Howard Blackburn. Separated from his schooner in a blizzard in 1883 while fishing off the Canadian Grand Banks, Blackburn rowed for five days with his hands frozen to the oars. Although he lost all of his fingers to frostbite, Blackburn became a successful tavern owner in Gloucester and twice sailed solo across the Atlantic Ocean.

Halfway through his own epic journey, Nathaniel Stone was honored to meet a Canadian named Mark Robbins who twice attempted to row alone in a small boat from Coney Island in New York City, around the coastal United States, to the Yukon in Alaska. Robbins was thwarted twice by sickness and had to abandon his quest, but he managed to complete 5,000 miles of the 6,500 mile trek. His average distance, consistently day in and day out, was forty miles, more than twice the distance Wagner had to cover on that single fateful night.

Stories of locals making the journey are legion. One Portsmouth businessman regularly rows his ocean shell to the Shoals and back before breakfast. Portsmouth-born novelist and sport fisherman Rodman Philbrick, author of *The Young Man and the Sea*, recalls rowing to the Shoals as a boy after hearing about the Wagner murders. "I rowed it from Rye Harbor in a crappy little flat-bottomed rowboat with a short pair of oars when I was about fourteen," Philbrick recalls. "It took me three or four hours and I blistered my hands badly. Then I realized I had to row back."

John W. Downs, the grandson of the last fisherman at the Isles of Shoals, recalled making the journey frequently. "In the early days when we had no power, we thought nothing of rowing a boat eight to ten miles, and hauling in from sixty to one hundred lobster pots, and rowing back again." The colder the weather for these rugged men, the better, since the cod and the mackerel were then most abundant.

In an age of muscle power, seacoast Victorians accepted Wagner's rowing ability without question, but as engines replaced oars, journalists and pulp crime writers exaggerated the story. An August 1964 issue of *Front Page Detective*, for instance, shamelessly mixed facts from the Wagner case with a wholly imaginary set of murder suspects in a semi-fictional piece titled "The Beast from Smuttynose." The blaring introduction to the article says it all: "Nothing human could row so far in stormy seas—except a man inhumanly possessed by visions of hoarded gold and lovely girls left alone on a barren island."

In May of 2013, to quell all doubts, a Maine engineer named Dan O'Reilly took the Wagner challenge. Dan is a ruddy-faced former shipyard worker with a thick gray mustache and a thicker Maine accent. Catching an identical outgoing tide to the one the killer took at eight p.m. on March 5, 1873, O'Reilly pulled out of Portsmouth's South End on a crisp May morning, not far from the dock where Wagner stole his wooden dory. O'Reilly was the sole figure in his replica Piscataqua wherry. He bought the flat-bottomed seventeen-footer more than forty years ago from Aubrey Marshall for five hundred dollars. Half a dozen observers in a thirty-five-foot lobster boat shadowed O'Reilly as he paced himself, pulling smoothly on his oars, not rushing. Within half an hour, Dan had already reached the lighthouse at New Castle, where the swift river meets the sea, a distance of about three miles.

"You're a rock star, Dan!" someone on the chase boat shouted as the rower, following Wagner's proposed path, glided past the historic Portsmouth Harbor Lighthouse and the granite walls of Fort Constitution where the mainland turns to open ocean. Soon he was moving beyond Whaleback Light, just off the Kittery shore. The rower paused only twice during the next seven miles, once to bail out his dory from a "weeping" leak, and once to take a long drink from a bottle of Gatorade. When he eased his dory into Smuttynose Cove, Dan O'Reilly wasn't even breathing hard.

"You made it with time to kill," the captain of the lobster boat shouted. It was a sick joke, but everyone laughed.

O'Reilly's official time from Portsmouth to Gosport Harbor was two hours and fourteen minutes. Admittedly, he was using more streamlined modern oars and better oarlocks than the wooden "thole" pins in Wagner's dory. O'Reilly rowed in the daylight in May, while Wagner rowed on a calm moonlit night in March. But Dan O'Reilly was a seventy-five-year-old amateur rower out for a morning jaunt. Wagner was a strapping twenty-eight-year-old professional dory fisherman in a race with the devil. It was only after proving his point that the white-haired rower revealed that he was a bit "under the weather."

"If I didn't have that damned strep throat, I'm sure I coulda done her in less than two hours," O'Reilly said apologetically as his dory was loaded onto the lobster boat for the return trip to Portsmouth.

Whether Wagner stole David Burke's dory and did the terrible deed for which he was executed in 1875, these pages must prove once again. But to all those landlubbers and flatlanders who question whether Wagner could travel the distance in the allotted time, the verdict is already an unequivocal yes.

Chapter 2

OUR FOUNDING FISHERMEN

From the air, the New Hampshire seacoast is barely a blip on the New England shore. It spans just seventeen miles as the crow flies, compared to an estimated 3,500 miles of twisting waterfront property along the coast of Maine to the north. Yet the city of Portsmouth, the only seaport in the Granite State, teams with tales of the sea. It is only within this rich heritage of maritime facts and maritime myth that we can begin to make sense of the Wagner case.

People were paddling to the Isles of Shoals in wooden boats long before the rise of the first pyramids in Egypt. For millennia, Native Americans hunted and fished here, arriving from the mainland in canoes initially carved out of hollow logs and later fabricated from birch tree bark stretched over wooden frames. We know precious little about the First People of northern New England. The bits we do know come from the oral traditions of their modern Wabanaki descendants, from spotty historical records, and from archaeological digs along the seacoast. We know that nomadic "Paleo-Indians" traveled along the coast of Maine when the last Ice Age receded about twelve thousand years ago. Before that, bison and wooly mammoth populated an ancient tundra that would be covered by a sheet of ice thousands of feet thick.

It was the slow ebb and flow of these glaciers, grinding and scraping, that created Maine's rocky coast and gouged out the undersea fishing area known as the Gulf of Maine. This deep basin or giant bowl of water stretches from Nova Scotia in Canada to Cape Cod in Massachusetts. The Gulf of Maine, often called a "sea within a sea," is so large that it has its own complex system of currents and weather. These currents continually stir up microscopic life forms to the surface where they thrive in the sunlight. The result is a rich protein soup that feeds an array of fish, whales, dolphin, shellfish, and other marine life.

These same glaciers created the nine Isles of Shoals, a lonely archipelago, by flattening and rounding the tips of a flooded mountain range. The origin of the name may come from the large number of fish (called "shoals" or "schools") that migrate close to the islands. Four of them—Lunging, Star, Seavey, and White—represent the only offshore islands belonging to the tiny New Hampshire coastline. The other five—Cedar, Smuttynose, Malaga, Appledore, and Duck—are the first of more than three thousand islands off the long jagged coast of Maine. All nine islands combined make up little more than two hundred scattered acres. From the highest point on Smuttynose, just thirty feet above sea level, all the islands are visible. It is the ideal prehistoric observation point. From here, a Native American could see the entire sweep of the coastline, from modern-day Boon Island and Mount Agamenticus in the county of York, Maine, to the north, past what is now Portsmouth Harbor and the Piscataqua River, and south to Cape Ann on the Massachusetts shore en route to Boston.

"The earliest Indians we've found on Smuttynose Island arrived here about six thousand years ago," says archaeologist Nathan Hamilton. With his summer crew of student diggers working from the Shoals Marine Lab on nearby Appledore, Professor Hamilton has been uncovering the island's history one artifact at a time. More than three hundred thousand artifacts have been unearthed at this writing from the triangular two-acre front lawn of Smuttynose where the Hontvet "murder house" once stood. There is scarcely any soil here, a meter deep at best, but what soil has managed to cling to the bedrock is thick with clues about life on this once-populated fishing outpost.

The aboriginal people of coastal Maine were skilled fishermen who could capture swordfish, shark, other large fish, and even small whales. The Shoals must have been an ideal base camp and rich Indian hunting ground for flightless birds like the great auk, a member of the puffin family, now extinct, and whose bones have been unearthed on Smuttynose. The Isles abound with seals too. Some five hundred of them lounge today on the rock cliffs of Duck Island nearby, and their curious pups occasionally pop up in Smuttynose Cove. Hamilton's diggers have uncovered prehistoric ceramics, burned or "calcined" fish bones, arrowheads, and other stone tools, each meticulously extracted from deposits of clay trapped deep in the island bedrock.

"We know for certain," Hamilton says, pointing to a square hole in the island soil, "that Native hunters sat right here. Here are the stone flakes they left while making their hunting tools. We know that Indians visited here during at least eight separate periods, perhaps hundreds or thousands of years apart. Then the archaeological evidence shows that European fishermen arrived in large numbers on Smuttynose starting in the 1620s—again on this precise spot. By then the Indian fishermen had disappeared."

The first European explorers, at least the first who kept written records, encountered no evidence of Native Americans at the Isles of Shoals. English explorer Martin Pring, the first known European visitor to sail up the deep Piscataqua River to salt water Great Bay estuary, saw only abandoned campfires in 1603. He wasn't looking for fish. Pring was searching for valuable sassafras trees, then considered a popular (though ineffective) cure for "the French Pox," or syphilis. That fact is rarely mentioned in the founding history of New Hampshire. Maine coast explorer Christopher Levett, who visited the Isles of Shoals in 1623, wrote: "Upon these Islands are no Savages at all." Between the visits by Pring and Levett, as many as 90 percent of Native Americans in the region had died in a great pandemic brought on by contact with diseases carried, most likely, by some of the first European traders, trappers, and fishermen. Local historians noted through the centuries that Indians had never lived on the Isles of Shoals until Hamilton's research discovered the truth in 2008.

The first European explorers missed seeing Indians at the Isles of Shoals, but they did not miss the huge commercial potential of the abundant fish and whale populations that thrived in the cold plankton-rich waters of the Gulf of Maine. Captain John Smith, best known for his earlier connection to Jamestown, Virginia, and Indian princess Pocahontas, visited the region in 1614. Smith wrote a glowing report of this area, which he named New England. Smith imagined the first New England settlements not as religious havens, but as high-profit fishing stations. He suggested creating an English industry like that already active in the Canadian Maritimes. Smith wanted to found his American colony on large Atlantic cod—the perfect, portable, protein-rich, low-fat food. The thick, white cod flesh was not fishy-tasting. Amazingly, when freshly split, salted, and dried in the sun, cod could survive for months, even years. Then when soaked in water and cooked, it was still flavorful and nourishing. Dried cod was a welcome change from fish like herring, which was regularly stored wet and pickled in wooden casks that could go rancid. Dried fish from New England, Smith promised his investors, could be as valuable as pearls, silks, and diamonds.

Captain Smith failed in three attempts to found a colony in the Gulf of Maine and died impoverished in London. But his book, *A Description of New England* (1616), contained his famous map of the region and was like a beacon to settlers who followed. Those arrivals include the now-famous band of religious Separatists who settled at Plymouth, Massachusetts, in 1620. But the nation's "Pilgrim fathers" were farmers, as Nathaniel Philbrick points out in his bestselling history *Mayflower* (2006). "Even though they lived on the edge of one of the world's great fishing grounds, the Pilgrims were without the skills and the equipment required to take advantage of it," Philbrick notes.

By 1623, the starving Plymouth colonists were forced to purchase fish, probably salted cod, from the first European settlers in what would become the province of New Hampshire to the north. David Thomson, his wife, Amais, their young son, John, and ten fishermen from England had recently built a fishing outpost at what is now Odiorne State Park, at Rye, New Hampshire. Thomson's original fortified settlement, often called Pannaway, was likely within sight of the Isles of Shoals. New Hampshire proudly takes its starting date of 1623 from the Pannaway fishing settlement.

Thomson had received his patent for land from the same Council of New England that had authorized the Plymouth venture. The Pilgrim military protector Myles Standish, usually depicted as short and stocky, red-haired and with a fiery temper, accompanied Thomson in a fishing shallop from New Hampshire to Plymouth, much to the delight of the desperate Pilgrim settlers in the summer of 1623. Two hundred and fifty years later, following his deadly deed, Louis Wagner would drag his dory ashore not far from the site of David Thomson's first fishing outpost.

While the Pilgrims were rescued from obscurity by nineteenth-century Christian historians and catapulted into American folklore, David Thomson and the first European entrepreneurial fishermen of Maine and New Hampshire remain all but unknown. Captain John Smith himself is scarcely remembered along these Yankee shores except, perhaps, at Monhegan Island, Maine, where he set up his experimental fishing operation, and at the Isles of Shoals. Locals like to think that Smith favored the Shoals and planned to establish the first American colony as a fishing outpost here. In his 1614 New England map, Smith may have named these islands for himself. "Smyth's Isles are a heap together, none near them," Smith wrote during his coastal exploration.

But Smith was only saying about the southern portion of the fertile Gulf of Maine what others had been saying about the Canadian maritime region long before him. In 1597, for example, sea captain Charles Leigh, while fishing for cod in the Gulf of St. Lawrence, reported that: "In little more than an hour we caught with four hooks two hundred and fifty." Atlantic codfish leapt from the sea directly into the fishermen's wicker baskets, he reported. Cod were so numerous that in 1602 one fisherman recorded tossing them back because his boat was quickly overloaded and in danger of capsizing.

Famous explorers named Cabot, Cartier, and Champlain filed similar glowing reports about the abundant sea resources in the New World even before Smith arrived. Rumors persist that the mysterious Basque people, who lived along the borders of France and Spain, secretly fished on the North Atlantic coast before Christopher Columbus "discovered" America in 1492. They were certainly busy at the Grand Banks off Labrador and Newfoundland in the 1580s and 1590s. Shoals historians have long suggested that the Basques may have fished as far south as the Isles of Shoals. Perhaps they gave the Spanish-sounding name Malaga to the tiny island that forms the other side of Smuttynose Cove. It is possible, but there is no evidence, according to archaeologist Nathan Hamilton, that Basques operated on Smuttynose Island prior to the arrival of the Pilgrims at Plymouth. And even if they had, the early history of New England would still be written primarily by Protestants, most of them of British descent, and many of them clergymen. These historians often had little respect for the French to the north and the Spanish to the south who had colonized America before the English arrived. They usually depicted the indigenous people as savages and heathens. And the early chroniclers had few kind words for the lawless, godless, hard-drinking fishermen who led the way to the founding of New England.

The discovery of a seemingly endless supply of fresh cod in the North Atlantic was as important to seventeenth-century Europe as finding an untapped source of oil or natural gas might be to an energy-starved nation today. By the early seventeenth century, the prime fishing grounds of Europe were overfished and in sharp decline. Catholicism, meanwhile, was on the rise, requiring more and more people to abstain from eating meat during frequent holy days. Meat, as Brian Fagan explains in his book *Fish on Friday* (2007), was associated with carnal desires of the flesh, while fish, a popular Christian symbol, was connected to purification, fasting, and atonement. By the 1620s, as the *Mayflower* Pilgrims were settling in, the fishing industry was expanding southward from Canada to the tiny Isles of Shoals. These flat, barren islands, smack in the path of migratory fish, made the ideal staging site for processing dried cod or "stockfish" that was then shipped back to the ravenous European market.

Initially, the English fishermen worked seasonally at the Shoals, making the six-thousand-mile round trip with surprising frequency and safety. As many as six hundred men, mostly living aboard ships, worked at what can only be called island factories on Smuttynose, Hog, and Star Islands. Some fished in teams from small shallops, hooking as many as two hundred to three hundred large fish per man per day. Paid per catch, British fishermen could earn three times their annual salary by making the long trip to America. Each man kept track of his catch by cutting out the fish tongues and impaling them on metal spikes.

While some men worked their boats at sea, crews known as "dressers" processed the caught fish back at Smuttynose Cove. Standing in a row, assembly-line fashion, the skilled dressers performed the same task over and over. The "throater" cut the cod from belly to anus and passed it to the "header" who, after ripping out the entrails, tossed the liver into one basket and the roe into another. Then he neatly sliced off the head of the fish and kicked it into the sea through a hole in the staging platform. The "splitter" then separated the fish flesh from the backbone with lightning-fast movements of his sharp knife. Then the fish were dried, turned, and salted on rocks or wooden platforms called "flakes." Having filled their quota, the ships packed up and sailed home to market. Because fishermen like to keep their prized spots secret, history knew little about the extent of the Smuttynose operation until twenty-first-century archaeological digs.

By the 1640s, it appears, some of these men, mostly from the region around Devon, England, were overwintering on the Isles of Shoals or on the mainland nearby. They began setting down roots in the New World, buying land, building homes, and marrying. Two entrepreneurs who set up operations at the Isles of Shoals, Richard Cutt and William Pepperrell, later became the primary landowners in Portsmouth, New Hampshire, and Kittery, Maine, on opposite shores of the Piscataqua River. In 1647, Cutt complained to the Maine Court that one fisherman had illegally moved his wife, goats, and hogs to Appledore Island, then known as Hog Island. This is the first written record of females at the Isles of Shoals. The ban on "womanhood" was officially lifted in 1650 by which time there were sixty residents at the Shoals. The first fishwife, by the way, was allowed to stay, but the livestock had to go. The animals were ruining the fish stocks and fouling the limited fresh water supply on the island.

By 1675, the population of the Isles of Shoals had reached 275 souls. Fishing families lived mostly in cramped windowless huts. Star Island had its own fort with two cannons to ward off marauding pirates and French mercenaries. The meetinghouse was located on Smuttynose. Both Maine and New Hampshire were then governed by the Puritans of Massachusetts. Then in 1679, New Hampshire regained its status as an independent British province. In 1715, Star Island officially became the town of Gosport, New Hampshire, while Maine remained under the thumb of Massachusetts for another century. Living on a rock at sea was harsh in the best of times. The population of Gosport declined almost to zero during the American Revolution and the War of 1812. It rebounded in the 1800s and crashed with the sale of Star Island in 1873, the year of the murders across the ocean harbor at Smuttynose. In 1876, Gosport Village voted itself out of existence.

Back on Smuttynose Island, archaeologist Nathan Hamilton has laid out a display of artifacts on a rickety picnic table on the front lawn. There are large rusted fishhooks, colorful ceramic shards, glass trade beads, a few flat faded coins, blobs of lead musket shot, and a prized six-sided gambling die carved from bone. The broken neck of a bellarmine jug, what Hamilton calls "the Coke can of the seventeenth century," shows the embossed face of a bearded man. Among the bones of seabirds, pig, goat, and fish, student diggers at the edge of the cove have cataloged more than nine thousand fragments of clay smoking pipes. One broken pipe bowl depicts a rare image of Sir Walter Raleigh being consumed by a crocodile. This rich cache of early trash, Hamilton says, is positive proof that long before Louis Wagner, Smuttynose Island was a key staging area for fishing and trading.

The Golden Age of fishing here, he estimates, was from 1640 to about 1680.

"There was a tavern right here at the cove long ago," Hamilton says. "It was patronized by tough and adventurous men and women. These were the founding American outlaws of the Eastern Frontier—fishermen, ship captains, and maybe some pirates and smugglers in the mix. They were living on the edge in dangerous times. They ate, drank heavily, smoked powerful tobacco, and played games. They haggled over the price of fish, talked radical politics, and traded stories. And we know from the historical record that they broke every law ever written."

The men at the Isles of Shoals broke every law, that is, except the commandment "You shall not murder." That crime would be reserved for a Prussian fisherman named Louis.

Chapter 3

THE WILD WILD EAST

Despite its dangerous association with shipwrecks, pirates, storms, and drowning, the Isles of Shoals have seen few violent criminal acts. A popular rumor says Edward Teach, best known as the fearsome pirate Blackbeard, abandoned his thirteenth or fourteenth wife at the Shoals to guard his treasure, but the claim is pure fantasy. Ghost stories about Bloody Babb "the Butcher of the Shoals" have evolved from the historical character Phillip Babb who was, in reality, just an island hog butcher back in the seventeenth century. And Betty Moody may or may not have smothered her own child while hiding among the cavernous granite cliffs on Star Island. Legend says she accidentally suffocated the infant while attempting to keep it quiet during an attack by Native Americans. The source of the incident may be a raid in 1724, when an Indian party managed to cut loose a few fishing boats and set them adrift—hardly a massacre. There is no evidence that the Betty Moody story is true. It sounds suspiciously like tales told in other New England towns. Another version suggests that Betty Moody was swept away by a towering rogue wave, probably an adaptation of the factual drowning of a Shoals teacher named Nancy Underhill in the mid-1800s. Both women have rock formations named in their honor, a source of much delight to Victorian tourists who picnicked along the granite cliffs.

So Louis Wagner stands alone as the only known and legally convicted killer in four centuries at the Shoals. That statistic seems almost disappointing in a landscape so harsh and treacherous. Jedidiah Morse, one of the many missionaries sent to Christianize the fishers of Gosport wrote in 1800 that "these islands have a dreary and inhospitable appearance, and but for their advantageous situation for carrying on the fisheries, would probably never have been inhabited."

Yet in the early days of colonial New England, an offshore island was an ideal shelter from whatever hostile enemies and wild animals might be lurking in the dense, dark, primal forests of the mainland that stretched endlessly westward. Wolves threatened the first settlers at Strawbery Banke, the 1630 settlement that would become Portsmouth, New Hampshire. While relations with Native Americans remained peaceful ashore for the first half century, conditions changed. Indians, often influenced by the French, finally struck back against broken treaties and mistreatment by English colonists. In 1691, for example, a surprise raid killed twenty-one white settlers at Sandy Beach, the original name for the modern town of Rye, New Hampshire, just inland from the Isles of Shoals. The village of York, Maine, was nearly wiped out by Indians in 1692, and there were deadly attacks at key settlements along the Piscataqua River including Dover, Durham, Exeter, Hampton, and Portsmouth, all named for English cities.

The 1600s represent the heyday of the cod fishing industry during which a tight-knit community evolved at the Shoals. The historic record shows the arrival of men with such colorful English names as Gabriel Grubb, Myles Pyles, William Wormwood, Phillip Babb, Hercules Hunkins, and Fortunatus Home. But these early founding Yankees were then British citizens more closely tied to the world of post-Shakespearian London than to anything we consider "American" today.

"If you met a seventeenth-century fisherman," Professor Emerson Baker is fond of saying to his students at Salem State University, "he would be about as familiar as a Martian." Dressed in thick canvas smocks encrusted with fish guts, fishermen spoke through rotting teeth in English dialects that would be unintelligible today. They imbibed great quantities of beer, rum, and wine, having learned that the polluted water of their homeland was unfit to drink. They had no concept of modern sanitation and believed that immersing the body in water to bathe was unhealthy. Although they lived their lives upon the sea, most fishermen never learned to swim.

"What they did believe in," Baker says, "was the Devil, who they saw as a living, breathing person who walked among them. Our ancestors were highly superstitious. They also believed in a tightly structured immutable universe in which some men were born to be kings and others born to be servants. Women were considered inferior to men and children were created to work, not play."

History has not been kind to the early fishermen of Gosport Harbor. They are often depicted as violent, lawless, poor, godless, stupid, drunken, inbred, and lazy—but question the sources. The written history of the early fishers at the Isles of Shoals came either from records of the Puritan court or from reports by a long string of Christian missionaries. The early provincial court records, often flawed and fractured, included only a litany of crimes and legal squabbles, the colonial equivalent of a newspaper police log or televised courtroom reality show today. The church reports came from ministers seeking more funds in their battle to Christianize the "heathen" islanders.

There is no doubt that the fishermen of the Shoals were heavy drinkers, as was the custom of the time for men who worked on boats at sea in cold weather, and this put them at odds with the pious Puritan lawmakers of Massachusetts. In his well-researched history, *The Isles of Shoals*, published coincidentally the same year as the 1873 murders, John Scribner Jenness recounted cases from the colonial record books. Shoals' fishermen were frequently found dead after heavy drinking. Drunken fishermen fell out of boats, fell off rocks, or were found frozen in their dories or along the shore. The Puritans passed laws against drinking and toasting and against the unlicensed manufacture, import, and sale of spirits. But the Puritans passed laws against just about everything. Besides treason and murder, citizens under their rule could be put to death for a long list of crimes including witchcraft, buggery, and burning a house or ship. Slavery, however, was fully legal and many Puritans were slave owners. Women, or "scolds," who talked back to their husbands or to male officials could be stripped, whipped, fined, or submerged underwater in dunking stools. Even children could legally be put to death for cursing their parents.

In 1667, according to Jenness, a fisherman from Smuttynose named Roger Kelly was hauled into court in the county of York for selling liquor without a license. Kelly's ten customers reportedly drank twelve gallons of wine in a single day while bowling ten-pins over on Appledore Island. These records, as obscure as they may seem to us today, had a direct impact on the Smuttynose murder trial two hundred years later. The case of Mr. Kelly and others were read into the Wagner court record when a legal scuffle arose over which islands were officially located in Maine and which were in New Hampshire.

As we will learn, Wagner's defense attorneys, Rufus Tapley and Max Fischacher, had only their client's word that he was innocent. No witnesses could be found to corroborate Wagner's detailed alibi, so Tapley made many attempts to get his case thrown out of court on a legal technicality. There was no evidence, Tapley claimed, that Smuttynose was actually in the county of York, Maine. Better yet, there was no evidence that Smuttynose was under the jurisdiction of any court. Tapley implied that Wagner could not be convicted by jurors from York if Smuttynose was located outside their jurisdiction.

During the Wagner trial, prosecutor George Yeaton was forced to prove in front of the jury that Smuttynose Island was truly within the state of Maine. This is why Amos Allen, clerk of the records of the County of York, took his place on the witness stand in Wagner's trial. Allen carried with him some of the oldest surviving documents concerning the Isles of Shoals, among the oldest court records in America. Allen handed the ancient records, dating back to 1653, to attorney Yeaton, who read them into Wagner's trial record.

In a sample case from 1681, Robert Marr was on trial for using "opprobrious language" against one Mr. Roger Kelly (likely the same Roger Kelly fined for selling booze to Shoalers a few years before), and to his wife,

Mary. The historical record does not tell us what Robert Marr said that so offended the Kellys, but his punishment was swift. Marr was given the choice of retracting his slander and apologizing in public or he could suffer ten lashes "well laid on" at the island whipping post and pay seven shillings court costs. Marr quickly "declared his sorrow" rather than accept the flogging and promised never to malign the Kellys again. To be certain Marr would keep his word, he was required to post a huge bond of ten pounds to the king and the province of Maine.

The recounting of such ancient crimes at Wagner's trial in 1873 was a questionable tactic at best. The prosecution claimed that colonial court records proved conclusively that Smuttynose and Hog (Appledore) were the only two occupied islands at the Isles of Shoals under the jurisdiction of the county of York, Maine. In addition, a 1684 act named four men from York County "to repair unto Smutty Nose Island and there to hold a Court of Sessions," thereby allowing ancient Shoalers to seek justice without sailing all the way to the mainland. Attorney Yeaton was able to prove, beyond any doubt, that the murders of Karen and Anethe had been within the jurisdiction of York County, Maine. And yet, in all the early records, no crime matched the fearsome deeds of Louis Wagner.

In his history of the Shoals, John Scribner Jenness pointed out that enforcing laws among the independent-minded Shoalers was a risky assignment. The seventeenth-century York constable, for example, identified himself when on the islands by carrying a black stick about five feet long that was topped with six inches of white brass or pewter. In at least one incident, Jenness noted, a gang of ten Shoalers, including one woman, assaulted the visiting constable "by words and blows, and threatening to break his neck on the rocks."

Yet the nasty reputation of the early Shoalers, historian Tad Baker says, may have been exaggerated by the Mass Bay colonists. The more the citizenry of Maine and New Hampshire felt threatened in the seventeenth century, Baker notes, the more they were inclined to remain under the protection of the Massachusetts government.

"The fact that the early Shoalers were repeatedly asking the courts for law and order and pleading with the church to send them ministers suggests to me that these people are not a tribe of wild, drunken fornicators as they are often depicted," Baker says.

Dozens of ministers did their best to save the souls of the island fishermen, but few lasted long. College-educated men, these Christian ministers and their wives often found life intolerable among the impoverished fishing families. Yet when the parish of Gosport called John Tucke to be their minister in the early 1700s, the young Harvard grad embraced the islanders lovingly. Rev. Tucke served more than forty years as their spiritual adviser, doctor, dentist, financial manager, and teacher. He was a true father figure. In return Tucke received a house at Gosport with a garden plot and free firewood, a luxury item on the treeless islands. The minister also was paid a quintal of marketable fish per man per year. At roughly 100 pounds of fish multiplied by 100 fishermen, Rev. Tucke became one of the highest paid clerics in all of New England.

John Tucke and his wife, Mary, had eleven children, but only three survived to adulthood. They kept four enslaved Africans in their household on Star Island. As shocking as that may seem today, slavery was not uncommon in wealthy eighteenth-century New England homes, even the homes of Christian ministers. Tucke died on the brink of the American Revolution in 1773, leaving his dwindling Gosport parish in ruins. Fearing that the British might blockade or even attack Portsmouth Harbor, most Gosport residents abandoned the Isles of Shoals or were cleared off by government decree. Some even dismantled their homes, floated them on barges to mainland New Hampshire or Maine, and rebuilt them there. A forty-six-foot granite obelisk built over the gravesite of Rev. Tucke on Star Island in the early twentieth century is considered New Hampshire's tallest tombstone.

Perhaps two dozen individuals weathered the war years in the near ghost town of Gosport. A single family, the Haleys, lay claim to Smuttynose Island during that era. The New England fishing industry collapsed during the American Revolution along with any system of recordkeeping at the

Isles of Shoals. But by 1800, as the postwar population began to revive, conditions on Star Island seemed to worsen. Legend says that the residents of Gosport even burned their only church for firewood. An observer from the mainland in nearby Newburyport, Massachusetts, was shocked to find squalid living conditions at Gosport. Both adults and children were addicted to alcohol while unmarried couples were raising families. One legally married woman, the visitor reported with horror, had left her husband to cohabit with her uncle "by whom she has a number of children."

"I am convinced," the Gosport observer wrote in the early 1800s, "they are as wretched a little community as ever excited the charity of man."

Chapter 4

THE FIRST TOURISTS

Captain Sam Haley refused to go ashore. During the worst of two American wars against Britain, when most Shoalers fled or were forced to relocate to the mainland, this crusty old sea captain, with his wife, Mary, and the twelve Haley children, carved out a hardscrabble kingdom on Smuttynose, then known locally as Haley's Island. "The people who remained," one historian wrote of this era at Isles of Shoals, "were ignorant, degraded, and worthless." But while the wretched fishers of Star Island barely survived the American Revolution and the War of 1812, it appears that the Haleys on Smuttynose thrived. Besides fishing and running their island store, the Haleys also operated a ropewalk for making rope, a windmill-powered granary, distillery, brewery, cherry orchard, salt-works, boathouse, hotel, bakery, a cooper's shop for making barrels, a brickworks, and a blacksmith shop. Today the stewards who oversee the island still sleep in the squat two-room Haley Cottage, built perhaps as early as 1770. Modern visitors can also see Sam Haley's handiwork in the stone pier and the stone breakwater to Malaga Island that encircle the cove. Legend says that the old captain paid for the breakwater after he discovered five bars of pirate silver, but there is no evidence of that. Like all islanders, the Haleys salvaged whatever gifts the sea delivered, from driftwood to the cargo of shipwrecked vessels.

The most famous shipwreck at the Shoals occurred in the winter of 1813, two years after the death of the old captain. So it was his son, also named Sam

Haley and also wed to a woman named Mary (they had eleven children), who discovered the bodies of fourteen Spanish sailors one frigid January morning. The ship *Concepcion* en route from Cadiz, Spain, had crashed onto the south-easterly tip of the island during a blinding storm. Legend says that a few of the men survived long enough to crawl toward the lamp in the window of Haley's house, but died of exposure before reaching shelter. Gosport town records incorrectly listed the wrecked ship as the *Sagunto*. What booty Haley and his children salvaged from the Spanish ship is unknown. A single sentence in the Haley family bible offers only this brief complaint from Sam Haley: "My sons & what other men I hired picked up 14 of the dead men & buried them in my burying field; but I did not get my pay from any man." Tourists routinely snap photographs of an historic marker at the supposed burial site. However, archaeologists using ground-penetrating radar have yet to find any evidence of the lost Spanish sailors.

Haley and his family managed to gain legal title to Cedar, Smuttynose, Malaga, and Hog islands in Maine. But by 1839, the Haley kingdom was played out. A sketch of Smuttynose at that time shows a complex grid of miniature subdivided lots along the cove and as many as ten wooden buildings of various sizes. Largest of all was the three-story Haley House, built early in the 1800s, that was possibly the first ocean hotel in the region. Little is known about the Mid-Ocean House of Entertainment other than its provocative name. In 1839, just before his death, Sam Haley Jr. sold all four islands and their contents to a mainlander from Portsmouth named Thomas Laighton.

In many ways, Thomas Laighton is the lynchpin of this entire story. Although he died in 1866, years before the infamous murders, Thomas Laighton purchased Smuttynose from the Haleys. His sons, Oscar and Cedric, later rented the house to John Hontvet, a fisherman from Norway. Laighton's wife, Eliza, hired Karen Christensen to work at the Appledore Hotel and "let her go" just days before she was murdered in her sister's house. Laighton's daughter Celia Thaxter first comforted survivor Maren Hontvet on Appledore Island the morning after the murders. Celia later published the gruesome story in the pages of *Atlantic Monthly*. Again, Thomas Laighton's successful hotel led to the tsunami of tourism on the Isles of Shoals that washed away all traces of the ancient fishing village of Gosport.

Like Sam Haley before him, Thomas Laighton was part-hermit and part-entrepreneur. Laighton too preferred scratching out a living on a deserted island to the company of other human beings. Brilliant, energetic, and outspoken, Laighton was forever in search of the ideal occupation to suit his iconoclastic nature. Before leaving the mainland, never to return, he had been the editor of a Portsmouth newspaper, ran a family grocery store, dabbled in politics, and invested in a failed whaling company. In 1839, he took a temporary post as lighthouse keeper at White Island, within view of the four islands he purchased from the Haley family. Laighton brought his wife, Eliza, his four-year old daughter, Celia, and a newborn son named Oscar to the forlorn lighthouse station. They lived in near isolation in a storm-battered house where there was barely enough soil for a backyard garden. Celia later romanticized her childhood days on White Island in her first book *Among the Isles of Shoals*, published the same year as the murders.

Laighton's original plan, once he got his bearings, was to revive the flagging fishing industry at the Shoals and make his fortune. He also tried raising sheep and growing tobacco on his islands. None of his original ideas panned out. He did revive Haley's store on Smuttynose, built on the site of the seventeenth-century fishermen's tavern and six-thousand-year-old Indian hunting ground. The store alarmed the island missionaries across the harbor. They saw Thomas Laighton as little more than a "rum-runner" and a threat to the sobriety of the fishermen of Gosport. Laighton promised not to sell booze to the local fishermen, but that vow did not apply to the patrons of the old Haley hotel. Beginning in the summer of 1842, the Laighton family, now with a third child named Cedric, left their lighthouse to summer on Smuttynose Island. Here, little Celia could run free over twenty-seven wild acres. And here, Thomas Laighton finally had an inspiration that changed not only his life, but also the lives of all the fishers at the Isles of Shoals. The Mid-Ocean House that he had purchased from the Haleys was in "ruinous" condition and yet it still attracted a few adventurous seasonal guests. They arrived with purses full of money to rusticate on the primitive Isles. They craved the healthy salt air, loved the sport of deep sea fishing, gazed upon the scenic sunsets from the hotel porch, and enjoyed a shot or two of Laighton's rum, along with endless bowls of wife Eliza's famous seafood chowder.

When Richard Henry Dana, a lawyer and the author of *Two Years before the Mast,* landed on Smuttynose Island in 1843, he found Thomas Laighton sitting idly by the stone pier gazing out to sea. Dana had taken a room in a fisherman's house on Star Island but found it less than tourist-friendly. "The whole island had a strong fishy smell," Dana later wrote, "and in going ashore we had to walk over a surface of fishes' heads and bones, which the fishermen leave on the beach, just where they throw them."

At Smuttynose, Dana found the irascible Mr. Laighton only a bit more appealing. "I found that he [Laighton] had read a great deal, and was a sagacious man, but had strong prejudices and a dislike of established laws and orders, and of any person who has positions other than his own."

But by 1846, Laighton was reluctantly ready to become an innkeeper. According to his spare diary entries, Laighton gave the old Haley hotel a fresh coat of paint, added new wallpaper, and imported clean linen and potted plants. He planted a little garden in the thin but fertile soil and found it brimful of vegetables and flowers. He even brought over busts of Beethoven and Shakespeare and a piano. He added a bowling alley in the basement. The renovated Mid-Ocean House drew paying customers principally from Portsmouth, Boston, and the North Shore of Massachusetts. Crippled with a lame leg from a childhood disease, Laighton claimed that the "healthful air" of the Shoals had cured him of all illnesses. He considered building a bigger summer sanatorium for invalids on Hog Island. Laighton, a former editor, knew how to manipulate the media. He told a visiting newspaper reporter that he intended to change the name of Hog Island to "Friendly Isle," but he wisely selected the name Appledore.

In the summer of 1846, the Mid-Ocean House guest list included Levi Thaxter, the son of a Boston area banker and a graduate of Harvard Law School. Thaxter was drawn to Laighton's bright young children and agreed to tutor them during a lengthy stay at White Island the coming winter. Thaxter also agreed, using his parent's money, to become Laighton's financial partner in a risky venture. With $2,500 from the Thaxter family, Thomas Laighton was able to build his dream hotel on Appledore. The Appledore Hotel opened for its first season on June 15, 1848, well ahead of the New England tourism boom that was still more than two decades away.

But the deal came at a heavy price. Mr. Thaxter, then twenty-four, had fallen head-over-heels in love with his partner's bright-eyed thirteen-year-old daughter, Celia, and wanted to marry her. Thomas Laighton rejected the union and broke off the business partnership but eventually relented. Celia and Levi were married on the porch of the Appledore House three years later when she was sixteen. That same year, in 1851, Maine approved a total ban on the manufacture and sale of alcohol, making it the first dry state in the nation and a pioneer in the growing temperance movement. But there were always spirits to be found at Appledore, many miles out to sea.

Celia quickly found herself the mother of three rambunctious sons, one of them mentally and physically handicapped. She also found herself married to a much older man who preferred reciting poetry to finding a steady job. Raised at the Isles of Shoals and fiercely independent, Celia did not take easily to marriage or to motherhood. She grew to dislike living off the largesse of her wealthy Boston in-laws, who, at first, called her "Levi's mermaid." There were good years at their house in Newtonville, a town outside of Boston, but she grew lonely. Celia took her frustration out in Victorian verses that were composed, as she told her literary friend, Annie Fields, "between the pots and kettles." In her first published poem, Celia Laighton Thaxter described her sadness at being "land-locked" so far from her beloved islands and family. "I but crave the sad, caressing murmur of the wave that breaks in tender music on the shore," she wrote. Although they never divorced, Celia and her husband soon grew apart. She lived much of her time among family and friends at Appledore, while Levi made his home on the mainland.

While the history of the early Gosport fishermen comes to us from the stern judgmental reports of Christian missionaries, life at the Appledore Hotel usually comes with a romantic or literary turn of phrase. Despite Levi Thaxter's connection to famous artists of New England, it was the beautiful and brilliant Celia who joined their ranks. The summer salons in her cottage next to the Appledore Hotel were attended by the likes of painters Childe Hassam and William Morris Hunt, actor Edwin Booth (brother to Lincoln assassin John Wilkes Booth), musicians Julius Eichberg and John Knowles Paine, and writers from John Greenleaf Whittier and Harriet Beecher Stowe to Sarah Orne Jewett, William Dean Howells, and Henry Wadsworth Longfellow.

As early as 1852, we see the Shoals through the eyes of none other than Nathaniel Hawthorne, who had recently published *The Scarlett Letter* and *The House of Seven Gables*. Hawthorne spent ten days at the Isles of Shoals, meeting up with Franklin Pierce, his former Bowdoin College classmate. Pierce was a New Hampshire native on his way to the White House, where he served one term as the fourteenth president of the United States. Four years later, having set the nation squarely on a course toward civil war, Pierce purchased land at Little Boar's Head in nearby North Hampton, within view of the Isles of Shoals. There he planned to build his own summer resort, but never did.

Writing in his journal in 1852—with the Civil War, the Thaxter's failed marriage, and the Wagner murders still far in the future—Nathaniel Hawthorne painted word pictures of a carefree life at the summer resort. The author chatted with old Thomas Laighton and rowed a dory among the islands with his young son Oscar. Hawthorne played whist and exchanged salty legends and ghost stories with Celia, whom he called "the pretty Miranda." Like so many tourists to come, Hawthorne was captivated by the primitive beauty of the Shoals. "Here one may sit or walk, and enjoy life, while all other mortals are suffering," he wrote.

One overcast day, Levi Thaxter rowed Hawthorne over to Smuttynose Island. Hawthorne was intrigued by the man then managing the Mid-Ocean House for the Laightons. He was an old soldier of Prussian descent who claimed he had fought at the Battle of Waterloo. Hawthorne described him as "a gray, heavy, round-skulled old fellow, troubled with deafness." The author was equally taken by a forlorn, middle-aged skipper in a rotting little fishing boat who stopped in the cove for a shot of rum.

"I know not why," Hawthorne wrote about the skipper, "but there was something that made me smile in his grim and gloomy look, his rusty, jammed hat, his rough and grisly beard, and in his mode of chewing tobacco, with much action of the jaws, getting out the juice as largely as possible, as men always do when disturbed in mind."

Levi Thaxter and Nathaniel Hawthorne wandered all over Smuttynose Island together. They visited the grave of Captain Sam Haley just a few yards behind the dilapidated Haley Cottage. They paused at the moss-covered stones that marked the graves of the shipwrecked Spanish sailors. They wandered past stone walls built centuries before by hands unknown. They hiked to the primitive unoccupied end of the island. Here, the waves smashed against sharp granite boulders, piled up, as Hawthorne observed, as if God had carelessly tossed his leftovers here after creating the Earth. Returning to his sparse but comfortable room at the Appledore Hotel, Hawthorne jotted his impressions into his journal. Describing Smuttynose Island, he concluded, "I have never seen a more dismal place."

Chapter 5

THE NORWEGIANS

After their permanent move to Appledore Island in 1848, the Laightons all but abandoned Smuttynose, renting out buildings to various friends and to Gosport fishermen. Formerly the hosts of the weather-beaten Mid-Ocean House, the Laightons moved on to become the royal family of Appledore. Thomas Laighton, a Portsmouth poet wrote, was now "King of the Shoals." Their famous hotel, publicized in newspapers throughout the East, eventually could support up to four hundred guests attended by one hundred staff members. Smuttynose continued to decline. So when Henry Ingersoll Bowditch, a prominent Boston doctor and son of the great navigator Nathaniel Bowditch, rowed from Appledore to Smuttynose in the summer of 1858, he had little good to say. Bowditch wrote to his wife about his trip into the cove:

"A beautiful, smooth beach (very rare in the islands) would make this a most desirable bathing spot, but now through the transparent water from 5 to 25 feet deep we see horrid jaws, shark bones & occasionally huge dead bodies of immense sharks that have been killed & thrown as useless by the fishermen [...] It was certainly one of the most curious of spectacles, to lean over the gunwale & to watch the various heads and glazed eyes & bits of vertebral columns that met our vision, as the boat glided slowly over them into very deep blue ocean."

Bowditch had this to say about the old Mid-Ocean House: "One large whitewashed house with rags in the windows has a sign of 'hotel' boldly printed on it—but suggestive eminently of bed-bugs, and ominous from the odors that surround it."

The arrival of the Hontvets and other Norwegians after the Civil War brought balance and purpose back to the former fishing outpost. Maren and John Hontvet were, after all, a fishing family from Norway, a country of hardy maritime families, rocky fiords, lighthouses, and long cold winters. Although the Isles of Shoals can appear "stern, bleak, and unpromising," Celia Thaxter wrote in her island history, the Hontvets considered themselves blessed to find it. They were mere immigrants who had arrived separately in America speaking a foreign tongue, and yet they were quickly married and settled on what amounted to their own private island with expansive fishing grounds and a sheltered cove. John's independent fishing venture brought in a living wage and their house, with two small but comfortable apartments, gave them room to expand.

The Hontvets had relatives back in Larvik, a village on Norway's south coast not far from the capital city of Oslo and the border with Sweden. Larvik is best known today for its Viking archaeology sites and as the hometown of Thor Heyerdahl, the twentieth-century adventurer who sailed five thousand miles of the Pacific Ocean in the Kon-Tiki, a raft that he built himself from reeds and balsa wood. The Norwegians who came to the Isles of Shoals were part of a major migration to America. As many as 250,000 of their countrymen and women, a quarter of the population, left their homeland in this era to find work, buy farmland, avoid taxes, and escape an unpopular political regime. They were, after all, a nation of adventurers and explorers with a centuries-old seafaring tradition. It was the ancient fishermen of Norway who had perfected the process of drying protein-rich codfish on rocks and wooden racks. And it was this portable, long-lasting food source that historians believe fueled the seemingly impossible Viking journeys across the North Sea to colonize the Americas more than five hundred years before Columbus.

John Christian Hontvet was born in 1842 near Larvik in a place called Tønsberg, considered the oldest city in Norway. An archaeological site there shows evidence of a fortified trading post dating to 870 AD. John's medieval ancestors may have fished from a sturdy, easy-to-build, wooden boat with overlapping planks called "faering." Broad of beam and highly seaworthy, the faering functioned then, and now, like the Scandinavian version of the sturdy Piscataqua dory, familiar to Shoals' fishermen. John appears to have arrived in the port of New York as early as 1862, four years before Maren. Whether they knew each other back in Norway is unknown. It is possible that theirs was an arranged marriage or began as one of convenience through correspondence after John had successfully established himself in America and could afford a spouse and helpmate.

Maren Sebeille Christensen, born in 1835, was seven years older than her husband. She grew up in the little village of Kvelde along a riverbank in the municipality of Larvik. She arrived with fellow Norwegians aboard a steamer from Oslo, then called Christiana. Maren first docked at Quebec and found her way to Boston. Arranged marriages were the norm in Norway in the Victorian era, often among cousins or distant relatives. Romance was not usually a factor in such cases. Unless revealing documents turn up, it is fair to assume that the Hontvet match followed the traditional pattern. John was a successful breadwinner and Maren was an excellent housekeeper well over the average marriage age.

Many Norwegian farming families ended up in Minnesota, the Dakotas, and Wisconsin, but New England was attractive to fishermen like John. Maren and John were married on August 17, 1866 in Boston, about two months after Maren's arrival. We have no photograph of them together. In the rare undated photos that survive, John is fair-haired with close-set eyes, a high forehead, and a thick mustache. With her hair pulled tightly back, in her high Victorian collar, and with her large jaw firmly set, Maren looks inescapably stern. There are no known images of John's brother, Matthew, who soon followed, or of Maren's "spinster" sister, Karen, or her attractive sister-in-law, Anethe. A faded group photograph taken in Boston decades after the murder reportedly includes Maren's brother, Ivan Christensen, by then gray and bearded and remarried. It is likely that John, as the successful patriarch, paid their passage, or more likely that he loaned his relatives the funds that they were obliged to pay back in cash or labor.

John and Maren initially stayed in Boston at 295 North Street in the city's North End melting pot. Katherine Brown, born in Ireland, and her husband, Edward, born in Germany, took in "boarders of all nations" in Boston. John met Louis Wagner here briefly as the Hontvets were leaving Boston two years later and heading to Portsmouth, New Hampshire. Katherine Brown, who also knew Wagner, would later become a key witness for the prosecution in the murder trial. Their connection to the Isles of Shoals appears to have been a fisherman named Christian Johnson, a transitional figure in this saga, who lived with his family at Gosport. Records show Johnson was living on the second floor of a small house on Star Island facing Smuttynose as early as 1860. That winter, Cedric Laighton, writing from Appledore to his married sister, Celia Thaxter, noted that Mr. Johnson of Star Island was traveling in to Portsmouth once or twice every week and keeping the Laighton family well connected with the news on the mainland. Soon afterward, Johnson became a tenant of the Laightons and rented the Red House on Smuttynose, soon to be home to the Hontvets.

A scorecard may be necessary to distinguish the many Johnsons in this story. It is likely that Christian Johnson, while in Boston, met the Hontvets and another Norwegian family, the Ingebretsens, and convinced them to join his fishing operation on the Laighton-owned islands at the Isles of Shoals. Arriving on the Portsmouth waterfront, the Hontvets stayed briefly with Matthew Johnson, whose boarding house would become a prominent scene in the Wagner murder investigation. Matthew Johnson's wife, Ann, his son, Charles, and his daughter, Mary, would become key witnesses at the trial. And it was Marshal Frank Johnson, head of the Portsmouth police force, who arrested Louis Wagner the day of the murders.

Christian Johnson makes a final appearance here in a strange incident. With prizefighting illegal in the 1860s, big city promoters had been known to stage secret bouts at the isolated Isles of Shoals, far from the prying eyes of the law. On October 2, 1867, two 145-pound contenders, one from

New York and the other from Rhode Island, faced off at Smuttynose. The sloping lawn in front of Johnson's house was roped off to form a twenty-five-foot square outdoor boxing ring. Spectators arrived by steamers and sailboats to see the two pugilists hammer away at each other. The twenty-five-round slugfest lasted roughly an hour and a half. Cedric Laighton, who with his brother Oscar was Johnson's landlord, opposed the "accursed prize-fight" as a "beastly and disgraceful exhibition." The following year, another boxing match fell apart when some of the visiting ships got lost in a dense fog and the fighters were too seasick for combat after their journey. That same year, the mild-mannered Hontvets apparently set up housekeeping at Smuttynose. Christian Johnson's lease on Smuttynose ran out in 1871 and he soon disappeared, reportedly drowned at sea.

Celia Thaxter, as her writing proves, was enchanted by the Norwegians who found their way to the Shoals. In her history of the islands, published in the *Atlantic Monthly* before the murders, Celia told the story of two brave Norwegians caught in a blinding snow squall off Portsmouth. One, possibly Christian Johnson himself, died of exposure while the other was carried helplessly by the sea for two days until he was rescued off Cape Cod. She makes light of a fisherman named Jorges (or "George") Ingebretsen, whose family was living on the south side of Appledore facing Smuttynose Island. It was Jorges and his son, Waldemar, who would rescue Maren Hontvet on the morning after the murders. His name was so hard to pronounce, Celia wrote, that the Shoalers called him "Carpenter" for no particular reason. In an 1869 letter to his sister, Celia, brother Cedric took the joke one step further, referring to the immigrant with the funny name from Norway as "Carpenter Vultimer Orroarer Inglebrizen." The Ingebretsens had so many children in their small cottage, Cedric joked, that he could not count them all, and he theorized that the family kept their kids stacked up behind the door like sandwiches. But it was all affectionate fun. Everyone in the Laighton circle had a pet name. In his letters, Cedric referred to himself as "Cedy," his brother Oscar as "Bocky," and his sister Celia as "Gwammie." Smuttynose Island was sometimes called "Smyrna."

Danes, Swedes, Finns, and Norwegians were all the rage among Victorians. Singer Jenny Lind, "the Swedish Nightingale," had taken America by storm during her 1851 concert tour under promoter P. T. Barnum. A fascination with the ancient Vikings was sweeping across New England. Influential poets, including James Russell Lowell, John Greenleaf Whittier, and Henry Wadsworth Longfellow, all composed romantic verses based on Nordic sagas, and all three men were mentors and island guests of Celia Thaxter. The theory that "Northmen" may have discovered America five hundred years before Christopher Columbus was the topic of serious scholarly lectures and the source of considerable Yankee pride. Despite a paucity of evidence, citizens along the seacoast wondered if the bold blonde explorer Leif Ericson himself had stepped foot within the borders of their town.

"The more I see of the natives of this far-off land," Celia later wrote in the *Atlantic* about the Norwegians, "the more I admire the fine qualities which seem to characterize them as a race. Gentle, faithful, intelligent, God-fearing human beings, they daily use such courtesy toward each other and all who come in contact with them, as puts our ruder Yankee manners to shame." Brother Oscar recalled hiring an immigrant named Mr. Bernsten who was an excellent boat builder. When Mr. Bernsten begin pining for his wife and children in Norway, the Laighton brothers loaned him the money to bring them over and let them live in the Haley Cottage on Smuttynose for free.

But Celia's rose-colored impression of domestic life among Scandinavians may have been wishful thinking. Her husband, Levi, had not been a good provider and her own marriage was on the rocks. Her view of the Hontvets was formed less by observation than from the idealized "simple folk" depicted in English translations of popular Norwegian novels like those of Bjørnstjerne Bjørnson. What Celia saw, on the surface, was an orderly but strictly patriarchal society in which men managed the money while the wife, or "keeper of the keys," managed the household. The married couple worked with great efficiency, but often with repressed, unspoken tensions. Arguments between married Norwegian couples were rare and divorce was almost unheard of.

The smattering of clean, hard-working, humble, and literate Norwegians who found their way to the Shoals stand in contrast, for Celia, to the decaying race of Gosport fishing families in the mid-1800s. Celia praised the few hardy fishermen still living on Star Island, men she described as "Saxon-bearded, broad-shouldered, deep-chested." But for the most part, she pitied and parodied the bickering crone-like women and the lazy men who lived on Star Island in tiny huts stinking of coal and tobacco smoke. The natives spoke in a unique Shoaler dialect that was barely intelligible to citizens on the mainland just a few miles away.

In *Among the Isles of Shoals* Celia described coming upon a chubby baby on Star Island. He was tied to a highchair in a fishing family's hut. The two-year-old was happily eating beans swimming in chunks of fat while drinking hot black coffee. "Aren't you afraid such strong coffee will kill your baby?" Celia asked the mother. "Oh, no," the fishwife replied and, pouring the boiling black liquid into the infant, said, "That'll make you hold your head up." The child and the entire family soon died of consumption.

Celia's father, Thomas Laighton, who had purchased four of the Isles of Shoals in 1839 with grand plans to revive the once-profitable fishing industry, died in 1866, leaving his two young sons and his widow, Eliza, in charge of the sprawling Appledore Hotel. This was the same year that Jorges Ingebretsen, the first of the kindly Norwegian patriarchs and his expanding family, settled at Appledore. One branch of the same family, calling themselves the Brentsens, lived for a time in the old Haley Cottage, next door to the Hontvets at Smuttynose.

For Celia and her brothers, following the loss of their powerfully important father, the Norwegians were a godsend. They made great neighbors and they brought renewed hope and centuries of maritime experience to the dying fishing village at the Isles of Shoals. The Scandinavians appeared to be the perfect law-abiding, family-friendly, industrious alternative to the ragtag fishers of Gosport.

And the feeling was mutual. On the arrival of Maren and John Hontvet, Celia wrote, "They rejoiced to find a home just such as they desired in this peaceful place." Maren was the perfect housewife, Celia noted, keeping the rustic duplex as neat as a pin, putting up curtains and shelves for houseplants, hanging colorful pictures, tending their few chickens, and frolicking with their little dog, Ringe, who reportedly immigrated from Norway with Maren. John was the dutiful husband, earning a decent living fishing aboard the *Clara Bella* with his brother, Matthew, who also arrived from Norway. The Hontvets also took on extra help when needed from among the unemployed fishermen at Gosport. One wonders, while they were digging privy holes or planting a garden, whether the new residents of Smuttynose turned up chards of pottery, rusted hooks, and the bones of the extinct giant cod left by the bustling fishing operation two centuries before.

Celia's hope that the people arriving from Norway might establish a permanent "colony" at the Shoals was not a new idea. "The Norwegians are industrious, frugal, intelligent, and moral, and are a very desirable class of emigrants," the *Milwaukee Free Democrat* reported a decade before the Civil War. Some Norwegians, mostly Lutherans and Quakers, came seeking religious freedom, but most were seeking jobs in the expanding American labor market. Here, laborers could earn five times the average pay offered in Norway. While some hoped to settle down in the "Land of the Free," many were simply planning to strike it rich and return to the homeland with their spoils. The great surge of Scandinavians crossed the Atlantic with the Hontvets and the Ingebretsens soon after the Civil War. But the most famous resettlement experiment was the work of one charismatic and wildly popular musician named Ole Bull.

A native of the Norwegian capital of Christiania, the same home region as the Hontvets, Ole Bull and his violin arrived in the United States in 1842 for a two-hundred-site whirlwind concert tour that covered one hundred thousand miles. Ole Bull fell in love with America and with the people who flocked to his performances where he mixed classical standards with Norwegian folk tunes. Powerfully built and "as beautiful as Apollo" with long flowing hair, the young Bull played his violin with a "seraphic rapture" that American audiences had never seen. His athletic movements produced music that was "beyond words," a newspaper critic reported, and one might as well "imprison the gorgeous colors of the rainbow" than to describe his performance.

A decade later, Ole Bull was wealthy and famous and disenchanted with the politics in his native land. Bull returned to America amid great publicity to found a "New Norway" for the people of his homeland. Bull spent a fortune to establish a utopian settlement on one hundred thousand acres in the Allegheny Mountains of Pennsylvania. The first one hundred colorfully-clad immigrants arrived from Norway in 1852 and named their colony Oleana in his honor. But Ole Bull, for all his compassion and desire for human rights, was not a successful leader and the experimental colony soon failed.

Undaunted, Ole Bull continued to perform and to tour the world. His journey eventually led him to the Isles of Shoals, very likely in 1869. According to Oscar Laighton, the virtuoso enraptured audiences with a benefit concert in the music room of the Appledore Hotel. The master musician, his flowing mane of hair now gone white, played "divinely," Oscar reported. Bull raised $365 for the Norwegian families then settling in at the Isles of Shoals. The historical record does not reveal whether John and Maren Hontvet attended the concert, but it is more than possible that they did and were its beneficiaries. Sitting proudly, surrounded by the cultural elite of Boston, the Hontvets were serenaded by the most famous Norwegian of their era. America, it seemed, was truly a place where dreams come true.

Chapter 6

POOR KAREN AND MR. POOR

By 1870, the scene was set for two island tragedies, the infamous Smuttynose murders in Maine and the demise of the ancient fishing village of Gosport, New Hampshire. These events may never have happened if not for the arrival of two key characters. It was Karen Christensen, sleeping in the dark kitchen of the Hontvet House, whose sudden cries of terror exposed the midnight robber who became a vicious killer. And it was the wealthy Boston merchant John R. Poor who greedily bought up all the property of the Star Island fishing village to build a luxurious Victorian hotel.

Maren Hontvet was sometimes lonely in her isolated Smuttynose home, Celia Thaxter wrote, until her sister, Karen, arrived from Norway in March 1871, bringing her own spinning wheel. Celia offered few physical details of Maren, describing her only as short with bright gray eyes. But Celia was charmed by Maren's "beautiful behavior" and her intelligence. Maren was "so gentle, courteous, decorous, she left on my mind a most delightful impression." The author was less taken with Maren's spinster sister who began working for the Thaxter family at the Appledore Hotel soon after her arrival.

"Karen was a rather sad-looking woman, about twenty-nine years old. She had lost a lover in Norway long since, and in her heart she fretted and mourned for this continually. She could not speak a word of English, at first, but went patiently about her work and soon learned enough, and proved herself an excellent servant," Celia wrote years later in the *Atlantic Monthly*.

By all accounts, Karen was unhappy with her life in America and perhaps unhappy with life in general. Despite Celia's upbeat picture of the Norwegian "settlement" at the Shoals, there was much sadness below the surface. Members of the community almost starved during long winter storms. One Norwegian fisherman was shipwrecked and another drowned. An elder Ingebretsen went insane. Annie Berntsen, whose family lived briefly at Smuttynose, suffered from profound depression. In the winter of 1881, Annie was found dead at age eighteen of "brain fever," most likely a suicide. Ovidia was "raving mad" and taken by boat, by train, and by carriage, screaming all the way, and installed at an insane asylum outside of Boston. Celia's biographer Rosamond Thaxter assigned their condition to the prolonged isolation and loneliness of the islands, to their homesickness for Norway, and to a general sadness that overtook the Norwegian community following the murders of Karen and Anethe in 1873.

The tragedy of the Appledore maids Ovidia and Annie Berntsen was still in the future when Celia Thaxter wrote about Karen Christensen in her essay "A Memorable Murder." Karen had been "in service" to the Thaxters at the Appledore Hotel for almost two years prior to the murders and had left her job just two weeks earlier. Besides visiting occasionally with her sister at Smuttynose, Karen had also lived briefly with the family of Joseph Pettigrew, a boot and shoe salesman with a store in the heart of downtown Portsmouth. Curiously, the top floor of Pettigrew's store housed the studio and darkroom of a popular Portsmouth photographer, and yet no photograph of Karen is known to exist. We have only Celia Thaxter's word picture of Karen as a very neat and clean woman, sitting at her spinning wheel by the fire wearing a gown made of blue cloth she had woven herself in Norway. Karen's standard uniform included a crisp white apron and a white muslin bow attached to her linen collar.

"She had a pensive way of letting her head droop a little sideways as she spun," Celia wrote, "and while the low wheel hummed monotonously, she would sit crooning sweet, sad old Norwegian airs by the hour together, perfectly unconscious that she was affording such pleasure to a pair of appreciative eyes."

Celia Thaxter is best known today for her island garden, her decorative painting, and for romantic poems focused largely on the sea and the flora and fauna at the Isles of Shoals. She applied the same clinical observation to her Scandinavian servants, studying them as she would a sandpiper, a wild rose, or a colorful species of kelp. "My little Norwegians are such treasures!" she confessed in a letter to writer Annie Fields. "So sweet to look at, so gently bred, with manners as near perfect as can be." And as with the birds and flowers of the Shoals, Celia turned these observations into verse. Her short poem about Karen Christensen was aptly titled "Karen." It appeared in the *Atlantic Monthly* and then in her first book-length collection of poems entitled *Driftweed* that appeared in 1879. "These little verses are like weeds that sprang out of the rock and never knew cultivation," Celia told her Boston publisher. And, indeed, her candid view of Karen—"She is not pretty, she is not young"—may seem downright unkind.

In the poem, Celia added a fictional young man named Waldemar who is secretly in love with Karen, but Karen is so consumed by grief over her lost lover back in Norway that she is blind to Waldemar's affections. The poet clearly borrowed the name Waldemar from one of the Ingebretsen boys who lived on Appledore Island. In the poem, Celia warns her housekeeper to stop pining away and to live for the moment.

> O homesick Karen, listen to me:
>   You are not young, and you are not fair,
> But Waldemar no one else can see,
>   For he carries your image everywhere.

Students of the Smuttynose murders have suggested that Waldemar may have been based on Louis Wagner, who, according to the local gossip, had feelings for Karen and killed her in a jealous rage. The *Boston*

Traveller, soon after the murders, even theorized in print that Wagner killed Karen "out of revenge because she would not marry him." The theory is unfounded. Karen was ten years older than Wagner, who was generally considered a ladies' man. According to John Hontvet, who insisted that the newspaper retract the false story, Louis and Karen met on no more than half a dozen occasions and only when others were present. While living with the Hontvets on Smuttynose, Wagner spent most of his time with Maren and later with Anethe. Nothing supports the theory that Karen and Louis had a romantic connection, but despite public denials by the Hontvets, by Karen's friends, and by Wagner himself, the rumor lives on.

Karen was very likely on duty as a maid at the Appledore Hotel in August 1872 when a wealthy Boston businessman named John R. Poor stepped off the ferry from Portsmouth with his wife and daughter. It was a banner year for tourists, Oscar Laighton recalled in his memoir, and there were no vacancies to be had at any price. Guests were sleeping on the piazza and on billiard tables. But Mr. Poor was an important man from Massachusetts who insisted on spending the night. Oscar dutifully gave up his own room to accommodate Poor's family, while the owner of the world famous Stickney & Poor Spice Company slept on the sofa in the hotel's letter-writing room. This inauspicious event would soon lead to the disappearance of the town of Gosport.

Stickney & Poor got its humble start in 1815 when Boston grocer William Stickney began grinding mustard seeds by hand and delivering the spice to customers in a wicker basket. By the Gold Rush era of 1849, mustard was not only a table spice but a medical necessity. Mustard plasters, a hot poultice made of powdered seeds spread on cloth, were placed on a patient's chest or back to prevent colds, improve breathing, and relieve pain. By the Civil War, using steam-powered machinery in their Charlestown factory, the company's familiar yellow-and-red mustard box was an American icon. Widely promoted with colorful advertising and a team of aggressive salesmen, Stickney & Poor became a household name for a wide range of peppers, exotic spices, herbs, yeast, ground coffee, and even patent medicines. A bottle of Stickney & Poor's Pure Paregoric, for example, was a potent mixture of opium and alcohol. Five drops of the soothing liquid was recommended in the Victorian era for crying babies as young a five days old and twenty-five drops could put teething infants or restless children quickly to sleep, sometimes permanently. Such drugs, described as "baby killers," were eventually taken off the market in the twentieth century.

According to Oscar Laighton's memoir *Ninety Years at the Isles of Shoals*, Mr. Poor was captivated by the burgeoning tourist business at the Appledore Hotel. Poor asked the Laighton brothers if he could purchase Smuttynose Island. Oscar and Cedric declined the offer, explaining that Smuttynose was then occupied by a Norwegian fishing family. "Mr. Poor had been with us a few days," Oscar recalled, "when we discovered that he was secretly buying out the inhabitants of Star Island and the whole village of Gosport."

Seeking to diversify, Poor was ready to invest a lot of cash into the lucrative summer resort business. On Star Island, according to Rosamond Thaxter, Poor found that the surviving fishermen were "a rather pitiable and worthless lot." The Spice King did not do the dirty work himself. Poor employed a go-between named Mr. Nathan F. Mathes of Portsmouth, who gobbled up the deeds for all but two of the island properties for a reported cost of fifty-four thousand dollars. By September 1872, following a unanimous vote of the townspeople of Gosport, Mr. Mathes was given title to all the houses and land with the exception of two holdouts, fisherman John Bragg Downs and the Reverend George Beebe. Downs, who was financially stable and had been born at the Shoals, refused to capitulate to the developer from Massachusetts and kept his home and tiny plot of land. Rev. Beebe had even deeper emotional ties. Rev Beebe had served since 1857 as the last Christian missionary to the fishing families of the island. Like Rev. John Tucke a century before, Beebe had been their spiritual leader, doctor, attorney, teacher, justice of the peace, carpenter, tax collector, and more. When the preacher's daughter, Mitty, attended school on the mainland for the first time in 1863, she contracted scarlet fever. Back on the island, the deadly disease spread to Mitty's two younger sisters, who died in quick succession. The graves of the three Beebe girls are still visible among a jungle of cedars, lilacs, and poison ivy at the far end of Star Island. Most tourists miss the hidden spot. Eventually, the sad Rev. Beebe and his wife detached their hearts from the island and moved on like the others.

Why did the Shoalers sell out? While some served honorably in the Civil War, others were in debt for fees paid to avoid military service. To make things worse, the fishing had not been good in recent years. Fish stocks were declining in the Gulf of Maine and a number of species had been fished almost to extinction. The giant cod weighing up to 120 pounds that had so attracted Captain John Smith were long gone, and by the mid-1800s, the teaming schools of mackerel and the all-important menhaden, or "pogies," used for bait were getting harder and harder to find.

There was a technical revolution going on too. Men who traditionally caught fish using hooks and lines from small boats could no longer make ends meet. Trawl, or "tub," fishing vessels employing hundreds of baited hooks, were taking over. But the costs of such a boat and all that equipment was beyond the means of most Shoalers. The lack of fish, the cost of high-tech trawling, overdue state taxes, and the lingering Civil War debts were more than the impoverished villagers could handle. The offer from Mr. Mathes to buy up the island property, at first blush seemed like a godsend. To sweeten the deal, Mathes offered to pay off the Gosport war tax and to clear the books of $3,800 in overdue New Hampshire taxes.

The local paper soon revealed that Mathes was merely the front man and that the secret "Boston capitalist" behind him was the wealthy John R. Poor. And just as quickly, Poor's workers razed the fisherman's huts and renovated the more substantial buildings for use as summer rentals. They cleared a large footprint of land on Star facing Smuttynose across the ocean harbor. Construction teams graded the rocky land and began to erect an enormous skeleton of what was to become the luxurious Oceanic Hotel. The 265-foot structure, according to Cedric Laighton's letter to his sister Celia, would cost Mr. Poor thirty-five thousand dollars to construct. The final cost was double that amount and Poor's new company would invest nearly three hundred thousand dollars to obtain the island and fit out the hotel. The Oceanic promised to open 147 sleeping quarters for 300 guests, boasted wide corridors, modern conveniences, a fine spacious dining room, a dance hall, and elegant fixtures. A large new stone pier would outstrip anything seen at the Appledore.

In a single swipe, one of the oldest continually-occupied European fishing outposts in the United States was obliterated. Removed permanently to the mainland, most of the displaced Gosport villagers quickly came to regret their decision to sell.

"Nearly all the Gosportians have been over here lately and they, one and all," Cedric wrote to Celia, "bitterly regret having sold their homesteads." The displaced Shoalers cursed Mr. Mathes and protested among themselves. Most begged John Downs to lease them a tiny parcel of his land on Star Island and pleaded with the Laightons to sell them building lots on Appledore or Smuttynose, but to no avail. Lemuel Caswell, whose family had lived on the Isles for generations, told Cedric that "if he don't get a place on the Shoals to live, he shall be crazy." It was no idle threat. Ten years earlier, Lemuel's uncle (also named Lemuel Caswell) had killed himself at the Shoals by cutting his own throat "from ear to ear" with a razor.

But the die was cast. Fishermen at the Shoals were suddenly on the verge of extinction. Only men like John Hontvet, who could afford a bigger boat, more hooks, and more bait, stood a chance of surviving. Beside his brother, Matthew, John was so successful that he could occasionally afford to take on extra help aboard the *Clara Bella*. One of those men was a Prussian immigrant named Louis Wagner, who had found his way from New York to Boston to Star Island exactly at the wrong time in history. Like a fish out of water, Gosport Village was gasping its last. Wagner, too, unable to make ends meet, was in desperate straits in 1872.

Unlike the Hontvets, Wagner had not yet gotten his fair share of the American dream. And unlike the old Shoalers whom he was living among at

Gosport, he had no property to sell to the wealthy hotel developer. He was about to become homeless again. So when John Hontvet offered Wagner not only a fishing job, but also a place to stay in his home on Smuttynose Island, it was a rare stroke of luck. If Wagner had been a religious man, which at the time he was not, he might have seen the hand of God at play. Finally, things were looking up.

II

MURDER

"Murder, to be fully effective, should be done out of doors, and if possible amid surroundings agreeably savage."

—William Roughead, early true crime writer

"No such awful story as this, in all its details, has been told for many years. The circumstances of the murder, the loneliness of the situation, the romance of the sea about the place, and the determination of the murderer, combine to make this tragedy long memorable on the coast of New England."

—*The New York Times,* June 26, 1875

Chapter 7

WITH AN AX

The ax used to end the lives of Anethe and Karen rests in a flat, square, wooden display case in the Portsmouth Athenaeum. The old membership library in Market Square, founded in 1817, is among the last of its kind. The interior looks like something out of "The Raven" by Edgar Allan Poe. Pallid plaster busts of forgotten men loom above leather-bound volumes on dark wooden shelves. Athenaeum regulars take no notice of the murder weapon. It is just one curio among so many in the collection—leather fire buckets, the wooden half-models of long lost ships, the twisted horn of an Oryx, a human arm bone from the Battle of Waterloo, a stuffed armadillo, or a carved Fiji paddle.

Visitors who spot the dull metallic blade with the now-wobbly broken handle inevitably ask, "Is that the real murder ax?"

It very likely is, the Athenaeum curator confirms. The provenance is strong. What looks like dried blood, however, is merely rust. The gory evidence was washed clean on the evening of the murder when a member of the coroner's team brought the ax back from Smuttynose Island. He tossed it on the floor of a fishing dory where it sloshed around in the icy spray from a heavy sea before it was ferried back to Portsmouth aboard the USS *Mayflower*. But the manufacturer, the Blodgett Edge Tool Company, is consistent with the time period. Blodgett operated in Manchester, New Hampshire, from 1853 to 1862 before it became the Amoskeag Ax

Company. Exhibited at the Wagner trial, the ax became part of a collection of murder weapons owned by a local judge. When the judge died, it was purchased by an antiques dealer in York, Maine, who sold it to a woman in nearby Dover, New Hampshire, who donated it to the Portsmouth Athenaeum in 1997. There was discussion among the library trustees at the time about whether the ax was an appropriate item to accept or to display, but in the end, it was just too intriguing to pass up.

Ax murders occupy their own dark corner in the American house of horrors. Even within our culture of violence, there is something especially wild and brutish about swinging a heavy sharpened blade attached to a long wooden stick. The modern killer, by choosing this primitive weapon, is instantly set apart from the more traditional and, dare we say, the more sophisticated user of guns, swords, or knives. These things are, after all, weapons of defense, while the ax is a common household tool available in any hardware store. Ax murderers rarely plan ahead. Theirs is a weapon of opportunity and proximity, grabbed in the heat of passion and wielded with savage fury and punishing intent. Thus the ax murderer in popular American culture is generally seen as depraved or insane, a person driven by passion and rage who is acting out of raw instinct. While threatening an enemy with an ax may be an effective deterrent, planning to use one in a close-range, bloody, mutilating act, for most of us, is unthinkable.

Although humans have killed one another with every object imaginable from pills to pillows, the lowly ax enjoys a celebrity status not shared by many deadly household objects such as bricks, hammers, rocks, and baseball bats. Ax murderers inhabit their own genre in the annals of true crime, as unique and recognizable as serial killers, poisoners, slashers, hit men, mad bombers, school shooters, and mass murderers. Perhaps it is the fearsome shape of the weapon itself or the rarity of its use or the crazed implausibility of the act itself, but murder with an ax has become both an iconic and a comic figure in American pop culture. Halloween superstores offer an ax murder costume in a plastic bag, complete with an escaped prisoner's jumpsuit and a plastic hatchet. The rap duo Axe Murder Boyz market their brand of music with T-shirts emblazoned with two crossed-axes. Even the once-demure cartoon character Minnie Mouse can be seen with ax in hand at Disneyland's Haunted Mansion.

The image is ubiquitous in western culture, from fearsome curved Viking battleaxes to double-headed blades used by hooded executioners at public beheadings. Ax murders may be as old as civilization itself. Hand-held stone axes with no handle (or "haft") date back three hundred thousand years. The ancient Roman "fasces" is a bundle of rods with an emerging ax blade symbolizing justice and power. This design still decorates the door-way to the Oval Office of the White House, the seal of the US Senate, the emblem of the Knights of Columbus, the insignia of the National Guard, and the seal of Harvard University. The short-handled tomahawk, ideal for cutting, throwing, and hand-to-hand combat, was used by both Native Americans and colonists.

Curiously, the parts of the modern ax, other than the "blade," sound quite benign, if not downright human. The elements of the steel "head" of the ax, from back to front, are known as the butt, eye, cheek, toe, heel, and beard. The elements forming the haft, from the top to the curved bottom of the handle, are called the shoulder, belly, throat, grip, and knob. And yet, in the wrong hands, the sum of these innocuous parts add up to carnage of the highest order. Shocking pictures of ax murder crime scenes were consid-ered unprintable except by the sleaziest of pulp magazines in the twentieth century or in similar websites today. But in the film industry, recreating gro-tesque murders with gallons of stage blood and countless prosthetic limbs has become a profitable industry.

Among a litany of horror classics is the 1964 feature *Straight-Jacket*, created as a comeback vehicle for aging Hollywood superstar Joan Crawford. The film poster shows Crawford, ax raised. The bold headline reads: "WARNING: *Strait-Jacket* vividly depicts axe murders." Crawford's character, enraged to find her young husband in bed with another woman, chops off their heads. The scene is laughably campy and the victims are as unrealistic as store mannequins. Comedian Mike Myers continued the psycho killer theme with his 1993 film *So I Married an Ax Murderer*. The genre hopefully reached its outlandish peak with *Abraham Lincoln: Vampire Hunter* (2012), in which the killer is also the president of the United States. In this mixture of horror and history, Abe the "rail-splitter" learns to twirl his ax like a Hollywood ninja warrior and uses it to defeat an army of flesh-eating undead monsters during the Civil War.

True tales of murder by ax are as old as America itself. They are indigenous to regions like New England, where people regularly cut down trees to clear land and chop wood to build warming fires. Colonists on both sides of the Piscataqua River were hacked to death during the Indian uprisings in the seventeenth century. Among those killed, then scalped and dismembered, was a woman with the unfortunate name of Ursula Cutt. Murdered while working on her farm in Portsmouth, Ursula was the wife of John Cutt, New Hampshire's first royal governor, whose brother, Richard Cutt, was among the early successful fishermen at the Isles of Shoals. A few years later in 1697, Native Americans kidnapped a woman named Hannah Duston (also spelled "Dustin") from nearby Haverhill, Massachusetts. Duston had recently given birth to her eleventh child, whom her captors quickly killed. As she was being carried off to Canada, possibly to be enslaved or added to dwindling tribal numbers, Duston managed to kill the sleeping Indians with their own tomahawks. She returned home with ten Indian scalps—men, women, and children—for which her family was paid a sizable bounty from the provincial government. A nineteenth-century bronze statue of Hannah Duston, the bloody ax gripped in her hand, still stands in downtown Haverhill. While some honor Duston as a heroine, critics, including writer Nathaniel Hawthorne, considered her murderous rage unjustifiable.

Inevitably, the Wagner murders draw comparison to the killing of Abby and Andrew Borden in Fall River, Massachusetts, nearly two decades later in 1892. Their daughter, Lizzie Borden, was arrested a month later, tried, and acquitted of killing her father and stepmother with a hatchet in their home. Both accused killers knew the victims. Both Wagner and Borden were widely suspected, but maintained their innocence. Both ax murder cases were based on a combination of circumstantial and forensic evidence and both were widely publicized, galvanizing newspaper readers and court-room spectators. Both crimes may have been motivated by money—the Hontvet's fishing profits and Borden's family fortune. And while most true crime enthusiasts today assume that Lizzie Borden got away with mur-der, a few still cling to the theory that Louis Wagner was wrongly hanged. Without the strange weapon and the shocked reaction of the Victorian public, however, the Wagner and Borden cases have little in common.

The Lizzie Borden story has spawned dozens of publications and documentaries plus a recent TV movie. The murder house in Fall River is currently marketed as a bed and breakfast, while cult Lizzie Borden follow-ers even have their own newsletter. Interest in the Wagner murder at the Shoals, by comparison, remains largely a local phenomenon, similar to a case in rural Iowa. Around midnight on June 9, 1912, a stranger picked up an ax in the backyard of a modest home in the town of Villisca and slaughtered six children and two adults. Witnesses found "somebody mur-dered in every bed," including Joshua and Sara Moore, their four children, and two visiting friends from Sunday school. Expecting to find an insane blood-soaked vagrant, locals came up empty. Hundreds of citizens followed two bloodhounds shipped in from Nebraska, but the trail was already cold. Suspects were identified, including an itinerant preacher and a prominent businessman but, to the great frustration of the citizens of Villisca, no killer was convicted. As with the Wagner case, the Villisca murders remain con-troversial and of undying interest to a core group of locals. Both murders have spawned a novel, a documentary, plus a number of books and conspir-acy theories. The Moore house, site of the still unsolved Villisca murders, has been restored to its 1912 appearance and opened as a museum.

Such crimes are often weighed against others in the region. When the story of the Smuttynose tragedy first broke, it was instantly compared to another, now-forgotten, seacoast New Hampshire murder. The day after the Shoals tragedy, with Wagner already in jail, the *Portsmouth Daily Evening Times* reported: "Not since the day when the murderer Pike killed the aged couple at Hampton Falls, have the people of this vicinity been so horror stricken and excited." The reference was to a sudden home invasion five years earlier. On the evening of May 7, 1868, an elderly Mrs. Brown responded to a knock on her front door and was immediately struck and killed with an ax. Her husband, Thomas Brown, was still sitting by the fireplace reading his newspaper when his skull was crushed by a sudden blow. Brown, however, lived long enough to identify the killer as their former hired hand, Josiah Pike of nearby Newburyport, Massachusetts. Pike had become friendly with the aged couple under an assumed name to rob them, but like Wagner, he discovered only a small portion of their savings before fleeing into the night. Pike was captured and convicted, then hanged the following year.

Coincidentally, Wagner would be forever paired with another Maine ax murderer. John True Gordon, as we shall see, joined Wagner on the gallows in 1875. According to the *New York Times* coverage, Gordon was "shiftless" and a "ne'er-do-well" with a penchant for liquor. He was violently jealous of his older brother, who inherited their father's small farm. Gordon reportedly crept into his brother's bedroom in 1873 "armed with the axe from the door-yard and deliberately chopped him to pieces, together with his wife and one of his children who was sleeping with him." Gordon's conviction, also based on circumstantial evidence, hung on the testimony of his eight-year-old niece who survived the attack. "Here were two men so clearly convicted of murder that that there can be no reasonable doubt remaining of their guilt," the *New York Times* concluded.

These unspeakable crimes seem to stick to the community where they occur. Their shocking details, passed from one generation to the next, leave a permanent stain. The questions they raise become fodder for decades of analysis and speculation. The murder sites become dark shrines. The murder weapons become artifacts. Their memory echoes the same inescapable warning—be afraid, be very afraid. In the words of one citizen of Villisca, "You're never safe—in your own town, in your own house, in your own bed." You're not even safe among friends.

Chapter 8

BEST OF FRIENDS

We can never truly know Louis Wagner. Although there is a significant canon of commentary about the Prussian fisherman, plus extensive news interviews and the lengthy transcript of his court testimony, every word of it was produced after the murders. So even the scraps of Wagner's life prior to March 6, 1873, are speculative or colored by the tragedy at Smuttynose. To poet Celia Thaxter, who got her description directly from Maren Hontvet, Wagner was "tall, powerful, dark, with a peculiarly quiet manner." Wagner seemed to hover on the edge of things, watching, but uninvolved.

"He was always lurking in corners, lingering, looking, listening, and he would look no man straight in the eyes," Maren reportedly told Celia. After arguing about some point of navigation with a group of sailors, Maren overheard Wagner muttering, "I know I'm wrong, but I'll never give in!"

By comparison, people who met the "Prussian devil" in person during his trial and incarceration often came away much surprised. "We would not select him in a crowd as one who would commit murder, as his expression is one of kindness," a local paper reported. The fair-haired blue-eyed man was tall, handsome, powerfully built, and was often perceived as friendly and honest, though with a sometimes strange and vacant stare. Even after being attacked by a mob in Portsmouth, he looked soulfully into the eyes of his captors and the press. "Wagner does not look like a villain," the *Portsmouth Evening Times* reported on March 8. "Put him

J. DENNIS ROBINSON

among a dozen respectable laboring men, and none would select him from the others as a bad man."

Louis H. F. Wagner arrived in the United States in 1866 at age twenty-one. He grew up in Ueckermünde, a seaport in what is now northeastern Germany. Today a popular resort in Pomerania on the border with Poland, the historic region dates its founding as a fishing settlement back to roughly 1200 AD. By his own account, Wagner began working on fishing boats in his early teens. Whether he came to America to avoid military service in his native land, as is often rumored, is doubtful. He became a man for hire, a short-term worker, often with no fixed address. He usually lived aboard a fishing boat, then spent a week in port before shipping out again. Like John Hontvet, Wagner migrated from the port of New York to Boston, where he stayed for two years, off and on, at a low-rent sailor's bethel and bordello in the North End. Then he moved on to Portsmouth and the Shoals. It was a tough, dangerous, lonely lifestyle with low wages and little chance to accumulate friends or funds.

Wagner arrived too late to the fishing party at the Isles of Shoals. By his own account, he lived at Star Island for just three months in the winter of 1871–1872, likely through the influence of Christian Johnson who, with the help of the Laightons, had attracted the Ingebretsens and the Hontvets to settle at Appledore and Smuttynose. Wagner's timing could not have been worse. The centuries-old fishing community would be dead within the year with only a single Star Island fishing family remaining. Celia Thaxter vaguely recalled Wagner living at Star Island where she saw him working alone aboard a wherry, "but he made very little money," she wrote.

Whether Wagner was a criminal at heart we shall never know. Rumors of previous dark deeds have not been substantiated. We have only a third-hand report from Celia Thaxter that Wagner once told his shipmates "not many had done what he had done and got off in safety." A witness at the trial swore under oath that Wagner had been using the alternate name Louis Ludwig while living in Boston. This story, first reported in the *Boston Herald* two days after the murders, must be taken with a grain of salt, but it

62

is intriguing. According to the newspaper account, while working as a ship's mate out of Boston Harbor, Wagner was a steady man, always in funds, but with "a morose and retiring disposition." He was generally unpopular with his shipmates and had a reputation with the dance hall girls of the North End.

The word on the street was that Wagner had convinced a fellow sailor, whose name was Henry Ludwig, to bring his trunk and bank book aboard a fishing vessel where Wagner was employed as ship's mate. Wagner reported that the sailor fell from aloft and broke his back on the rail of the ship before falling into the sea. Wagner is said to have impersonated Ludwig while attempting to collect the money from the dead man's bank account, but the bank refused to issue the funds. This led to rumors that Wagner had killed his shipmate and tossed his body overboard to rob him. We cannot know whether Wagner plotted a crime or if this was a case of mistaken identity.

There were also accusations, although no evidence, that Wagner had stolen money from an elderly couple in his homeland. One newspaper reported that Wagner was "ugly when in liquor," but Maren, who knew him better than anyone, confessed that she had never seen him drunk. Of his brief stay on Star Island, we have two snippets of information. One comes from John Downs, grandson of the "last Shoaler," who included this note in his 1943 memoir *Sprays of Salt*:

"When I was a baby Louis Wagner used to come in and out of our house. My mother has often told me that more than once he held me in his big, brawny arms and cuddled me with his broken English. She always said he could swear more than any man she had ever heard. His committing the murder was a surprise to most of the Shoalers, for they had liked and respected Wagner in many ways."

Downs recalled long, dark winters on Star Island, huddled indoors against icy gale winds with the windows permanently shut and the air thick with coal, wood, and tobacco smoke. He remembered the last of the Shoalers were mostly of Scandinavian, Scotts, or English descent. These were cautious and highly superstitions people who drew meaning and guidance from the slightest incident. Setting an empty rocking chair in motion, for example, portended bad luck. A dog howling at night meant someone had died. A person who sang before breakfast was doomed to cry before dinner. Picking up a lost pin could bring a day of good fortune, but too much happiness was a sure sign of coming misfortune for the islanders. A broom falling across a doorway or a dropped piece of silverware was a sure sign that a stranger was about to visit—a spoon indicated a child, a fork was a woman, and a knife meant that a man was coming.

Downs was only three years old at the time, but Mollie Lee Clifford was about seven when Wagner visited her family one Sunday in the only house on nearby Lunging Island. Typically, Wagner was seeking a free meal. In an unpublished memoir, Clifford claimed that, after dinner, her father read from the Bible. Following the reading of the scriptures, Wagner said, "I would rather be a devil than an angel anyhow, for your angels have nothing but shimmering hair and wings, while devils have power!"

Clifford also recalled overhearing Wagner tell a lengthy story to her father that she titled "The Wickedest Man." The narrative centered on an unnamed German youth who robbed his own mother of her small savings before leaving home. The money quickly spent, the man took a job as a handyman for an elderly couple. After gaining their confidence, he discovered they kept their savings in a strongbox in a room adjacent to their bed chamber. Finding no opportunity to rob his employers stealthily, the wicked man killed them both and set their bed on fire to cover the robbery. The murderer escaped to Italy where he quickly spent all the money, then immigrated to America. Whether Wagner was talking about himself, whether the story was entirely fiction, or whether it was ever spoken at all, we cannot know.

Clifford's childhood memory appears to have been heavily influenced by Celia Thaxter's "Memorable Murder," by local gossip, and by the passage of many decades before she jotted down the details. She described Wagner as "tall, dark, and powerful, a veritable giant" who was "extremely fascinating, and at the same time, repelling."

During another visit to Lunging Island, Wagner reportedly asked Clifford's father where a man should hide his money while he was out fishing. Although he had significant cash savings, Clifford's father told Wagner he never had enough money to need a hiding place. When the girl asked her father why he had lied to Wagner, he told Mollie, "I don't know. I just had a feeling come over me that I did not want him to know that I even had any money." If Wagner hoped to befriend Mollie Clifford's family on Lunging to rob them, his plan did not work. Clifford's family moved permanently to the mainland that same fall along with the rest of the residents of Gosport.

John Hontvet first met Wagner on the docks in Boston. Testifying at trial, John said he took Wagner in as a boarder at Smuttynose on April 11, 1872, and that Wagner lived with his family until early in November of that year. The Prussian likely came to Smuttynose, as he had at Lunging, destitute and in search of free food. Celia Thaxter suggested this and says Maren "gave him food when he was suffering from want" and Wagner always received her "utmost kindness." Whether Wagner contributed to the rent of the Red House owned by the Laighton family or whether he was living entirely on charity is unclear, but his considerable strength, stamina, and fishing experience were certainly potential assets to the small Hontvet clan. By all accounts, the group got along famously, with John and Maren living on the right side of the duplex and Wagner on the left. John's brother, Matthew, was likely upstairs. Karen rarely visited when she was working at the Appledore Hotel and she never once spent the night on Smuttynose when Wagner was there, Maren later said.

Instead of being crammed into a hammock aboard ship or sharing a room with other men in a flophouse, for a few months in 1872, Wagner finally had room to stretch out and call his own, possibly for the first time since his arrival in America. According to Maren's testimony, he slept in the large kitchen on the easterly side of the house and hung his clothes in the small adjoining first-floor bedroom, the room where Karen's body was later discovered. When he returned from a fishing trip, Wagner was in the habit of hanging his wet, smelly "oil pants and oil jacket" on a peg on the wall two steps up the stairway in the entrance to the Hontvet side of the building, rather than in the identical space on his own side. He also had ample time to explore the large wooden trunk that Karen stored in Wagner's sleeping space while she was working at the Appledore Hotel. It contained her winter clothes and the feather bed that she brought from Norway.

For the bulk of his stay at Smuttynose, Wagner was ill, or more likely he was feigning illness. Once he had established residence on Smuttynose, at age twenty-seven, he complained that he was too sick to work regularly, and was grateful to be given a comfortable place to recuperate. In his own words spoken at the trial, Wagner said: "I was glad to keep me there. I had to look out for my own living while I was sick, crippled with the rheumatism. I did my day's work and minded my living. The women were always kind to me; most of the time there was only one woman there, Hontvet's wife."

If one accepts, on his word, that Wagner suffered from rheumatism, it casts doubt on his ability to reach the island by rowboat on the night of the murder. If one believes, as Celia and so many others did, that his condition was faked, then Wagner becomes even more shady and nefarious as a character.

Although subject to her husband's will in all matters pertaining to business and money, Maren ruled the domestic life on Smuttynose. It was her job to tend to the needs of her guest. Following Norwegian traditions of the Victorian era, she was obliged to be polite and kind to visitors, giving them the best food served on the finest dishes. In Celia's words, Maren "sheltered, fed, nursed, and waited upon him [Wagner] the greater part of the season." And it is reasonable to assume, based on Wagner's unctuous nature, that she may have enjoyed his company.

In the seven months that Wagner boarded with the Hontvets, he worked as a regular crewman for John on the *Clara Bella*, for little more than two months, from the first week of September to the first week of November. With another harsh winter fast approaching, perhaps Wagner found it expedient to make himself useful to keep his room. He would also have known that the arrival of Maren and Karen's half-brother, Ivan, and his wife, Anethe, was imminent. The young couple arrived from Norway on October 12, 1872. Mary Johnson, who worked at her parents' boarding house, recalled seeing Ivan's attractive Norwegian wife waiting on the dock for her first trip to Smuttynose aboard the *Clara Bella*. In less than six months, Anethe's disfigured body would lie in a pine coffin inside Mary Johnson's house on Water Street.

It was Anethe's youth (she was twenty-five) and "innocent beauty," combined with the haunting isolation of the island, plus the savage use of an ax, that made this story so shocking to Victorian audiences. "Anethe, everybody says, was a regular fair beauty, young and strong, with splendid thick yellow hair, so long she could sit on it," Celia Thaxter wrote. Ultimately, it was for the killing of Anethe Christensen alone, and not Karen, for whom Wagner was tried, found guilty, and hanged. The killing of innocent Anethe, even though few in the region had ever seen or met her, came to symbolize the very essence of evil. "It seemed to me," Celia wrote, "that beauty had fled out of the world, and that goodness, innocence, mercy, gentleness, were a mere mockery of empty words."

And yet in the fall of 1872, the only occupied house on Smuttynose Island was a warm and happy place. The addition of Ivan and Anethe was the fulfillment of the American dream that promised hardworking immigrants a new start in a new world. And by uniting the Christensen family once again, John had certainly fulfilled a promise to his wife, Maren. An impressive re-creation of this brief joyous moment can be seen in the film *The Weight of Water* (2002) based on the novel of the same title. Although both book and film are fictions inspired by the historical double homicide, director Kathryn Bigelow came as close as can be imagined to capturing the look, the language, the music, the clothing, and the setting inside the Hontvet House in the months before the tragedy. The film presents Wagner living like an honorary member of the Hontvet family.

The film also shows what great comfort and friendship Wagner was about to lose. It is unknown whether John asked Wagner to leave the crowding house as winter approached or whether Wagner moved on of his own accord. But within weeks of the arrival of Ivan and Anethe, Wagner was living on the mainland in Portsmouth. There he signed on as a crewman aboard a fishing schooner named the *Addison Gilbert*. That journey would not end well, and Wagner was soon back in Portsmouth, sharing a room with two other seamen in a cheap boarding house on the city's rundown waterfront. Once again he was broke and alone. His rent was already many weeks overdue. His clothes were old and ragged. By early 1873, Wagner had no prospects and nothing to show for his seven years in America.

Later that year in June, sitting upright in the witness box in the county courthouse at Alfred, Maine, a well-dressed defense attorney questioned Wagner as a roomful of spectators looked on.

"Had you any difficulty at any time with either Karen Christensen or Anethe Christensen?" the attorney asked.

"No, sir," the defendant said politely.

"Had you any ill-will against Anethe or Karen?" the attorney probed.

"I never had," Wagner replied.

"Any difficulty with any of the Hontvet family?"

"No, sir," the prisoner said.

"They were your personal friends?" the lawyer asked.

"Yes," Louis Wagner said, his eyes filling with tears, "the only friends I had."

Chapter 9

ON WATER STREET

Louis Wagner just happened to be standing on Walker's Wharf around four o'clock in the fading afternoon light of Wednesday, March 5, 1873, as the *Clara Bella* came alongside. He grabbed the ropes and tied the lines fast as the schooner settled against the dock just off Water Street in Portsmouth's rough and tumble South End. As John Hontvet stepped ashore, Wagner asked him how many fish he had caught that day. John, his brother Matthew, and brother-in-law, Ivan, had done well enough fishing at a spot south of the Shoals. John estimated their catch at between 1,600 and 1,800 pounds. Wagner asked John if they would be heading back to the Shoals that night. In fact, according to John's courtroom testimony, Wagner asked that question three times.

The men of Smuttynose had no intention of leaving the women alone all night. They had left the island about six o'clock that morning and checked their lines at a good spot further to the northeast of the islands. They intended to stop back home and pick up Karen, who wanted to do some shopping in Portsmouth while the men picked up more bait. (There is no indication that John mentioned Karen to Wagner in their brief meeting.) But a strong southeasterly headwind had made it more convenient to head directly into Portsmouth to sell their catch. John had sent word to Maren and Anethe via one of the Ingebretsen boys from Appledore whom they met at sea. The boy delivered John's message to the women at Smuttynose, telling them that the *Clara Bella* should return home by ten p.m. But the train bringing the bait north from Boston was late, a fisherman told John, and was not expected to reach Portsmouth until eleven p.m. Wagner overheard this critical detail while standing on the wharf.

For the previous eight weeks, through January and February, Wagner had been prowling the many private docks along the Portsmouth waterfront looking for work. He complained bitterly to anyone who would listen about his lack of money, poor wages, ragged clothes, and bad luck. He hinted to others that he knew where to steal some money. Whether this was just a boast or whether Wagner was growing increasingly desperate and waiting for the perfect opportunity to commit robbery, is unknown. He later denied ever making such statements. If nothing else, Wagner was always very interested in how much money John was earning. While working on the *Clara Bella* in the fall, Wagner learned that John had money coming in from Boston and had accumulated at least six hundred dollars toward the purchase of a new boat.

"Through the winter," John later testified, "he [Wagner] used to come down about every time we came into Portsmouth, and used to ask us how many fish we got and what price we got, and knew pretty well what we were doing. From the time we started until this [murder] happened I had got one thousand odd dollars."

To Wagner, this must have seemed an enormous sum in an era when a crewman on a fishing boat often earned just $200 to $250 per year. Compared to Wagner and other struggling Gosport fishermen, John Hontvet was "forehanded," that is, he was well off because he knew how to plan for the future. John was a thinker and an entrepreneur who could adapt to new ways. During his one decade living in America, John had managed to find steady work, get married, establish his own business, buy a boat, find a house, build a crew, and bring his relatives across the Atlantic from Norway. Wagner, in the same period, had nothing to show for seven years of back-breaking labor. Cast out of his comfortable accommodations on Smuttynose, he was back in a cheap sailor's boarding house, this time at the home of Matthew and Mary Johnson at 25 Water Street adjacent to the docks. Already in arrears on his rent, Wagner had been forced so low that he had to beg for thirty-five cents from another fisherman to buy tobacco. He complained to all who would listen that he was down on his luck and near destitute.

The tipping point for Wagner may have been his disastrous experience aboard the *Addison Gilbert*. After leaving Smuttynose, he had secured a job and a bunk on the fishing schooner and things were looking up. But early in January 1873, the *Addison Gilbert* was struck abreast by the sloop M.M. *Hamilton* out of Portland, Maine, laden with heavy railroad iron. The two ships collided at one-thirty on a foggy early morning just off Portsmouth Harbor Light at the mouth of the Piscataqua River. In just ten minutes, the *Addison Gilbert* sank in five fathoms of water. It is unclear from reports whether Wagner was aboard during the accident, but the eleven crewman, including Wagner, lost all their personal effects, which the *Portsmouth Journal* valued at a total of one thousand dollars. The crew was rescued by the M. M. *Hamilton* and Wagner found himself once again back on the hard-knuckle wharves of Portsmouth with nothing but a few articles of clothing to his name.

Water Street, now Marcy Street, was the oldest road in Portsmouth. In fact, the first house in the city was constructed there in 1631 when the first permanent European settlers arrived. The spot began as an English plantation called Strawbery Banke, named according to legend for the wild strawberries growing there. The two-story four-gable "Great House" may have stood on the same ground as the Johnson's boarding house, where Wagner now shared a second-floor room with two other sailors. But a lot had happened to Water Street in the 242 years since the original settlers arrived. Water Street had evolved into the hub of a prosperous colonial American port with rows of sturdy wharves welcoming as many as thirty ships per day from across the globe. Revolutionary heroes like Paul Revere, John Hancock, and John Paul Jones had found their way to the neighborhood known as Puddle Dock. President George Washington stopped by in 1789 with his secretary Tobias Lear, who had grown up in Portsmouth's South End. But those days were gone. New Hampshire's only seaport had peaked economically by the early 1800s, then crashed. The city center moved half a mile to the west. The rich merchants died off and their children quit the town for greener pastures, leaving crumbling docks and fading mansions behind. By Wagner's time, Portsmouth was a city in decay.

Formerly the home of powerful maritime businessmen and the state's royal governors, the waterfront devolved into a seedy line of saloons, warehouses, boarding houses, and bordellos. The city's "red light district" catered to the ebb and flow of sailors and laborers who worked at Portsmouth Naval Shipyard directly across the river. Before the current bridge was built linking Kittery to Portsmouth, sailors as young as fourteen were ferried by the hundreds to the top of Water Street. There, among the coal pockets and fishing wharves, stood the city brothels and a glitzy world of sin. The sex trade along Water Street was expanding in Wagner's time, but would not reach its peak until the Gay Nineties and early twentieth century. Official records on white slavery and prostitution in Portsmouth are nonexistent and the newspapers turned a blind eye to the elicit business that thrived for decades under the protective eye of city officials and police.

Among the storied institutions was the Four Tree Island House, located at what is now a picnic area a few yards offshore from modern-day Prescott Park. Charles E. Gray purchased the tiny island for forty dollars in 1877. A rare ticket about the size of a playing card has survived and promises the bearer "Free Dances Tuesday & Friday Evenings." Known locally as the "menagerie" and the "museum," Gray's saloon reportedly featured a stuffed alligator, a stuffed cow that dispensed beer from its udders, and a pair of boots that once belonged to outlaw Jesse James. The back of the bordello ticket includes a ribald poem about a boy and a maiden whose encounter leads to an unwed mother and an absentee father. The Four Tree Island House disappeared in a spectacular blaze in 1907. A lengthy legal circus began after Gray's death when five women claimed to be his widow.

By the mid-nineteenth century, the tidal inlet called Puddle Dock had devolved into a stinking bog, clogged with silt and debris and ripe with human waste and garbage. Johnson's boarding house was located eight buildings up from the historic Liberty Bridge, the site of a colonial Stamp Act riot against the King of England in 1760. By Wagner's time, Water Street was no longer a desirable address in the "Old Town by the Sea." One Victorian guide to Portsmouth, published the same year as the murders, points out the historic Liberty Pole, an ancient cemetery, and the home of New Hampshire's first governor in Puddle Dock. Pausing only for a moment, the author adds, "Let us get into some cheerfuler neighborhood."

Even before the sinking of the *Addison Gilbert*, Wagner may have been planning a robbery at Smuttynose or simply dreaming about it. Waldemar Ingebretsen, an Appledore fisherman, testified that he and Wagner had been aboard the *Gilbert* in December when it was tied up at Rollins Dock in Portsmouth. They were dressing to go ashore and Wagner was polishing his shoes when he found a torn spot in the leather. "This won't do any longer!" Wagner muttered to Ingebretsen. "I am bound to have money in three months if I am going to murder for it." Wagner reportedly made the same comment to Charles Johnson, whose father owned the boarding house, to Emil Ingebretsen, and even to Captain John Hontvet, all of whom testified in the murder trial.

As soon as John stepped off the *Clara Bella* on March 5 and discovered his bait would not arrive for at least another seven hours, he asked Wagner if he would like to make some quick money baiting trawls starting at around eleven p.m. that night. Wagner said he would be back to help them later on.

"You have been quite a stranger to me," Wagner told John on the dock. "I have not seen you since three weeks before Christmas."

This slice of conversation comes from Wagner's court testimony, which is riddled with inconsistencies and inventive lies. In his version, Wagner seemed to take offense at the presence of Ivan Christensen, Anethe's husband, who was serving on John's crew rather than remaining on Smuttynose protecting the women.

"Why have you brought your brother-in-law?" Wagner claims he said. "You never brought him in before."

"I brought him in once in a while to show him Portsmouth," John reportedly told Wagner. "The women at home can keep the house safe through the night."

New England storyteller Edward Rowe Snow suggested that Wagner's devious plan was sparked by John's casual comment that all three men, thinking they were returning home, had left their wallets back on the island. They didn't even have money to buy dinner or visit a bar. Perhaps Wagner imagined those wallets lying out in the open at the house, easy pickings for a thief with a boat. That information, plus the delayed arrival of the bait supply, was too tempting to pass up. In his impulsive way, Wagner may even have believed he could row to the island and back and still have time to join Hontvet's baiting party, or at least to get out of town before the robbery was discovered.

Wagner then went to Johnson's for his supper, although reports differ whether he showed up. Both men stated in court they saw each other once more an hour or two later near the wharf. They talked for about five minutes. Wagner again asked John if the men planned to return to the island that night. John said no. He knew it would take most of the night to bait hundreds of hooks. They talked about the weather. It was a clear night with a fair breeze blowing out toward the islands. Wagner said something to John about a boat he wanted to buy but could not pay for. Then they parted company. It was a Wednesday evening. They would not speak again until Friday afternoon when Wagner was a prisoner inside the Portsmouth jail.

John testified that he went looking for Wagner two or three times on the evening of March 5. He searched for him at Johnson's boarding house, then wandered along the many wharves on Water Street to see if his former crewman had picked up another odd job among the fishing boats there. By the time the bait train finally arrived from Boston, it was twelve-thirty a.m. on Thursday, March 6. Ivan Christensen, unaware that his wife Anethe had only minutes left to live, pitched in to help his brother-in-law bait trawls. Fisherman George Lowd helped, too, while Matthew Hontvet stayed aboard the *Clara Bella*.

The three men set up operations in the shop at Matthew Johnson's boarding house. The shop was located at ground level in the brick first floor facing Water Street. The top two floors where the family and boarders lived were constructed of wood. At the rear of the shop was a sitting room with a small bar and counter, a stool, three or four chairs, an antique claw-foot sofa or lounge, and a coal stove. John went back and forth from the shop to the sitting room all night to warm up and to drink water from a pitcher on the counter. Both Ivan and George Lowd took naps on the sofa. George quit at two or three a.m. and reportedly slept on the sofa until dawn. The two Norwegian men from Smuttynose continued their task until around six a.m. Thursday morning. The back door was locked and no one else came or left the two rooms during the entire time, John testified at trial.

Baiting trawls was a laborious process, especially in a cold winter workshop at night by lantern light. The men stood or sat in a group, each taking a long line with hundreds of attached hooks. They speared bits of bait onto the sharp metal barbs and then coiled the baited lines into wooden tubs to be deployed at sea. John preferred herring as bait, but herring was in short supply that year. Clams, menhaden shad (better known as "pogies"), and alewives were also popular bait among New England fisherman. The problem in 1873 was getting enough bait to supply the new "tub trawl" system. For centuries, fisherman had used single handlines with one or more baited hooks per line. They sailed or rowed to the most promising spots and waited for the fish to find them. And even with this simple technique, European fishermen had managed to deplete the available stocks and drive overfished species into near extinction. The desire for richer fishing grounds had been a driving force in the exploration of New England and the fertile protein-rich Gulf of Maine

Now history was repeating itself on the American side of the Atlantic Ocean. Fish along the New England coast were growing smaller and scarcer. Fishermen were forced to cluster in larger boats and to travel farther out to sea to find schools of fish. This process had driven the single dory fishers at Gosport into debt, factoring into their decision to sell off their meager homes and property at Star Island to hotel developer John Poor. Only the modern high-tech commercial fisherman like John Hontvet with their long trawl lines and sturdy schooners could survive the changes and compete in the marketplace.

By the 1870s, a process called "purse seining" was also catching on. Giant nets 1,350 feet wide and 150 feet deep hung down from the surface of the ocean, buoyed up by floating corks or hollow glass balls. When closed up like the drawstring on a purse, fishermen could capture everything inside the net, including egg-laying females and small fish. These immense nets and hooks were dragged along the ocean floor destroying shellfish beds. Besides fish, the crew hauled in tons of organic material, now called "bycatch," that was dumped back into the sea as waste.

Deep sea trawling and purse seining were dangerous and capital intensive methods. If John could not afford a bigger boat, more lines, more bait, and more crewmen, his little operation would also be killed off by the newer, faster, larger, steam-powered trawlers on the horizon. Attempts to pass regulations to ban or control trawl fishing in the late nineteenth century were unsuccessful. Environmental science was in its infancy and, despite significant evidence that trawl fishing might destroy entire underwater species, just as hunting from trains might wipe out the western buffalo, the warning went unheeded. Professor W. Jeffrey Bolster, who has written extensively about the history of Atlantic fishing, says most Victorians clung to the belief that "the immortal sea would buffer itself somehow from human-induced catastrophe."

But by 1873, the sea was proving to be mortal indeed. In that very year, the US Fish Commission announced that "restoration of our exhausted cod fisheries" was a federal priority. The impact of depleted fish stocks could be devastating to solitary fishermen in small boats, but it also cut into the profits of trawl fishermen. By the summer of 1873, the *Portsmouth Chronicle* reported: "Trawl fishing at the Shoals is to a large extent abandoned, owing to the scarcity of fish." The *Chronicle* blamed the new breed of trawl fishermen for "breaking up the schools of fish" that annually visited the area and "destroying the mother fish." Yet while times were tough, especially for members of the fishing community wiped out at Star Island, John Hontvet appeared to be doing better than ever. Although it is speculation, we can easily imagine that John's enviable situation and increasing profits fueled Wagner's resentment, especially in light of his recent expulsion from Smuttynose and the sinking of the *Addison Gilbert*. His personal animosity toward John not only enhances Wagner's motive for secretly robbing the Hontvets, but may help explain his homicidal rage at being discovered and his later efforts to blame the murders on his former boss.

With local bait suppliers unable to satisfy the growing demand by trawl fishermen, large specialty companies were springing up in Boston to fill the void. They shipped tons of processed bait daily by rail to waiting customers like John Hontvet. In a way, John's success on Smuttynose had set the stage for the unfolding tragedy. His small trawling operation could range farther and extract more fish than the old-fashioned hand-line system. But it was costing him more to keep pace. He was forced to build up a stash of money to upgrade and stay competitive. He needed to import, house, and feed an extended family to keep a steady crew. And once locked into the modern trawling system, John Hontvet was at the whim of the distant factory that supplied him with bait. If the train from Boston was late, John would be late returning home to Maren. And when Louis Wagner failed to show up to help, as he had promised to do, the men from Smuttynose were forced to work through the long, cold night.

Chapter 10

ROWING

Here the story splits sharply in two. On one side, we have Louis Wagner's elaborate but unsupported version of where he went and what he did in Portsmouth over the next eleven or twelve hours. On the other side, we have the case against Wagner assembled from snippets of information gathered from dozens of witnesses and assembled by the prosecuting attorneys. After chatting with John Hontvet on Water Street, Wagner all but disappeared until he was spotted at nearby New Castle early the following morning. He did not show up for supper at Johnson's boarding house on the evening of March 5. No witness could be found to confirm, as Wagner later claimed, that he had worked baiting trawls for another ship on the docks, that he wandered sick and drunk through the streets after visiting two bars, that he vomited and passed out by the town water pump, or that he was sleeping on the sofa in the sitting room at Matthew Johnson's while Hontvet's crew baited trawls in the next room.

In three months of investigation, Wagner's defense attorneys could find only a single witness, a six-year resident of Portsmouth named Timothy Chellis, who was willing to swear in court that he had seen Wagner that evening. "I saw him about half-past seven on that night, I should judge, in my shop, it might be a little later," Chellis told the jury. "He called for some ale." When he was arrested the following evening in Boston, a police officer told Wagner they had found the baker who sold him bread before he left for the Isles of Shoals. Wagner challenged the accusation, saying he had visited a Portsmouth bakery, but on the morning after the murders.

So no one actually saw Louis Wagner steal David Burke's dory from the small dock where it was tied at the base of Pickering Street in the city's South End. Wagner had been fishing aboard Burke's schooner, the *Iris*, three weeks earlier with Burke's sons, and with fishermen named James Lee and Peter Johnson. All four men testified they knew Wagner and he had been with them when they used the dory to travel back and forth to Burke's fishing schooner. On March 5, James and Peter had taken the dory into Portsmouth for provisions. They arrived at the base of Pickering Street at seven-thirty p.m. and tied it securely "with two half hitches round a post." That detail tells any sailor that the boat did not drift away on its own. When they returned an hour later, the dory was gone. It would be discovered early the following morning adrift in Little Harbor in the neighboring town of New Castle.

For once, Wagner's timing was perfect. It was a good fifteen-minute walk from the downtown saloon run by Tim Chellis to the end of Pickering Street, and it was a mere three hundred yards from the dock to David Burke's house where the two fishermen were picking up their provisions. Another few minutes and they would return, taking the rowboat with them. Wagner may have been prowling the waterfront in search of a boat to take to the Shoals or he may have been searching, as he testified, for a quick job unloading fish or baiting trawls. He was wearing his worn-out cold-weather fishing outfit, among his only possessions not lost in the sinking of the *Addison Gilbert*—blue overalls, a blue jumper or sweater over a brown jumper, and a pair of size-eleven rubber boots.

By nature, Wagner was both calculating and impulsive. It is entirely possible that the daring plan suddenly coalesced the moment he saw the familiar dory bobbing in the water with its two oars attached. The calculus was clear. With all three men off Smuttynose, with the moon on the rise and the sky clear, with the wind low and the tide right, with a boat at hand, there was time enough. He could reach the Isles of Shoals, slip silently into the house, grab the Hontvet's savings, and have the dory back in its place well before dawn. It might be days before anyone noticed the money was missing. By then, he would be far away. Murder, it is possible, was the last thing on his mind. If the women were asleep and did not wake, Wagner later told the judge in a semi-confessional moment at his arraignment five days later, he could have easily stolen the Hontvet's money.

It would have taken no more than a minute for Wagner to step onto the dock, unfastened the dory line, position the oars, and push off into the dark Piscataqua River. New Hampshire has only three ocean lighthouses and Wagner would pass them all as he pulled toward the Isles of Shoals. The swift flowing tide, one of the fastest in North America, would whisk the dory and its passenger the first three miles almost without effort. Quickly came the glow of Portsmouth Harbor Light at Fort Constitution on New Castle Island, the last chunk of land before the mouth of the river turned into open sea. The beam from this wooden tower, built in 1770 under British colonial rule, was fixed like a spotlight, but would scarcely have illuminated a lone rower. The granite block fort had been the site of what locals still proudly call "the first battle of the American Revolution." The whitewashed cast-iron tower that stands today near the ruins of the old fort was built in 1877, two years after Wagner's death.

The second benchmark was the station on tiny Whaleback Ledge in the center of the river. It was actually two towers. The original brick lighthouse had been replaced just months before by a new tower of dovetailed granite blocks but the old tower had yet to be removed. The light from the expensive new Fresnell lens swept repeatedly across the dark water. Until he reached the sea, even at night, Wagner was at constant risk of being seen. A few years earlier, the keeper at Whaleback Light had counted 380 vessels as they passed by in a single day. The lamp exposed the dory with each pass, but Wagner was swiftly out of range.

From here, Wagner would have to row in earnest. During a recent reenactment of his journey, an amateur rower in a replica dory took only thirty minutes, borne by the powerful tide and traveling at over five knots, to reach this point from Pickering's Wharf in Portsmouth. But here the sea becomes frighteningly vast and the intermittent glow from the third lighthouse at the Shoals seven miles away would be no bigger than a firefly. If Wagner had doubts, this was the point to turn back. There was still plenty of time to return to the city and to bait trawls. But the powerful undercurrent still tugged at his dory, urging it seaward. The Hontvet's treasure, perhaps hundreds of dollars, lay waiting. Turning around now meant fighting the mighty Piscataqua tide. The return trip, Wagner knew, could take as long and expend as much energy as rowing the rest of the way to Smuttynose. By dawn he could earn a dollar from John Hontvet, or he could have it all. So the die was cast, and he pressed on.

The next few hours belong to fiction writers and to poets. The image of Wagner in his tiny boat, pulling relentlessly at the oars in the near darkness while his victims sleep is hypnotizing. Celia Thaxter imagined the scene as if in slow motion with the grim figure of death inching closer to his innocent victims. "It seems to take an eternity of time," Celia imagined, as if she were in the dory with Wagner.

Instead of thwarting the murderer, she wrote, Mother Nature appeared to be assisting Wagner on his deadly mission. Two weeks earlier, the thermometer had dropped to thirteen degrees below zero in a "cold blowy snap" with plenty of snow and white-capped waves. Suddenly it was like spring with fair westerly winds, calm seas, and just enough moonlight to guide his journey while disguising him from view. Even God sat idly by as "this planned piece of deliberate wickedness" was enacted, Celia wrote, quoting from a play by the poet Robert Browning. The horror of Wagner's journey stood in sharp contrast, she wrote, to the peaceful snow-covered scenery as he rowed "with his heart full of darkness, blacker than the black tide that swirled beneath his boat and bore him fiercely on."

Maine poet John Perrault captured the seemingly endless journey by repeating this refrain after every stanza in his "Ballad of Louis Wagner." The chorus goes: "Louis, Louis Wagner, rowing through the night/ Louis, Louis

Wagner, the noose will fit you tight." While it is tempting, in retrospect, to imbue Wagner at this point with homicidal intent, he may have had little on his mind except the dull meditative rhythm of the oars. He apparently brought no weapons with him.

He was a dory fisherman and familiar with the ocean at night and in all weather. He knew the risk of being seen by a passing schooner, the mercurial changes of New England weather, and the dangers of the sea. If his boat was swamped by a sudden wave, he would most certainly drown minutes later in the frigid waters. In the dark, facing away from the bow of the boat, Wagner could strike a rocky ledge and sink or spring a leak. He could snap a precious oar and find himself drifting aimlessly toward open ocean, eventually to die of exposure. There was even the chance that John Hontvet, tired of waiting for his bait to arrive, had left Portsmouth and that the *Clara Bella* would suddenly appear out of the darkness.

On the same spot off the Isles of Shoals decades later, two men hauling their trawls had a fearsome encounter with a seventy-foot whale. It circled them and thrashed the water into foam with its tail, filling their dories to the railings with water and forcing the men to bail or sink. "The whale seemed to be disappointed and angry," they told a trade publication called *The Fisherman* in 1895, "for he headed right after us and poked his big nose up to the tall rail of the sloop. He chased us about two miles then went to the eastward."

The brightest of the three lighthouses was now dominating the night sky, its rotating lens flashing endlessly red, then white, then red every thirty seconds. As the narrow beam from White Island grew closer and the low dark islands appeared, Wagner must have feathered his oars with more confidence, pivoting them parallel to the water with each stroke to reduce the sound of splashing and the muffled squeak of the wooden paddles. His destination was almost a mile north of the pulsing lighthouse, its beam too distant to reveal his coming. If he arrived at the Shoals in good time,

Wagner may have seen lanterns still sputtering in Celia Thaxter's cottage on Appledore. ("What fearful thing passed by!" she later wrote, "but we slumbered peacefully.") Or he may have seen lights winking out among the surviving houses on Star Island where John Poor's workmen were retiring from another long day building the Oceanic Hotel. He may even have seen Maren Hontvet's lamp go out on Smuttynose. The three women, after waiting in vain for the men to return, turned off their lamps and went to bed sometime after ten p.m.

It has been suggested that Wagner slipped silently between the stone pier and Malaga Island to see if there were any other boats in Smuttynose Cove. He was clever enough not to tie up his stolen dory there in full view but apparently landed some distance away. He may have gone all the way around the islands, killing time, passing around Star and Cedar. More likely he pulled his boat up among the rocks near what is now a stone breakwater connecting Smuttynose to Cedar Island. A hand-painted sign now marks the rocky spot as Wagner's Cove.

March 5 had been an uncharacteristically lucky day for the Prussian fisherman. All the pieces of the perfect robbery had so far fallen into place. He knew the island intimately having lived there seven months. And he knew, or thought he knew, where John Hontvet hid his money in the family home. Just another hour or two and he would be a wealthy man. But as midnight loomed and Wednesday turned to Thursday, Wagner's bad luck would return with a vengeance.

The problem was Karen. It is probable that Wagner believed there were only two women, Maren and Anethe, sleeping soundly in the house, not three. Karen had left her job at the Appledore Hotel two weeks earlier after serving the Laightons for almost two years since her arrival from Norway. In "A Memorable Murder" Celia reveals that Karen was planning to go to Boston and obtain work at a sewing machine "for she was not strong and thought she should like it better than housework." Suffering from severe toothaches, Karen had also recently been to Portsmouth where a dentist had removed all of her teeth, an extremely painful process in Victorian times. According to Celia, Karen had told Mrs. Johnson, the woman who ran the boarding house on Water Street, that the waiting period for a set of false teeth was three months. Wagner may have overheard this conversation between Karen and his landlady in Portsmouth, and Celia says that Wagner then muttered to himself, "Three months! What is the use! In three months you will be dead."

While Celia Thaxter is often a reliable source, this whispered threat is almost certainly untrue or highly exaggerated. According to one of her contemporaries, when it came to her prose writing, "Celia was always given to coloring in a little," and this may be one of those times. Wagner's comment was overheard by Mrs. Johnson's daughter, Mary, as told to Maren Hontvet, as told to Celia Thaxter after the murders. It makes no sense that Wagner would threaten Karen's life within earshot of a witness, and especially to do so with a three-month timeline. Neither of the Johnson women mentioned this incriminating comment at Wagner's trial, nor did Maren. So if Wagner's motive was robbery and Karen's murder was not premeditated, why would Celia Thaxter include this damning detail?

Celia may have had personal reasons to demonize Louis Wagner. Maybe she felt more than a little guilt surrounding Karen's sudden departure from Appledore. We get a fuller story from Cedric, who wrote to sister Celia on February 23, two weeks before Wagner's dory slid silently into Gosport Harbor. While Celia downplayed the story of the firing of Karen in her famous essay, Cedric described it in epic terms as one of the most memorable days in the history of the Appledore Hotel.

With his usual comic wit, not knowing Karen's death was days away, Cedric described the battle that ensued when Karen was instructed to clean out the apartments that housed the hotel workmen. The men would soon arrive to begin the annual spring preparation and their rooms had barely been washed or swept since the previous fall. Eliza Laighton, the widow of Thomas Laighton, apparently ordered Karen to get to work in a harsh manner. Karen, already unhappy with her job, embarrassed by her missing teeth, and heartsick for her lost lover, responded with righteous indignation. Karen stood in mother's doorway, Cedric reported to Celia, "clutching the doorknob in her feverish grasp and with the fire of her pent up emotions flashing from either eye." Karen then "annihilated" her boss in "a whirlwind of broken English" and stalked off.

The next day, Karen made a sorrowful apology but Eliza Laighton was unforgiving. She gave Karen some money, Cedric wrote, and then ordered her to, "depart and never come in my sight again." On hearing that her favorite servant had been fired, Cedric's Aunt Caroline, then living at the hotel, erupted in an "earthquake" of protest. Aunt Caroline "burst out into some of the most fearfully dismal and piercingly heart wrenching yells I ever heard," Cedric wrote. The windows rattled, the cows mooed, and the horses in the barn pulled at their reigns in fear, Cedric joked. Karen Christensen's departure from the hotel was a fearful scene that "will long be remembered in the annals of Appledore." The truly fearful scene, however, was yet to come.

Karen's untimely return to Smuttynose now appears as a cruel twist of fate. Worse yet was the sudden shift in the breeze on the afternoon of March 5. Karen had planned to go shopping in Portsmouth that day. John Hontvet was coming to get her. He intended to drop off Ivan at Smuttynose after fishing, eat dinner with his wife, Maren, and sail with Karen and Matthew aboard the *Clara Bella* to Portsmouth. While the men sold their fish and baited trawls in the city, Karen planned to run a few errands, then they would all return to the Shoals that same evening.

Karen was dressed for a trip into Portsmouth all day, Maren later told Celia. Karen had "lots of copper money" that day, too, Maren testified at the trial. Anethe gave her sister-in-law three quarters and Maren had given her a dime to buy some braid. Anethe also took a white button from Maren's sewing basket. She gave the button to Karen and asked her to look for matching buttons while she was in the city. Karen put the coins and the button in her purse and snapped the lock shut. But then the wind shifted and the men went to Portsmouth and the bait train was late. So Karen did not go to Portsmouth on Wednesday as planned. She did not go on Thursday or on Friday. She did not go to Portsmouth until Saturday afternoon when she and Anethe arrived aboard the USS *Mayflower*. The tugboat delivered their battered bodies in pine boxes to the warehouse of funeral directors Woodbury, Gerrish & Company.

Chapter 11

LOUIS! LOUIS!

How long the thief in the night stalked the island before striking we cannot know. In his detailed analysis of the Smuttynose case, true crime writer Edmund Pearson suggested that Wagner spent "an hour of silent reconnoitering, spying, and listening" after stowing his stolen dory. He was known to be methodical, calculating, quiet, even voyeuristic. Wagner may have had as long as two hours for spying, giving him plenty of time to peer through the windows, if he dared, after the lights went out at ten p.m. It was a pleasant night, Maren later testified, and she had left the shades up, although Karen's makeshift bed in the kitchen corner remained invisible to peering eyes. The robber tuned his ears for any sounds in the "westerly" end of the dark duplex. He watched the smoke drift from the central chimney towards a dazzling 360-degree canopy of stars. His large rubber boots crunched too loudly in the last of the winter snow, but the sound was muffled by the distant rhythm of waves washing over seaweed-covered rocks.

Maren would be sleeping in the Hontvet bedroom farthest to the right with its single small window facing Gosport Harbor and the rising Oceanic Hotel on Star Island. Anethe, Wagner would assume, was sleeping upstairs. For the moment, Wagner had the advantage of surprise. According to John Downs, whose grandfather was the only fisherman left on Star Island at this time, "robbery on the island was an unheard of crime." The close-knit Shoalers had traditionally been "hard-faring honest people" and they were "loathe to touch the cent of another," Downs tells us. The Hontvets, like most Shoalers, kept their money hidden somewhere in their house. The nearest bank was miles away on the mainland. John's fortune, as much as six hundred or one thousand dollars Wagner had learned, might be sewn into a mattress, or more likely, could be hidden in one of the large trunks that had come with them from Norway. Certainly Wagner had run the scenario through his head many times and was confident that he could find some or all of the money. Although maybe, after hours outdoors in the winter cold, faced with the reality of what he was about to do, his confidence was fading. He was stealthy by nature, but under no circumstances, once he entered the house, could he allow himself to be identified. Not even the boldest lie could explain away his presence on Smuttynose at midnight with a stolen boat nearby.

If John's wallet was on the table, he could grab it and run. If the trunk with John's fortune was in the kitchen, then the robber had a solid chance of getting away with a windfall. But if the trunk was in Maren's bedroom, how could he expect to extract it without waking her or rousing her damned little dog, Ringe?

Did Wagner plan to knock the women unconscious as they slept? Or was the plan to blindfold, gag, and tie them up, then ransack the house at his leisure? Or was there no plan at all? What had seemed a golden opportunity just a few hours ago at Pickering's Dock was now looking risky, even foolhardy. One loud creaking floorboard and the jig was up. But to turn back now, to row all those miles to Portsmouth with nothing to show for his efforts but a few blisters, that too was madness.

It is entirely possible that Wagner spent time contemplating the coming deed while hiding inside the "easterly" apartment to the left. Had the money been stashed on that side of the house, now used as a workshop, this could have been the perfect crime and Louis Wagner would be unknown to history. This apartment was familiar territory for Wagner. The large kitchen on the left side of the duplex had been his bedroom for many months the previous year. With a window on each end of the large room, he had watched the spectacular golden sunrises and the purple and scarlet bands of sunset over Malaga night after night. From spring until the fall of 1872, Wagner had enjoyed the same cool breezes and the healthy salt air that drew throngs of city tourists to the scenic Isles of Shoals. Here was the room where Maren had nursed and fed him as he suffered, or pretended to suffer, from crippling bouts of rheumatism. Here, despite his poverty, he had lived in comfort, cleanliness, independence, and dignity.

But it was his room no more. With the arrival of Ivan and Anethe, the Norwegian clan was complete. John and Matthew had since turned the room into a spacious workshop. Louis, meanwhile, had survived a shipwreck, lost most of his possessions, and moved into a flop house, sharing a room with two other sailors. He had been reduced to begging for tobacco, while John Hontvet enjoyed a privileged life of fortune and family. Later Wagner would blame his former employer for orchestrating his arrest, for bribing witnesses, and for committing the murders with his wife. But now, as Wagner hovered outside the Red House, it was John Hontvet's turn to feel the sting of bad luck and the loss of his hard won savings.

The robber eventually plucked up his courage and tested the knob on the narrow front door of the Hontvet apartment. The door, as he suspected, was unlocked. His sudden wave of incredible luck was holding. A gentle pocket of warm air welcomed him into the familiar, cramped entranceway. It was too risky to climb the creaking stairs. Instead, Wagner silently pushed open the door to the Hontvet kitchen. He was rewarded by another whoosh of warm air from the embers still burning in the kitchen stove that vented to the central chimney. There was the lingering scent of food, perhaps herbs, baked goods, and fish chowder.

Wagner's eyes adjusted to the vague shadows cast by the light of the three-quarter moon coming through the windows. He scanned for a trunk where there might be money. So far, so good. Perhaps he removed his large wet boots before he felt his way silently along the table and chairs in the center of the room. The door between the kitchen and the downstairs bedroom had been left open to draw warmth from the stove. The robber took a moment to carefully close the door to Maren's bedroom and wedged a stick into the latch. Maybe the door squeaked against its frame or the latch rattled or the floorboards sagged or some other sound woke Ringe the dog who barked from inside the bedroom. The robber froze, heart pounding. But in the next room, Maren did not stir. Then a disembodied voice came out of a dark corner of the kitchen just beyond the iron stove.

"John, is that you?"

The robber barely breathed. Someone else was in the room. Was it Anethe? He had been standing right next to a sleeping figure all these minutes. Roused from sleep, speaking in Norwegian and with all of her teeth removed, Karen Christensen's garbled voice may have been unintelligible to Wagner at first. She was lying on a makeshift bed that her sister had assembled from a lounge and two chairs. Drowsy, she naturally assumed that the three Norwegian men had returned from Portsmouth.

"What is the matter?"

This was clearly Maren's voice, Wagner knew, coming from the bedroom, edged with concern and barely muffled by the thin plaster wall.

"John scared me! John scared me!" Karen repeated to her sister in the next room.

Wagner's split-second response changed everything. Rather than run and row home and return to his life of poverty, the robber lashed out. All the frustration and disappointment he had endured over the years filled his large powerful frame. All the jealousy and anger he felt for John Hontvet came back. He picked up one of the heavy kitchen chairs and savagely struck the figure lying in the corner of the kitchen, now partially visible in the moonlight. Karen shrieked in pain and confusion at what she still mistakenly thought was her brother-in-law.

"John killed me!" she cried over and over.

Maren jumped out of bed and tried to rush to her sister's aid, but the bedroom door was fastened from the other side and she could not get it open. Anethe sat up with concern. With her husband gone, and unwilling to sleep alone upstairs, she was sharing Maren's bed downstairs.

"John killed me!" Karen cried again.

The dark figure rained blows on Karen until she fell off the makeshift bed. Karen managed to crawl underneath the kitchen table. The clock on the wall above the bed crashed to the floor. Somehow, according to Maren's account, whatever was blocking the bedroom door fell away at this point and she was able to get into the kitchen. In the moonlight, she saw only the silhouette of a tall man standing by the window. The figure looming above her held a chair in both hands. Still gripping the bedroom door with one hand, Maren reached her other arm toward Karen and grabbed her sister firmly. As she pulled Karen toward her, Maren was struck twice on the back with blows from a chair but she managed to hang onto the door while helping Karen into the bedroom.

Anethe was out of bed now and all three women, dressed in their winter nightclothes, were trapped in the small first-floor bedroom with an unknown maniac in the next room. Maren told Karen to hold onto the door latch while she and Anethe tried to push open the small bedroom window. It was only a short drop, about nine narrow clapboards distance, to the snow-covered yard below. But Karen was too weak to defend the door.

"I can't do it," Karen said. "I am so tired."

Karen threw her arms over the bed and dropped to her knees, unable to rise. Her traumatic firing at Appledore, her longstanding depression, her fresh wounds had robbed her of the will to carry on. So it fell to Maren to barricade the door as the intruder tried to force his way in. Maren commanded the frightened young Anethe to gather up some clothes and to jump out the window and escape. Anethe opened the window as she was told and clambered out, but she clung to the side of the house unwilling to flee into the cold and dark of the island.

"Run!" Maren told her sister-in-law, but Anethe only moved a few feet away from the house and refused to go farther.

"Run!" Maren told her in desperation as the intruder beat again on the bedroom door.

"I can't run," Anethe called back through the window, shivering in the snow.

"If you cry out," Maren told her, "somebody from the other islands might hear you."

"I cannot cry out," Anethe said from just beyond the window.

The stranger in the kitchen hammered on the bedroom door a third time, but he did not speak a word. Then the pounding suddenly stopped, and moments later Anethe did cry out when she saw a man she knew coming around the corner of the house.

"Louis! Louis!" Anethe shouted.

Hearing her sister-in-law's voice, Maren jumped away from the bedroom door and looked cautiously out her only window. Anethe had seen Wagner coming around the side of the house, and he had seen her. The dark figure in a short hat with a white brim stopped right outside Maren's window. He stood so close, she later said, that he could have laid his elbow on the window. The intruder kept his back toward the window and never spoke. Maren did not see his face. But that no longer mattered to Wagner. He had been identified. The women, by waking, had ruined his perfect plan. They had given him no choice. Whatever happened next was their fault, not his. He could not leave a witness alive on the island. After a moment, he turned and went back around the corner to the front of the house, then quickly returned holding a large ax. Maren recognized it as the ax she used to chop ice off the surface of their fresh water well. They kept it propped near the front door.

Wagner stood in the moonlight holding the ax, expecting the beautiful blonde woman to run. But Anethe, frozen with fear, only continued to plead his name —"Louis! Louis! Louis!"—as he approached. Then, as Maren watched in horror from her window, he began striking Anethe with the ax.

"He hit her on the head," Maren later testified to an equally horrified jury of twelve men. "He struck her once, and she fell down. After she fell down, he struck her twice."

Leaving Anethe for dead, her dark blood melting into the snow just a few yards from the house, the killer walked back around the corner toward the front door. With the ax, he could make quick work of the bedroom door. Maren grabbed a skirt, wrapped it around herself, and jumped out the window. Leaning back in, she begged her sister Karen to come with her, but to no avail.

"I am so tired," Karen whispered. "I can't go."

Maren ran across the sharp icy rocks in her bare feet, down the hill past Anethe's motionless body, and she disappeared in the direction of the water. Wagner, meanwhile, reentered the house. He returned to the kitchen, this time carrying the blood-stained ax. He stood again outside the bedroom door. The clock at his feet, broken in the attack on Karen, still registered 1:07 a.m. A few minutes before that, he had been on the verge of the perfect robbery. Now he was a murderer with two witnesses left to dispatch.

Back in Portsmouth, the bait train had finally arrived from Boston. Wagner still was nowhere in sight, and after many fruitless searches, John Hontvet had given up on hiring his help that night. Thanks to Matthew Johnson, the fishermen could at least work indoors at Johnson's shop rather than aboard the *Clara Bella*. It was after one o'clock in the morning by the time John, George Lowd, and Ivan Christensen were each settled around a wooden tub baiting their long trawl lines. In Portsmouth, it promised to be a tiring but uneventful night. Come dawn, the men would sail home to the women sleeping peacefully on Smuttynose.

Chapter 12

HUNTING MAREN

After leaping out her bedroom window into the snow, Maren ran instinctively down the low sloping island toward shelter. She opened the door of a small abandoned house near the water where she kept her henhouse. Maren stepped inside thinking, momentarily, of hiding in the old root cellar, which was little more than a coffin-like crawlspace framed by the stone foundation. Then Ringe appeared.

"I saw the little dog coming, and I was afraid to hide away," she later said. "I was afraid the dog would bark, and out I went again."

She passed Anethe, who lay silent and motionless a few yards up the hill toward the house, her vivacious spirit reduced to a dark shape in the fading moonlight. Maren ran along the decaying buildings near the water, past the stone pier, hoping to find Wagner's boat hauled up in the cove. With luck, she could take it and row across the harbor for help, leaving the killer stranded on Smuttynose. But there was no dory in the cove. She considered hiding among the ramshackle fish houses but again was afraid that Ringe would give their position away. So Maren ran, stumbling over icy rocks and brambles in her bare feet with her little dog at her heels, tripping and rising, and running again. She was still within view of the house when she heard Karen cry out one last time.

"I heard her so plain, I thought she was outside of the house," Maren recalled. Then the silence of the winter night returned and Maren was alone.

A lamp flickered on inside the kitchen of the Red House. Maren noticed that Wagner had pulled down the shades. "I ran to find rocks to hide myself away underneath the rocks on the island," she later testified.

Her risky decision to secrete herself and her dog among the cold jagged rocks was the right one. Footprints in the snow made from large rubber boots later showed that the killer had methodically moved from house-to-house and room-to-room hunting his final victim. Wagner knew the unused buildings on the island and it is easy to imagine him, bloodied, wild-eyed, with a weapon clutched in one hand and an oil lamp thrust forward in the other. With the moon now set, the glow of the lantern would illuminate only a small circular space as the killer moved from outhouse to henhouse and down to the cove. With each swing of the lantern, the shadows jumped and shifted. Maren, he knew, might be anywhere, crouched in the darkness of the rotten smelling fish house, among the barrels of the old Laighton store, or burrowed among decades of island debris inside the long wooden warehouse atop the stone pier.

All this searching took valuable time and sapped his energy, time and energy he badly needed to row his stolen dory back to Portsmouth before daylight where he must establish an alibi. But he could not leave Maren alive. She might not have seen his face through the bedroom window, but she had undoubtedly heard Anethe call out his name again and again until he silenced her with the ax. But Maren was not hiding in the ancient Haley Cottage next door. Nor was she crouched behind the many guestroom doors of the looming two-story Mid-Ocean House. And yet, left with no choice, the killer had to search every dark hotel room, every closet, every privy, every cellar. If she survived the night, Wagner knew, he was doomed, so the hunt continued.

"What a picture!" Celia Thaxter wrote. "That blood-stained butcher, with his dark face, crawling about those cellars, peering for that woman!"

What weapon Wagner carried in his search, if any, is unknown. The "big ax" that killed Anethe was broken. It would be discovered in the morning hours lying outside the house, the handle snapped and jagged. A broken piece of the wooden sill outside of Maren's bedroom window, it has been suggested, was made by the pole of the ax as Wagner swung fiercely from inside the bedroom. Perhaps the handle snapped as the killer made one wild swing at Maren as she leapt to freedom. Wagner "struck at her with the axe as she leaped and drove it deep into the window ledge," Celia wrote to a friend a few days later.

Or more likely it was Karen, having recovered slightly, who crawled out the window just as Wagner burst into the bedroom with ax held high. Having just butchered Anethe, he was at the peak of his rage. He swung at her and missed. The blow gouged the inside of the window sill and shattered the exterior as the haft snapped and the bloody head of the ax tumbled into the snow where it lay until the fishermen, the spectators, and the coroner's team later arrived. Karen managed, somehow, to make her way into the other apartment of the duplex. She stumbled through John Hontvet's workshop, where Louis Wagner had lived the previous year. Pausing to light a lamp, Wagner quickly found Karen still alive, shivering beneath the bed in the room he had once used as a clothes closet. Karen screamed again loudly as Wagner withdrew a white handkerchief. She could see his face now. He may have tried to coax her into revealing where John kept his money. If so, she did not know, or was too tired to say. Then the killer drew the handkerchief around Karen's neck, knotted it at the back with a sailor's precision, and tightened the cloth until her tongue protruded and her breathing ceased.

After an exhausting and fruitless search for Maren, Wagner returned to the warmth of the Hontvet kitchen. Here, he began another frantic search for the king's ransom that had drawn him ten miles across the ocean and cost the lives of two innocent women who had been his friends. Wagner tore through trunks upstairs and down. He tossed out clothes, emptied drawers, and upturned furniture on both sides of the Red House. He left bloody stains and hand prints wherever he went. Exactly what denominations of coins and paper money were stolen that night would become a key element of the prosecution's case against Louis Wagner. But there was no one thousand or six hundred dollars, the amounts John Hontvet had told Wagner he was owed for selling fish in Boston, to be found in any room. There was $10 in a pocketbook inside the trunk belonging to John and Maren. The thief broke the lock, emptied the purse, and tossed it aside. There was another $145 in cash tucked between two sheets at the bottom of the same trunk. Wagner fumbled through the contents with his bloody hands, but he did not find the larger cache of money. It is a telling fact that the only unopened trunk was the one belonging to Karen, which contained her summer clothes and a featherbed. Wagner would have known it held nothing of value, since Karen's trunk had been stored in his bedroom all the previous year. Wagner did steal a few dollars from Karen's purse, the one she had planned to carry on a shopping trip to Portsmouth the previous morning. There was a silver half dollar, and unseen among a handful of coins, there was a white button, the one Karen was hoping to match for Anethe during her shopping. The killer's total booty, when the search was finally concluded, came to roughly $16, or $8 per corpse.

At some point Wagner returned to the body of Anethe that lay freezing a few yards from the dark house. Perhaps he reached down and grabbed her cooling ankles to drag her over the snowy rocks, pulling up her nightgown and exposing her naked flesh. Another report suggests that he wrapped a shawl around Anethe's neck and used that to drag her inside. Either way, he pulled the body up over the single wooden front step of the Hontvet apartment, leaving a trail of blood. He hauled it through the small vestibule where he let Anethe drop just inside the kitchen. Although both bodies were initially found naked below the waist, no whisper of sexual crimes ever appeared in the Victorian press, in the coroner's report, in the trial transcript, or in any other serious study of the case since. The possibility, as unlikely as it may be, has been too horrifying to contemplate.

We cannot know the precise sequence of events early on March 6, but at some point the killer also washed up and ate a meal before departing Smuttynose Island. A basin and bloody towels were found later that morning by the open well that can still be seen about thirty feet behind the site of the Hontvet House. That the killer knew where to find the well in the darkness—a well that was nothing more than a circle of stones less than two feet high—is further evidence that he was familiar with the layout of the island. Most likely he washed in the icy water before returning again to the warm kitchen where, to the abhorrence of writers like Celia Thaxter, Wagner ate a meal.

"But how cool a monster is he!" Celia wrote in the *Atlantic Monthly*. "After all this hard work he must have refreshment to support him in the long row back to the land; knife and fork, cup and plate, were found next morning on the table near where Anethe lay; fragments of food which was not cooked in the house, but brought from Portsmouth, were scattered about. Tidy Maren had left neither dishes nor food when they went to bed. The handle of the tea-pot which she had left on the stove was stained and smeared with blood. Can the human mind conceive of such hideous nonchalance? Wagner sat down in that room and ate and drank! It is almost beyond belief!"

Based on his arrival on the mainland at about six-thirty a.m. Thursday, Wagner may have lingered on Smuttynose until three or even four o'clock that morning. Perhaps he turned off his lamp and waited in vain for Maren to stumble back home half-frozen. Perhaps he explored each of the empty buildings again and again, or wandered along the shore, shined his lamp behind the tombstones in the Haley cemetery, or along the low stone walls that crisscross the island. But eventually, with sunrise and the arrival of the *Clara Bella* imminent, Wagner reclaimed his hidden dory and made his escape. In an era before fingerprints, blood typing, DNA analysis, and other forensic evidence, the killer left a crime scene littered with clues unreadable to Victorian eyes.

Chapter 13

ESCAPE

Legend says Maren Hontvet concealed herself and Ringe deep among the storm-tossed boulders at the uninhabited southeastern tip of the island. A jutting rock formation there is now called Maren's Rock. If so, then she had walked some three-quarters of a mile in the frozen darkness over treacherous terrain and past scores of equally isolated spots. Celia's description of the hiding place could be taken for almost anywhere on the Smuttynose shore. It is more than possible that Maren hunkered down not far from where Wagner secretly stowed his dory near the fragmented granite breakwater that now connects Smuttynose to Cedar Island. (The breakwater from Cedar to Star Island, the channel separating New Hampshire from Maine, did not exist at the time and was then a key shipping lane through Gosport Harbor.) If she was hunkered down there, then Maren narrowly missed discovering the killer's boat in the darkness, and Wagner narrowly missed uncovering her sanctuary.

Celia dramatized Maren's escape this way: "She creeps, between two rocks, upon her hands and knees, and crouches, face downward, with Ringe nestled close beneath her breast, not daring to move...She is so near the ocean she can almost reach the water with her hand. Had the wind breathed the least roughly, the waves must have washed over her."

The sun had been up for half an hour before Maren dared to crawl from her rocky hiding place. Her first thought, as she trudged painfully back toward the heart of the island, was that Louis Wagner might still be on Smuttynose.

"I thought he must be there, dead or alive," Maren told Celia Thaxter. "I thought he might go crazy and kill himself after having done all that."

But Wagner was not a man inclined toward suicide, or even toward remorse and guilt. Maren was alone on the island. Inching her half-frozen feet painfully along the sharp rocks facing Gosport Harbor, Maren attempted to signal the men working on the Oceanic Hotel. John Poor's new luxury hotel was fully framed and Maren could clearly hear the workman's hammers ringing out in the morning breeze. She waved the skirt that she had grabbed before leaping from her bedroom window and "hallooed out" for help, always wary that Wagner might still be hunting her. But she was merely a tiny figure hundreds of yards distant. Her cries went unheard and she received only a friendly wave from the carpenters on Star in return.

It was a calm and peaceful morning with the sun glistening off the water. Eyes wild, hair drenched, face bruised, nightgown bloody, feet savaged, Maren worked her way along the shoreline, apparently avoiding her house and whatever lay inside. She crossed Sam Haley's breakwater, her feet bleeding into icy pools, and reached tiny Malaga Island, not fully two acres, on the far side of the cove. The northern side of Malaga faces Appledore Island across a quarter-mile-wide channel of fast flowing water. From this vantage point, she could see the cottages of the other Norwegian families. It was the two small Ingebretsen boys who eventually spotted Maren's distress signal. They alerted their father, Jorges Edward Ingebretsen, who quickly set out for Smuttynose in his fishing dory. Maren was in "an over bad condition," fatigued, frostbitten, and in shock, when he reached her sometime between seven and eight o'clock in the morning, Ingebretsen later testified.

"She was in her night-dress crying and halooing, and blood all over her clothes," Jorges told the court. "I got her into the boat . . . I searched her feet right off and they were stiff. I carried her over to my house."

Again we must depend on Celia Thaxter's account for what happened next, although she was not an eye witness to the actual rescue. Jorges

Ingebretsen told Celia that he found Maren "distracted, half senseless with cold and terror."

"Maren, Maren, who has done this?" Jorges asked her, but at first she was incoherent.

"Louis, Louis, Louis!" was all Maren could say as Jorges gently ferried her to Appledore and delivered her into the nursing care of his wife and family. Then Jorges went up the hill to alert workers at the hotel with the scattered bits of the story he had been able to decode from Maren. He did not, at first, visit the murder scene or view the carnage.

"As I sit at my desk I see him pass the window," Celia wrote of Jorges's arrival, "and wonder why the old man comes so fast and anxiously through the heavy snow," Celia reported. Then she saw Jorges and a small group of Norwegians heading back toward Smuttynose armed with guns.

"What has happened?" she called downstairs.

"Some trouble at Smuttynose; we hardly understand," one man answered.

Assuming it was just another drunken brawl among Gosport fishermen, Celia went back to her work, only to be roused half an hour later by the cries, this time, of Norwegian women shouting, "Karen is dead! Anethe is dead! Louis Wagner has murdered them both!"

Running to the servants' quarters, Celia finally got the gruesome details. A posse set out to search for Wagner on Appledore. Then they rowed across the channel to Smuttynose. Celia rushed to the Ingebretsen cottage, once home to her estranged husband, Levi, who was then living on the mainland.

"Oh, I so glad to see you! I so glad I save my life!" Maren said through cracked dry lips and a bruised jaw as she gripped the hands of the poet. Celia was also Maren's landlady, her dead sister's former employer, and the reporter who would eventually tell Maren's story to the readers of the *Atlantic Monthly*. Celia comforted Maren as if she were a wounded puppy:

"Poor little creature, holding me with those wild, glittering, dilated eyes, she cannot tell me rapidly enough the whole horrible tale. Upon her cheek is yet the blood-stain from the blow he struck her with a chair, and she shows me two more upon her shoulder, and her torn feet. I go back for arnica with which to bathe them."

But before Celia could run back to her house for the liniment, Ivan Christensen burst into the room. Having baited their hooks all night, Ivan and John and Matthew had left Portsmouth in the *Clara Bella* at six a.m. By 6:45, they were happily setting their trawls on a crisp, beautiful morning that signaled the end of winter. When they later approached Appledore, John told the newspapers, some women on the island hailed them frantically. John stayed on his fishing schooner, but sent Matthew and Ivan ashore in a dory. On Appledore, the two men heard a scattered and frightening report. "Louis has been here and Mary is crazy," the fisherwomen of Appledore reported. Matthew rowed back to the *Clara Bella*. "There is trouble at the house," he breathlessly told his brother John and the two men headed directly to Smuttynose, leaving Ivan on Appledore.

"Anethe, Anethe! Where is Anethe?" Ivan shouted as he ran half-crazed into the Ingebretsen cottage where Maren lay on a bed.

"Anethe is at home," is all his sister could say, and Ivan ran out again. Grabbing a dory, he rowed like a madman across the channel. By the time Ivan arrived in the cove, three of the Norwegian fisherman carrying weapons had met up with John and Matthew and were standing outside the Red House. The blood in the snow, the myriad boot prints, the broken bloody ax, and the dead silence all spoke volumes, but, as yet, no one had gone inside.

It was Ivan who pushed through the group and first opened the door to the apartment to find his wife's body stripped and scarred on the kitchen floor. Ivan told the jury three months later that he turned and ran back outside. Celia Thaxter, once again, offered her version of the scene:

"There upon the floor, naked, stiff, and stark, is the woman he idolizes...stone dead! Dead—horribly butchered! Her bright hair stiff with blood, the fair head that had so often rested on his breast crushed! Cloven, mangled with the brutal ax! Their eyes are blasted by the intolerable sight:

both John and Ivan stagger out and fall, senseless, in the snow. Poor Ivan!...And he was not there to protect her!"

The *Portsmouth Daily Chronicle* reported the following day that Ivan was "nearly crazed" by the murder of his wife and "his friends have kept him away from her mutilated body."

The advance party searched the rest of the house and found Karen, bruised, cut, and strangled, in the bedroom of the apartment on the left. It was ten a.m. before John Hontvet was able to reunite with his wife on Appledore. Maren was soaking her frozen feet in water when he entered the Ingebretsen home. Celia Thaxter had returned with the arnica lotion for Maren's feet. Ivan, who arrived with John, became a figure of over-whelming sadness and pity. Celia described him in epic language as "a young man of the true Norse type, blue eyed, fair-haired, tall and well-made, with handsome teeth and bronzed beard....He is superb, kindled from head to feet, a fire-brand of woe and wrath, with eyes that flash and cheeks that burn."

Celia offered Ivan a few pale words of comfort, but she knew that his true comfort was gone. The excited fishermen who had gathered in the next room parted as if for royalty as the famous island poet passed through them on her way back to the Appledore Hotel. Turning, she saw Ivan "crouched with his arms thrown round his knees and his head bowed down between them, motionless, his attitude expressing such abandonment of despair as cannot be described. His whole person seems to shrink, as if deprecating the blow that has fallen upon him."

III

CAPTURE

"So strangely was the mind of man constructed, that pleasure could be gathered from the elements of pain, and beauty seen in the Gorgon head of horror."

—Daniel Webster

"Portsmouth, New Hampshire's only seaport, is one of the few places in America touched with the hue of decay."

—Annie Fields

Chapter 14

THE AMERICAN KILLER

Louis Wagner was about to become a media sensation. At six a.m. on the morning of March 6, his muscles aching and hands blistered and bloody, he pulled desperately through the low rolling waves toward the nearby coast of New Hampshire. Small icicles clung to his beard and clothes. Ten hours ago, he had been an ordinary and anonymous fisherman. Now he was the slaughterer of two innocent women, the first official murderer in the history of the Isles of Shoals. For the moment, however, his crimes were unknown to anyone but Maren, still hiding beneath the rocks on Smuttynose.

He had searched far too long among those rocks and abandoned buildings for Maren. Now the glare from the rising sun was in his eyes, blinding his view of the distant Shoals as he neared a point on the mainland where the first New Hampshire fishermen had settled 250 years ago, almost to the day. To avoid the main channel up the Piscataqua River, Wagner veered southward at a jut of land called Jaffrey's Point. The Little Harbor route was slightly less traveled. He could not afford to be seen by the men aboard the *Clara Bella* who were, at this very moment, setting sail from Portsmouth after a long night of baiting trawls at Matthew Johnson's shop on Water Street. Soon they would reach the Shoals, he knew, and find the savaged bodies of Karen and Anethe.

With luck, they would find Maren frozen from exposure or drowned or perhaps too traumatized to speak. If so, then he had a prayer of avoiding capture. He could establish his alibi at Johnson's boarding house and make up some tale to explain his absence the night before. Then he could slip away to Boston, melt into the city, and sign on with the first departing ship, never to return. Eventually no one in Portsmouth would remember his name. But if Maren was alive, then they would come after him. She knew, and soon everyone would know.

Maren was alive. And even as Wagner drew his boat into the "back channel" known as Little Harbor, she was stepping tentatively out of her hiding spot among the rocks of Smuttynose. Maren alone had heard her sister-in-law scream the killer's name with her dying breath. As soon as Wagner reached the mainland, he set his boat adrift and walked hurriedly along the roads of New Castle toward his lodgings in Portsmouth. Maren, meanwhile, was about to reveal the killer's name to Jorges the fisherman, to Celia Thaxter, and to all the angry fishermen of Appledore. Then her husband, John, would carry that cursed name aboard his schooner to the police. The story would reach the Portsmouth newspapers in time for the evening edition. The press and the police would telegraph the details to Boston and Portland and New York City. Within a single day, Wagner's name would be on everyone's lips as a mob of thousands chanted, "Lynch him! Kill him! String him up!"

Wagner's infamy, the reason we are still talking about him today, is certainly rooted in the gothic horror tradition. The facts of the case read like genre fiction. Wagner could be the handsome beguiling stranger with the secret sordid past who destroys the innocent young beauty in a dark mysterious setting before, in the dénouement, he is justly punished for his sins. The gothic genre was spawned in titillating romantic novels of the eighteenth century and often credited to Englishman Horace Walpole, author of *The Castle of Otranto* (1764). The genre includes such classics as Mary Shelley's *Frankenstein* (1818) and later Bram Stoker's *Dracula* (1897). The Victorians adapted the gothic style, for example, in atmospheric works by the Bronte sisters—Charlotte, Emily, and Anne—whose female characters were trapped in a domestic world and controlled by powerful, even demonic, male characters like Heathcliff, the tortured outsider in *Wuthering Heights* (1847). In the same vein, Celia Thaxter referred to Wagner as the "Prussian devil" who destroyed the domestic tranquility of what she imagined to be an idyllic Norwegian colony at the Isles of Shoals. For Celia, Wagner was: "this unknown terror, this fierce, dumb monster who never utters a sound to betray himself." Celia's silent night stalker was every bit as terrifying as Stoker's vampire or Shelley's Frankenstein monster.

The idea that reading about horrible acts could bring pleasure and even moral comfort to the reader was well established in American culture by 1873, thanks especially to the works of Edgar Allan Poe. Experiencing pain, danger, and death vicariously through literature, critics pointed out, could induce strong, sensual, even sublime feelings in the mind of the reader. The more violent and lurid the writing, some believed, the more sublime, even "beautiful," the emotional response.

This ghastly fiction, advocates of gothic horror claimed, could have a positive effect. The sympathetic reader, in theory, is repulsed by the awful events in the book and driven away from acting in the same manner. As a result, the reader is pushed toward a healthier and less sinful lifestyle. Others, including the famed New Hampshire–born editor Horace Greeley, claimed that continued exposure to increasingly violent material tended instead to dull human sensibilities. It is an argument familiar to those who oppose violent films, song lyrics, and videogames today. Too much exposure to gothic fiction, Greeley argued, might even cause the reader to engage in deviant and criminal acts himself. In an age of expanding technology, scientific discovery, and realism, Americans were becoming hooked on horror. Works like *The Telltale Heart* or *The Strange Case of Dr. Jekyll and Mr. Hyde* may seem tame today when Americans routinely dine in front of television sets depicting psycho killers, flesh-eating zombies, gory crime autopsies, or high-definition war and disaster on the evening news.

The American public's hunger for shocking realism was not limited to fiction. Weekly newspapers were giving way to cheaply printed publications created for a growing population of literate middle-class Americans.

The new dailies offered sensational "true" stories about shipwrecks, pirates, strange foreign lands, cannibalism, distant wars, massacres, newly discovered animals, sexual intrigues, strange inventions, and, especially, tales of actual crimes. While traditional weekly newspapers had given little ink to these taboo topics in the past, the new "penny press" offered daily content tuned to the interests of the working public. Those interests included such lowbrow topics as police reports, theater reviews, sports scores, and want ads. And while newspapers of that era tended to support a single powerful political party, the cheap new dailies promised to report fearlessly and candidly on stories that interested the masses in America's crowding cities. The more sensational the stories, editors soon discovered, the more newspapers they sold.

Historians point to April 10, 1836, as a landmark date in the evolution of journalism, an evolution that helped make Louis Wagner a household name across New England decades later. Curiously, it was another brutal ax murder of a woman from Maine that sparked an irrevocable shift in the way American newspapers reported on heinous crimes and courtroom trials. The furor centered around the murder of Dorcas Doyen, a beautiful young housekeeper from Portland, Maine, who became a New York City prostitute under the alias Helen Jewett. When the body of the twenty-three-year-old sex worker was discovered, hacked and set afire, in the bedroom of an elegant New York bordello, suspicion immediately fell on a nineteen-year-old clerk named Richard Robinson who had been a frequent customer of Jewett. A hatchet was discovered in the backyard.

James Gordon Bennett, editor of a new penny daily called the *New York Herald*, seized the story, promising objective, exclusive, and unbiased coverage of the sordid affair. The case was not outstanding. Some twenty prostitutes in as many nearby bordellos had been killed in the city in the previous three months. But the "Jewett affair," Bennett instinctively knew, offered the inquisitive public a heavy daily dose of sex, horror, and mystery. Editors of the *New York Sun* and the *Transcript* joined the media circus, claiming they were reluctantly featuring the story in hopes of reforming the morality of the public. Exposing the "disgraceful" details of the five-day trial in June, one editor told his readers, was a "painful part of our duty as public journalists." In the murder of another fallen woman like Jewett, Bennett told *Herald* buyers, "We are all guilty alike."

The circus turned into a war of words as Bennett flexed his editorial muscle in front page coverage of the case favoring young Richard Robinson, the accused killer. The use of an ax and the burning of Jewett's body in her own bed, the *Herald* editor boldly claimed, was more likely "the vengeance of female wickedness" than the hand of any man. Bennett blamed the bordello madam, the corrupt police, society in general, and the seductive Jewett herself—everyone except Robinson, whom he characterized as the "innocent boy" victim. Rival editors accused Bennett, in turn, of accepting bribes from Robinson and of fabricating some of his "evidence," which he likely did. While investigative reporting came alive in the era of the penny post, fiction was frequently substituted for fact due to small newspaper staffs and constant deadlines. But hyper coverage of the Jewett-Robinson case also forced the church and traditional press to acknowledge the existence of the thriving sex trade in New York City, if only to deny tabloid estimates that there were twenty thousand full- and part-time prostitutes currently at work.

Robinson had good lawyers, good family connections, and the support of the boisterous *Herald*. Bennett later claimed that he quadrupled his circulation to twenty thousand copies during the Jewett affair. Fifteen minutes after the five-day trial wrapped up, the jury acquitted Robinson and set him free. The public, in general, believed he was guilty, but that there had been reasonable doubt in the prosecutor's circumstantial case. Robinson fled to Texas where he changed his name and lived a full life. Bennett's *New York Herald* went on to dominate the penny newspaper trade in New York City for decades.

Murder, thanks to the penny press and its avowed search for objectivity, had found its way permanently onto the newspaper front page. The American public, horrified, yet unable to look away, grew familiar with daily courtroom coverage, grisly forensic details, intimate jailhouse interviews, crime scene reenactments, and even to the personal opinions of reporters and editors who speculated openly on the guilt or innocence of the accused. All these media elements would play a part in the sensational capture, trial, and execution of Louis Wagner, the next antihero in an endless lineup of notorious American killers. His story is replete with the factual errors, exaggerations, dueling editorials, conspiracy theories, commercial exploitation, and outright fictions that inevitably accompany crimes that get caught up in popular memory.

Reaching shore after an exhausting journey, Wagner abandoned his dory at Little Harbor near a spot marked by a deep cleft in the rocks. The rock formation known as Devil's Den can be seen today along the boardwalk at an exclusive marina packed with luxury vessels and monitored by online security cameras. He climbed onto a rock on a hill near what is now the historic Wentworth by the Sea Hotel in New Castle. He scanned the horizon to get his bearings, not knowing he was being observed. Then he set off along the river across dangerously thin ice in the direction of Portsmouth. He did not know if Maren was alive or dead, but he knew that, soon enough, people would come after him.

Besides the grieving members of the Hontvet family, Wagner had made two powerful enemies. He had tapped into the smoldering anger of the dispossessed fishermen of Gosport and their families. The former residents of Star Island, having just sold their tiny huts and gardens to hotel developer John Poor, were now landlocked permanently on the mainland near Portsmouth. They would soon congeal into a vengeful mob intent on Wagner's immediate death. Their centuries-old fishing kingdom was no more, and the killing of women in the fishing family on Smuttynose by one of their own trusted members was a final betrayal beyond bearing.

And he now had a powerful opponent named Celia Thaxter. Celia took the murders of Anethe and Karen on her beloved Isles of Shoals personally. Wagner had struck too close to her heart, killing her former maid in a house that her family owned, and shattering her happy childhood memories of

Smuttynose Island. As a writer for the prestigious *Atlantic Monthly,* and as host of her polite and artistic summer salon at Appledore, Celia was an influential member of the Boston literary elite. Her friends formed the very hub of American culture in the 1870s. Her goal, in time, would be not only to see Wagner hanged, but to blacken his name for all eternity.

Chapter 15

THE STRANGER

When Sarah Campbell of New Castle got up to make her husband's breakfast on the morning of March 6, she spotted a stranger through the window. He was standing atop a rocky bluff looking in all directions. Sarah and her husband, Charles, lived below the hill on a small peninsula called Campbell's Island that poked into Little Harbor, the back channel to Portsmouth. They had been renting rooms in their home to summer visitors since the 1840s, but the Campbells had big plans to build a tourist hotel on that same overlook. It was an ideal spot for the rising wave of tourists, offering scenic views of the ocean and the distant Isles of Shoals to the west, with views of Little Harbor to the east. From this spot, one could see the ancient forty-two-room mansion of New Hampshire's colonial governor Benning Wentworth and glimpse the church spires of Portsmouth, about two miles away as the crow flies. The stranger, having apparently gotten his bearings, moved quickly down the hill toward Sarah's house sometime after six a.m. Not long afterward, Charles Campbell returned home from his full-time job as night watchman at the Portsmouth Naval Shipyard on the Kittery side of the Piscataqua River.

"After arriving home," Charles Campbell said later, "my attention was called to a stranger in the vicinity of my house. . . . He was back towards me."

The stranger threw a jacket over his shoulders, not bothering to put his arms into the sleeves, and walked "in a hurried manner" in the direction of

Portsmouth. At first, Campbell admitted, he did not pay particular attention to the man. But his neighbor Israel Fletcher, the other night watchman at the shipyard, also saw the stranger. Both men had arrived home in New Castle from work in the same boat. When Fletcher looked out the window of his house, at 6:40 a.m. by his watch, the unknown man was moving "at a quick trot" over a frozen patch in Little Harbor called the Mill Pond. Walking over the thin ice was a risky thing to do, Fletcher knew, with spring so near at hand. The stranger disappeared in the direction of Riverside Cemetery that connects with the main road from New Castle to the South End of Portsmouth.

Trained to be cautious, after lunch the two watchmen went to the spot where they had first seen the stranger. They tracked a set of large boot prints backward in the snow along Little Harbor. The trail stopped mysteriously at the water's edge about a quarter mile from the Campbell home. It was a point too deep to wade and directly across from the rock formation on the Rye, New Hampshire, border called Devil's Den. Campbell and Fletcher were unaware that two hours earlier, another man named Charles Place had come upon an unattended boat floating no more than 175 feet from Devil's Den.

"I took her in tow and towed her up to Portsmouth," Place told investigators. "I knew she belonged to some of the fishermen, so I towed her up; it was what we call a dory."

Unable to find the owner at first, Place had towed the boat home before Campbell and Fletcher arrived on the scene. The next day, Place learned the dory belonged to David Burke, a Portsmouth fisherman, who had reported it stolen from a wharf off Water Street the night before. Police investigators gave the dory a thorough examination before returning it to Burke. It would become a key piece of evidence in the coming murder case.

Meanwhile, back at Little Harbor, the stranger had successfully crossed the icy Mill Pond and was making his way among the tombstones in the New Castle graveyard. This shortcut allowed him to avoid the central village and to meet up with the narrow road that joins New Castle to Portsmouth.

Originally called Great Island, the ancient fishing village is connected to the mainland by three bridges that hop and skip over two smaller specks of land known as Goat Island and Shapleigh Island. In the Victorian era, these were privately owned toll bridges that extracted a few pennies from carriages and pedestrians. On any other day, the stranger might have walked on in anonymity, pausing only to drop a coin at the toll house located at the base of Water Street. But a few days before, heavy chunks of melting ice had knocked out two sections of the wooden bridge over the swift river, leaving only the posts, or "spiles," sticking out of the water. As he exited Riverside Cemetery before seven o'clock, the stranger could see a small cluster of New Castle men traveling to work by foot in the morning. They were waiting patiently about five hundred feet ahead of him at the washed-out bridge. In its place, a ferry boat was carrying passengers across the narrow channel to Portsmouth.

George Amazeen, a shoemaker, saw the stranger coming from the cemetery, but did not recognize him as a resident of the tiny town of New Castle. The man was wearing a white hat and a bluish frock that was simply buttoned around his neck with the sleeves unused and hanging. He had on a fisherman's jumper, a pair of blue overalls, and large rubber boots. He also wore a black and red scarf around his neck. Someone in the group told the stranger that the ferry would be along soon, but the man, who appeared agitated and in a great hurry, only turned his face away.

George's brother, Joseph Amazeen, a stonecutter, spoke to the stranger as he stepped onto the broken bridge.

"It is a good chance to walk overboard," Joseph said to the nervous man.

"Yes, it is," the stranger replied, catching the man's meaning. Then, with the help of the Amazeen brothers, the stranger picked up a heavy twenty-five-foot wooden rail that was lying nearby. They managed with effort to position the long board over the missing section of the bridge, balancing it on one of the recently replaced foundation posts sticking out of the swirling water.

"I don't think it is down far enough," Joseph said.

The three men then shoved the heavy rail a little farther until it was safely balanced on the opposite side. Without another word, the stranger stepped onto the board with his big rubber boots and tried to walk across like a gymnast on a balance beam. But he quickly stepped back and, straddling his legs over the board in a sitting position, used his hands to inch rapidly forward on his butt. When he reached the intact portion of the bridge on the other side, the stranger disappeared down the road without even turning around.

A cooper named Joshua Frasell (elsewhere Freizell) was also among the group waiting for the ferry. He saw the stranger in the white hat coming. The man appeared to be exhausted.

"You'll weather it," Frasell had said to the stranger as he tentatively inched his way along the plank to the opposite shore. "I guess so," the stranger called back. Frasell was certain he had seen the stranger weeks before in his barrel-making shop on Bow Street and among the fishermen on the wharves. The stranger's name, he later recalled, was Louis Wagner.

The closer he got to town, the more Wagner was recognized and identified. As he moved toward the second bridge, he was spotted through a window by a woman named Anne Carlton at about seven o'clock. Her house was only a dozen feet from the road, so she got a good look at the man with the white hat, blue overalls, rubber boots, red scarf, with a knit jumper buttoned around his neck. Carlton had grown up on nearby Water Street and, while visiting her parents there recently, she had seen the same man outside Matthew Johnson's house.

"I thought he had fell overboard," Mrs. Carlton later testified, "because he seemed to be so wet. His overalls seemed to be wet and icy around the bottom. And another thing, he was a stranger in New Castle, and I thought it was queer he should be down there." Like Sarah Campbell, who had first spotted the man craning to get his bearings at Little Harbor, Mrs. Carlton thought the man looked so curious and out of place that she alerted her husband to take a look.

John Lyons, who worked on the last New Castle bridge, met a similarly dressed stranger moments later and asked him how he got across the washed-out span. Wagner told Lyons he had to "hove a pole across," then rushed on toward Portsmouth where he was spotted by Alonzo Greene, who was heading into work at his father-in-law's store. The two men passed one another at Liberty Bridge in Puddle Dock, only eight densely-packed buildings away from the boarding house where Wagner lived at 25 Water Street. It was now seven-fifteen a.m. Wagner made such a marked effort to avert his face from being seen that the witnesses found him especially memorable. He was up to something, but they did not know what.

At this point, after eleven mysterious hours, Louis Wagner's story begins to coincide once more with the testimony of future witnesses at his trial. Key among them were Ann Elizabeth Johnson, Wagner's landlady on Water Street, and her daughter, Mary. Although well in arrears on his rent, Wagner had managed to charm and flatter Ann Johnson. Her husband, Matthew, was crippled and had been confined to a wheelchair for the past twelve years. Even though Wagner sometimes "told pretty bad yarns about himself," Ann recalled, he had always been respectful and never gave her a saucy word.

Ann had not seen her tenant since supper at six-thirty p.m. the previous night. Water Street was the roughest neighborhood in town, so on nights when he planned to be out late baiting trawls, Wagner always told his landlady in advance and she would leave the back door unlocked. Having heard nothing from Wagner the night before, Ann bolted the back door sometime after midnight. She unlocked it the morning of March 6 between five-thirty and six a.m. During that entire time, John Hontvet and his two assistants had been baiting trawls in the back shop.

Now Wagner and his landlady crossed paths briefly as he entered the back gate of the boarding house at seven-thirty in the morning. Ann was walking through the backyard toward the woodshed as he appeared.

"Hello, Louis," Ann said. "Where do you come from? John was looking for you to help him bait trawls."

"I was baiting trawls and I was asleep," Wagner said curtly and went directly into the house via the back door. Wagner's two roommates, a sailor named William Kenniston and a navy gunner named Frederick Moore, were in the kitchen when he came in. He looked "like a wild man" Moore recalled. Kenniston noted that his pants were wet with snow and ice.

"Where have you been? You look like the devil this morning," Moore said.

Wagner did not reply, but turned and looked at himself in a mirror in the kitchen.

"I guess you have had a good tramp anyhow," Moore continued. "You have been somewhere."

"If I was, I was not drunk," Wagner said defensively and went up the stairs to the bedroom he shared with the two men.

Ann Johnson did not question Wagner openly at first but she knew he had not been in the house all night. His bed had not been "tumbled" and the back door had been locked. When she called Wagner down to breakfast a few minutes later, she noticed that his face was "awful red." She later told the newspapers that her tenant was "much agitated" and "his hands trembled violently."

Wagner could not eat. He had no appetite. He stood up, slid his chair under the table, and went from the kitchen into "the shop" where Matthew Johnson was sitting in his Victorian-era wheelchair. Frederick Moore overheard their conversation.

"Here comes the lost sheep," his landlord joked. Wagner explained that, rather than wait to work for John Hontvet the night before, he had gone down to the wharf to bait trawls for someone else, then he had fallen asleep on the lounge in the back of the room they were in.

"How is that, Louis?" Matthew Johnson said. "Hontvet has been here all night, never left here until five o'clock in the morning."

Wagner absorbed each new piece of information about his appearance and about the time when he was missing. If people thought he looked drunk or sick, for example, then he would incorporate those details into his story. He would continue to adapt and shape his alibi over the next days and months, cleverly bending it around the testimony of others. After taking off his rubber boots and putting on a pair of shoes and changing his pants at the back of the shop, Wagner spoke again.

"I feel kind of bad," he said.

"If you feel bad, you better take some composition and turn in a while," Mr. Johnson said, referring to a dose of medicine and a nap.

"I don't want that. I want something else." Wagner said and went back up to his room at the head of the stairs.

Mary Johnson, aged nineteen, had last seen Wagner at tea the previous night. He was then wearing his blue pants, reddish jumper, his dirty scarf, and a white shirt she had mended for him a few days earlier. She did not take much notice of him the next morning when he first arrived, although she thought he "acted very queer." She was busy doing chores and helping her seventeen-year old sister, Olava, get ready for school. Mary noticed that Wagner was going up and down the stairs from his room and at one point, he seemed to have a bundle hidden under one arm as he went out the back door toward the privy.

At 8:45 a.m., Olava called down to Mary and told her sister she was late for school, then hurried off to do her hair. Mary was in the kitchen alone, writing a note to Olava's teacher, when Wagner approached and took her hand.

"Mary, I am in trouble," he told her. "I have got myself into trouble and I feel as if I am going to be taken."

According to Mary Johnson, Wagner was sobbing as he spoke. When he heard Mrs. Johnson coming into the kitchen, he dropped Mary's hand and wiped away his tears. Mary noticed that there were deep scratches on his hands and on three of his knuckles.

"Louis has been drunk last night," Ann Johnson said in passing.

"No," Wagner replied. "I had a little beer, but I was not drunk."

"Better go upstairs, and turn in," Ann told Wagner, but he said he felt like walking, not sleeping.

"Go and walk it out, if you don't want to sleep," Ann said.

"You say you were tight last night," Mary added, looking into his reddened eyes. "But you do not look so. You look as though you had no sleep."

According to Wagner, he then took Mary's other hand. He stared back into her eyes and then he kissed her.

"I must be going," Wagner told Mary.

Wagner turned and saw Olava sitting at the breakfast table.

"I left Mary Johnson and went over to Lava Johnson," Wagner told a packed courtroom three months later. "I put my right arm around her neck, and kissed her. It was not the first morning I done so. I done so every morning. Any time a day I received it when I wanted it."

It was a curiously intimate and, in retrospect, a creepy exit.

As soon as Wagner walked out the door of the boarding house, never to return, Mary and her mother chatted about their tenant's strange appearance and bizarre behavior. Perhaps, they reasoned, he had gotten drunk and been in a fight the night before. Such brawls among local fishermen, visiting sailors, and shipyard workers were common on the streets of Portsmouth, especially among the bars and brothels of Water Street. But if Wagner had been arrested and had spent the night in jail, they reasoned, why would the police release him so early? The truth, more horrible than they could imagine, was a few short hours away.

Chapter 16

THE ARREST

The dreamlike imagery of blood on the snow in the mists of a deserted island may appear timeless. But this gothic horror is equally a modern tale of trains, trials, and tourists. Within fifteen minutes of his tearful exit from the Johnson women in the South End, Louis Wagner had purchased ten cents' worth of pie at a bakery on Daniel Street and was boarding a train on the opposite end of town. He paid $1.45 for a one-way ticket to Boston. The Thursday morning train steamed out of the Portsmouth station at 9:10 a.m. Wagner had been awake since the previous morning. Now, as he began to doze, Ivan Christensen and John Hontvet were opening the door to the murder scene on Smuttynose. In less than two hours, Wagner's train arrived at Charlestown, Massachusetts, today the site of the historic Freedom Trail, Old Ironsides, and Bunker Hill. By this time, John and Ivan and a frenzied group of Appledore fishermen were about to dock the *Clara Bella* off Water Street en route to alert the Portsmouth Police of the biggest crime in their record books to date.

According to Wagner, the Boston trip was a spur of the moment thing. He fully intended, he said, to return home in the evening or the next day. He checked out the ships on the Charleston wharves, likely hoping to find one ready to embark immediately for distant shores, but without luck. Walking along Commercial Street, still wearing his bloody fishing clothes, Wagner spotted "a little colored man" in his barber shop.

"I thought my whiskers had been growing three weeks, and I thought I better go in and have a shave, and look better," Wagner later explained. "He [the barber] asked me if I was going to try to go to sea again. I told him no, that I came there to look for work ashore."

He paid the barber thirty-five cents for a shave and a haircut. On Hanover Street, Wagner went into a familiar store to buy a hat for a dollar. The Dutch shop owner talked him into also purchasing a pair of pants, a cheap coat, vest, and suspenders for a total of ten dollars. Wagner, who had been destitute of funds not twenty-four hours before, paid the Dutchman with two five-dollar bills, the equivalent of two weeks' wages. Around two p.m., he stepped into a shop at 39 Fleet Street owned by a shoemaker named Jacob Todtman, whom he had known during his earlier years fishing out of Boston.

"Halloo, Louis," the shopkeeper said, remembering his name. "Where are you come from?"

"From Portsmouth," Wagner replied.

"How long ago is it since you have been here last?" Todtman asked.

"Nearly two years," Wagner said.

Todtman asked Wagner if he was still fishing. Wagner told him that he was finished with the sea and wanted to find other work in Boston. Again, as with the barber, Wagner's later testimony implied he had no intention of escaping to a distant port, but was only scouting for new work. He showed the shoemaker his tattered boots. They were so torn, he said, that he needed to wear a cheap pair of rubbers over them to keep the boots from falling apart. And again, his explanation backed up his alibi. He was not disguising himself with new clothes, he claimed, but merely replacing a worn-out wardrobe.

The shop was busy, but between customers the two men negotiated a price of $2.50 for a new pair of footwear. While he was waiting, Wagner set the package he had purchased at the previous store on the cobbler's display case and opened it. He changed into his new clothes in the aisle of the tiny shop. In Wagner's version of the story, the shoemaker's wife, Ansetena, and their servant girl, Johanna, watched him as he undressed. According to Todtman's testimony, the two women were not even in the room at the time. Under his blue overalls, Wagner was wearing "a pretty good pair of green-striped pants," Todtman noticed. Wagner put the pants he had just purchased over those green pants and changed into his new coat and vest, setting his old white hat and clothes aside. Then, as the cobbler worked at his bench, Wagner made another strange remark.

"I have seen a woman lay as still as that boot," he said.

Wagner later denied making that peculiar statement, but the shopkeeper was adamant that it was an accurate quotation. In his court testimony, as he did frequently, Wagner offered an entirely different conversation. Todtman, according to Wagner, had taunted him about women. The cobbler advised Wagner to settle down in Boston. "Pick out a girl with plenty of money and get married," Todtman reportedly said. Wagner replied that he was not interested in marriage.

"I told him [Todtman] that I had a girl at home [in Prussia], for six years, but that I heard no news about her the last two years. Perhaps she is dead." It was another in a series of odd semi-confessional comments that Wagner revealed to members of the courtroom at his trial. Todtman insisted, under oath, that Wagner's version of their conversation about the women was fabricated.

Both men agreed they shared a celebratory glass of "kimmel," a popular European liqueur flavored with caraway and cumin. And Wagner then purchased two cigars from the cobbler's wife who had come upstairs. After half an hour in the shop, Wagner left, but he returned at four p.m. and picked out a pair of slippers, which he traded for a broken watch. He also asked if he could leave his old clothes, temporarily, in Todtman's shop and the shoemaker reluctantly agreed. These items would become another key element in the prosecutor's case.

By this time, Louis Wagner had spent almost all of the fifteen or sixteen dollars later reported missing from the Hontvet House on Smuttynose. Exhausted, broke, and with nowhere left to go, he instinctively sought out familiar territory. Just as he had run to Johnson's boarding house that morning, Wagner now went looking for sympathy in Boston. Rather than run for cover, he made his way to the boarding house at 295 North Street where he had lived some three years before.

"It must be remembered," true crime writer Edmund Pearson says of Wagner, "that although he could be sly, and at times seem almost clever, he was really stupid, dull, brutal."

There was a saloon on the first floor at North Street, and as soon as Wagner entered and took a seat by the window, he was greeted by a woman he later said was a prostitute named Emma Miller. She knew him as Louis Ludwig (or Ludwick), a name he denied using. She asked if he would like to "stand a treat" with her but he said his pocketbook was empty and he had no money for sex. When Miller asked why he looked "awful bad" despite his new clothes and haircut, Wagner made another strange remark.

"I am just after murdering two sailors, coming from New York," he suddenly explained to the woman in the bar. "The mate put me ashore in a boat. I ran away and came to Boston. I had my whiskers shaved off in New York so that the officers would not know me."

Emma Miller laughed, assuming Wagner was joking, but he continued.

"There is another girl I want to murder and then I am willing to go," he said. His juxtaposition of "two sailors" and "another girl," assuming the trial transcript is correct, is one more seemingly confessional outburst.

Wagner then left the bar and went up a rickety flight of stairs to the boarding house. Katherine Brown, an Irish immigrant, was standing in the kitchen. Her German-born husband would arrive soon after.

"Halloo, Louis," she said after they shook hands. "Where have you been to so long, and what is the matter? You look so curious. You look like somebody that has lost all his friends."

"I have happened with great misfortune," Wagner told her, "and am cast away."

As he had done so often and effectively in the past, Wagner spun his tale of woe, describing, not the murders, but the shipwreck of the fishing schooner *Addison Gilbert* months earlier. It was the same hangdog approach he had used to get free meals from the fishermen's wives at Gosport, Lunging Island, Johnson's boarding house, and Smuttynose. When Katherine revealed she had recently suffered the death of her young son, Wagner was unmoved and unsympathetic. She found herself, instead, comforting Wagner, who said he was "destitute of everything." Wagner begged to spend the night, noting he might "ship on a vessel" in the morning or in a day or two. This was in direct contradiction to what he had told the barber and the storekeeper. Katherine said she would ask her husband when he returned from work if Wagner could stay. While waiting for Mr. Brown to show up, Wagner dozed by the kitchen stove and Katherine had to shake him awake when it was time for supper.

The Browns knew John and Maren Hontvet well. The Hontvets had lived at Hamburg House at 295 North Street after they were married in 1866. In the bustling hub city of Boston, the Browns proudly accommodated "boarders of all nations" including the kindly Norwegians. For old time's sake, the Browns agreed to let Wagner stay a night or two on credit, since he was out of money. Wagner told Katherine he had been baiting trawls with John the previous night in Portsmouth, another lie, but he refused to speak a word about Maren. Wagner instead complained to Katherine that his feet hurt. His new leather shoe gaiters were too tight. After eating, he returned briefly to Todtman's shop for the new pair of comfortable slippers. Back at the Browns' he put on his new slippers and the landlady, who by now knew the Boston police were looking for Wagner, suggested he retire to the sitting room downstairs with the other men in the boarding house. She would not see him again until she stepped into the witness box at the murder trial in Maine.

Wagner's actions after the murders have confounded many. Instead of leaving the New England seacoast behind, he spent precious hours returning to Johnson's boarding house. Instead of disappearing into a city of three hundred thousand Bostonians, he patronized familiar stores, spent all his blood money on new clothes, and quickly returned to begging favors and sympathy from old friends. It was as if, historians have suggested, he wanted to be caught. He would follow a similar pattern in a future break from jail.

Back in Portsmouth, the police wasted no time. After learning that the alleged Smuttynose killer had previously lodged at the Browns' boarding house in Boston, Marshal Frank Johnson and his assistant Thomas Entwistle telegraphed a message asking the Boston police to be on the lookout for a man matching the description of Louis Wagner. Then Johnson and an officer from New Castle named Benson took the evening train out of Portsmouth, bringing photographs of Wagner for identification. They did not have long to wait. Sometime after eight p.m., even as the USS *Mayflower* was arriving with the coroner's jury on the Isles of Shoals, Wagner stepped into the doorway of the Browns' house wearing his new slippers. Two Boston Police officers approached him.

"Halloo Louis," officer James Haley said.

Wagner took a sudden step backward, but Haley caught hold of the suspect's right arm while patrolman William Gallagher grabbed the left. They muscled him out onto the busy sidewalk.

"What do you want?" Wagner said.

"We want you," Haley replied.

"Let me go upstairs and put my boots on," Wagner said.

"Your slippers are well enough," Haley said as they met Officer William Currier and walked the prisoner along the crowded North Street toward the station house a quarter-mile away.

"How long have you been in Boston?" Gallagher asked about a minute later.

"Five days," Wagner said. Later he explained that he was scared by the sudden arrest and misunderstood the question. He thought the officer had asked him how many years he had lived in Boston, to which he had intended to say "five years." Then the police asked if he had not just come from Portsmouth, and he admitted that he had.

When they arrived at the police station at 8:45 p.m., Marshall Johnson from Portsmouth was there.

"That's the man we are looking for," Johnson said. "Gentlemen, you have got a murderer."

"That's the man, but perhaps the wrong one," Wagner retorted.

The police searched their suspect. They placed the contents of his pockets on a shelf in the station—a silver half-dollar, some little five-cent pieces, some coppers, three or four buttons, a ring to a watch, a piece of tobacco, and what looked like the wick to an oil lamp. Wagner's personal property was sealed in an envelope and locked in a closet until his coming trial.

Suspicious that he had recently changed his blood-stained clothes, a Boston police sergeant named Thomas Weir asked Wagner to strip. Officer Johnson claimed that Wagner had changed his underclothes that morning. Wagner insisted he had been wearing his underwear for eight days. They accused him of shaving his beard in Portsmouth, but he said he had done so in Boston. Wagner freely admitted he had purchased new clothes to look presentable to his friends. When he told police that he had left his old clothes at the shoemaker's shop on Fleet Street, an officer rushed off to retrieve the evidence from Mr. Todtman.

Wagner was then ushered into the police captain's private room where Marshal Frank Johnson of Portsmouth questioned him intensely. No one yet had told Wagner why he was being arrested and he had not asked. Officer Benson of New Castle, according to Wagner, asked him if he could read the English newspapers. He said he could not.

"If you could," Benson reportedly told him, "you would have seen what was in it and you would have been in New York at this time."

During questioning, Johnson finally told Wagner they knew he had been down to the Shoals and killed two women. The woman who had escaped knew him.

"My God, I never done any such a thing!" Wagner said. Over the next two years, even standing on the trapdoor of the gallows, his denial never wavered.

Chapter 17

LYNCH MOB

Poor unmarried Karen and beautiful young Anethe, their lives already reduced to media stereotypes, lay in their private morgue at the Red House on Smuttynose as an angry crowd gathered at the Portsmouth depot on the evening of March 6. But rumors that the captured prisoner was being returned on the late train to Portsmouth were false. Wagner was fast asleep in his Boston cell. Eventually the frustrated citizens, many carrying weapons, dispersed. "Had Wagner been brought on that train," the *Portsmouth Daily Evening Times* predicted, "it is probable that he would have been attacked by the enraged fishermen and perhaps killed."

On the morning of Friday, March 7, the prisoner was fed and photographed. Then the policed escorted Wagner (he said "dragged" him) in handcuffs through the streets of Boston to the jeers of a "hooting mob." The word was out, although the dispatches sent by big city correspondents "dealt more largely in fiction than fact" the *Portsmouth Chronicle* complained. By evening, the name Louis Wagner would be reviled across the land.

The prisoner was not happy to find himself returning north to Portsmouth on the ten a.m. train that encountered angry protestors at many Massachusetts stops along the way. "The prisoner was surly and answered the shouts of the crowd with obscene and defiant language, inviting them to the place that he is evidently booked for," the *Chronicle* reported. As word spread that Wagner was to arrive in Portsmouth soon after noon, thousands of noisy and impatient citizens stormed toward the depot. Fearing the worst, Portsmouth Mayor Thomas Marvin and assistant marshal Thomas Entwistle wisely called for backup. A squad of marines crossed the Piscataqua from the Portsmouth Naval Shipyard in Kittery to guard the incoming prisoner, who was due to arrive at twelve-thirty p.m. The soldiers were ordered to charge their bayonets to keep the raging crowd at bay.

Hoping to evade the mob, Marshal Frank Johnson stopped the train fifteen minutes before it reached the depot at the outskirts of town. Entwistle, who had returned from the grisly scene on Smuttynose at three a.m. that very morning, rendezvoused with Johnson and the other police officers who had joined the train en route. They attempted to sneak Wagner, handcuffed between two officers, through the back streets to the police station in the heart of the city, but the ruse did not succeed for long. By the time the small posse reached Bridge Street, hundreds of men had surrounded them. Enraged citizens led by about two hundred fishermen made several attempts to blockade the streets and rush the officers to "strike the wretch." Wagner "trembled like a leaf" and was so terrified that the officers had to hold up the six-foot 170-pound prisoner to prevent him from being trampled.

"I did not look at them," Wagner recalled. "I was scared at them for fear they would knock me down. I just kept my head away from them as much as I could."

It was the gruesome nature of the crime, according to Shoaler John Downs, that so fired up the fishing community. Like others at Gosport, Downs's parents had trusted Wagner and had taken him into their home for a meal. He had played with their baby boy. Now Downs's father was among the hooting mob "in their clumbering fishing boots and waving their old tar ropes," hoping to land a stone or two against the prisoner.

Amid oaths and curses, a few blows hit their mark. On Congress Street, the city's main artery only a few blocks from the station house, the crowd surged, screaming, "Lynch him! Kill him! String him up!" Police officers were forced to draw their revolvers, but with the help of the marines, the prisoner was safely escorted into the station and locked up.

In 1873, the official jail was on Islington Street just beyond the city center. While the jailer's house remains standing, the attached "old jail" made of granite and brick is gone. Whether Wagner briefly stayed there or at another temporary site downtown is unclear because Portsmouth likes to move and repurpose its city buildings. After serving since 1782, the walls of the Islington Street jail were recycled into a downtown furniture store. The earlier colonial jail on Prison Lane is now the site of the historic Music Hall. The "new" jail on Penhallow Street has since been turned into office space, and the holding cells used today at the Portsmouth Police Department stand in what used to be the city hospital.

Historically, New Hampshire's only seaport had seen its share of public protests. In 1765, for example, at the height of the Stamp Act rebellion, a colonial mob hanged the local stamp agent in effigy and set his image on fire in Haymarket Square. When Paul Revere rode into Portsmouth late in 1774, only months before the battle at Lexington and Concord, hundreds of locals stormed King George's fort in nearby New Castle and carried away the king's powder and muskets. A century later, in reaction to the Draft Act calling men to serve in the Civil War, a protest in the city streets turned violent. After quelling the crowd, Marshal Frank Johnson, who would manage the Wagner case a decade later, discovered a stray bullet from the mob had just missed his head and pierced his hat. Two years later in April 1865, joyous and drunken citizens were celebrating the end of the Civil War. Amid the revelry, a horde of two thousand decided to trash the offices of the city's only pro-slavery newspaper. The crowd threw the offending printing press into the Piscataqua River as the editor escaped with his life from an attic window.

For the moment, at least, Wagner was safe inside his cell. Although the defense lawyers would later vilify the local police, Professor David Ferland says Wagner was treated courteously and with no roughness or abuse. Ferland, an expert on the history of local crime, notes that Portsmouth was not incorporated as a city until 1849 and formed its first official police force the following year. Entirely untrained and poorly paid, patrolmen often worked solo. They usually carried only a foot-long wooden "billy club," as much a symbol of authority as a weapon.

"I think they were terrific people," Ferland says of the city's early policemen. "They were popular and they were fair. Remember, there was no job protection back then and not much of a command structure. You could not walk a beat by yourself in a small tough town like this back then if you were an ass. You had to have a good sense of justice and be respected by the community. If you were brutal, you would be railroaded out of town."

It was not until 1866 under incoming Marshal Frank Johnson that members of the force all wore uniforms. The long, double-breasted blue coat with brass buttons, belt, badge, and hat "adds very much to their appearance and efficiency," Johnson said. While police watchmen often wore the tall distinctive helmet adapted from the British "bobby," ranking officers Marshal Johnson and his assistant Mr. Entwistle wore a round, flat, military-style cap with a sharp square visor.

Ferland, a retired Portsmouth police chief, says murder was uncommon in the city in the Victorian era. When it occurred, the police were unschooled in crime scene analysis, so it was left largely to the coroner's jury. Besides the usual drunkenness, brawling, and robbery found in a hard knuckle seaport, Portsmouth police officers routinely dealt with abusive husbands, vandals, and runaways. A typical day might include complaints of lewd behavior, profane language, bathing in public, cruelty to animals, violating lobster laws, giving away liquor, and stealing railroad ties.

As soon as Wagner arrived at Portsmouth jail, Marshal Johnson and others asked him about the scars and blisters on his hands. The scars, Wagner explained, came from baiting trawls and the blisters were from a recent "sculling" expedition on the river. The prisoner had been in his cell about three-quarters of an hour when John Hontvet, Matthew Hontvet, and Ivan Christensen arrived at the side door of the station. John had come from bringing his wife, Maren, by boat to Portsmouth. Too crippled to face Wagner, Maren had to be carried to Matthew Johnson's boarding house on Water Street where she was under the care of a Dr. Whittier.

"Oh, damn you murderer!" John cursed Wagner. "You kill my wife's sister and her brother's wife."

"Johnny, you are mistaken. I hope you will find the right man who done it," Wagner replied, gripping the bars of his cell with two blistered hands.

"I got him," John said.

Too overcome with emotion to speak directly with Wagner and not fluent in English, Ivan whispered a question to John, who translated it to the prisoner.

"Could you not get the money without killing the women?" John asked.

"I never tried to steal money, but if I was a thief I could get money without killing people," Wagner said in his typical convoluted manner. Matthew then showed him two pocketbooks taken from Smuttynose Island. Wagner denied having robbed them.

"Hanging is too good for you, and hell is too good for you," John shouted. "You ought to be cut to pieces and put on to fish-hooks."

John's threats come from Wagner's memory of their encounter, and while they may be accurate, Wagner was careful to present himself as cool and collected and John as violent and emotional. "The net that you spread out for me to drop in, you might drop in yourself," Wagner claimed he told John. If so, this was the first of many subtle attempts he made to shift the blame for the murders onto others, particularly to John and Maren Hontvet. Although he never dared to make direct accusations in court, over the coming months Wagner would exhibit an innate genius for dissembling the facts, vilifying others, creating doubt, and garnering sympathy. His mercurial responses, sometimes meek and sometimes bold, worked surprisingly well with the Victorian media and in the court of public opinion. Most of the Smuttynose murder "conspiracy theories" that have made their way into modern debates and popular fiction were seeded by Wagner and nurtured by the press.

Gaining public approval was an uphill battle, to be sure, with a mob ready to crucify him and the popular press in a feeding frenzy. But Wagner was his own best press agent. Since the rise of the penny post and the infamous Jewett case in 1842, murder had become front page news in America. The media wars and the quest for "objective" independent reporting was evident even in a small city of ten thousand like Portsmouth. Here, too, dueling publishers with competing morning and evening editions battled to increase circulation that, in turn, boosted advertising sales. As in colonial days, newspapers continued to copy the juiciest content from one another, often spicing up the language and adding fictional details. According to the March 7 edition of the *Bath Daily Times* of Maine, for example, Maren Hontvet had pleaded, "Louis, don't murder me!" The Bath paper falsely reported that Maren then "escaped through a door, ran to a boat, and pulled out in the stream." Deadlines frequently trumped the truth as the *Portsmouth Daily Chronicle* revealed, also falsely, that Wagner had been seen the night of the murders "at 9 o'clock at Tucker's Wharf with an axe in his hand."

Sickening details from the coroner's visit to Smuttynose had begun appearing in print. Karen Christensen, the *Chronicle* reported, was "clothed only with a chemise, the lower extremities being exposed" and her "face was straightened out as if she had been in great agony." The *New York Times*, while getting the name of the victim wrong, delivered details as if their reporter had been an eyewitness to the crime. "All at once," he reported, "Wagner seems to have become possessed of a demon and heaped the blows of the ax thick and fast upon the head and body of the unfortunate woman. Miss Lawson's head was literally crushed to a jelly."

It was on March 7, as Wagner settled into the Portsmouth jail, that David and James Burke reclaimed their lost dory. Meanwhile, John Hontvet and his grief-stricken brother-in-law Ivan revealed to the papers that the killer had made off with between thirteen and sixteen dollars. That same day, while recuperating on Water Street, Maren Hontvet repeated her harrowing story to the coroner's jury. Much of it would appear word for word in the evening paper. The police were certain they had their killer and, at first blush, the media agreed. "There is no doubt he [Wagner] deliberately planned the murder and rowed out the ten miles on that cold night intending to kill three defenseless women," the *Portsmouth Daily Evening Times* concluded. But there was a new problem. It was becoming clear that the crime had not taken place in New Hampshire, but on an island attached to the county of York in the state of Maine across the river. This battle over jurisdiction would become the centerpiece of the case by Wagner's defense attorneys. With the state of Maine "soft" on capital punishment, as the newspapers pointed out to the chanting mob, once he was taken to Maine, Wagner might yet go free.

At four p.m., according to an officer named William Jellison, the prisoner was invited into the office of the Portsmouth marshal for a two-hour interrogation. Jellison had witnessed the meeting earlier that day between Wagner and John Hontvet. While Wagner depicted himself as defiant, Jellison saw a weeping, frightened figure, possibly on the verge of confession.

"I am sorry I went to Boston," Wagner sobbed in his cell. "If I had not went to Boston, they would not have thought I done this thing."

Officer Jellison was also present when Judson Randall, a Portsmouth fisherman, met with Wagner. The Randall family had a long history at the Isles of Shoals that had come to an abrupt end with the sale of Gosport to hotel developer John Poor. John Hontvet was leaving the police station and Wagner was still crying when the fisherman arrived. Randall told Wagner that he "had been out to see the corpse and the deed that was done."

Randall asked Wagner what he thought about the whole sordid affair at Smuttynose. Wagner replied, "I felt as bad as if I had done it." This statement was taken as another of the prisoner's subliminal confessions, but Wagner would insist that Randall had twisted his words. He felt bad, he later told the jury, because "people thought I was a murderer." Wagner never expressed the slightest sympathy for the victims or their family, and Judson Randall swore to his version in court. As he left the jail cell, Wagner thrust out his hand, but the fisherman refused to shake it.

After Randall, the police paraded a series of potential witnesses and curious onlookers past the prisoner, hoping to build their case. By the four p.m. interview in the marshal's office, they were doubly convinced they had their man. Assistant Thomas Entwistle would testify that no one ever asked Wagner if he was guilty. There was no need. It was during that afternoon meeting or soon afterward, Wagner claimed, that Entwistle tried to trick him into confessing. The officer, in Wagner's words, said "they would do all they could" for him if he admitted his guilt.

"Louis," Entwistle reportedly confided to his prisoner, "there is some proof against you. They will hang you. But if you say you done it in drunkenness, they might give you six or eight years." The testimony comes from Wagner.

"I told him that I rather would die innocent, than to take my liberty as a murderer," Wagner said. It was a convincing line he would use often in the months to come.

As Entwistle pushed for a confession, Wagner revealed what would become his most powerful public relations tool. Although never known to be religious, and in fact, to be among the most profane of the hard-swearing fishermen, Wagner was reborn in Jesus. He told the story of his religious revival to a packed courtroom.

"I have been twice in greater danger than this," he said after evading the lynch mob. "I have been once overboard, and I have been saved again." (Here, according to the trial transcript, the defendant burst into tears.) "And once I dropped into a vessel's hold, and was crippled up all over. God saved me that time, and he will save me this time again."

There would be no confession that day, or ever, and Wagner was led back to his cell. Entwistle swore in court the confession conversation never took place. Outside the Portsmouth jail, the angry fishermen continued to curse and shout and call for Wagner's death until well after midnight.

"What the [curse deleted] are you in here this time o'night for?" Wagner shouted at the rowdy men. "You'd better be abed."

Chapter 18

EVIDENCE AND ALIBI

By Saturday morning, he was a full-fledged celebrity. According to the daily news "many hundreds of people of both sexes were admitted to see Wagner on Saturday as on the previous day." Locals, children included, hung around the jailhouse door in droves hoping to catch a glimpse of the celebrated Smuttynose murderer. They "begged for a moment's admission" and many got their wish. Those who came to view a freakish ax murderer locked in a cage were shocked to find him a gentle and attractive young man of Teutonic origin. Wagner stood quietly at his cell door. "He said little and seemed not at all displeased that the populace were allowed to come in and gaze at him," one reporter noted.

The first glimpses of Louis Wagner as a truly sympathetic character come from the pen of William Thayer, editor of the *Portsmouth Daily Evening Times*. Judging that this case would be among the biggest stories of his career, Thayer planted himself in the city's police station for much of the prisoner's brief stay. Although completely convinced of Wagner's guilt, Thayer made a journalistic effort to pull together an unbiased profile of the killer from personal observation, accounts in other newspapers, interviews, gossip, and police records. His coverage, others claimed, leaned in favor of the prisoner.

"He is a large strong man, ugly at times, but has not been considered a dangerous character," the *Times* first reported. "The prisoner was a steady man who always had funds, but tended to be morose and withdrawn. His shipmates knew him as shrewd and close-fisted and had little affection for him."

The *Portsmouth Times* reported that all visitors to his cell "were much surprised to meet a man with so honest, [and] kindly a face. Wagner does not look like a villain. Put him among a dozen respectable laboring men, and none would select him from the others as a bad man." Despite his Prussian accent, the prisoner spoke "frankly and freely . . . and in all respects acts and talks like an honest, intelligent man."

Frank W. Miller of the competing *Portsmouth Daily Chronicle* was even more convinced of Wagner's guilt and amazed by his strangely calm demeanor. "We would not select him in a crowd as one who would commit murder, as his expression is one of kindness" the *Chronicle* suggested. Miller's observations, however, appear more detached and well-rounded. He noted that the prisoner "sometimes hid himself" in his cell from visitors and "bursts into tears when spoken to . . . A more wretched condition than he is in can hardly be imagined." Yet, a few sentences later, Miller noted, Wagner "liked the ladies" and told one "that he had never been happier in his life."

Miller's characterization is of a man more mercurial and complex than Thayer's and presents Wagner as duplicitous and conniving. While Miller was equally willing to report on Wagner's quirky behavior, the *Chronicle* suggested it was playacting. Wagner "looks squarely at everyone who takes a glance at him and evidently has made up his mind to play a game of bluff," Miller's paper suggested. It is clear that both Miller and Thayer made an effort to be objective, but always with an eye toward keeping the controversy going and selling newspapers. Despite the strong circumstantial evidence against Wagner, the *Times* reported on Saturday "it must be admitted that there is room for a reasonable doubt about his guilt."

The newspaper debate over Wagner, though good-natured, was born out of a strong and longstanding local rivalry. Miller had founded his pro-Republican *Chronicle* in 1852 as the first daily in the city. In 1867, he also took over an ancient weekly known as the *New Hampshire Gazette*. Established in colonial Portsmouth in 1756, the *Gazette*, Miller proudly proclaimed, was "the oldest newspaper in America." His *Chronicle* had been the only daily paper in the region until 1868. That year, a hard-bitten Democrat named Joshua Foster began a rival daily called the *Portsmouth Times*. It was Foster, as publisher of a pro-slavery or "Copperhead" newspaper, who had seen his printing press tossed into the river by a drunken Portsmouth mob at the close of the Civil War. So it makes sense that Charles Thayer, as the newest editor of the *Times,* might lean slightly in favor of the latest underdog, who in this case was Louis Wagner.

Both Miller and Thayer came from publishing families and had printer's ink in their veins. And both knew how to build circulation and advertising revenue by milking a good story. Miller has been described as a "vigorous, imaginative newspaperman who had a flair for making a dollar." He was elected mayor of Portsmouth by a wide margin in 1874, but that same year the Democrats gained control of the governorship and both legislative bodies in New Hampshire. Miller was targeted for his Republican views and gerrymandered out of office after serving only six months as the city's mayor.

Both newspapers offered lengthy coverage of the prisoner's own version of events from seven-thirty p.m. on Wednesday until six-thirty a.m. Thursday morning. Wagner insisted to the press that he never left Portsmouth during that period. From nine until eleven o'clock at night, he was down on the Portsmouth docks, he said, baiting trawls for a fisherman he had just met. Then he drank two or three glasses of ale in an oyster bar on the left side of Congress Street. Wagner said he could not recall the names of the boat, the captain, the wharf, the bar, or the bartender.

"Load me down with irons and chains if you must," Wagner reportedly told the police, "but I ask you, carry me out there that I may point out the saloon. I will show you them people I was with that night." Unwilling to risk the prisoner's safety with the jail surrounded by blood-thirsty protestors, the police instead brought in every potential witness they could find to identify Wagner. One bartender testified that he had served Wagner one glass of ale at seven-thirty that evening, but no one could be found who had seen him after that.

Unused to drinking and drowsy from the ale, Wagner said he walked to Court Street downtown. There he slipped and fell on the ice near the town pump. He lay there for a long time. He returned to Johnson's boarding house through the back door at about three a.m. Wagner swore he could see John Hontvet and his crewmen baiting trawls through a window, but by this time he was too tired and ill to join them, so he fell asleep on a sofa in the back room of the shop. By the time he awoke, Hontvet was gone. Wagner said he went to the breakfast table at Johnson's, but was too sick to eat. With a sudden urge to visit friends in Boston, he hopped on the morning train. Arriving in the big city, he decided to make himself more presentable by getting his whiskers and hair cut. Then he bought a new set of clothes and shoes, leaving his old fishing outfit behind.

The essential details of his inventive story never wavered. And it was upon this fragile skeleton of events that Wagner's life hung. Proving his alibi, without a single corroborating witness, would be no easy task for his yet unnamed defense attorney. Deconstructing that skeleton of events, bone by bone, was the job of county attorney George Campbell Yeaton. Born in 1836 in nearby South Berwick, Maine, Yeaton was a local boy with deep family roots. His ancestor Richard Yeton (an earlier spelling) had petitioned the royal court for leniency in 1715 on behalf of the poor fishermen at the Isles of Shoals who were, as always, overdue on their tax payments. "The people are very few in number [and] most of them are men of no substance," Yeton wrote of the early Shoalers. "They live only by their daily fishing and not one-third of them are single men and threaten to remove and leave us, if the tax be laid which will prove our utter ruin if our fishermen leave us."

George Yeaton's father owned a sawmill on the Salmon Falls River that flows into the mighty Piscataqua. His father's success allowed George to attend Berwick Academy and Bowdoin College and to settle on Academy

Street in the center of the picturesque village. In 1870, Yeaton's office and many valuable papers were destroyed in a fire, perhaps influencing his decision to accept the job as attorney for York County the following year. Yeaton also served as the lawyer for the burgeoning Boston & Maine Railroad. He was a prominent local Mason and served as the president of local banks. He and his wife, Harriet, had only one daughter who died at age four. Yeaton dedicated his life to practicing law in Maine and was best known for the Wagner case that was hailed as "a classic in criminal prosecution." Following his death in 1918, Yeaton was eulogized as "the last of the polished, highly-cultivated legal minds of the old school."

By Saturday morning, March 8, 1873, Yeaton was "virtually certain" that Smuttynose Island fell under the jurisdiction of Maine, not New Hampshire, so he headed to the Portsmouth jailhouse to collect his celebrity prisoner. But before delivering the defendant to Maine, Yeaton needed to visit the murder scene on Smuttynose where the bodies of Karen and Anethe still lay. Yeaton shipped out aboard the USS *Mayflower* at noon headed toward the Isles of Shoals.

At that same moment, the back door to the station house opened. Still unable to walk, Maren Hontvet was carried from her carriage by two police officers and set on a lounge in the city marshal's office. She "seemed to be suffering" and was accompanied by her husband, John, and the near comatose Ivan Christensen. The prisoner was led into the office to confront the woman he had tried to destroy. Wagner looked at Maren with a mournful expression.

"Louis, you killed my two sisters, you know you did!" Maren shouted repeatedly in "broken English," raising herself up painfully on one arm on the lounge.

According to William Thayer of the *Portsmouth Daily Evening Times*, who was a witness to the conversation, Wagner showed no excitement. Then with a voice "full of feeling and earnestness" he responded.

"Mary, I did not do it. I did not go out to the Shoals that night. I never put my hand on any woman to hurt her. You can't say that for true, Mary."

Half-sitting, half-lying down, Maren continued to fiercely condemn her former friend and lodger.

"Louis, didn't we take you in and feed you while you had no money and might have starved?" the *Chronicle* reported. "Did we deserve to be treated so by you?"

"No Mary, not by me or anyone else," Wagner said.

"Would you not like to kill me?" Maren then asked, according to Wagner's version. But when he tried to respond, he was told by the marshal to keep silent.

"I had no right to answer her," he later testified. "I was not allowed to."

After a lengthy confrontation with the prisoner, a city solicitor named Frink asked Maren to tell her full story once more, for the record, and her words were set down on paper. Wagner listened, his face unchanged, as Maren described the figure in the dark who struck down Anethe with an ax. She said she heard Anethe cry out "Louis! Louis!" But Maren admitted that the killer had remained silent and kept his back toward her, so she did not see his face or hear his voice.

"No one who was there," William Thayer wrote, "could fail to be impressed with the fact that Mrs. Hontvet firmly believes that she saw Louis."

"I'm glad Jesus loves me," Wagner said as the Hontvets prepared to go.

"The devil loves you!" John shot back.

As soon as Maren was carried back to her carriage to return to Johnson's boarding house, Mary Johnson, the landlady's daughter, was ushered into the Portsmouth police station. Her real name, according to the not-always-reliable *New York Times*, was Mary Ramsey, "a fine looking woman" who was in the process of being divorced although she was not yet twenty years old. Mary had been friendly to Wagner during his recent eight-week stay, but as the weight of circumstantial evidence mounted, she was now deeply suspicious. She had last seen him with a long beard wearing his signature rubber boots, overalls, blue and brown jumpers, with a dark dirty scarf around his neck. In his cell, he was well-dressed and clean shaven, handsome even.

Mary told Wagner he could not possibly have slept on the lounge in the back of her father's shop on the night of the murders as he claimed. Mary had seen her mother lock the back door around midnight. Besides, Mary told Wagner, another tenant named George Lowd had been napping on that same lounge after baiting trawls with John Hontvet in the next room. Mary accused Wagner of acting strange and looking wild when she met him at breakfast on Thursday morning. She reminded him that he had said, "Mary, I have got myself into trouble and I feel as if I am going to be taken."

Mary was especially bothered by a missing shirt. Wagner had only four white shirts and, having done all his ironing, mending, and washing for weeks, Mary told the police, she knew precisely what shirt he had been wearing the week of the murders. But despite numerous searches, Mary and Marshals Thomas Entwistle and Frank Johnson could not find that shirt. It was not in Wagner's room at the house on Water Street as he claimed or in his clothes bag or in the drawer in the shop where tenants stored clean clothes. It was not on Wagner in his Portsmouth cell and it had not been among his old clothes the police recovered during his arrest in Boston. Mary recalled that Wagner had been acting suspiciously before he took the train out of Portsmouth. She had seen him with a mysterious bundle sticking out beneath his jumper. He was holding something under his arm as he went from his bedroom to the outhouse in the backyard.

"I watched him to see how queer he acted," Mary later told the police, who returned many times to search the Johnson house and to interview Maren, who was recuperating there, "but he [Wagner] went out the back door; went out into the yard."

Despite the tense and revealing meeting with Mary Johnson, Wagner kept his poker face intact, never showing resentment, guilt, or fear. According to his testimony, he and Mary parted with a friendly handshake. But according to the newspapers, as the prisoner was ushered back into his cell, Mary snapped, "What a liar!" and refused to take his proffered hand.

"I don't want to shake hands with a murderer," she told him. Time and again, Wagner's view of events differed from that of everyone around him.

The only time Wagner's deadpan expression cracked, according to the *Portsmouth Journal*, was when a gentleman asked him—if he had truly been such close friends with the Hontvets, why were they so willing to believe he had turned to murder? Wagner's reply was as inscrutable as ever.

"I don't know," he said, his face reddening. "John wanted me to bait trawls, and I didn't go to help him...and I thought John was mad." In Wagner's world, his best friends were accusing him of murder because he had not shown up for work.

Link by link, according to the media, the circumstantial evidence was beginning to bear out Maren Hontvet's theory that the true killer was already in custody. David Burke reported that the wooden pegs, or "thole pins," that attached the oars to his recovered dory were suddenly and significantly worn down.

Although they had just been replaced and used only once, the wooden pegs had overnight been worn down by a quarter of an inch as if they had been heavily used for hours. Someone resembling Wagner had been spotted near Devil's Den on the morning of the murder. Eyewitnesses waiting for the ferry at the first New Castle bridge on March 6 now swore that Wagner had been there. He had not returned to the boarding house all night. A white handkerchief found "twisted around Karen's neck" reportedly belonged to Wagner. He had run away to Boston. And there was a bombshell yet to burst. In two days, Portsmouth police would discover a white shirt, bloody and torn into three strips, stuffed behind the vault of the privy in the back of Matthew Johnson's house. Mary Johnson was called to examine the shirt that lay in the snow. She immediately recognized the stitching she had done and the new collar. It was the missing shirt that belonged to Wagner.

"The chain of evidence seems to be tightly closing around Wagner as the murderer," the weekly *Portsmouth Journal* concluded. But on Saturday, as the bodies of Karen and Anethe finally arrived in Portsmouth and an armed and angry throng congregated once more outside the police and railway stations, Wagner's biggest problem was getting out of town alive.

Chapter 19

THE FUNERAL

Of the four lawyers who brought the Wagner case to trial, two for the defense and two for the prosecution, only George Yeaton visited the murder scene on Smuttynose and saw the mangled and strangled bodies. Before extraditing his prisoner to the state of Maine on Saturday, March 8, Yeaton and a party of naval officers and local citizens were ferried to the Isles of Shoals aboard the steam tug USS *Mayflower*. He was accompanied by doctors Parsons, Whittier, and Rogers of Portsmouth, and by a surgeon from the Navy Yard named Buell.

Judging by the vacuum of news coverage from Smuttynose that afternoon, it appears the press corps stuck close to the prisoner back in Portsmouth jail. Dozens of curious visitors had already flattened the snow and tainted the crime scene on the island when Yeaton arrived. The bodies of Karen and Anethe had been lying in the Red House for nearly sixty hours, their faces hacked and frozen in agony. Yeaton's entourage arrived to find that undertakers from Woodbury Gerrish & Co. had finally come to collect the remains. Having placed the corpses in fresh coffins, the morticians were preparing to depart in a small boat for their funeral home in Portsmouth. Yeaton had the coffins transferred to the USS *Mayflower*. It was a more dignified vessel. Three years earlier, naval hero Admiral David Glasgow Farragut had died suddenly while visiting the Portsmouth Naval Shipyard in Kittery. The man who had said, "Damn the torpedoes, full speed ahead" was treated with the highest military honor. Farragut's gleaming metal coffin bedecked in flowers had been transferred through these same waters aboard the USS *Speedwell*, the sister ship to the *Mayflower*.

The *Mayflower* arrived back in town that afternoon. Yeaton's next job was to visit the Johnson's house to study the scene on Water Street and to interview potential witnesses. But first, the prosecutor instructed the doctors that no major invasive autopsy was required on the two victims. This was not an unusual request since autopsies were rarely done at the time. The final examination should, however, offer a detailed description of the wounds that caused the death of each woman, primarily to confirm what the coroner's jury of Kittery had learned two nights before.

Dr. John Parsons, who had been part of that original group, now managed the team assembled in the back room of the funeral parlor on Daniel Street. Parsons would deliver key testimony at the upcoming trial. To mollify the media, Parsons now reported briefly that Karen, aged thirty-nine, had fifteen cuts around her face and head with many bruises and fractures. There was a compound fracture on the back of her skull and another at the forehead, either one of which "was sufficient to produce instant death." The head of Anethe, aged twenty-five, had been "terribly hacked to pieces." The temple bone above her eye was "completely smashed" and both ears were nearly severed, with many bruises all over the body. One earring was cut out and dangled in her hair. When the coroner's jury rendered its official verdict that afternoon, no one was surprised. Preliminary evidence, they said, indicated that the women had met their death by an ax in the hands of Louis Wagner.

After the morticians did their best to repair the bodies for view, the caskets were delivered by carriage to the Johnson house on Water Street. They arrived around nine p.m. Saturday evening just as solicitor Yeaton was preparing to secretly extract his prisoner from Portsmouth to Maine. According to the *Times,* someone inside the police department leaked the news that Wagner was being shipped out on the evening train. The *Chronicle* offered a more sardonic view of the secret plan.

"One of the knowing ones, however, doubtless thinking that York county would be saved several thousands of dollars of expense and the murderer punished if he did not reach Maine, told a few people, the result being the assembling of a thousand people near the North Church just before 10 o'clock."

Again the prisoner was handcuffed between Marshals Frank Johnson and Thomas Entwistle, who were not halfway to the depot before the mob had doubled in size and intensity. Wagner, wearing Entwistle's police cap, was flanked by three Maine deputies and Portsmouth mayor Thomas Marvin, all armed with pistols and "billies" to protect the prisoner. By the time they reached the church at the center of Market Square, about two hundred fishermen from up and down the seacoast, also armed with pistols, clubs, and brickbats, began shouting and fiercely jostling the small posse of officers. To the angry fishermen and former Shoalers, Wagner was slipping out of their grasp. "Tear him up," someone cried. "Pull him to pieces." Others called for a rope to hang the prisoner on the spot.

Two blocks farther at Vaughan Street, a stone or brickbat found its mark, striking Wagner above his left ear "causing the blood to flow freely." A brick whizzed by Marshal Johnson but only nicked his nose. Entwistle was hit on the shoulder, the leg, and then on the side of the head, the blow stunning him momentarily. Another officer was struck in the chest. At Hanover Street, now the city's new hotel district, Entwistle cocked his revolver and threatened to shoot anyone who tried to lay hands on the prisoner. The crowd scattered briefly. The officers took shelter in the freight office until the train pulled into the station and then, forming a human shield, they smuggled their prisoner onto the Pullman smoking car. Moments later, a brick crashed through the train window in a spray of broken glass but no one was injured.

"A fisherman, a relation of the murdered girls, ran about with a revolver, trying to get a chance to shoot Wagner," the *Portsmouth Journal* noted, "and had it not been for fear of shooting the policemen, the body of the murderer would have been riddled undoubtedly."

Seeing Wagner safely aboard the eastbound train, the crowd grew even louder and the chanting and swearing more violent. The prisoner appeared "astonished," according to one report, to see a figure with a gun chasing the train as it chugged slowly out of town in clouds of smoke and steam. In his trial testimony, Wagner named names.

"Rocks and bricks was flying around my ears," he told the court three months later. "I then turned around and looked and saw Mr. Hontvet nearest to me; hove a brick or rock at me, but struck that little policeman [Entwistle]. Half way down the depot, a rock struck me in the head, cut a hole through the hat, cut my head. The blood was running down my neck. I then bent down so far that I was not a great deal higher than the policeman, to save my head; but still the rocks was flying, another rock struck me on the leg. The crowd was so thick around that we hardly could move. They might have killed me if it were not for the Portsmouth police."

But despite the heroic lifesaving efforts of the Portsmouth lawmen, Wagner and his attorneys would later blame them for lying, for conducting a shoddy investigation, and for falsifying evidence in a corrupt effort to railroad an innocent man onto the scaffold. The defense would further accuse the Hontvets, although never directly, of bribing witnesses in an attempt to cover up a crime of their own making.

When John Hontvet arrived back at Johnson's boarding house, Karen and Anethe were there. An unknown number of mourners were allowed into a private viewing Saturday evening and through the early afternoon on Sunday. "The bodies were nicely prepared and lay in two handsome caskets," the *Chronicle* reported, "their faces, though bruised and discolored, looking calm and peaceful."

The funeral service, based on the snippets of information the newspapers found it acceptable to publish, was a strange and brief affair. The next day, March 9, was a Sunday and the ceremony was held at St. John's Episcopal on Chapel Street at three p.m. Formerly Queen's Chapel, the Anglican church occupying the highest point on the Portsmouth waterfront had been the social center of the rich and powerful in colonial days.

The stone burying vaults that open onto the steep winding road to the left of the church contain the bones of three colonial New Hampshire governors. A Brattle organ in the upper gallery, the oldest working pipe organ in the United States, was imported to the colonies in 1708. The church owns a rare "Vinegar Bible," named for a conspicuous misprint of the word *vineyard* made in 1717. St. John's has a steeple bell once repaired by Paul Revere and a mahogany chair where President George Washington reportedly sat while attending services there in 1789. All these items were saved when the wooden church burned and was rebuilt in brick in 1807 and most remain on view to the public today.

The caskets containing the remains of Karen and Anethe Christensen were placed side by side in front of the St. John's altar, each covered with a wreath. Today that spot is decorated by a towering scalloped ceiling, and behind where the coffins lay, is a triptych of panels bearing the words of the Apostles' Creed, the Ten Commandments, and the Lord's Prayer. Although the dead women had known scarcely a handful of Portsmouth citizens, the capacity crowd of mourners spilled into the aisles. People stood at the back of the sanctuary and flowed out the door to the steep street. The only flowers were two wreaths hastily donated by "a sympathetic lady" from another church when she discovered that no other flowers adorned the sanctuary. To the disappointment of the ghoulish in attendance, both casket lids remained shut.

"The murdered women were of irreproachable character, and quite remarkable for their personal beauty," the *New York Times* reported, although their coverage was entirely secondhand. But the victims of whom we know so little remain largely forensic specimens in the Wagner story rather than fleshed-out human beings. We have only Celia Thaxter's simple impressions to cling to. The melancholy Karen was memorialized in the brief poem that bears her name. "She is not pretty, she is not young," Celia wrote.

In a letter addressed to a friend the day after the funeral, Celia mentioned Karen in passing. "Karen was quite one of the family here; it was she of whom I wrote the little spinning ballad, you know." No mention was made of the traumatic scene in which Celia's mother had fired Karen.

In describing Anethe in the same letter, Celia framed the words she would later recycle into her essay in the *Atlantic*. "Anethe, everybody says, was a regular fair beauty, young and strong, with splendid thick yellow hair, so long she could sit on it." Only in this letter did Celia reveal the reaction of her younger brother Oscar, when she confessed: "Oscar was so impressed with her beauty. We begged her to come over as often as she could, it was such a pleasure to look at her! You can't imagine how shocked and solemnized we have all been. Oscar walks up and down, now ejaculating, 'Oh poor, poor things, and Anethe so beautiful, so beautiful!'"

While the *Manchester Daily Union* called the funeral service "appropriate to the occasion" and "solemn and impressive," others had hoped for a less formal and more "sympathetic" service. No mention of the crime or the cause of death was made in the ritualistic Episcopal burial service. The music, the *Chronicle* complained, "was not worthy of the church," since the organ needed repair and the new choir was not at their best. After a few brief readings, the rector "dashed off to his room," leaving the members of the congregation looking blankly at one another, unsure if the funeral was over. Then they slowly dispersed. Many in attendance, having been shocked and enthralled by the tragic events of the week, "turned away dissatisfied, disappointed" the *Chronicle* reporter concluded. Except when mentioned by the rector at the beginning of the church service, the only acknowledgments of Karen and Anethe at their own funeral were their names along with their birth and death dates inscribed on the side of their caskets.

After the ceremony, a parade of citizens followed the two horse-drawn hearses about three-quarters of a mile from the city center to the cemetery on South Street. The coffins were placed in a cold granite receiving vault where they would remain for weeks until the spring thaw. Their long journey from Norway complete, the two women had become permanent residents of Portsmouth, New Hampshire. Karen and Anethe were later buried in an attractive section of the city's expansive South Cemetery called Harmony Grove. Their matching white-marble tombstones, the inscriptions now faded, are embedded in a single slab of granite.

Louis Wagner would never set foot in the city again. "After a scene of confusion and turmoil that cannot be described," the *Chronicle* announced on the day of the funeral, "the prisoner was at last safely put on board the train, and Portsmouth was rid of him." During his thirty-six-hour stay in Portsmouth jail, the handsome Prussian killer with the kind face had sparked two riots and captured the attention of readers nationwide. And the headlines had just begun.

"Lots of newspapers came with such distracted accounts of the murder that it is enough to make anybody sick," Celia wrote to her friend on March 12. "As if a Star Islander did it! If they do not hang that wretch, law is a mockery."

IV

TRIAL

"That is a honeymoon pair at the end of the carriage," whispered the commercial traveler.
"Yes," said the modern Sherlock, "and I'll wager two pounds he kissed her going through the tunnel."
"Did you see him?"
"No, but I see something now. He had a smutty spot on his nose when the train entered the tunnel, and now she has one, too."

—From a cartoon titled "Circumstantial Evidence" in a 1907 newspaper

"How ready people are sometimes to transform the man into the criminal."

—Defense attorney Max Fischacher at Wagner's trial

Chapter 20

OPENING CEREMONIES

The summer of 1873 was a game changer at the Isles of Shoals. Most conspicuously there was a massive new hotel preparing to open. The gleaming white monolith dominated the forty acres at what used to be the island village of Gosport. The villagers had vanished and many of their ramshackle huts had been leveled. The workmen who had ignored Maren Hontvet's plaintive cries for help in March were now hammering in the final nails. And what had been the peaceful island of Smuttynose across the ocean harbor was now an infamous murder site.

For twenty-five years, the Appledore Hotel had reigned supreme at the Isles of Shoals. A generation of summer visitors had come to know the Laighton family. Guests roamed every rocky cove, cliff, and cairn. They heard the familiar island tales of ghosts, pirates, and shipwrecks. Eliza Laighton, whose doctor described her as "morbidly obese," served up three enormous meals each day to hundreds of hotel patrons. A typical supper menu offered the following bounty from the sea: broiled fresh mackerel, salt mackerel, broiled scrod, fried halibut, fried cod, broiled saltfish, fish balls, fish chowder, hashed fish, perch, pickled lobster, plain lobster, spiced or smoked salmon. And that was in addition to heaping plates of beef, turkey, chicken, ham, tongue, all varieties of eggs and potatoes, baked beans, fresh baked breads, and preserved fruits. The only competition ten miles out to sea had been the Laighton's own dumpy Mid-Ocean House hotel on

Smuttynose and the three smaller guest houses on Star Island run by Origen and Lemuel Caswell.

Besides the cool "healthful air" and the spectacular sunsets, visitors to Appledore were often treated to celebrity sightings. Classical musicians gave impromptu concerts while famous painters set up their easels on the hotel piazza. American poets and writers, the rock stars of the Victorian era, were ubiquitous in Celia Thaxter's cottage salon. But it was her connection to the prestigious *Atlantic Monthly*, founded in 1857, that made Celia herself the most sought-after celebrity on the island. Due in large part to its two-hundred-year connection to Harvard University, many Americans, especially New Englanders, saw Boston as an intellectual capital, a "latter-day Athens" according to one historian. If Boston was the nation's cultural hub in the 1860s and '70s, then the *Atlantic Magazine* was the hub of the hub. And when the elite magazine's authors and editors took a vacation, they frequently found their way to the Laighton family hotel.

James Russell Lowell, the first editor of the *Atlantic*, had been among the original guests at Appledore in the 1850s. Considered America's first "man of letters," Lowell was also a bit of an alcoholic, suicidal, and absent-minded. But he set the bar high for the new *Atlantic* magazine by paying a decent rate to big name nineteenth-century writers like Emerson, Hawthorne, Holmes, Whittier, Melville, and Longfellow. An abolitionist and advocate of women's rights, Lowell's own four-hundred-line poem titled "Pictures of Appledore" is a perfect example of the lofty (most readers today might say "stuffy") literary style that characterized the magazine in its early days.

The first five editors of the *Atlantic Monthly*, including Lowell, James T. Fields, Thomas Wentworth Higginson, Thomas Bailey Aldrich, and William Dean Howells, all had strong connections to Portsmouth, to Kittery, or to the Isles of Shoals. So it was only natural that readers of the magazine became familiar with Celia Thaxter's poetry and her legends of the Shoals region.

As *Atlantic* readers moved westward with the expanding nation, so did the reputation of the Isles of Shoals. Like Celia Thaxter, the second *Atlantic* editor, James T. Fields, was Portsmouth-born. His wife, Annie Fields, became Celia's closest friend. As a partner in Ticknor & Fields, James became the most important Boston literary publisher of his age. According to a contemporary, Fields was "the shrewdest of publishers and the kindest of men." It was Fields who pushed Hawthorne to complete *The Scarlet Letter*, who urged Henry David Thoreau ahead in his writing, who made Quaker poet John Greenleaf Whittier wealthy, and who published the works of Charles Dickens in the United States.

Ticknor & Fields purchased the ailing *Atlantic Magazine* in 1859 and Fields served as editor until 1871. Fields encouraged Celia to write her classic *Among the Isles of Shoals* that first appeared as installments in the magazine in 1869 and 1870. Journalist Horace Greeley, no easy critic, found Celia's *Atlantic* essays on the Shoals, with their vivid "pen pictures," to be "the best prose writing I have seen for a long time." William Dean Howells, who succeeded Fields as editor of the *Atlantic*, had also been smitten by young Celia's natural beauty during early visits to the Appledore Hotel before the Civil War. Howells continued to publish Celia's poems and championed her bold, realistic essay on the Wagner murder in 1875. Each mention of Celia and the Shoals in the *Atlantic* was free publicity for the Appledore Hotel. It was Celia's depiction of her romantic isolated kingdom that lured *Atlantic* readers to the islands. And it is likely that this publicity attracted Boston spice merchant John R. Poor to open the competing Oceanic Hotel on Star Island in 1873.

"One of the brightest figures in literary Boston for many years, was Celia Thaxter," a critic wrote after the poet's death. "She was the best of good company. Everybody wanted her." Professor Jane E. Vallier, a scholar of Thaxter's work, reminds us that Celia was among the most popular and frequently published poets of her time. She "set the moral tone" of the Appledore resort, Vallier says, and turned the island into a sort of utopia. It is against her high standard of behavior that the murders appear especially abhorrent.

Celia's rock star status does not translate well in the roughly two dozen surviving photographs we have of her. Even as a child, she appears perpetually solemn, thoughtful, dour, and shy. She frowns and averts her eyes from the camera. She never ever smiles and grows matronly as the years pass. Yet contemporaries remember her not only as fearless and independent but also as endowed with an infectious laugh. Her "broad chest" and "vigorous physique" erupted with peals of laughter, one hotel guest recalled in later years. Always social, rarely intimate, Celia was the ideal hostess. Yet she confided in letters to friends like Annie Fields that the crush of admirers often left her exhausted and depressed.

The Oceanic Hotel offered no such celebrity host when it opened in the summer of 1873. While the Appledore resort had evolved from the mind of Celia's eccentric father, Thomas Laighton, the Star Island project was a financial investment pure and simple. John Poor was among a number of newly rich Boston businessmen seeking to diversify his holdings by cashing in on the tourism boom then sweeping the New England coast. In the coming years, a glut of summer hotels would spring up along the sandy beaches and rocky bluffs close by. On a clear day, hotels stretching from Boar's Head in Hampton to Bald Head Cliff in Ogunquit, Maine, were visible from the Shoals. These big wooden hotels sported big names like the Sagamore, the Passaconaway, the Champernowne, the Farragut, and Wentworth by the Sea. Many would, as wooden hotels often did, expire in flames.

In the same month as the murders, with Louis Wagner languishing in a Maine jail awaiting trial, details of the rising Oceanic Hotel began to leak into the local newspapers. Although the Laighton family complained privately of John Poor's devious acquisition of Star Island, Oscar declared publicly that the new hotel was no threat to the Appledore. "There is business enough for all," the *Portsmouth Journal* reported, "and there will never be hotels enough built on the Isles of Shoals to accommodate all who wish to rest there."

At four stories high and 262-feet long, the Oceanic could not quite match the enormous 500-guest peak capacity of the Appledore House. But it was newer and boasted a sturdy stone dock 350-feet long and 20-feet wide.

An enormous circular cistern carved into solid rock could hold 100,000 gallons of water at Star Island. The Appledore, by comparison, looked and operated like a pre–Civil War hotel for an exclusive set of carefully vetted guests based largely in the Boston area. The Laightons depended on referrals and on Celia Thaxter's literary fame to draw paying guests. John Poor, however, had deep pockets and used his fortune to advertise the Oceanic as a metropolitan-style hotel, targeting vacationers from Chicago, New York, Philadelphia, St. Louis, and beyond.

The final incorporation of the Oceanic was a rocky process. New Hampshire legislators wondered why Mr. Nathan Mathes, who had scooped up all the Gosport real estate in his own name, was not part of the Oceanic Hotel Corporation. The five incorporating parties included John R. Poor, John A. Poor, and Daniel E. Poor, a family name also associated with lucrative railroad speculation and the Standard & Poor investment agency. The new hotel company boasted $300,000 in operating capital. But with the peak summer season about to begin on July 1, New Hampshire legislators continued to table the Oceanic Company's requests. The state finally sanctioned Poor's corporation on July 3, 1873, and the doors opened five days later.

In the first month of operation, 1,098 guests signed the Oceanic register, filling 182 rooms and the many converted fishing cottages on the island. A renowned Boston caterer prepared and served meals in a spacious dining room and the kitchen featured an ornate meat-carving table, marble coffee urns, enormous stoves and grills, "hot closets," and patented fish fryers. The Oceanic boasted modern steam-powered elevators and superior plumbing, special baggage rooms for long-stay guests, a bowling alley, separate men's and ladies' billiard rooms, and the best ferry service on the east coast. Oceanic advertising promised perpetual ocean breezes that were not only healthy, but free of dust and mosquitoes. The thermometer, according to a visitor testimonial, was permanently "nailed at 70 degrees."

That summer, John Poor personally hosted a private charter and sumptuous banquet for members of the press corp. After coffee and cabanas and many hearty toasts, the reporters were treated to a tour of the murder site on Smuttynose, followed by cod fishing and yacht sailing. A grand "hop" with a live orchestra topped the evening. In the spirit of camaraderie, Mr. Poor invited Appledore Hotel proprietor Oscar Laighton and 150 of his guests to dance the night away in the grand Oceanic ballroom.

As part of his 1873 media blitz, Poor contacted yacht clubs up and down the New England coast, hoping to stir up more elite business. His promotional efforts led to the first-ever Gosport Regatta the following summer. More than fifty boats entered a thirteen-mile race from Star Island to Boon Island in Maine and back. The winner was the yacht *America* for which the famous America's Cup race later took its name. But according to Celia's biographer "Rozzie" Thaxter, this new wave of wealthy summer tourists left much to be desired. "So many noisy and objectionable people came to the new Oceanic Hotel," Rozzie noted, "the more discriminating guests moved to the Appledore House where the atmosphere continued one of refinement and culture."

The opening of the Oceanic killed the Gosport fishing village. It also ended the chance for summer visitors to meet the hard-bitten old Shoalers in their natural habitat. The strange synergy that had existed between the early hotel guests and the quirky fishing families was gone forever. By the summer of 1873, the former inhabitants of the island had faded into the misty realm of legend along with ghostly pirates and frozen shipwrecked sailors. The family of John and Maren Hontvet, living and dead, had moved to Portsmouth, never to return. Their Red House had become the "must see" attraction of the summer. Victorian visitors bought hundreds of stereoview picture cards of the Smuttynose murder site as naturally as if it was the Grand Canyon or a battle scene at Gettysburg. Others took more palpable keepsakes, cutting away chunks of the blood-stained house with pocket knives.

Author William Leonard Gage watched the transition firsthand. For fifteen years, beginning in 1860, Gage took the summer ferry from Portsmouth to the Isles of Shoals. ("I know of no steamer ride in the United States more delightful," Gage once wrote.) Before the arrival of the Oceanic, Gage had often lodged at the Gosport House on Star Island operated by Origen Caswell and his wife, Mary, whom the writer greatly admired. Origen was the bravest, truest, noblest man Gage had ever met and never allowed a drop of liquor in his lodging house. Gage would come to miss the quaint simpler times among the poor folk of old Gosport village. He recalled exciting days on the ocean, fishing in a small boat with the Caswells. One time, they hauled in a hundred cod and mackerel in a single trip.

But Gage had little sympathy or respect for the "degraded islanders" of Gosport whom he described as lazy, drunken, and bickering. "He who could swear the hardest was the best fellow," he wrote of the last of the Shoalers. Gage admired the new Oceanic Hotel, but was not always impressed by its clientele.

"From the Boston or New York point of view, it is certainly a success," Gage wrote of the Oceanic in 1875, "and whether in beds, or electric signals, or grand piano, or spacious dining hall, or noble piazza, or spacious corridors, or billiard or bowling alleys, or elegantly appointed tables, with their perfect galaxy of waiters—it has few if any superiors."

"There was no style, no fashion, no excess of ornamentation," among the old Shoalers and early rusticators who visited the island, he recalled. Those authentic Yankee characters had been replaced by a new generation of socialites and partygoers. "People went out to the Shoals to enjoy the ocean and the rocks, not to waste the summer and criticize one another," Gage wrote, comparing the very different eras. "Among the crowds who frequent the Oceanic, you not infrequently meet some who have never taken the pains to walk out and see and hear the dashings of the sea."

Despite his nostalgia, Gage was honest about the good old days at Gosport. "Would I go back to them? I hardly think it," he wrote.

In 1869, before the arrival of John Poor, a travel writer named B. F. DeCosta had described Gosport as "the most perfect picture of a fisherman's village that I have seen on the New England coast." Four years later, it was gone.

"The Isles of Shoals have been transformed from a fisherman's paradise to a famous summer resort," the *New York Times* declared, "to many, the most attractive on the New England coast." But the change took its toll. "Like the Indians, however, [the fishermen] have disappeared before the onward march of civilization."

Samuel Adams Drake, another prolific author of Victorian travel guides, said it best. Drake found it ironic that the hotel industry at the Shoals began with Thomas Laighton, a man who was pathologically reclusive and downright antisocial. It was stranger still, Drake wrote, that John Poor believed that his "monster hotel" made Star Island a better place.

"Thus by the so-called hand of improvement," Drake wrote with undisguised sarcasm, "was the ancient village of Gosport swept off the face of the island to which, like some lonely sea bird, it had clung with precarious hold for more than two hundred years. In all New England we do not recall a similar instance of a whole village being *improved out of existence.*"

But the grand Oceanic Hotel, as John Poor first imagined it, would not survive for long. Like Louis Wagner, its days were numbered.

Chapter 21

THE EXAMINATION

Louis wept. Through much of Sunday, March 9, since arriving in Maine, Wagner had been his usual stoic self. Even when hordes of visitors came to stare at the infamous Smuttynose murderer, his blank face revealed nothing. But the moment a local reporter asked about his harrowing escape from the vengeful New Hampshire mob the previous night, Wagner turned pale, his body trembled, and the tears flowed.

Those evil Portsmouth people had tried to kill him, Wagner told the reporter in sad tones. And why? He was an innocent God-fearing man. They had wounded him, not only with flying rocks and sharp ice missiles, but with their taunts and their insults. He had received a nasty cut on his head by a flying object, but thanks to the heroic efforts of the Portsmouth police, the prisoner had not been torn to pieces. The police had safely smuggled him aboard a Pullman car, its windows smashed by a well-aimed brick. The train carried him over the Piscataqua River Bridge and out of Portsmouth forever. It chugged steadily through the winter darkness, moving north some forty miles along the coastal towns and white sandy beaches of southern Maine—past Kittery, York, Ogunquit, Wells, and Kennebunk to the mill town of Saco.

Like its sister city of Portsmouth, Saco's first permanent English residents settled in 1631. Both riverside ports relied initially on fishing, then on the timber trade and shipbuilding. By Wagner's arrival in 1873, Saco, along with its sister city Biddeford across the Saco River, was best known for its textile mills. These factories were operated initially by an influx of Yankee farm girls, then by French-speaking Canadians, Greeks, Armenians, and Jews who immigrated to New England. The waters that powered the mill wheels flowed from the scenic White Mountains in New Hampshire and out to the Atlantic Ocean. So, like the Isles of Shoals, the scenic Saco River Valley had seen a smattering of summer visitors as early as the 1840s. Then in 1873, the Boston & Maine Railroad opened its newest terminal at Saco's seven-mile-long Old Orchard Beach, now a separate town, ushering in a thriving summer tourist business that continues today.

Most New England towns have at least one murder victim who refuses to stay buried. In Saco, it is Berengera Caswell, a Canadian mill-worker who died during a botched abortion. Caswell's rat-chewed body was discovered floating in the Saco River, lashed to a wooden plank, after a winter thaw in 1850. Like so many child victims of the Industrial Revolution, Caswell had begun working in the textile mills of Lawrence, Massachusetts. She moved to the sprawling brick millyards in Manchester, New Hampshire, before "losing her virtue" to a boyfriend in Maine. Her killer, a homeopathic doctor and abortionist from Saco, was convicted of manslaughter, but he served only a brief jail sentence. Caswell's tragic tale was fictionalized into a cautionary book written for young women titled *A Thrilling and Exciting Account of the Horrible Murder of Mary Bean, the Factory Girl* (1852). Fallen virtue, the story implied, could have deadly results.

Two decades after the sensational Caswell murder, residents of Saco and surrounding towns pressed their way into the town jail to catch a glimpse of Wagner. He was sitting on his bed when the reporter from the *Portland Press* was ushered into his cell. The reporter spoke a few words of greeting in German to the fair-haired, blue-eyed man and then handed him a cigar. Wagner chatted amiably, puffing on his stogie.

"He possesses one of those faces to which you would naturally take a liking, though there is about it a weak appearance, which grows upon you, the more you look upon him," the journalist wrote. Again Wagner declared his innocence. He had been close friends with the murdered women, he said, and promised he could prove he was not on the island that fateful night. Like William Thayer of the *Portsmouth Times*, the *Portland Press* reporter quickly felt sympathetic toward the prisoner.

"There were about him no marks of guilt, and the quiet, composed manner in which he spoke went far to induce a belief in his innocence," he wrote.

"My God, how think you I could ever go to kill them! It is not so," Wagner repeated, which well may have been true if his intent was robbery. The killings were an unfortunate byproduct of being recognized by Anethe. Yet Wagner's delivery, as he painted himself as the true victim of Smuttynose, sounded sincere to many who did not know the man or the preponderance of evidence pointing in his direction.

"The sad tone in which he said this and the slightly marked accent made it very effective," the reporter at Saco concluded. "I came away, certainly not impressed with a conviction of his innocence, but still cherishing a reasonable doubt, and feeling much kinder toward him than on entering the cell."

Wagner's seduction of the *Portland Press* still resonates today. Its sympathetic coverage of Wagner appeared word-for-word in the *New York Times* and other newspapers, setting off a groundswell of public support in the three months before the trial that still lingers. Wagner began carrying a copy of the Holy Bible, declaring that "Gott is good" and that God would never let an innocent man be hanged. Women sent him handkerchiefs in solidarity. Even Celia Thaxter later admitted that Wagner's demeanor in jail and at trial "was a wonderful piece of acting" that "really inspired people with doubt as to his guilt."

On Wednesday, March 12, Wagner was delivered to the courtroom at South Berwick, Maine, under the protection of York County sheriff Edmund Warren. South Berwick, formerly Salmon Falls, is a peaceful village on the New Hampshire border just up the Piscataqua River from

Portsmouth. There, the prisoner was officially arraigned for the murders, Justice Alexander Dennett of York presiding. Prosecutor George Yeaton presented testimony from Portsmouth and Boston police, from Mary and Ann Johnson of Water Street, and others. The probable cause hearing lasted from eleven a.m. until five p.m.

"An immense crowd of people from the surrounding towns flocked to see him," one paper reported. The prisoner's stolid, sad face "seems to excite the sympathy of all who see him."

A week after the murders, Wagner still had no lawyer. According to prosecutor Yeaton, Wagner waived his right to counsel and testified freely at South Berwick. At trial, however, Wagner claimed that Yeaton had asked him, before the hearing began, if he wanted a lawyer. Wagner said he did, but when he got into the hearing room, he was on his own. Wagner spoke "on the record" for a full half hour and much of his testimony appeared in the local newspapers. Wagner's defense team would later claim their client was tricked into testifying and had been denied his right to an attorney. Retired Maine criminal attorney John Perrault, an expert on the Wagner case, reminds us that prisoner's rights were less evolved in Victorian days. The damage to the prisoner's defense or his newfound public sympathy was minimal. "I'm not under the impression Louis said anything at South Berwick that severely prejudiced him at trial," Perrault says. "On the other hand, I'm not sure it was in the prisoner's best interest to say anything."

As in Portsmouth, Wagner took the opportunity in South Berwick to condemn Maren Hontvet for unfairly naming him as the killer, but he did not go so far as to directly accuse Maren and John of the murders. That would come later. He also made a few statements at South Berwick that ring strange. As proof of his innocence, for example, Wagner suggested that, if he had committed the robbery, he could have pulled it off successfully.

"If I wanted money," Wagner told Judge Dennett at the hearing, "I knew every trunk in the house; knew Hontvet was in Portsmouth; could have gone there and taken the money *if they were asleep* without murdering them."

While his alibi remained consistent, Wagner occasionally nuanced his story to include new details he heard from witnesses. Here he was likely responding to John and Ivan's agonized plea on the day after the murder: "Could you not get the money without killing the women?"

Picking up on this point, the *Portsmouth Chronicle* implied that, like so many desperate criminals, Wagner was either stupid or a terrible planner. The trunk with the largest amount of cash (the money he did not find when frantically searching) had been three feet from the foot of Maren's bed. Instead of slipping smoothly in and out of the Red House, the thief had managed to trap all three women inside the bedroom with the money he was seeking.

"Our theory is that Wagner might not have committed murder if he could have driven the women out of the house without being discovered," the *Chronicle* suggested. That theory holds water. Even if Wagner had been dreaming for months about stealing the Hontvet's money, he likely considered it too risky and too complex to attempt, and therefore had not worked out the finer details of his plan. The events of March 5 played out rapidly, leaving him little chance to strategize.

He had been standing idly on the Portsmouth dock on March 5 when suddenly the *Clara Bella* had appeared with the men from Smuttynose. The bait was late, the men had forgotten their wallets, the women were alone, and Burke's abandoned rowboat beckoned. It was only upon his arrival at Smuttynose, after his ten-mile effort with the oars, that he realized that carrying away the trunk undetected was the most difficult element of the robbery. Wagner's plan was simply "TOO THIN!" as the *Chronicle* headline announced.

True crime writer Edmund Pearson, whose 1926 essay on the Wagner case remains the best analysis to date, cautioned readers against the modern trend toward amateur psychoanalysis. The mind of Louis Wagner mystified those who knew him. And it is unlikely, Pearson suggested, that people who never met him and who are unfamiliar with the life of a New England fisherman in 1873, can do anything except jump to conclusions. Based on his own extensive research, Pearson, though reluctantly, concluded that Wagner was not just a boaster, but "a complete egotist."

"To him," Pearson wrote in *Murder at Smutty Nose*, "his poverty, his torn shoes, his want of the comforts of life were cosmic tragedies; compared with these, the slaughter of two or three innocent women, and the heart-rending grief of two men, were of no consequence whatever."

We cannot know from newspaper clippings and trial transcripts whether Wagner was what we would currently call a sociopath or psychopath. But he scores high on the armchair therapist's checklist of related characteristics—glibness, superficial charm, cunning, grandiose thinking, pathological lying, lack of remorse, failure to accept responsibility, living a parasitic lifestyle, having no long-term goals or friends, and impulsivity.

We see evidence of this in his tendency, even when fleeing from a murder scene, to head directly to familiar and comfortable places, like Johnson's boarding house in Portsmouth and Brown's boarding house in Boston, where he sought sympathy over safety. When Mrs. Brown revealed her beloved son had recently died, Wagner seemed uninterested and complained about his aching feet. Although charming at first contact, Wagner had no close male friends. He preferred the company of women, especially those who cooked for him, mended and laundered his clothes, provided sexual favors, sympathized, and nursed him when he was sick or feigning sickness.

He was a boaster, Pearson reminds us, and enjoyed being the center of female attention, whether on the witness stand or in jail. He had perfected the passive stare, the hangdog look, and the ability to weep at a moment's notice. It was important to Wagner that people knew he had kissed Mary and Olava Johnson before boarding a train to Boston. "I done so. I done so every morning. Any time a day I received it when I wanted it," Wagner told the packed courthouse that summer. And in South Berwick, even as he refused to accept responsibility for killing Karen and Anethe, Wagner wanted people to know he could have completed the robbery on Smuttynose *"if they were asleep."* But the women did wake up, and in Wagner's twisted mind, what happened next was not his fault.

At one point during the proceedings in South Berwick, a man spoke up claiming to be Wagner's defense attorney. He was not the first. According to prosecutor Yeaton, three men in Saco and several in Portsmouth "had the impudence to push himself as counsel for the accused." Yeaton told the man, later identified only as Mr. Collins from Boston, to hold his tongue or he would be ejected from the courtroom or arrested. Judge Dennett ruled that the "shyster lawyer" was not authorized to practice law in Maine and vowed that that Wagner would not be "gobbled up by any foreign counsel who wished to gain notoriety through the press."

The judge at the hearing determined, based on Yeaton's compelling evidence, there was sufficient cause to hold Louis Wagner for trial on the third Thursday in May. He would appear before the Supreme Judicial Court of York in the pastoral little farm town of Alfred, Maine. But the new jail cells being built at Alfred were not yet completed. And the jail in nearby York was out of commission. And the jail at Saco was scheduled to be torn down to make way for the coming Boston & Maine Railroad line to Old Orchard Beach. So the prisoner was shipped north to Portland, currently Maine's largest city and primary seaport, to await his trial.

A gathering of thirty to forty people, mostly fishermen in solidarity with John Hontvet's family, met Wagner's train at Portland. In a miniature reenactment of the Portsmouth mob scene, the protestors shouted, "Kill him! Kill him!" Portland police rushed the prisoner from the train into a waiting horse-drawn hack. According to the *Portland Argus*, the officers "whipped up" the horses and got Wagner safely to jail where he remained "perfectly calm." Readers of the morning newspaper were duly informed the Smuttynose murderer was being held in Cell 49 on the ground floor on the north side of the west wing. It was as good as drawing a map.

The *Portsmouth Chronicle* reported that Wagner still retained his "amazing sangfroid," a French term that translates literally as "cold blood." The accused settled in to his new cell about fifty miles north of New Hampshire's only seaport. Despite an official order that no one was allowed to visit the prisoner until he had met with an attorney, the curious continued to stream past his cell. "The sympathy of most of the visitors at his jail has certainly been won by his calmness and his general appearance, which is quite prepossessing," the *Argus* observed.

Among the visitors was a Christian lady hoping to save the prisoner's immortal soul from eternal damnation. After their pleasant conversation with Wagner, as she left the woman turned to say, "I hope you put your trust in the Lord."

"I always did, ma'am," Wagner said sweetly, "and I always shall."

Chapter 22

DREAM TEAM

The public was ravenous for more information. On March 15, the *Portsmouth Journal* ran a detailed summary of the murders including a sketch, rare for this era. It showed a crude floor plan of the crime scene at the Hontvet house on Smuttynose, delineating the location of the rooms, doors, windows, beds, trunks, and dead bodies. While such forensic details are common to twenty-first-century crime enthusiasts for Victorians, the chance to play detective on a bloody case ripped from the headlines was captivating. Then suddenly the data flow stopped.

With Wagner on ice for a few months, the major newspapers moved on to juicier topics, leaving the local media to scrounge for crumbs of information, bicker among themselves, and speculate on the Wagner case. It was rumored, for example, that the Portland police were charging visitors, including many ladies, ten cents apiece to view the alleged killer in Cell 49. The money was reportedly being used to offset the Portland city debt. Wagner complained he was getting "rheumatic fever" (probably "rheumatism") in the damp lower cell where he was on exhibition. Prosecutor Yeaton quickly stepped in and the prisoner was transferred to an upper cell in the city jail. The press then reported Portland was no longer "making a show of the villain."

No detail was too trivial to print. When a jail guard suggested that Wagner had "an evil eye," his comment made the evening news. "When

Wagner is called the 'Smutty Nose murderer,'" the *Chronicle* pointed out to readers, "it is not meant that he has a smutty nose, but that he murdered two women on Smutty Nose Island." By early April, photographs of the "Isles of Shoals murderer" taken during his arrival in Maine, could be purchased by sending twenty-five cents to the studios of Mr. H. L. Webber of Sacco.

In the Victorian era, anonymous editorial comments were often sprinkled among the tightly packed columns of local news. For example, the *Chronicle* theorized Wagner dragged Anethe's body back into the kitchen of the Red House because he intended to torch the building to cover up three murders. With Maren still alive, however, Wagner had reportedly changed his mind, fearing the fire would attract nearby islanders to her rescue. Although this was pure speculation, the fire theory was passed from one newspaper to the next.

Despite vehement denials by the Hontvets and their friends, the *Boston Traveller* continued to falsely suggest Wagner killed Karen in a fit of revenge because she had spurned his proposal of marriage. With 20-20 hindsight, *The Traveller* further theorized the three rugged Norwegian women should have stood their ground together against Wagner. Barricading the bedroom door with a bed, rather than attempting to flee out the window, would have been a better plan. "No murderer would have remained long in the house when he found that resistance was earnestly made," the editor wrote. There were documented cases, the paper offered, where women had successfully defended themselves against men. Although women "are not apt to be cool," the *Traveller* concluded, when they are suddenly awakened at night.

Not all the attention was lavished on the prisoner in the months leading up to the trial. Frequent one-sentence updates in the Portsmouth papers noted that Maren Hontvet was on the mend. A thank-you card from John Hontvet and Ivan Christensen appeared in the *Portsmouth Journal* on March 10. The two fishermen expressed their sincere appreciation to the citizens of Portsmouth in the time of their bereavement and to the Portsmouth

Naval Shipyard for the use of the tugboat USS *Mayflower*. The "sympathetic woman" who provided the only flowers at the funeral was revealed to be the wife of Frank W. Miller, editor of the *Chronicle*. One reporter, waxing poetic on the subject of the island murders wrote that "all the angels in heaven must have shrieked aghast at the inhuman butchery; all the fiends incarnate rejoiced thereat."

The victims were not entirely forgotten. In mid-April, with the first thaw, the two wooden coffins were removed from the grim granite mausoleum on South Street at a spot once called Gallows Hill. Ruth Blay, the last woman hanged in New Hampshire, had met her end here in 1768. The Christensens, united in death, were carried down the hill where Blay had been hanged a century before, past a little pond, and up a slow rise to a peaceful spot called Harmony Grove. The two Norwegian women were buried not far from a copse of cypress trees that still hide the grave of Portsmouth historian Charles W. Brewster. New Hampshire governor and United States Supreme Court Justice Levi Woodbury lies nearby. Alemaker, robber baron, and politician Frank Jones, the city's richest man in the nineteenth century, would eventually build his towering ornate monument here near the two simple markers of Karen and Anethe. The granite slab linking their tombstones offers this sobering verse:

A sudden death, a striking call,
A warning voice which speaks to all,
To be prepared to die.

Louis Wagner, the papers suggested, should also be prepared to die. "If Wagner is found guilty of the awful crime," the *Times* editorialized, "the public will demand his execution." Capital punishment was a hot topic. While New Hampshire, at this writing, still teeters on the brink of banning the death penalty, Maine was already close to abolishing it in the 1870s. As Wagner sat in the Portland jail, the debate in the Portsmouth newspapers reflected the classic arguments.

"Is the gibbet a failure?" editor William Thayer asked in a March 24 headline of the *Times*. Hanging, or what Thayer called "strangulation by the officers of the law," was increasingly considered an inhumane method of execution, even among death penalty advocates. If a prisoner's neck was not broken by the noose in the sudden fall from the scaffold, he could struggle for many minutes, twisting and suffocating horribly in a "dance of death." This awful method, Thayer argued, made jurors reluctant to issue the death penalty and states reluctant to carry out executions, greatly increasing the number of men living out their days on death row. But for hanging to be an effective deterrent to future crime, the *Times* argued, once the sentence was passed, the hanging must be carried out. On the barbarous inhumanity of hanging, Frank W. Miller of the *Chronicle* was in full agreement. Miller made no secret of his complete opposition to the death penalty for any crime.

On the same day as the *Times* editorial, Miller reprinted an op-ed or "think piece" he copied from the *Portland Press*. In the past, according to the *Press*, public hangings had served as a deterrent to sinful citizens, so the more gruesome the spectacle, the better. But hangings were no longer public. By 1873, statistics showed that, in the three states where the gallows had been abolished (Michigan, Rhode Island, and Wisconsin) capital offenses had actually declined. The only legitimate goal of the gallows, the *Press* therefore explained, must be to provide a swift, merciful death by "breaking the neck by a single jerk" from the weight of the condemned man's falling body. But it was common knowledge, the article presumed, that this goal was unsuccessful in nine out of ten attempts. "To stop the breath without at the same time depriving the victim of consciousness, is to inflict protracted torture beyond the power of the imagination to realize," the *Portland Press* concluded. The guillotine, poisons, shooting, even the garrote were more humane methods of ending a life.

Curiously, it was during this time, as Wagner awaited trial in Portland, that the only lynching in Maine history (some say in all of New England history) occurred at Presque Isle on the Canadian border in late April 1873.

It all began, legend says, when an impoverished James Cullen stole a pair of boots. Cast out by his young wife in favor of another man, Cullen took twenty-five dollars in goods from the general store in Mapleton, Maine. He reportedly needed the supplies to walk back to his former home in New Brunswick, Canada. Searching for the petty thief among the wild woods of Aroostook County, Sherriff Hayden Granville and his deputy caught up with Cullen, who was staying with a friend. Out of sympathy, Sheriff Granville decided to let the robber "escape" in the night and continue his journey to Canada. The sheriff planned to return the stolen goods the next day.

The group settled into an isolated cabin by an old sawmill for the night. But as the sheriff and his deputy slept, Cullen killed them with an ax and set the cabin on fire. The murderer was quickly recaptured hiding in the cellar of his own home. Two days later, as Cullen was being transported to the nearest jail, a group of hooded men, possibly members of the late sheriff's Masonic order, waylaid the local constable and hanged Cullen from a tree. A large lynch mob then arrived to find Cullen already dead and his body placed in a pine coffin. His corpse was put on public display outside the local store. An inquiry determined that Cullen had been killed by "parties unknown."

The only solid news for Wagner watchers during his Portland period was the appointment of his dream duo of defense attorneys. First to make headlines was Max Fischacher, a "well-known attorney of Boston," with offices at 45 Milk Street, although his name was far from a household word in Maine or New Hampshire. A proud German Jew, Fischacher had emigrated at age six in 1853 with his parents and three siblings aboard the paddle steamer *Germania*. His parents were apparently well-to-do and Max graduated from Harvard in 1868. His motives for taking on the Wagner case appear transparent. As president of the Hebrew Young Men's Association in Boston, Fischacher was dedicated to serving American immigrants, particularly young men from Poland, Russia, and Germany. He wanted to help them gain independence in a strange new land where the odds were stacked against foreigners, especially poor foreigners. In a four-month period, for example, his charitable Jewish organization had assisted 181 people by finding them jobs and shelter, obtaining peddlers licenses, supplying food, fuel, clothing, and legal aid.

There is no reason to assume Fischacher was anything but altruistic in taking on the alleged Smuttynose murderer. "It is because he [Wagner] is a foreigner and I a German that I was suggested," the defense attorney would tell the jury at the upcoming trial. "I said I could not refuse to act, but would gladly lend my services to a man who represented himself innocent, as did the prisoner." Wagner was a stranger in America with no close friends, family, or supporters. As a foreigner, the defense attorney would argue, his client had been the "subject of prejudice and calumny and prejudgment."

In a rural Maine courtroom, Max Fischacher was himself a stranger in a strange land. Henry Munroe Rogers, another Harvard lawyer who lived almost to age one hundred, recalled in his memoir how truly isolated minorities were in Boston in the days following the Civil War. Rogers wrote: "There was then one negro lawyer, Robert Morris. There were no Jews, so far as I recall, excepting perhaps Max Fischacher." Rogers remembered seeing Fischacher's own newspaper advertisement that read: "the only Pollock Jew lawyer in Boston."

Fischacher was second in command to Col. Rufus Prescott Tapley, lead counsel for the defense. Tapley was born in Danvers, Massachusetts, back when James Monroe, America's fifth president, was in office. By 1873, Tapley was a respected fifty-year-old Maine lawyer. Thin, balding, with narrow, deep-set eyes, Tapley was clean-shaven, but sported two fluffy white "muttonchop" sideburns that flowed to his shoulders. He had served briefly with the 27th Maine Volunteer Infantry Regiment in the Civil War, although he served only five months and saw no action. Days after the assassination of Abraham Lincoln in 1865, Tapley delivered a funeral oration to five thousand mourners in his hometown of Saco, Maine, for which he was well remembered. Since the war, he had served as associate justice to the Supreme Court of the State of Maine, a position from which he retired in 1872. He had also served as a representative to the Maine state legislature. As "the honorable" Rufus Tapley—judge, soldier, politician—he was a man of considerable experience, notoriety, and clout in York County when he was appointed to the Wagner case.

Anticipating a damning timeline of circumstantial evidence from the prosecution, Fischacher quickly set out to assemble a list of witnesses for the defense. If he could find even a single person willing to swear that Wagner was in Portsmouth on the night of the murders, he could quickly prove reasonable doubt among jurors and knock the legs out from under George Yeaton's case.

The aggressive young defender fought back against press reports that had branded Wagner as the killer from the first day. The "Prussian lawyer" launched his own media campaign. It was "pure fantasy," Fischacher told reporters, that a white handkerchief tied tightly around Karen's throat had belonged to his client. He disputed evidence that "so-called experts" had found traces of human blood on Wagner's clothes. He ridiculed reports that a red pencil with his client's teeth marks had been found at the scene of the crime. But his attempts to locate evidence that favored his client made Fischacher unpopular along the "combat zone" on Water Street. The Boston lawyer found that key witnesses were being "kept out of the way" and would not speak to him. He was required to ask the city marshal for help and protection in the city's South End.

"The friends and acquaintances of the murdered women are very unwilling to admit even established facts that are in any degree favorable to Wagner," the *Chronicle* reported late in March. "Some of them even go so far as to threaten personal violence to Mr. Fischacher if he persists in doing his duty to his client."

The *Times* reminded its readers that "Wagner is entitled to all the defense he can make." A brief tiff arose when Thayer's newspaper announced the defense team had successfully uncovered evidence "that Wagner may be innocent of the terrible crime with which he stands charged." The *Concord Monitor* in New Hampshire's capital city reprinted this information but added a postscript to its readers: "It should be understood, however, that the *Times* inclines to the side of the defense, and its statements may not, therefore, be altogether impartial."

Portsmouth Times editor Thayer fired back a denial that his paper was in any way biased. But he admitted his paper was inclined toward the "possibility" that Wagner was innocent even when "the mob were crying for his life." Agreeing things looked bleak for Wagner, Thayer stated that the *Times* was "inclined to give him a fair hearing, and we are sorry to know that others are inclined to judge him before the evidence is heard." Back at the *Chronicle,* Frank Miller jokingly referred to Thayer's competing daily as the *Lyre.* Wagner's much-trumpeted religious conversion and Fischacher's new exculpatory evidence were "mere inventions," Miller wrote.

In fact, the dream team quickly hit a wall. Wagner's alibi, although richly detailed and delivered in a heartfelt tone, could not be validated. With hopes of raising a reasonable doubt, Wagner's lawyers would instead have to derail Yeaton's freight train of circumstantial evidence. They could put Wagner on the witness stand and pray his charisma could sway the jurors as it had the media. But they desperately needed a backup plan. So Fischacher and Tapley constructed legal landmines designed to derail the prosecutor's case and to save their client from an agonizing death by strangulation on the gallows.

Tapley immediately requested a change of venue, hoping to move the trial to Cumberland County next door, away from the howling mob of Hontvet sympathizers to a spot where jurors might be less informed and more sympathetic. When that effort failed, the defense team managed to move the trial date from May to early June, the beginning of tourist season along the coast. And then there was the nagging issue of jurisdiction. If the defense team could not prove Wagner was innocent, then perhaps they could prove that Smuttynose Island was not located in Maine as the prosecution claimed. If the offshore island was not legally part of York County, then technically, how could York County condemn Louis Wagner to be hanged?

Chapter 23

ALFRED

William Thayer would have to eat his words. As media coverage of the Smuttynose murders faded with the winter snow, the editor of the *Portsmouth Daily Evening Times* predicted the upcoming trial "will develop nothing new and will attract but very little attention, except among the friends of the murdered women." Two months later, the "trial of the century" was about to begin and the little town of Alfred, Maine, was a beehive of activity.

"The hotels are full and the jurors are boarded at the jail," Thayer's paper reported early in June. Private homes were boarding visitors from all over Maine, New Hampshire, Massachusetts, and beyond. In an age before television and film, everyone wanted to glimpse the handsome prisoner and the fisherman's wife who had survived the murderer's hatchet. "The courtroom was crowded to suffocation," the *New York Times* correspondent telegraphed to his editor on the first day of testimony, "and the excitement hourly increases. Large numbers of people are arriving by every train."

Standing in the quiet heart of Alfred today, it is easy to see why residents there still talk about the Wagner trial. The York County Courthouse is but a short tree-lined walk from the village center that includes a few elegant white houses, a country store, an antiquarian bookshop, a white church, a cemetery, and the white town hall. There is a small granite library building and an even smaller post office. During Wagner's era, a sturdy oak known as the Whipping Tree was among the most historic sites in the village. Criminals convicted of lesser crimes were publicly flogged while pressed against the tree. The practice was so brutal, legend says, that men begged to be hanged rather than submit to the lash. The whippings ended in 1830 and the "most famous tree in Maine" was felled by a hurricane in 1959.

The Alfred Historical Society occupies the former fire station and currently is open to visitors for a few hours each week in season. Inside the red firehouse doors is a "gramma's attic" of artifacts from an age when this was a community of farmers and lawyers. In 1873, the town population was 1,200 residents. A century later the population was still 1,200. Currently, the picturesque town is in the throes of a growth spurt. With busy highways on every side, Alfred has become a bedroom community for nearby Sanford, Biddeford, Kennebunk, and Portland. According to the most recent census, the population now tops 3,000, and residents are struggling against urban sprawl to maintain Alfred's country charm.

Two accidents of history distinguish Alfred from its neighbors. In the late 1700s, it became the center of the Shaker religious movement in Maine. An inventive and industrious community of "shaking Quakers," best known for their quivering dance, and their simple and celibate lifestyle, settled on a large tract of land and constructed dozens of buildings in town. Alfred was also the geographical center point of York County, the oldest and today the second most populous of sixteen counties in Maine. In 1806, when Maine was still governed by Massachusetts, Alfred became the official county seat for York. Twenty-first-century residents proudly refer to Alfred as a "shiretown," using the old-fashioned English term *shire* for the county seat of authority. As a result, many of the handsome homes that line the primary streets were built for the lawyers and judges who have worked at the bar. A worn plaque outside the two-story brick courthouse reminds us that "the oldest continuous court records in the United States," dating to 1636, are stored inside. Those same record books were taken down, dusted off, and used as evidence in the Louis Wagner trial. They were almost lost in 1933 when the center of the courthouse burned, but the documents survived in a fireproof vault in an adjoining wing.

We have no photograph of the interior of the Supreme Judicial Court of York as it appeared in Wagner's time, but it was typical of the scene we all know from countless legal films and television dramas. In June 1873, the robed judge sitting behind the raised bench and flanked by colorful flags was the Honorable William Griswold Barrows, age fifty-two. A native Mainer and graduate of Bowdoin College, Barrows had a distinguished face, deep-set eyes, long stylish hair, and a well-ordered salt-and-pepper beard. He had been a judge for ten years. The jury of twelve white men sat on wooden chairs to the left of the witness box.

The court recorder, Josiah Dunn Pulsifer, was a white-haired man with no mustache, but a thick square goatee. Famous in his own quiet way, J. D. Pulsifer was a pioneer in the emerging field of stenography and became the first official court reporter in the state of Maine. Pulsifer scribbled his unique brand of shorthand rapidly in four-hundred-page leather-bound notebooks using a pen. He was sometimes accompanied by his wife or one of their five children, all of whom were accomplished at shorthand. At the Wagner trial, Pulsifer was assisted by his son William Pitt Pulsifer and his daughter Abbie.

Although overlooked in every study of the Wagner trial, J. D. Pulsifer had an enormous impact on the case as we know it today. Educated in the classics, a Civil War veteran, teacher, journalist, and trained as a lawyer (he found the legal profession too boring), Pulsifer developed what he called "the Maine system" of stenography. He adapted the Pittman system of shorthand based on phonetics, or the sounds of words, rather than on spelling. Although he was "a stickler for detail," according to his 1896 obituary in the *Lewiston Evening Journal*, his transcripts were not word-for-word as one might assume. He often did not include questions asked by the lawyers, but gave transcript readers only the answers spoken by witnesses. In instructing his students, Pulsifer wrote "give all the evidence, but not all the words." By cutting out "useless words," he was able to reduce the size, and therefore the cost, of printing trial transcripts, making them more appealing for the future use by lawyers. It was up to the judgment of the trained stenographer, he wrote, to decide what was relevant and what was not.

"The sands of life run out too fast to allow of printing and reading of everything," Pulsifer instructed his students in the *Shorthand Review* newsletter. "Even shorthand writers must be allowed to winnow out some chaff, and the more, the better success and greater satisfaction."

So we do not have all the words. Critics who blame Wagner's defense attorneys for being too soft on cross-examination or too sparse with their questions should consider the trial transcript itself was weighted in favor of the prosecution. Pulsifer wrote: "In murder trials where the prisoner takes the stand, the very minimum of his testimony is given. In admissions of parties, conversations, and statements of verbal contracts, of course, the notes are transmitted verbatim, as are also the notes of the judges' charge. The notes of testimony are cut down in transcription from one-half to two-thirds, and in cross-examinations often more than that."

Wagner's senior counsel, Honorable Rufus P. Tapley, the balding man with the massive sideburns, had already served as a judge in the Supreme Court of Maine. So he knew the territory well. Tapley and co-council Max Fischacher from Boston had managed to delay the trial from late May to June 9. Their effort to move the entire proceedings north to Cumberland County, however, had failed. Days before the opening of the trial, the duo was still pushing to shut down the trial on a technicality.

"Wagner was brought into court at Alfred by request of his counsel, Tuesday," the *Chronicle* reported on May 30, "and entered a protest against the further cognizance of his case on the ground of want of jurisdiction, claiming that Smutty Nose Island is not in Maine." Judge Barrows was unmoved by the plea, but with little else to work with, the defense team would continue to hammer on the question of jurisdiction, forcing the prosecution to read pages of dull seventeenth-century court documents into the record.

By this time, Wagner had been in Alfred for a month after brief lockups in Boston, Portsmouth, Saco, and Portland jails. He was transferred without fanfare on April 29 to a modern prison facility that stands to this day. Wagner was among the first inmates of the three-story brick jail that was then the pride of the Maine penal system. Forever scrounging free room and board, Wagner appeared pleased, at first, by the cramped, but comfortable new cell. Today, the dilapidated three-tier cell block still stands at the heart of the building. Rows of metal cell doors hang open. Paint chips curl off the crumbling walls. The asbestos-coated ceiling leaks. Much of the glass in the six cathedral windows, blocked with thick iron bars, has been smashed by vandals. Closed to prisoners since the 1970s, then briefly used as a homeless shelter, the cell block is currently hidden inside an antiques shop.

As we will see, Wagner came to know the new jail and its jailers intimately in the weeks to come. In what would prove to be a prophetic pun, the *Portsmouth Journal* announced the prisoner had "broken out—in song." Wagner was "in excellent spirits" and taken to crooning "Home Sweet Home" in a loud and cheerful voice, according to the *Times*. The *Chronicle* version read: "Wagner has taken to prayer and psalmody, much to the disgust of the other inmates of Alfred jail. They don't object to the prayers, but they declare that his singing is terrific." (This was not a compliment. The word *terrific*, in its original form, meant "causing terror.") Wagner's voice was so abominable, the newspaper added with a Shakespearean flair, that it "doth murder sleep."

Although the newspapers insisted no one except Wagner's attorneys were allowed to see him at Alfred, the curious public continued to trickle in. George Lincoln Came, a thirty-seven-year-old bachelor farmer from Alfred recorded one such meeting in his journal, now in the Maine Historical Society. After church one Sunday in April, Came joined a few female friends and a local choir, perhaps the very group that inspired Wagner's musical outbreaks. "I went into the jail," Came noted in one of many crisp, colorless diary entries. "I saw and spoke to Wagner the supposed murderer of the two women at the Isle of Shoals." Later in June, Came would abandon more than a week of important farm work to attend the trial that, temporarily, turned the media spotlight onto the sleepy village.

It is a short, peaceful walk up Court Street from the Old Alfred Jail to the courthouse. With its towering white pillars and overhanging second floor porch, the courthouse looked, in Wagner's day, like the grand mansion in a southern plantation. Today the thick brick walls and many sturdy brick additions are reminiscent more of a fortress than a home. Modern visitors attending trials are searched and scanned for weapons. Anyone attempting to enter the building with a firearm, a sign at the door reads, will be subject to arrest and prosecution.

Wagner was transferred daily in handcuffs from jail to court. The first order of business, on Monday, June 9, was to select a jury from among seventy men. The entire group gathered in the courthouse at two p.m. It was not critical, Judge Barrows told the potential jurors, whether they had already formed an opinion about the guilt or innocence of the prisoner. What mattered was whether they could listen to witnesses from both sides without prejudice and be governed by their testimony. Then Barrows asked each man these questions: Did he hold any bias or prejudice for or against the prisoner? Did he have any feeling against the death penalty that would prevent him from rendering an impartial verdict? Was he related by blood or marriage "within the degree of second cousin" to either the deceased women or to the prisoner?

Thirty men were drawn from the pool. Wagner's attorneys challenged only three of them. Fifteen more men were removed because they had formed an unshakable opinion about the murders. The final twelve, mostly middle-aged men in beards and dark suits were:

Isaac Eaton of North Berwick
George A. Twambly of Shapleigh
Ivory C. Hatch of Wells
Horace Piper of Newfields
Levi G. Hanson of Biddeford
Nahum Tarbox of Biddeford
Benajah Hall of North Berwick

Charles Whitney of Biddeford
William Bean of Limington
Robert Littlefield of Kennebunk
Isaac Libbey of Parsonsfield
Calvin Stevens of Wells

The process of empanelling the jury took less than two hours. Defense attorney Max Fischacher, in another effort to delay the trial, suggested the new jury members should all take a boat trip to Smuttynose Island and view the murder scene. The idea found no favor with Judge Barrows, who had little patience with theatrics or demagoguery. The judge adjourned the court in plenty of time for supper. Wagner was returned to his cell and, with his life hanging on the outcome of the next few days, found nothing to sing about.

Chapter 24

A HAILSTORM OF EVIDENCE

Infamous court cases often create famous lawyers and launch successful careers, but Harris Merrill Plaisted needed no help. He was already a rising star before he became lead prosecutor at the Wagner trial. Born in Jefferson, New Hampshire, Plaisted was a practicing lawyer in Bangor, Maine, at the outbreak of the Civil War. He enlisted in the 11th Maine Volunteer Infantry Regiment, served bravely by all accounts, and rose to the rank of major general. By 1873, the soldier with the prominent forehead, slicked back hair, unkempt beard, dangling sword, and military braid had become the attorney general of Maine. Plaisted was now a mature attorney of forty-four years old. At Alfred, his beard was trimmed and combed and he was developing a slight paunch. The same year as the Wagner trial, he would successfully prosecute James M. Lowell for the murder of his wife, Elizabeth, whose headless skeleton wearing only a silk dress was discovered three years after her disappearance. Following these two gruesome homicide cases, Plaisted would move on to serve in the United States Congress and as governor of Maine.

With the prestigious Mr. Plaisted at his side, with the Alfred courtroom crammed to capacity, and with Wagner and his lawyers seated at a nearby table, attorney George Yeaton slowly rose to make his opening statement. He did not sit down until the conclusion of his speech two hours later. The jury, Yeaton began, must convict Louis Wagner for an atrocious crime, "a crime which startled and shocked the community as few within the recollection of the oldest man upon this panel ever have." The job of the prosecution team, Yeaton explained, was to lay before the jury a plain explanation of the facts of the case. From this evidence, the jury would either be convinced of Wagner's guilt or they would acquit him of the horrible murders. But before parading through an estimated forty-six witnesses, the prosecutor needed to define a few key terms.

First degree murder, Yeaton began, represented the "highest offense known to the law" except for treason. Wagner had unlawfully killed his victims with *malo animo*, or with an "evil mind," the prosecutor said, parsing the Latin term for *malice*. The murderer had acted with deliberation. "How long must a man deliberate before, in law, there is sufficient deliberation?" Yeaton asked the jury rhetorically. "I think, gentlemen, not one instant." If Wagner went to rob the Norwegians and had not considered murdering Anethe until the second he let the ax fall, then that instantaneous decision was reason enough to convict him, Yeaton said.

Anticipating a battle over tiny technical details from the defense, Yeaton explained it made no difference whether the victims died on March 5 or March 6 or whether they ultimately expired due to blows from an ax or other means. Yeaton went to great lengths to explain, using ancient court records, that Smuttynose Island was indeed within the jurisdiction of York County. The jury should focus on the overwhelming evidence, he warned, and not get distracted by the tactics of Wagner's attorneys.

It was a full hour of definitions and history trivia before the prosecutor finally got down to brass tacks. His star witness and the only survivor of the tragedy would soon tell her fearful story, the prosecutor promised. Yeaton then went on to vividly summarize the murders. He detailed Wagner's alleged journey from New Castle back to Johnson's boarding house in Portsmouth, his escape by train to Boston, and his capture. The prosecutor pointed to Wagner's abject poverty as the motive for the robbery. Burke's rowboat was his opportunity to reach Smuttynose, and his strange and conflicting comments were evidence he was an habitual liar. The state would produce the ax, Yeaton promised, then display the killer's bloody clothes and his distinctive size-eleven rubber boots that tracked blood all over the island. The state would introduce Karen's telltale white button found in the prisoner's pocket and offer a full accounting of the money stolen at Smuttynose, detailing the purchases that Wagner made in Boston. All this was forthcoming, but first, there was one sticky detail to clear up.

"A popular prejudice sometimes exists against what is termed *circumstantial evidence*," Yeaton told the jury. "Every man understands that the moon controls the tides. How do they arrive at that conclusion? Purely and solely from circumstantial evidence. Who ever saw the moon pulling the water from one side of this earth to the other?"

If we wake up on a winter morning and see human footprints in the freshly fallen snow, the prosecutor further explained, we can assume that someone recently walked by. We did not see the man. We have no direct evidence that he was there, but only the circumstance of the footprints from which to conclude that someone walked by. Most of our knowledge about the world comes, not from direct eyewitness proof, he noted, but from conclusions intelligently drawn from myriad connected clues.

Circumstances do not "add up" to a conclusion, Yeaton said. Rather, each new circumstance "multiplies" the others. If Wagner was desperate for money, for instance, and he knew the Hontvets intimately, knew that they had money, knew the women were alone on the island—each of these separate circumstances multiplied the possibility he might take dire action. So when two of the women were found murdered and Wagner was missing, when a boat with which he was familiar suddenly disappeared, when he was seen by witnesses in New Castle the morning after, when the same boat reappeared nearby, when Wagner denied he was in New Castle, when he suddenly had money to spend, when he fled to Boston, when he disguised himself—the sheer logical weight of these circumstances multiplied together could not be ignored by a rational person.

After two hours of pacing back and forth in front of the twelve-man jury, George Yeaton had reached the emotional and intellectual apex of his opening argument. Circumstantial evidence, he implied, when scientifically presented, was a valid and effective means for making important judgments. But it was incorrect, he concluded, to picture circumstantial evidence as an arch, rope, or chain. These often-used metaphors were flawed.

"You all know that no chain is stronger than its weakest link," Yeaton said. A reasonable doubt about Wagner's innocence, he therefore implied, could not be established merely by disputing one or two bits of circumstantial evidence. The argument did not fall apart if one or two factors were in doubt. Instead of a chain, Yeaton explained, the accumulation of circumstantial evidence when multiplied against itself should be compared to a hailstorm. And the hailstorm would last four days, burying the defendant under a deep and damning blanket of evidence that George Yeaton had meticulously organized. The York County attorney had personally visited the murder scene on Smuttynose even as the bodies of Karen and Anethe were being loaded aboard ship for Portsmouth. Yeaton had picked up his prisoner in New Hampshire amid the lynch mob riots and had successfully arraigned him in South Berwick. Now, with the learned Mr. Plaisted as his partner, he was going to see justice done and the guilty man hanged.

On Wednesday, Yeaton began by establishing the location of Smuttynose as affirmed by the testimony of York County surveyor Moses Safford. Then the prosecutor launched into the real action by delivering up two of his most appealing witnesses. Both men spoke in thick Norwegian accents. Jorges Ingebretsen of Appledore Island, the fisherman who had rescued Maren Hontvet when she was half frozen with fear and cold, took the stand. He described seeing the bloody ax with the broken handle lying on a rock in the snow outside the door of the Red House.

Ivan Christensen, widower of Anethe, came next. Since the murders, Ivan had been working at the Appledore Hotel. According to Celia Thaxter, he was no longer a handsome picture of masculinity. He had been transformed, in recent weeks, to a pale, thin, sickly shadow.

"He dragged one foot after the other wearily, and walked with the feeble motion of an old man," Celia wrote. Unable to pull himself away from the Shoals, but unable to ever look again at the house on Smuttynose Island, Ivan had given up fishing and taken a position as carpenter at the Thaxter's hotel. Celia yearned to comfort him, she said, but could not, "for he seemed to me to be hurt too sorely to be touched by human hand." Anethe's death, Ivan later told John and Maren, must have been part of God's mysterious plan. Otherwise, he said, "Why else did all things so play into Louis's hands?"

Witnesses were kept out of the Alfred courtroom except during their testimony. Now the wooden doors opened and Ivan Christensen, head bowed, stepped reluctantly toward the front of the room. Wagner, who scarcely reacted to most witnesses during the day, appeared to regard Ivan "with special interest and pleased recognition." Ivan swore his oath on the bible and took his place in the witness chair as the audience fell silent. Struggling to understand the prosecutor's questions in a language he scarcely knew, unnerved by the enrapt onlookers, his heart and soul broken, Ivan responded in clipped terms as evidenced in the trial transcript:

Ques. Where did you go from Appledore Island?
Ans. I went first up to Ingebretsen's house. After I left there I went to Smutty Nose. When I got to Smutty Nose, I went right up to the house and right in.
Ques. What did you see there?
Ans. I saw my wife lying on the floor.
Ques. Dead or alive?
Ans. Dead.
Ques. What did you do?
Ans. Went right back [out] again.

Yeaton then introduced one powerful witness after another. Calvin L. Hayes of Kittery, a member of the coroner's jury, recounted the ghastly scene in the kitchen where Anethe's body lay on the floor with her brains exposed. There was "a scarf or shawl, some colored woolen garment" around her neck. The furniture was thrown all around and the clock had fallen and shattered. Hayes found Karen on the other side of the duplex strangled with her tongue protruding. She was "covered with wounds, but not so bad as the first one," Hayes said. It was Mr. Hayes who had picked up the ax that was lying on a stone just outside the house. Now, upon request, Hayes produced the murder weapon, washed clean by the ocean spray as the coroner's team rowed back from Smuttynose to Appledore on the night of the investigation. The ax was exhibited in the courtroom and entered as evidence.

"I took the ax from the island," Hayes said. "It has been in my custody since . . . It does not now resemble its condition then at all; it was besmeared with blood and covered with matter entirely."

Next in the witness box was Dr. John W. Parsons of Portsmouth, who had examined Anethe's body at the Portsmouth funeral home on March 8. He described her condition in forensic detail: a flesh wound over the right cheek bone, two flesh wounds under the left eye, another on the upper right side of the forehead, and many more. The victim's left and right ears were nearly severed and there was a compound fracture of the skull. Attorney Yeaton asked the doctor if Anethe's death was likely caused from a severe blow by the heavy ax on display in the courtroom. Parsons said "yes."

Twenty-one-year-old Waldemar Ingebretsen, who had lived on Appledore, Star, and Smuttynose islands, said he knew Wagner well. Waldemar and four other witnesses testified that, weeks before the tragedy, they had heard Wagner say: "I am bound to have money in three months if I am going to murder for it." Another fisherman named Lars Nelson had seen large, bloody boot tracks on the island the day after the murders. Nelson also confirmed that, in recent weeks, Wagner had been penniless. James Lee, who had fished with Wagner aboard the *Addison Gilbert*, recalled a similar conversation. "He [Wagner] told me if he had money enough to buy a suit of clothes, he would leave Portsmouth and go to Boston, or some-where else. He told me that [if] he could get a boat and go to the Shoals, he would get money enough."

Throughout Yeaton's speech and the first cluster of witnesses, Louis Wagner sat unmoved. The defendant manifested no emotion except "an incredulous smile" the newspapers agreed. It was only when Maren Hontvet, dressed in black, entered the jam-packed courtroom that the prisoner suddenly appeared "eager to catch her every word." Maren pointed out her former friend and lodger for the court records. They had not faced one another since Maren lay on a lounge in the Portsmouth jail and asked Wagner, "Would you not like to kill me?" In her presence, according to the *Chronicle*, Wagner "threw aside or had lost that coolness previously shown."

In the film version of the novel *The Weight of Water*, adapted from a fictional version of the Smuttynose murder case, the courtroom encounter between Maren and Wagner is dark and moody. The fictional prisoner stands manacled in a narrow, waist-high, wooden cage in the center of a misty room, a scene more reminiscent of the Salem Witch Trial era than America in the Industrial Age. As Maren recounts her harrowing escape to the jury, an eerie soundtrack, ideal for a gothic horror movie, combines violin and cello music with the screams of women and the crashing of waves. The actor playing the fictional Wagner in the movie is older, darker, more reactive, more ragged and unkempt, and much less endearing than the cool and calculated historical Wagner at Alfred. But Sarah Polley's portrayal of Mary S. Hontvet may hover close to the truth. Although a decade younger and more camera-friendly than the historical Maren, Polley's character is equally hard-working, strong-willed, long-suffering, stern, and dignified. In the movie trial, she is conservatively garbed in a long, black, mourning dress and bonnet, likely in sharp contrast to the summer tourists and farmers' wives, with their lunch baskets and paper fans, who filled the Alfred courthouse.

Accompanied by her husband, John, and now fully recovered from her traumatic escape, the real Maren, the lone survivor of the March 6 massacre, faced off against her attacker at trial. "She is a very intelligent looking woman," the *New York Times* noted on June 12.

There was nothing new in Maren's testimony at Alfred. Her story had appeared numerous times in the press, and yet the *Chronicle* ran her full response to attorney Yeaton's questions. March 5 was, Maren recalled again, a pleasant night with the promise of spring. Three Norwegian women, no longer separated by thousands of miles, went to bed peacefully downstairs in the easterly end of the Red House at ten p.m. There was some tension in the air. The three men of the house, delayed in Portsmouth according to their message, had not arrived late in the evening as scheduled. But the weather was not threatening. The curtains were open. The lock on the door had been broken since summer. They slept. Then Karen cried out "John scares me!" and the nightmare began.

Although he had scarcely spoken since the trial began, defense attorney Rufus Tapley rose here to object to the admission of the statements made by Karen and Anethe as reported by Maren. This was merely hearsay, Tapley declared. But Judge Barrows accepted the comments, citing the common law principle of *res gestae*, an exception to the rule against hearsay. Although secondhand, the statements of the dead women were considered trustworthy and admissible as evidence.

This was a critical victory for the prosecution. While Karen had initially believed the intruder in the dark was her brother-in-law John Hontvet, it was undeniable that John was in Portsmouth all that night and not on the island. Karen had been mistaken. But Anethe's cry of "Louis! Louis!" gave Yeaton and Plaisted the next best thing to an eyewitness. Without it, Maren could only attest she had seen the shadowy shape of a tall silent man in the moonlight. She had seen his profile, not the front of his face. It was Anethe's dying words more than any other piece of evidence that placed Wagner on the island on the night of the murder with an ax in his hand. Because Anethe identified Wagner spontaneously and without deliberation as she was being attacked, under *res gestae,* her words were considered highly credible, a dying declaration, not subject to deceit or interpretation.

Tapley objected successfully to other hearsay conversations Maren had with her sister, Karen, and he managed, temporarily, to prevent Yeaton from entering the incriminating white button into evidence. Tapley briefly cross-examined Maren, but it was a delicate game. The defense could not appear to badger or even dishonor the surviving victim. Tapley managed only to get Maren to repeat the fact that she had not actually spoken to the killer and had seen him only momentarily from the back or side as she looked out her bedroom window. The defense scored a minor point with Maren's description of the killer's hat.

"He had a hat on his head," Maren said, "some kind of a dark hat, a short hat with a wide brim. Did not see his face."

Originally Maren had said the killer wore a "tall hat" or a "beaver hat." Wagner denied ever owning a tall hat. Witnesses later that day would describe Wagner wearing an old-fashioned military-style cap sometimes called a "slouch" or "Kossuth" hat when he crossed the bridge in New Castle. Wagner did own a light-colored Kossuth hat, probably made of felt with a broad black band around it. The confusion over Wagner's hat was a minor detail. It had been dark. He could have changed hats. But it was a tiny warm spot for the defense against the blizzard of evidence that engulfed them.

John Hontvet took his wife's place in the witness chair next. He retold the story of Wagner's extreme interest in the fishing profits on the *Clara Bella*, of their meeting on the docks on March 5, of Wagner's disappearance after he learned the women were alone on the island. Through Yeaton's clever questioning, John put to rest any doubt one could row a boat to the Shoals in three hours or less, even against the tide. He had made the trip by oar at least fifty times himself, John said. He recounted his frequent attempts to find Wagner along the Portsmouth docks that night. He confirmed beyond doubt, despite Wagner's claim, that no one except his men had been sleeping on the couch in the back room of Matthew Johnson's shop as they baited trawls. Rufus Tapley's cross-examination challenged none of this. He may have been lazy, as some insist, or he may have known he could not impeach John Hontvet's story.

Next came Charles Johnson, a fisherman and son of Wagner's Water Street landlords. Charles confirmed Wagner's poverty and his threat to murder for money. Charles Campbell, the night watchman at the naval shipyard, then recounted seeing a stranger running across the ice at Little Harbor toward the cemetery on the morning after the murders. He later found large, distinctive boot prints in the snow near Devil's Den. At this point, Judge Barrows recessed the court for lunch and media correspondents from New York to Boston scurried to telegraph their updates.

The hailstorm continued all afternoon, beginning with Sarah Campbell and Israel Fletcher of New Castle, who also saw the stranger heading toward the toll bridge en route to Portsmouth on March 6. Charles Place testified to finding a dory abandoned near Devil's Den that morning. James Burke confirmed the recovered boat was his and the same one stolen from the base of Pickering Street the night before with its "thole" pins significantly worn from recent use.

Defense attorney Tapley made a valiant attempt to insinuate the testimony of Joshua Frasell, a cooper from New Castle, had been heavily influenced by John Hontvet and the Portsmouth police. Frasell denied the veiled charge he had been fed false information and said he was certain the stranger at the toll bridge was Wagner. The Amazeen brothers, George and Joseph, took the stand in turn. They explained how they had helped the stranger, who turned out to be Wagner, cross the washed-out bridge. Anne Carlton, John Lyons, and Alonzo Greene swore they had seen Wagner, his hat pulled over his face and his dungarees wet with snow and ice, as he hurried the final distance from the New Castle toll bridge to Water Street in Portsmouth's South End.

By late afternoon on Wednesday, prosecutor Yeaton had fashioned twenty-two witnesses into an almost seamless chronological narrative. Defense attorneys Tapley and Fischacher had been unable to solidly dispute any of their testimony, and there were more tough witnesses to come. Wagner's landlady, Ann Elizabeth Johnson, was especially daunting. She had the memory of an elephant and the demeanor of a junkyard dog. Her daughter, Mary, would prove tougher still.

Chapter 25

FOUR WOMEN

Ann Johnson was irritated. Compelled to testify, she and her daughter, Mary, and her son, Charles, had come up from Portsmouth to Alfred by train and were staying in a house nearby during the trial. Ann was required to leave her crippled husband, Matthew, behind. Although a potential witness, Matthew had been confined to a chair for twelve years and, in his wife's words, "cannot go from one room to another." Wagner's former landlady had been sitting in a basement room of the Alfred courthouse all day as nearly two dozen witnesses preceded her. As the owner of a boarding house in the burgeoning waterfront "red light" district, Ann Johnson was clearly uncomfortable in the media spotlight. Earlier that day, in an effort to discredit the evidence of her son, Charles, defense attorney Fischacher had half implied the Johnson's themselves were running a disreputable house. It stood, after all, on a street known to sailors far and wide.

"Is there a bar there at your father's house for drinking?" Fischacher had asked. Charles had to admit, under oath, that his father kept a little bar there, but only for his boarders "and transient men that come there." The attorney pressed further, asking, "What is the sex of your father's boarders?" They were "mostly males, sometimes men with their families," Charles explained. When she was finally called as the last witness of the day, Ann Johnson would characterize her boarders only as "comers and goers."

She had quite liked Louis Wagner initially, she told attorney George Yeaton when she finally took the stand. Wagner had treated her with respect. She had cooked for him and done his laundry, while her daughter, Mary, made his bed and mended his clothes during his eight- or nine-week stay. Mrs. Johnson had allowed Wagner to fall $15 behind in his rent of $4.50 per week.

Yes, Ann told the court, she was certain she had bolted the back door around midnight on the night of the murders. Yes, she was absolutely positive Wagner had not been in the house until early that morning. His bed had not been slept in. George Lowd, her brother-in-law, had been sleeping on the lounge on the first floor that Wagner claimed to have used. She recounted how Wagner "looked kind of queer" when he came through the gate in the morning. She heard him tell her husband that "he never felt so bad in all his life" and that "he got himself into trouble, and felt as if he was going to be taken."

From the moment Max Fischacher rose to cross-examine Mrs. Johnson, she became a fiery, hostile witness. Back in Puddle Dock at 25 Water Street during his original investigation in March, she had refused to answer any of his questions. But not even death threats from enraged Shoals fishermen had deterred Wagner's lawyer. Fischacher had returned to Johnson's under police protection and forced her to respond. Now he was interrogating her again in front of a hundred witnesses and newspaper reporters. So Mrs. Johnson met Fischacher's every question with obfuscation and sarcasm. Asked, for example, what kind of clock she used to "fix the time" of Wagner's arrival, she replied "a pretty good one." When Fischacher asked her to describe the back door of the boarding house, the landlady shot back, "You saw it, I showed it to you."

The defense attorney pressed harder on the exact details of the landlady's testimony earlier at the South Berwick arraignment, but she continued to parry his questions. Fischacher obliquely accused Mrs. Johnson of reshaping her testimony in collusion with the Hontvets and the police. Her annoyance with the questions of Wagner's Boston attorney shines through the pages of the trial transcript.

> Ques. How many times have you told this story to anyone since?
> Ans. I ain't told it to nobody.
> Ques. To any one?
> Ans. If I have, I have told it straight. I could not tell but one thing, for I don't know anything else.
> Ques. How many times have you talked about this matter with any one since that morning?
> Ans. I don't know that I have to any one than my own folks.
> Ques: With anybody else?
> Ans. Nobody in particular.
> Ques. Who have you talked it over with?
> Ans. Could not tell you.

Of all the witnesses for the prosecution, Ann Johnson appeared the most sympathetic toward the prisoner. "Wagner always treated me well in my house," she testified. But when Fischacher pushed, Mrs. Johnson pushed back. Was Wagner "a man of peaceable habits?" the lawyer asked.

"For all that I ever saw of him," she replied, then twisted her compliment into a sharp attack. "I have heard him tell pretty bad yarns of himself. I heard about him taking a hatchet to a man. You don't want me to tell anything of that kind. He did not board with me at all then. Somebody else told the story."

Unable to impeach any of her ironclad testimony and bloodied by her rebukes, the defense attorney concluded his cross-examination for the day and asked Ann Johnson to step down. "That is all," Fischacher said, dismissing her. "I am glad of it," Mrs. Johnson snapped back. "I hope I never shall come here again, or to any such place."

Nineteen-year-old Mary Johnson was equally confounding to the defense during her lengthy testimony the following morning on Thursday.

Although as unflappable as her mother, Mary seemed to enjoy her sudden celebrity. She confirmed to prosecutor Yeaton that she had seen her mother lock the back door soon after midnight on March 5, and that Wagner's bed had been untouched on the night of the murders. The next morning, she said, Wagner sobbed as he confided to her, "I have got myself into trouble...I must be going." She noted seeing scratches on his hands and knuckles as he wiped tears from his face. "You look as though you had no sleep," she had told him.

Mary proved herself an expert on the topic of Wagner's wardrobe. "I know every article of clothing that Wagner had," she told the jurors, and proceeded to list them—a pair of pants, half a dozen woolen shirts, a couple of pairs of drawers, a coat, two jumpers, three white shirts, two dirty scarves, and a pair of socks worn out at the toes and heels.

She recalled ironing his white shirts and placing them in a drawer in the downstairs sitting room. The Johnson women routinely did this for male tenants so they would always have a clean shirt set aside. Mary testified she had given Wagner a white shirt from that drawer on the Sunday before the murders. It was, by her description, "a white shirt, plain, plaited bosom shirt, and there was a little collar to it; was a binding about an inch wide and then a little collar sewed on to that." Wagner was still wearing that shirt at dinner on March 5, Mary confirmed, before he disappeared. But when he returned the following morning, wind-burned and wild-eyed, she could not tell what shirt he was wearing because he kept his blue jumper buttoned up tight to his neck. A few minutes later, after Wagner had been up to his room on the second floor, she saw him come back down the stairs and go into the backyard with what appeared to be a mysterious bundle tucked under his jumper. Mary had mentioned that detail to the Portsmouth police the Saturday after the murder, she testified. They had been searching for days for the white shirt that Wagner had been wearing on March 5. He was not wearing it when captured. It was not among the items he left at the cobbler's shop in Boston. And it was not in his room at Johnson's or in his kit bag at the house. The shirt had finally been located in Johnson's privy on Monday, March 10, even as Wagner was being transferred from Portsmouth to Maine. The police had delivered the shirt to an avowed expert in the science of blood stains. His scientific analysis, rare for criminal cases in the 1870s, was yet to come.

George Yeaton asked Mary how she could possibly identify a single white shirt that belonged to Wagner. "Underneath the collar it is torn," she explained with forensic detail. "The button-hole is large. The button-hole was torn down some ways, and the button was small. I buttoned it over that afternoon of the fifth before the murder." Mary remembered precisely, she said, because Wagner "swore about it" when she mended the button "and said it would not stay over."

"When did you see that shirt next, if ever?" Yeaton asked.

"The next Monday after it was taken from the vault," Mary explained, referring to the privy in the Johnson's backyard off Liberty Street.

"Look at that," Yeaton said, producing the same shirt, now torn, soiled, and bloodstained. "See if that bears any resemblance to it." Mary examined the prosecutor's evidence closely. The spectators in the Alfred court held their breath.

"That is the shirt," she said with total conviction, and the crowd exhaled.

Here, Yeaton cleverly reintroduced the white button that Maren Hontvet had previously identified. It had been in Karen's purse with a cluster of coins before the murder and then gone missing with Karen's money. The defense had objected to this evidence earlier, but it was now on the record.

"Do you know of any buttons on Wagner's clothing at the house similar to those?" he asked.

"No sir, have not seen any like those," Mary said. Yeaton introduced the button as having been discovered in Wagner's pocket when he was arrested in Boston. This time Judge Barrows accepted it into evidence.

Max Fischacher did his best to break down Mary Johnson's testimony in a withering cross-examination that lasted the better part of an hour. He fell short of accusing the witness of planting the bloody shirt in the privy herself. Fischacher again implied that the Johnsons, the Hontvets, along with Portsmouth Marshals Frank Johnson and Thomas Entwistle, had concocted false testimony to bolster their case against the defendant. After all, the Johnsons were loyal to the Hontvets who were, even then, living with them at 25 Water Street during the summer of 1873. And the Johnsons were among the few people in Portsmouth who had actually met Karen and Anethe Christensen. The butchered bodies of the victims had lain in the parlor of Matthew Johnson's boarding house in the hours following the autopsy and before the funeral. Wagner was a stranger, the odd man out, the defense reminded jurors. Was he possibly the scapegoat for the real killer? It was a nice, neat conspiracy theory. It was Fischacher's job to cast a reasonable doubt on the government's case. But if his client was truly innocent, everyone knew, then a whole lot of people were conspiring and lying under oath.

Could someone have slipped into Wagner's room, Fischacher asked Mary, and stolen away his white shirt before the police confiscated his clothes on Saturday? Mary conceded it was possible, if, indeed, Wagner had left the white shirt in his room. But no one had found it there, she added. Could she swear the police had never secretly shown her the white button before her testimony at Alfred? Yes, Mary confirmed, she had never seen it before this day. Was it possible, the frustrated defense attorney tried again, that Wagner had buttons on clothes Mary had never seen? Mary admitted it was possible, but unlikely.

The defense hammered away at a range of topics, but Mary never wavered or grew impolite. She had not colluded with her mother on her testimony, she explained, because, "I had my story, and she hers."

Hoping to catch her up one last time, Fischacher asked Mary about comments she had made just the night before after leaving the courtroom. Was it also true she had been talking privately about Louis Wagner with her friends before taking the witness stand this very day? Mary admitted she had. And what exactly, the attorney demanded, had she told her friends about the prisoner?

"I said he looked quite nice," Mary confessed, "better than ever I saw him when I was acquainted with him." The trial transcript does not tell us whether the audience giggled openly at Mary's reply. Fischacher had made no dent in her testimony.

Next up were Wagner's former roommates on Water Street. William Kenniston confirmed he had tried to enter the boarding house through the back door around midnight and found it locked, then entered by the storeroom where the men were baiting trawls. He had seen Wagner arrive at about seven-thirty a.m., his dungarees wet with snow. Sailor Frederick Moore remembered Wagner looking like a "wild man" when he arrived at breakfast. Moore also was in the downstairs shop when Matthew Johnson jokingly called to Wagner, "Here comes the lost sheep!" Moore had overheard Wagner explain he had spent the night baiting four tubs of trawls for an unfamiliar fisherman on the Portsmouth docks. Moore last saw Wagner outside the Johnsons, standing at the corner of Court and Water streets, gazing toward the docks in the harbor. Perhaps he was hoping to see a ship departing or feared the return of the *Clara Bella*. Moments later, still wearing his boots and fishing clothes, Wagner walked downtown and hopped on the next train out of Portsmouth.

Sticking to the precise timeline of Wagner's journey, George Yeaton then moved his hailstorm of circumstantial evidence to seven witnesses who had traveled from the bustle of Boston's North End to sleepy Alfred, Maine. Katherine Brown, proprietor of a "boarding house" at 295 North Street and her "boarder" Emma Miller took the stand. (The quotation marks on "boarder," as used here by the *Portsmouth Evening Times,* may have been a subtle clue to newspaper readers that the women were of dubious moral character.)

Emma Miller, aged nineteen, lived in "the shop" on the ground floor below the boarding house. The shop was a bar that served drinks to sailors and stayed open until midnight. Miller had been taking care of Mrs. Brown's infant son until his recent death. She was working in the kitchen when Wagner entered the Boston house around four o'clock on March 6. She greeted him as "Louis," she told the jury.

"I guess you are mistaken," Wagner told Emma.

"I do not think I am," she replied.

"That is not my name," Wagner said.

"Louis, if it is not your name, it is the name you went by when you were here before. It was Louis Ludwick."

"I guess you are mistaken," Wagner repeated, and then suddenly he admitted, "Emma, it is me."

Here, Wagner made another of his dazed and strangely confessional comments. He confided to Emma that he had just come from New York where he had killed two sailors. The mate, he told her, had put him ashore in a boat. He had come to Boston and shaved off his whiskers so that the officials would not recognize him. Then he added, "There is another girl I want to murder and then I am willing to go."

In his cross-examination of Emma Miller, Fischacher did his best to present her as a prostitute from a ruined home, and therefore, not a reliable witness. Emma openly admitted she had previously lived across the street from the Brown's in a house "not of good character." And she had been "down on the Island four months" when she was sixteen for "disorderly conduct." But it was her brother's fault, Emma told the defense attorney, because "he wanted me to go home, and I would not go."

Katherine Brown's testimony presented Wagner as exhausted, friendless, distracted, desperate, and running low on his characteristic sexy charm and humor. "He told me he had happened with great misfortune," Brown told the prosecutor, "had a hard time of it, or some such word as that; that he was cast away." Wagner's canny former landlady had seen all this behavior before and instinctively knew he had gotten himself into serious trouble.

Wagner's veracity as a witness in his own defense was being eaten away by Yeaton's parade of strong and believable working-class women. Their stories, multiplied together, slowly exposed the prisoner's pattern of dependency and poverty, plus his seemingly pathological habit of bending the truth to gain sympathy, especially from women. Wagner had told a shop owner hours before visiting the Browns he was finished with the sea forever and wanted to work in the city instead. He later told police he was only taking a quick trip to Boston to visit friends and planned to return directly home. But Katherine Brown now testified he told her he "might ship on a vessel tomorrow."

Wagner told Mrs. Brown he had not seen the Hontvets since May, then told her husband he had been baiting trawls with John Hontvet just the night before. He refused to say anything about Maren. Something in Wagner's guarded, manipulative, and slightly incoherent manner set off alarm bells for the Browns. They hesitated when Wagner asked them for a free room for the night. They were no longer a sailor's bethel, Katherine Brown told him, hoping to put him off, but instead they catered to long-stay immigrant families "that won't make any trouble."

Wagner sobbed to Mrs. Brown that he had lost everything. She placated him, offering comforting words. "Don't mind that Louis," she said. "You have your life and health to earn more." But then as soon as he dozed off in the kitchen, the evidence suggests, she called for the police to pick him up.

Chapter 26

COPS AND BLOOD

Four Boston policemen briefly described the arrest of Louis Wagner in straightforward detail at the Alfred trial. Prosecutor Yeaton wanted them to establish, beyond doubt, they had acted properly. There had been no rough stuff, no badgering, and no trickery. The items found in the prisoner's pockets, officer William W. Currier confirmed, were laid out on a wooden shelf in the Boston police station, sealed inside a long envelope, locked in a closet, and stored. Sgt. Thomas Weir confirmed that the items had then been delivered to York county attorney Yeaton, who then emptied the contents of the same envelope onto a table in the courtroom in Alfred. The coins, button, watch ring, wick, and a piece of tobacco were entered into evidence.

James Haley Jr. and William Gallagher, the arresting officers, recounted picking up Wagner outside Brown's boarding house in Boston's North End around eight-thirty p.m. on the evening of the murder. Wagner did not ask why he was being arrested, Haley said, and they did not immediately tell him. The officers noted that Wagner, at first, lied about the time he had been in Boston. He said he had been in town for five days, although he later recanted the statement and admitted he had just come in from Portsmouth.

Yeaton then introduced cobbler Jacob Todtman of Fleet Street, who had sold Wagner his new boots, slippers, and two cigars for which he received most of the killer's remaining money and a broken watch in trade.

Todtman said he had allowed Wagner to change into his new clothes in the store and to leave his old clothes behind. Todtman swore that, when his boots were finished, Wagner said "he had seen a woman lay as still as that boot." Max Fischacher made a valiant attempt to undermine the cobbler's memory, but Todtman would not give an inch.

Portsmouth police officers William H. Jellison and Thomas Entwistle then picked up the narrative. Jellison testified to seeing large blisters on the palms of both the prisoner's hands and blood blisters on both thumbs when he arrived from Boston. Wagner said he had blistered his hands while "sculling" and baiting trawls the night before, but trawl fisherman Judson P. Randall told the jury that baiting trawls would not cause such blisters. Where and why Wagner had time to do some serious sculling on the same day as the murders, the defense was unable to establish. He was a practiced oarsman, we can assume, with the weathered hands of a sailor, and yet Wagner's large blisters were fresh when he was captured. While sculling currently indicates recreational or competitive rowing, Wagner was probably referring to the practice of propelling a small boat forward using the sweeping motion of a single oar from the stern or back of the craft.

Judson Randall, who had been allowed to visit Wagner in his Portsmouth cell, offered another controversial quote. When Randall asked what the prisoner thought of the horrible murders of his friends on Smuttynose, Wagner said that "he felt as bad as though he had done it." Assistant Marshal Entwistle confirmed these were, indeed, Wagner's words, following which he burst out crying. "I was four feet from Mr. Randall," Entwistle told the defense attorney during cross-examination. "My memory is as good as the average." It was Entwistle who had been injured while shielding Wagner from the lynch mob and who had been on the scene when the bloody shirt was pulled from the Johnson's privy. Fischacher wanted to know if the police had considered any other possible suspects in their investigation. "I never asked him [Wagner] to tell me whether he committed the murder or not," Entwistle said. "We were satisfied he did."

By Thursday afternoon, prosecutors Plaisted and Yeaton seemed to be running out of steam as their final handful of witnesses took on increasingly trivial topics. York County Attorney Edmund Warren, for instance, reported he had asked Wagner at South Berwick how his white shirt got into the privy. Wagner had replied he did not know, since he had left it on the bed when he went to Boston. Ivory Lord testified Wagner told him at Saco he did not wear a white shirt on the day the women were murdered, but instead had on a vest and "a dark, checked, plaid shirt."

Levi Mansion, a stonecutter, next testified he had seen Wagner sitting on a bench in Matthew Johnson's shop prior to the murders. Wagner was fiddling with a reddish brown pencil about two or three inches long, the witness said. There were teeth marks on the top of the pencil. Like a magician, Yeaton suddenly produced a short red pencil, chewed at one end. The stonecutter identified it positively and it was entered into evidence. Then young Emel Ingebretsen of Appledore Island, the son of the man who had rescued Maren Hontvet, took the stand.

"Look at that!" Yeaton said, pointing to his latest bit of evidence.

"That is the pencil," Emel said. It was the very pencil he had found in the entranceway of the Red House on Smuttynose. He had picked it up on Friday afternoon even as the bodies of Karen and Anethe lay inside the house.

"Do you think that is the pencil?" Yeaton asked again.

"Yes, that is the pencil," the boy confirmed.

The defense attorney rose confidently from his seat next to Louis Wagner and approached the Ingebretsen boy. Did he know, Fischacher asked Emel, there had been a coroner's jury of half a dozen men on the island observing the bodies, not to mention half a dozen newspaper reporters?

"Yes, sir," Emel said.

"Do you know if any of these gentlemen had pencils?" the defense attorney asked.

"No, sir," Emel had to admit.

It was a tiny victory for the defense attorney who, with Perry Mason flair, managed to cast a reasonable doubt on the pencil theory. It was, unfortunately, the weakest piece of evidence the prosecutor had introduced.

The dynamic case for the State of Maine against Louis H. F. Wagner might have ended with a fizzle, but the prosecutors were ready to detonate their most explosive testimony of the day. In a move that was rare for the 1870s, and especially so for a case against a poor foreigner, the defense introduced an expert in the analysis of blood stains. Dr. Horace Chase of 22 Newbury Street in Boston was able, he claimed, to accurately distinguish between the blood of humans and the blood of animals or fish. Dr. Chase had been hired by Yeaton and Plaisted to make a scientific examination of Louis Wagner's blue overalls, his jacket, and the bloody shirt retrieved from the privy.

Scientific and medical experts were not new to the courts in 1873; the field of "medical jurisprudence," the dawning of CSI-style research, was on the rise, but Yeaton was taking a big risk with Dr. Chase. Would his jurors from rural Maine really be impressed by the big-city authority with his new-fangled theories? Or would they suspect trickery? The Victorian era was fraught with "experts" offering scientific "proof" of just about everything from the heavenly messages decoded through astrology to the analysis of personality based on the shape of the human head as espoused by phrenology. Back on Appledore Island, poet Celia Thaxter was an avid follower of Spiritualism, a reportedly scientific method of communicating with the dead through Morse Code–like rapping and tapping. Science and technology were advancing so rapidly that the public was uncertain what to believe. Around the time of the Wagner trial, John Ordronaux, an early professor of medical jurisprudence, warned his students that "there is a growing tendency to look with distrust upon every form of skilled testimony."

The Wagner case falls into a dreamy transitional era in the history of American homicide. While it looks, on the surface, like any murder case pulled from Court TV today, the Victorian prosecutors were using a tricky mixture of circumstantial and forensic evidence. The crime scene in the

Red House on Smuttynose, for example, was smeared with bloody hand-prints on doorways and dishes. But the evidence was invisible to nine-teenth-century investigators. The first use of fingerprints in a high-profile murder would not occur until March 27, 1905, when the killer of two London shopkeepers left a perfect print on a metal money box. And while Victorians had not yet been introduced to either Sherlock Holmes or Jack the Ripper, the fascination with brilliant detectives and cold-blooded kill-ers was already imbued in popular American culture thanks to writers like Edgar Allan Poe and Charles Dickens. The expectation scientific deduc-tion and analysis might someday rid the world of crime altogether seemed wholly possible in 1873, but so was the realization the world was full of charlatans, quacks, and hoaxers. And there were legitimate scientists, inventors, and professors who, despite their scholarly Victorian efforts, were often dead wrong.

Before modern forensic detection, prosecutors had to rely on eye wit-nesses, snitches, prisoner confessions, and raw logic to get a murder con-viction. Because Maren Hontvet had not seen Wagner's face, and because Wagner had not confessed, George Yeaton chose to bring in Dr. Chase to buoy up his primarily circumstantial case. Historians point to the John Webster murder trial of 1849 as the first case in America based largely on scientific evidence. Webster, a Harvard lecturer, struck and killed his land-lord George Parkman with a cane in a fit of rage over an unpaid debt. Parkman was a wealthy Boston Brahmin and the trial became a media sideshow. Pieces of Mr. Parkman—including his thigh, pelvis, torso, and jawbone—were discovered in a privy and in a furnace at Harvard Medical School. The victim was identified from dental records. Professor Webster then confessed and was hanged. In his defense of Wagner, Max Fischacher would refer to the Parkman case during his plea to the jury. Although Webster was clearly guilty, Fischacher pointed out, eye witnesses swore they had seen Mr. Parkman on the street, even though he had been dead for days. Was it not then possible those people who saw Wagner on the New Castle road were equally wrong?

Even by the late nineteenth century, juries were beginning to realize that, for every expert opinion, there was another expert willing to swear the opposite was true. The theories of experts, according to one New Hampshire Supreme Court justice, was so "warped" in favor of the side they represented, they were "incapable of expressing a candid opinion." Worse yet, the skilled expert often swallowed up days, even weeks, "wasting the time and wearying the patience of both court and jury, and perplexing rather than elucidating the questions involved in the issue."

Despite the risk, Yeaton introduced his blood expert. It took Dr. Horace Chase a full two hours on Thursday afternoon to present his case against Wagner. The proof, Chase explained, was hidden in the corpuscles of dried blood on the defendant's clothing. Within days of the murder, Chase said, he had made scores of "microscopical" tests. First, he was able to bring the blood cells on Wagner's clothing back to their liquid state after soaking them in a serum of glycerin and distilled water for twelve hours. Then he was able to determine the blood came from a mammal, based on the shape and diameter of the blood corpuscles. While fish and birds possess an oval or elliptical red blood cell, Dr. Chase explained, humans and animals have round blood cells. A year later, testifying at another trial in New Hampshire, Dr. Chase told a skeptical jury he could tell the difference even on a bloodstain that was ten years old.

Seen under a microscope at four hundred times normal size, he told the jury, the human corpuscle "resembles very much a small India rubber ball pressed with the thumb and finger so that it leaves the edge rounded down to what is called a 'concavity' in the centre." Each human cell measured roughly 1/3200th of an inch, which Dr. Chase said he measured with a hand-held mechanical device called a micrometer. When comparing fish to human cells, "the difference is quite perceptible," the expert claimed and, with practice, he had even learned to distinguish human corpuscles from the slightly smaller cells of dogs and horses. The doctor had tested stains at many locations on Wagner's clothing, analyzing each test sample from five to ten times at intervals of twelve hours. Despite Wagner's attempts to wash or rinse off the stains at the Smuttynose well, Dr. Chase was absolutely convinced the defendant's clothes had been splattered with human blood.

"The science of bloodstains," according to Colin Wilson, author of *Written in Blood*, "is probably the most important single advance in the history of crime detection." Records show the Chinese experimented with bloodstain analysis as early as 1250 AD. Efforts at blood transfusion, from human-to-human and from animal-to-human, date to the mid-1600s. Sometimes transfusions worked, but more often the doctor ended up killing his patient. What was missing, until the twentieth century, was the knowledge there are four different "types" of human blood. It was not until 1900 that an Austrian immunologist named Karl Landsteiner was able to observe the clumping and repelling of different blood types. Armed with this knowledge, police detectives could finally compare blood sampled at a crime scene or on the killer's clothes with the blood types of the victim. And the age of forensic science was born.

Dr. Chase, however, arrived on the witness stand just ahead of this critical discovery. Telephones, electric lights, and automobiles would soon be in common use, but Chase's science was more closely tied to blood research made before the Civil War. Thanks to a healthy cross-examination by Max Fischacher, we know exactly where Dr. Chase learned how to analyze the stains on Louis Wagner's clothes. On bloodstains, he studied the "updated" 1858 edition of *Taylor's Medical Jurisprudence* by the British author Alfred Swaine Taylor. Science and the law were advancing at such a breakneck pace in the nineteenth century, Taylor noted in his preface to the sixth edition of his textbook, he had been required to add three hundred new pages since it first appeared. Taylor's text included medical updates for lawyers on poisons, pregnancy, abortion, drowning, insanity, rape, wounds, dipsomania, homicidal mania, and blood stains on clothing.

Max Fischacher, having done his homework, confronted the prosecutor's blood expert head on. Do you know, the defender challenged Dr. Chase, that Taylor's latest guidelines include a warning that efforts to distinguish between horse blood and human blood in criminal cases "is speculative and may be considered unsafe to rely upon"?

"It probably would be for a man that had no experience," Chase responded confidently. "I believe those persons who say they cannot distinguish with certainty, are not competent to make the examination." Chase was right, therefore, because he thought he was right.

Dr. Chase said he drew his authority about measuring the diameter of blood cells from the famous Englishman Thomas Southwood Smith, whose 1838 book, *The Philosophy of Health,* was the WebMD.com of the nineteenth century. As physician to the London Fever Hospital, Dr. Smith had been a tireless advocate of public health and sanitation in an era when the urban poor lived in the most squalid conditions imaginable. As an avowed "Utilitarian," Dr. Smith believed in making the best use of everything to promote human happiness. Smith campaigned against the wasteful burying of human bodies, for example, when corpses were desperately needed for dissection by medical students and researchers. Smith is best known today as the man who publicly dissected his friend Jeremy Bentham. A freethinker and philanthropist, Bentham donated his body to scientific study, and today it still sits inside a glass closet in a London medical school.

Unfortunately, when it came to cutting-edge research on identifying human bloodstains, Thomas Southwood Smith's textbook was hopelessly out of date. Fischacher pressed Dr. Chase to swear he could "say with certainty" that Wagner's clothes were spattered with human blood. Chase said he was certain, but admitted his conclusion should be "received with caution." Fischacher kept his composure, but he may have wished he could shout, as did one of his Victorian colleagues: "Gentlemen of the jury: there are three kinds of liars—the common liar, the dammed liar, and the scientific expert."

By the end of Dr. Chase's testimony, even Louis Wagner was at the end of his tether. He had listened for days to seemingly endless details about buttons and corpuscles and pencils, when all he wanted was to tell his side of the story. In a final burst of trivia, prosecutors Yeaton and Plaisted called a witness who presented statistics on the depth of water at the Isles of Shoals. Another expert listed every resident living on the islands according to the 1860 census. There was a heated discussion over the correct spelling of Anethe Matea Christensen's middle name.

On Friday morning, June 14, the prosecution was about to conclude its hailstorm of evidence when George Yeaton unexpectedly called Obadiah Durgin to the stand. As deputy sheriff, it was Durgin's job to guard the prisoner and to transfer him from the Alfred courthouse to his jail cell and back each day.

"What remark, if any, has Wagner made to you in regard to the progress of the trial, or case?" George Yeaton asked Durgin on the stand. Was it possible, the hushed courtroom audience wondered, that Wagner had let slip an incriminating remark to the deputy?

"He used profane language in relation to it," Officer Durgin replied, uncertain whether he was allowed to repeat a curse word in front of the many female spectators.

"Give us the language," the prosecutor demanded.

"God damn them!" Durgin said, repeating Wagner's words. "All they want is my life, and they can have it without making all this fuss about!"

"Thank you," Yeaton said, and the prosecution rested its case.

Chapter 27

WAGNER'S LAST STAND

Max Fischacher hit the jury with everything he had. But beyond Wagner's own words, the defense had nothing to counterbalance the circumstantial evidence weighing against the prisoner. Fischacher and Tapley would introduce nineteen witnesses in all, many of them "unwilling witnesses." But they would come and go quickly with little impact. Worse yet, Fischacher's lead-off witness turned out to be a disaster. Mrs. Benjamin Maggridge of Portsmouth had employed a young woman named Matilda Folsom, who had reportedly visited with Wagner, possibly on the night of the murder. This, perhaps, was the testimony that would vindicate the prisoner, but the evidence suddenly evaporated when Mrs. Maggridge admitted she had never actually seen the defendant in her house.

"You only know [Wagner] has been there from hearsay?" the defense attorney asked with a hint of desperation.

"Yes. She told me he was there," Mrs. Maggridge replied, referring to the mysterious Matilda Folsom, who was not on the witness list and nowhere to be found.

"You never saw his face till today?" Fischacher asked again.

"No, sir," the witness said.

"I am sorry I sent for you to Portsmouth," the embarrassed attorney concluded.

"I am very sorry you did," Mrs. Maggridge snipped and left the witness box.

Fischacher had broken the lawyer's cardinal rule—never ask a question unless you already know the answer. So if anyone was going to sway this jury of twelve "good and true men," it must be the Harvard-educated lawyer from Boston.

"I am not here for the purpose of throwing dust in your eyes," Fischacher told the jury and the large audience in his impassioned one-hour opening statement on Friday afternoon, June 13, 1873. "Louis Wagner is not the man who committed the fearful crime." Fischacher was a stranger defending a stranger, he said, and he hoped the men of Maine would not hold that against him. He had taken Wagner's case on faith. "All I knew is that he insisted that he is innocent," said the attorney.

His client, the defender said, had been treated with prejudice and calumny from the start. The newspapers had named him the murderer within hours. No other suspects had ever been considered. The police investigation and the prosecution's entire parade of witnesses had been biased toward his guilt. "The officers said it was Wagner, the excited populace said it was Wagner, the multitudes said it was Wagner," he explained. As a result, every utterance Wagner made and every action he took was seen as that of a guilty man.

But there was a reasonable explanation for everything, the defense attorney told the jury and a roomful of sympathetic listeners. When Wagner told Mrs. Johnson he felt bad, it was because he had drunk too much beer the night before. Wagner looked tired and exhausted to Mary Johnson because he had been up most of the night baiting trawls and being sick. He could not produce the name of the saloon he had drunk in, or its owner, or the owner of the fishing boat he had worked on, because he had not asked their names. He had gone to Boston simply to see friends. He had shaved his beard and bought new clothes to look presentable to them and later to do a little job hunting in the city. As proof of his innocence, Wagner had even gone directly to the Brown's boarding house in the North End because he knew if his friends in Portsmouth wanted to reach him, he could easily be found there. It was all just a case of mistaken identity.

Despite being attacked by a killing mob, Fischacher explained, his client had been cooperative and forthcoming. He had not resisted his sudden arrest. And while denied access to a lawyer at his South Berwick arraignment (and despite his request for one), Wagner had told his story freely on the record. While exhibited to the public like an animal in a zoo, he had been a model prisoner. Wagner's story, though unsupported, was too detailed to dismiss as a "mere fabrication," the attorney claimed. Wagner was a mere fisherman and "he could not have invented a theory so rapidly and have told his story so ingeniously without truth."

Fischacher knew he was walking on eggshells. He and co-attorney Tapley had scarcely objected to any of the selected jurors in the lead-up to the trial. And they had rarely raised objections during Mr. Yeaton's exhausting presentation. They did not want to appear "overzealous," Fischacher frequently noted, but rather wanted to show respect for Judge Barrows and the court at Alfred. The defense acknowledged a terrible crime had taken place on Smuttynose. They understood the Hontvets and their friends rightly desired to avenge the murders of Karen and Anethe. But this was a court of law, Fischacher told the jury, not a court of public opinion. And it was not the job of the defense to find the real killer, but rather to raise a reasonable doubt as to Wagner's guilt.

As compelling as the prosecution's case might seem, he said, the State had not proven "to a moral certainty" that Louis Wagner was on Smuttynose Island the night of the murders. "You cannot convict a man simply because he is found under suspicious circumstances," the defender warned. Witnesses make mistakes, he said. He offered an anecdote about a New Hampshire witness in another case who, mistaking the officer for the criminal, swore the deputy sheriff was the killer. Witnesses also exaggerate, he noted, they collude, and sometimes they lie, believing that "the end would justify the means."

The case for the defense, in a nutshell, was that, while Wagner's alibi could not be proved, neither could it be proved false. The prosecution's circumstantial case was simply not enough evidence, Fischacher argued, to hang a man. If any juror could not accept even a single part of the government's case, "then you cannot conscientiously assign this man to the gallows." And here was, perhaps, Wagner's greatest hope of survival. The prosecution was well aware Victorian juries had been demanding more hard evidence for a conviction. So Yeaton had given them the button, the pencil, the ax, the boots, and the bloody clothes. But Fischacher knew that Victorian juries were also less and less likely to condemn a man to death based mostly on circumstantial clues. So he pressed harder on their sympathies.

"This man's life is in your hands," he said to the jury. He hoped they would listen to the prisoner's story without prejudice. Or would they make the defendant "one more added to the list of the dead"? Fischacher's goal was to make each juror feel as if he was the hangman. And with that preamble, Louis Wagner rose and walked to the witness chair.

He was much taller than he appeared while sitting with his attorneys. The members of the public gallery, half of them women, noticed this right away. His muscular frame was visible beneath the cheap coat and vest he had purchased in Boston. His blue eyes and blonde hair were more attractive than advertised on those black-and white celebrity photographs on sale for "two bits." Throughout much of Fischacher's speech, Wagner had been sobbing to himself. But as all eyes in the courtroom focused on him now, he appeared to blossom and grow confident, even charming.

Wagner told his story eagerly, prompted by his attorney. Despite the thick German accent, his voice was strong and clear. He was twenty-eight, he said, and had worked aboard fishing vessels since he was thirteen. He had been in America seven years. He had first heard about the murders at the Isles of Shoals after he was arrested in Boston.

He recounted the now familiar story of his whereabouts hour by hour, but with subtle changes. When he met John Hontvet's fishing party on the Portsmouth dock on March 5, for example, Wagner now recalled telling John about a woman he'd met. Her first name was Johannah. (Curiously, she had the same name as cobbler Todtman's servant girl in Boston.) Wagner did not know her last name. She wanted a ride back to Star Island aboard the *Clara Bella*, Wagner claimed. John, according to Wagner, said that there was no room for Johanna on his boat, because the forecastle, a small sleeping or work area at the bow of the boat, was too cramped. There was only one bunk and they needed the space to bait trawls. The mysterious Johanna could not be found by the police or by the attorneys. She had not appeared in John Hontvet's testimony and was never mentioned again. In his Alfred testimony, Wagner amended his promise to bait trawls for John later that night. Now he recalled saying he would return conditionally "if I were not employed somewhere else." He was hedging his bets and adapting his narrative.

Wagner's testimony was peppered with subtle attempts to throw suspicion onto others. He implied, for example, that John was frustrated with the three females on Smuttynose, who were literally eating up his profits. "As fast as he made money," John reportedly confided in Wagner, "they were spending it on grub." Later, Wagner cheerfully identified John Hontvet as the member of the lynch mob who had struck Assistant Entwistle with a rock. He also claimed that Entwistle, whom he derided as "that little man," had tried to trick him into signing a false confession.

Wagner also attacked the reputation of Charles Johnson, a witness and the son of his Water Street landlady. Charles had once knocked down a drunken man in the streets of Portsmouth, Wagner told the courtroom. Charles had robbed the man of thirteen dollars, a sum very close to what Wagner had stolen at Smuttynose. "That's the way to make money," Charles reportedly bragged to Wagner, who advised Charles, in return, to lay low, tell no one, and not to spend the money. It was one more weird confessional remark, as if Wagner was warning himself, but too late.

To explain away his skinned knuckles, as observed by Mary Johnson, Wagner now suddenly recalled he had helped a lame fisherman load four or five boxes onto a cart on Pier Wharf near Caswell and Randall's store. He did not know the man's name. After a mug of ale in an unknown saloon on Congress Street, he said he returned to a different wharf where he baited nine hundred hooks by himself, a huge task, aboard a different boat. But he could not identify the captain or the boat. He then went to another unidentified bar on Congress Street, had two glasses of ale, got sick, vomited, slipped, and fell on the ice by the town pump on Court Street. Hurting his knee, he lay there for a long time. Eventually, he limped home with near-frozen feet. If Maren had suffered from frostbite, then so had he.

Despite contradicting testimony, Wagner stuck to his claim that he returned to Johnson's house via the back door, did not go up to his room, saw the Smuttynose men baiting trawls through a window, and fell asleep on a sofa there. He then went down to the docks again around five a.m. and bumped into Mrs. Johnson in the backyard when he returned home around seven-thirty that morning. Because witnesses swore they saw him on lower Water Street on the morning of the murder, Wagner now explained that he had, indeed, walked down there, still feeling ill, and possibly passed by these same men. From here, Wagner's updated alibi parroted the testimony of the four prosecution witnesses who saw him at Johnson's that morning. He was able to weave his story smoothly into theirs. As to his bloody shirt found in the privy, he could only recall asking Mrs. Johnson to rip it up and use it for rags. This, of course, took the bloody shirt off his own back and placed it in the hands of his landlady. It did not explain why he had told Judson Randall he was not even wearing a white shirt that day, but a plaid one.

By Friday afternoon, basking in the spotlight, Wagner had explained his impulsive trip to Boston to find work, a visit to the barbershop, and his purchase of a new outfit. Wagner denied making any statement to Todtman the shoemaker about a woman lying as still as a boot. Time and again, he flatly denied the testimony of others, attempted to discredit them, or colored their comments with his own unique memories. Wagner "remembers his statements more accurately than these witnesses," Fischacher told the jury. It was his word against theirs, and they were all wrong.

Instead of continuing the trial through Saturday, Judge Barrows recessed the proceedings until the following week. The reason for the unscheduled break was known only to the defense team. As he would reveal years later, Max Fischacher had stumbled across what appeared to be a surprise witness. Unseen by the gaggle of reporters, he slipped off to Portsmouth in hopes of finding the man who could turn the case upside down. Meanwhile, in the village of Thorndike, Maine, another man named John Gordon was being arrested for killing three members of his own family with an ax. Gordon and Wagner's fate would soon be irrevocably linked.

"I remember the point in my narrative where I left off," Wagner said on Monday morning, June 16. Picking up the story in the North End of Boston, he suddenly remembered an anecdote about Katherine Brown, his former landlady, who was now on his enemies list following her testimony. Mrs. Brown had quarreled with her husband years ago, Wagner said, and "pulled her husband's whiskers out."

"Mr. Brown was going to kill his wife that night," Wagner said. In fear for her life, Mrs. Brown "begged of me to stay that night the row was in the house, to save her life."

It was another wild Wagner memory, calculated to sully Mrs. Brown's testimony and present himself as a hero. Wagner then turned his attention to Emma Miller, the Boston prostitute. He denied making any statements to her about killing two sailors in New York. Emma had mistaken him, at first, for another man named Henry Ludwig, Wagner said. Ludwig was the sailor who had fallen overboard years earlier while the two men were on a fishing boat.

Emma came to him and sat on his knee in the saloon on the first floor of Brown's, Wagner told the jury. One night years ago, the Browns had been fighting, Wagner said, Emma "came into my room in her night clothes and tried, or did, turn into my bed." Now on the afternoon of March 6, Wagner said, she wanted to seduce him again. She asked if he might "stand a treat" and pay her for sex. But he told Emma that he had no money for her services and she would have to wait. His money, he told her, was coming on the next train. It was odd, having lied to a prostitute, that Wagner felt compelled to confess his lie to the jury. But this was consistent with his pattern of bragging about relationships with women. It was important everyone in the Alfred courthouse should know he was desirable, brave, almost irresistible to all females. He had befriended the murdered Christensen women, charmed Maren Hontvet and Mrs. Johnson out of their rent, kissed the two Johnson girls whenever he wished, saved Mrs. Brown from her husband in Boston, and kept a lover back in Prussia. Now, taking the moral high ground, he was rejecting the advances of a fallen woman.

"I looked at her and asked her if she was not in a family way," Wagner said of Emma Miller. "She answered, no. Then I pushed her away from me."

True or false, it was a shocking bit of Monday morning gossip to Victorian ears. Wagner then presented his version of the traumatizing events that followed. He explained how he had been abruptly strong-armed away from the Browns' boarding house by the Boston police. The officers scared him so greatly that he accidentally told them he had been in Boston five days. What he meant was he had lived in Boston five years. The police then "stripped me bare naked" at the station, he said, interrogated and accused him of murder, then tossed him into a cell.

In the morning, after being "dragged through the street," he had been transported back to Portsmouth where a howling mob led by a gun-toting John Hontvet did their best to end his life. He was then put on public display in jail. People pointed at him in horror. Witnesses said he was the man who had walked from New Castle. Maren and John Hontvet came to his cell, cursed him to hell, and threatened his life. Then his friend Judson Randall, a Shoals fisherman, sat in his cell and described seeing the butchered bodies of his good friends Karen and Anethe. When Randall asked how all this made him feel, Wagner began crying. "I told him I feel bad," Wagner sobbed, "because people *thought* that I was a murderer." Again, he felt sad for himself, not for the victims.

The most dramatic media moment in the trial came after Wagner denied hiding the white shirt in the privy. The scene anticipated the "bloody glove" episode in the celebrity trial of O. J. Simpson in 1995. Jury members asked the lawyers to "try the shirt on the prisoner's wrist." In front of everyone, Wagner exposed his muscular arm and placed it into a sleeve of the torn bloody shirt "which appeared to be too small to button." Although Wagner later admitted he owned shirts of different sizes, and not all of them fit him well, the spectators in the courtroom gasped at the sight. The evening newspapers gushed over the exciting revelation.

For many, Wagner's quirky testimony was too detailed, too candid, and delivered with too much passion to ignore. Perhaps he was a hapless fisherman, as his attorney claimed, who had merely "fallen into distress." Perhaps Anethe had mistakenly identified him in her dying moments or maybe Maren was lying. It was possible that John Hontvet, the last of the successful fishermen at the Isles of Shoals, had convinced other fishermen to exaggerate their testimony. Was Wagner really dumb enough to tell four men, including Hontvet, that he knew where to get money at the Shoals, but he might have to murder for it? Had the police been fooled into focusing their entire investigation against the accused prisoner while the real killer was still at large? Did someone plant the bloody shirt in the privy? Were attorneys Yeaton and Plaisted duped by the overzealous scheming locals?

On Wagner's testimony, the *Boston Journal* reported, "His appearance on the stand is such as to make a favorable impression. He tells his story in a very connected and assured manner." Always an advocate, Charles Thayer at the *Portsmouth Times* suggested the verdict could go either way. "Opinion now divided over guilt of Wagner," the *Portsmouth Times* announced. "Who can it be? asks the crowd."

Thayer used the opportunity, once again, to shift suspicion over to the city marshal. "He [Wagner] told how the police officers tried to frighten, coax, and bully him into making a confession that he was guilty of the murder," the *Times* told its readers. Even the *Portsmouth Chronicle* had to admit "Wagner bore his examination well, not contradicting any of his former statements and appearing at ease."

George Lincoln Came, the farmer from Alfred, may represent the best "man in the street" view of Wagner's appearance on the stand. Came had given up his farm work for a week to attend the exciting trial. Taking time from plowing his field, selling cranberries, building a piazza, and courting a local woman, Came wrote in his journal following Wagner's testimony: "Nice day. Wagner on the stand. He tells a plausible story."

Chapter 28

CIRCLING THE WAGONS

Wagner stayed cool even under intense cross-examination on Monday. With no dramatic confession likely, the prosecution chose to pick away at Wagner's alibi, forcing him to add details they hoped would stretch his explanation to the point of absurdity. He had purchased his extra-large rubber boots last winter on Market Street in Portsmouth, Wagner testified, where there were "a couple hundred there the same size." George Yeaton, incredulous, asked Wagner if there were really hundreds of size-eleven boots in a little Portsmouth shop. Didn't he mean "a couple hundred different sizes"? "No, sir," Wagner confirmed, "there were about ten hundred [boots] there, different sizes, a couple hundred from the same size."

Yeaton also found it amazing that a schooner captain, who was a complete stranger to Wagner, would pay him a dollar in advance to bait trawls unsupervised on an unidentified boat the night of the murders. "I might have seen him," Wagner dissembled, "but I did not thought I had seen him before; perhaps I had, but I could not make it out that night."

The prosecutor was equally amazed the Hontvets had reported being robbed that very night of two five-dollar bills, a silver fifty-cent piece, and a handful of "coppers," while the clever thief had been careful to leave all the telltale Norwegian coins and distinctive paper "scrip" behind. Although Wagner had been penniless days before, he was able to spend precisely the same amount of money and in same denominations while in Boston the

following day. The fifty-cent piece and a few pennies were still in his pockets with the white button when he was arrested. Wagner claimed he had
secretly saved up enough money to pay his overdue rent, about twenty dollars total, but then decided to use the money to go to Boston.

Wagner claimed he had been carrying the unspent silver fifty-cent
piece for four years. He said he had carried it in a pocket book, but then
claimed he had lost the pocket book two years earlier in Boston. So why did
he still have the half-dollar? That had been in his waistcoat pocket all those
years, he said. Silver coins were hard to come by in 1873, and this one was
practically uncirculated. Although he had spent the rest of his money freely,
Wagner may have been afraid to part with the silver because it could more
easily be identified than the other stolen money.

Point by point, Yeaton chipped away. If Wagner had been in the saloon
on Congress Street many times, why didn't he know its name? If he was
subject to bouts of rheumatism, why would he lie on the icy ground by the
pump for more than an hour? Why had it taken him forty-five minutes to
walk from Court to Liberty streets after he vomited near the pump, a distance the defendant agreed normally took five minutes to travel?

Under attack by the prosecutor, Wagner shot back. He denied he had
ever complained to anyone about his poverty. And while he refrained from
accusing his former boss of the murders while under oath, he did recall an
interesting story about John Hontvet, the wealthy fisherman of Smuttynose.

"He [Hontvet] said last fall," Wagner told the jury, "in some kind
of argument about the people in the United States, if he had power and
strength enough, that there was a great many people in the United States he
would kill and hang on lantern posts and skin them alive."

These darkly bizarre comments aimed at the Hontvets did nothing to
help Wagner's case. As soon as Yeaton was finished with his cross-examination, Tapley and Fischacher quickly ushered their client back to his seat.
Fischacher then introduced his own sad parade of witnesses in a desperate
attempt to make his client's alibi appear credible. There were fourteen of
them, in addition to Wagner. Henry Hunnerfeldt, for example, recalled

that Louis Wagner had "borrowed a needle of Edwin Burke" while fishing on Burke's schooner three weeks before the murders. Wagner had said he stuck the large sail needle into a blister and released the blood. This testimony was offered as the reason he had human blood on his clothes in addition to "fish goory." (It also implies the defense was fearful that Dr. Chase's blood analysis might indeed be legitimate or might sway the jury.) Edwin Burke and his shipmate Peter Johnson confirmed the story of the needle and the blisters. But during cross-examination, Yeaton used the opportunity to revisit the stolen boat incident. Jurors were reminded that Wagner knew Burke's dory, and that the thole pins on the recovered boat had been mysteriously worn down from heavy use of the oars in a single night.

On Tuesday, Tapley and Fischacher countered with their own blood expert. James F. Babcock, a professor and analytical chemist from the Massachusetts College of Pharmacy in Boston, took the stand. Fischacher asked Babcock point-blank whether it was possible for Dr. Horace Chase to positively identify human blood on Wagner's clothes.

"I should say that was quite impossible," Babcock stated firmly, and then went on to dispute Chase's bloodstain theory one corpuscle at a time. While he had no doubt that Dr. Chase "believed" himself a capable chemist, Babcock told Yeaton during cross-examination, his scientific method was flawed.

"I know of no discovery since 1861 that would authorize anyone to say with certainty which was human blood and which [was] other mammalian blood," Babcock said.

The blood expert was the high-water mark of a sinking case. After that, according to the Portsmouth papers, "nothing material was elicited." Previously, two clerks had read a few ancient York County documents into the record to bolster the flagging theory that Smuttynose Island was not in York County.

Then a hairdresser named Stephen A. Preble recounted a lengthy story about a customer who had come into his shop on the morning of the murders. The long-haired foreigner looked enough like Wagner to be his brother, the witness said, which is why Portsmouth police had originally reported Wagner shaved his beard in New Hampshire before leaving for Boston. Portsmouth's Assistant Marshal Entwistle had even collected samples of the other man's whiskers from the barbershop floor as evidence against Wagner. Fischacher raised this point to prove that, even as they were gathering evidence and interviewing witnesses, the Portsmouth police exhibited bias against their client. Judge Barrows threw out the line of questioning as irrelevant.

Timothy Chellis, the star witness for the defense, had waited six days at Alfred to tell his story. It was scarcely worth the wait. Chellis had seen Wagner in his saloon around seven-thirty p.m. on the night of the murder. Chellis had sold him a glass of ale. It was the best alibi Wagner would get. It proved he was in a saloon as he claimed, but it still gave him plenty of time to steal Burke's boat half an hour later and head to the Isles of Shoals.

More embarrassing tidbits followed. Deputy Richard Philbrick had seen the bloody shirt taken from the privy. Harrison Berry had been down on the Water Street wharves, but had not seen Wagner there on the fateful night. Jesse Getchell said he was rowing from Kittery to New Castle early in the evening of March 5, but had not seen Wagner on the river. Stephen Shaw, a member of the coroner's jury, testified the murder scene had been very bloody. This last witness was called in support of the defense's theory that, had Wagner been guilty, he would have been covered with much more blood. But as everyone knew, he had been wearing his oiled fishing clothes and the killer had washed off an ocean of blood at the island well.

Fischacher then recalled Dr. John Parsons, another member of the coroner's jury, who had testified earlier about the wounds on Anethe Christensen's body. It was another risky move, but he needed to plant the seed of doubt in one or more jurors and his time was running out. In polite, roundabout, Victorian language, the attorney asked Parsons whether Anethe's many flesh wounds might have been inflicted by "a person of not great muscular force." In other words (and this question has been asked by armchair detectives and conspiracy theorists ever since), could the killer have been a female? Was she, by implication, Maren Hontvet, rather than the muscular Louis Wagner?

But again, Fischacher's efforts were thwarted. Again, he had asked too many questions and had opened the door to damaging testimony. Dr. Parsons had his own theory about the murder and he was allowed to voice it. Based on his years of medical expertise and forensic analysis, Parsons said, he believed "that the flesh wounds were made...by one hand, while the person was held by the other. That being the case, a person being excited, would not be likely striking very rapid blows to get much force into them."

The visual image was explicit. If Dr. Parsons's expert theory was correct, then Anethe had attempted to flee as soon as she saw her attacker raise a long-handled ax in the air. At first she had been frozen in fear, and even after identifying Louis Wagner, and calling his name, she had remained pinned to the spot as Maren testified. When he returned with the ax, Anethe was still standing in the moonlight in her nightdress just a few feet from the house, her waist-long blonde hair floating in the icy island breeze. If Parsons's theory was correct, she must have turned at the last moment to run. The thief grabbed her with one hand, preventing her escape. Then, gripping the ax handle with his other hand, he swung awkwardly at his victim at close range. The death blow, Parsons reminded his listeners, had been made with crushing force against the side of the young woman's skull. This was the work of a powerful, muscular person, and by implication, not Maren. Wagner was still the likely killer, and worse, the defense attorney had given the doctor an opportunity to recount the gory details once more.

Convinced the Portsmouth police had suppressed important evidence that favored his client, the attorney called Charles Thayer, the editor and owner of the *Portsmouth Times*. Thayer had been a fly on the wall at the police station, gathering news during Wagner's thirty-six hours in the city jail. Thayer had watched as the police brought in potential witnesses, including those who had seen Wagner along the New Castle road heading toward Portsmouth early on March 6. According to Thayer, at least one man, on seeing Wagner in his cell, said he could not identify the prisoner as the man on the bridge in New Castle. But the same man, Fischacher believed, had then identified Wagner on the witness stand. The defense attorney smelled a conspiracy. Despite his best efforts, he had been unable to get the police to release the names of any men or women they had spoken with who had not seen Wagner in New Castle that morning. Judge Barrows was unsympathetic. It was not necessary for the police to inform the defense council of every single person they interviewed during their research, Barrows concluded. That was simply part of the investigative process.

So that was it. As the defense rested its case, attorney Yeaton slipped in half a dozen rebuttal witnesses, including three Portsmouth patrolman, all of whom testified they had walked the Court Street area on a regular beat on the night of the murder. They had seen no one lying in the snow near the town pump during several visits and there were no marks in the snow to indicate anyone had lain there. Thomas Entwistle reiterated his sworn statement that he had not attempted to trick Wagner into confessing by offering to keep him off the gallows.

With that, according to the *Times*, "the long, tedious examination was ended." Max Fischacher stood and announced that "Judge" Rufus Tapley would now present the closing argument for the defense. The courtroom was packed more tightly with spectators than on any other day. Tapley, however, had not expected to give his final speech until the next morning. The audience sat in respectful silence for a full twenty minutes as the lawyer gathered his notes. Then, at precisely eleven a.m., the Hon. Rufus Tapley stepped in front of the twelve seated jurors and began to speak. It was an oration worthy of an ancient Roman senator.

"What have we been doing?" Tapley asked, taking a moment to settle the jurors and get his bearings as he took center stage. "Think of it a moment." Echoing Fischacher's opening remarks, Tapley warned against a rush to judgment in the Wagner case. He reminded the jury they had been endowed by the state of Maine with an awesome power over the defendant. "Whether he lives or dies rests upon your determination," Tapley began. "You must pronounce the joyous or fatal word; you *cannot* escape it." But thanks to the maturity of the jurors, most of whom were fifty years or older, the defense attorney said he was hopeful and confident they would acquit. Louis Wagner was no more than "a stranger in a strange land," unfairly accused of killing the only friends he had.

Tapley spoke for almost five hours in an effort to unravel the noose that Yeaton and Plaisted had fashioned around Wagner's neck. And as he spoke, the prisoner wept bitterly and openly. Nothing in the government's chain of circumstantial evidence, Tapley declared, proved Wagner was guilty. It was only "a rope of sand" that would fall to pieces if the real killer could be found. The prosecutor's case, he said, was actually two separate and unrelated cases—a tragic murder on Smuttynose Island and a search for the whereabouts of Louis Wagner on the mainland that same night. There was no definitive proof, he said, that Wagner was the stranger who walked from New Castle to Portsmouth on the morning after. And it was that very lack of proof that had caused the fishing families of the Shoals and Water Street to invent false testimony. If Wagner had been stupid enough to tell four local fishermen, in advance, that he might rob and murder at the Shoals, Tapley said, then the prisoner belonged in the "Insane hospital," rather than the county jail. "Who ever heard of a man going around and making proclamation of his intention to commit such a crime?" the defender asked. And it was these same angry fishermen, Tapley noted, who organized and led the lynch mob.

It was Wagner's story, his defender argued, that was more probable than the trumped-up, circumstantial case against him. Otherwise, why would a man who was fleeing from justice run toward places where he was well-known? If Wagner was so shrewd, as many claimed, how could he be simultaneously so foolish? As to Wagner's many so-called "confessional" statements, his attorney tossed them off as mere misinterpretations of language caused by Wagner's Prussian accent. Or they were innocent off-the-cuff remarks that suddenly took on darker meaning after he was unfairly condemned by the newspapers and hauled into jail. Either that, or the witnesses for the prosecution were lying.

Norwegian immigrants John Hontvet and his brother, Matthew, ran a successful trawl fishing operation from Smuttynose Island. In 1872, they invited a twenty-eight-year-old Prussian named Louis Wagner (center) to join their operation and lodge with their family. This image comes from a short 1980s film called *The Ballad of Louis Wagner* based on a song by John Perrault.

Credit: University of New Hampshire

Opened in 1848, the Appledore Hotel (top) was a well-established resort and cultural Mecca for the Boston literati when "Spice King" John R. Poor bought Star Island nearby. His luxury Oceanic Hotel (bottom) wiped out the ancient fishing village of Gosport, New Hampshire, when it opened in 1873. It burned in 1875 and was replaced by the surviving hotel operated today by the Star Island Corporation.

Credit: Portsmouth Athenaeum

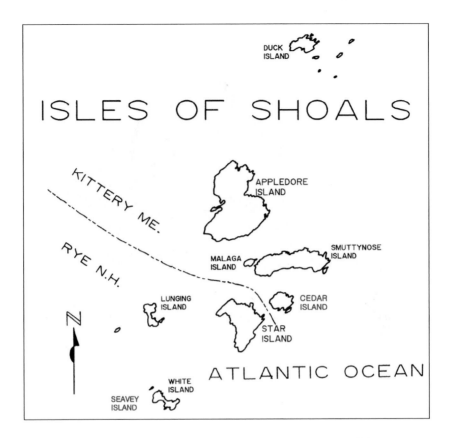

The nine Isles of Shoals are located just ten miles from historic Portsmouth, New Hampshire, named for the "shoals of fish" that drew English settlers here as early as the 1620s. They turned these rocky outcroppings into a vital colonial staging site for drying and exporting cod. The Maine–New Hampshire border runs between the islands.

Credit top: Peter E. Randall, Publisher
Credit right: SeacoastNH.com

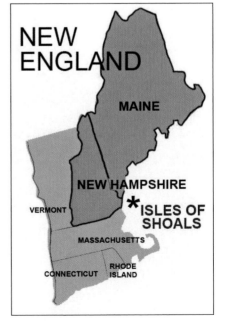

The ax with the broken handle found at the murder scene (top) is now in the collection of the Portsmouth Athenaeum in New Hampshire. An imaginative illustration (bottom) depicting the murders appeared in the March 29, 1873, edition of *The Day's Doings*, a sensationalist New York publication.

Credit: Portsmouth Athenaeum

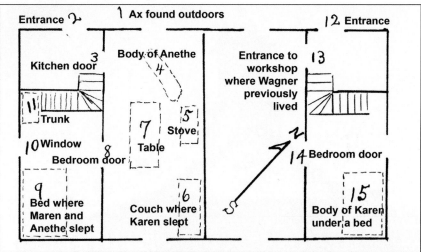

1 Ax found outdoors
Entrance 2
Kitchen door 3
Body of Anethe 4
Entrance to workshop where Wagner previously lived
12 Entrance
13
11 Trunk
5
7 Table
Stove
10 Window
Bedroom door 8
14 Bedroom door
9 Bed where Maren and Anethe slept
6 Couch where Karen slept
15 Body of Karen under a bed

One of many souvenir photos of the Hontvet House on Smuttynose Island (above) taken after the murders, here with an unidentified woman in the doorway and the Sam Haley Cottage in the background. A diagram of the murder scene (below) appeared in the *Portsmouth Journal* on March 8, 1873. This version is adapted from a similar sketch by historian Lyman Ruttledge.

Photo credit: Portsmouth Athenaeum
Diagram credit: Star Island Corporation

Assistant Marshal Thomas Entwistle, later promoted to city marshal, walking in the South End of Portsmouth, New Hampshire (above), and the city's Victorian train station (below) where police twice defended Louis Wagner from a violent lynch mob.

Credit: Portsmouth Athenaeum

Prussian immigrant fisherman
Louis H. F. Wagner (above)
murdered Anethe and Karen
Christensen on March 6, 1873,
while his former employer John
Hontvet (right) was baiting trawls
on the mainland ten miles away.

Credit: Portsmouth Athenaeum

Smuttynose Island, as seen from Malaga Island, in the late nineteenth century shows a number of buildings now gone. The Mid-Ocean House (left) and the surviving Haley Cottage (center) are visible, but the Honvret House is largely obscured here behind a store at the cove and by the long fish house that stood on the old stone pier.

Credit: Portsmouth Athenaeum

The site of New Hampshire's original plantation in 1630, the tidal inlet called Puddle Dock, was choked with debris by the Victorian era. The inlet was filled in during the early twentieth century and is now the site of Strawbery Banke Museum. The wooden houses along Water Street (now Marcy Street) are gone. Wagner crossed Liberty Bridge (now the Liberty Pole at Prescott Park) on his journey from New Castle to Matthew Johnson's boarding house on the morning of March 6, 1873.

Credit: Portsmouth Athenaeum

Celia Thaxter – 1882

"Island poet" Celia Laighton Thaxter moved to the Isles of Shoals at age four, married in 1851, and had three children. Her family rented the Red House to the Hontvets on Smuttynose and employed Karen Christensen at the Appledore Hotel. Celia's literary fame brought the toast of Boston artists, musicians, and writers to the Shoals, and her 1875 *Atlantic Magazine* essay "A Memorable Murder" is considered a classic example of true crime literature.

Credit Portsmouth Athenaeum

Rare image believed to be Mary S. "Maren" Hontvet, who survived the moonlight murderer and whose testimony sent Louis Wagner to the gallows. False rumors claiming that Maren was the killer are based on death row threats by Wagner and by a hoax "deathbed confession" reported—and then retracted—ten years before Maren's death in 1887. The inset shows graves of Anethe and Karen Christensen in Portsmouth cemetery.

Courtesy Portsmouth Athenaem

Louis Wagner's escape from the new high-security jail in Alfred, Maine, created a panic in the bustling tourist summer of 1873. The cell where Wagner was housed during his trial still survives inside the post–Civil War brick building.

Courtesy J. Dennis Robinson

An enterprising photographer recorded the recapture of "Isles of Shoals murderer" Louis
Wagner in Farmington, New Hampshire, only days after his dramatic jailbreak. Wagner (in
shackles at left) is seen here with local sheriff A. J. Scruton (center) and an unidentified man.
An earlier souvenir picture of Wagner, taken at Saco, Maine, sold for twenty-five cents.

Courtesy J. Dennis Robinson

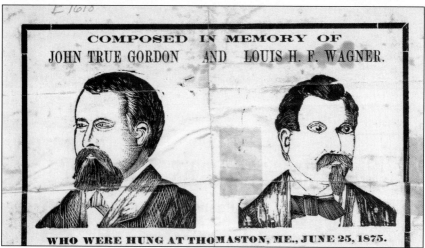

COMPOSED IN MEMORY OF
JOHN TRUE GORDON   AND   LOUIS H. F. WAGNER.

WHO WERE HUNG AT THOMASTON, ME., JUNE 25, 1875.

Populated by hundreds of seasonal fishermen in the 1600s, Smuttynose Island is now privately owned and a protected sanctuary (above) largely for hundreds of seagulls. A "bloody murder" broadside (below) souvenir memorialized the hanging of John True Gordon and Wagner in 1875 at Thomaston State Prison in Maine.

Credit top: Rodman Philbrick
Credit bottom: Portsmouth Athenaeum

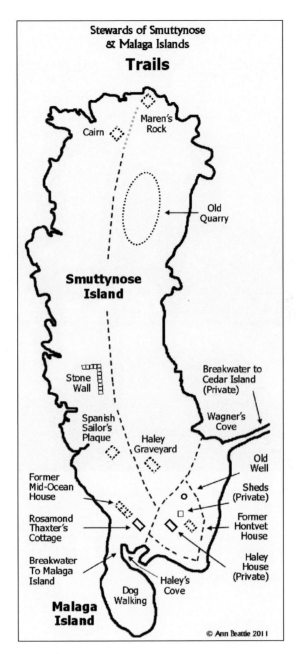

Although there are no public facilities whatsoever on the island today, visitors who have their own small boats are welcomed to tour Smuttynose in season following the regulations posted at the cove entrance.

Credit: Ann Beattie, ISHRA.org

This historic photograph was taken in 2014 on the four hundredth anniversary of the visit by Captain John Smith who named "New England." Taken by a flying "drone," this aerial shows (left to right) the tip of Appledore, then Malaga, Smuttynose, and Cedar Islands encircling boats in Gosport Harbor. The reconstructed 1875 Oceanic Hotel on Star Island is in the foreground.

Credit: David J. Murray, ClearEyePhoto.com

The defender derided the prosecution's theory that Wagner had dropped a little pencil at the crime scene. "Do they mean to argue that he had it out to make a memorandum of the fact he had committed murder, so as not to forget it?" Tapley's sarcasm was undisguised. And why had the prosecution not called for the testimony of George Lowd, the man who reportedly slept on the downstairs sofa? Why did they not deliver Matthew Johnson, the crippled landlord, for questioning, or put Marshal Johnson on the witness stand? The government's case against Wagner was so weak and so full of holes, Tapley claimed, that in their desperation to hang him, they were forced to admit false statements, bend the truth, and fabricate physical evidence. The prisoner, in Tapley's view, had heroically resisted every attempt by the police and prosecutors to "dragoon him" into a false confession. "I would rather die an innocent man than take my liberty as a murderer," Wagner had told Portsmouth marshals.

"Beautiful, beautiful, truthful, honorable, worthy of a hero. Hear it!" Tapley told the Alfred courtroom after repeating Wagner's statement. "It was a declaration that deserved to be engraved in gold," Tapley declared. Surely these words, spoken by a "poor, ignorant, fisherman" were divinely inspired and could never be uttered by a man with an evil spirit. Thanks to his attorney's rhetorical skills, Wagner sounded more like the reincarnation of Nathan Hale, an American patriot hanged by the British, than a cowardly thief who had slaughtered two innocent women with an ax for a fistful of money. Wagner's refusal to confess was not the cry of a man whose hands were "dyed with the blood of his best friends," Tapley said, but rather "the cry of injured innocence, and you can never forget it to the longest day of your life."

After a two-hour recess for lunch, the trial resumed. Wagner was not "the wild man or simpleton they would have us believe," the defense attorney stated. Yet the prosecutors had used every trick in the book, he told jurors, "to poison your minds and incite your prejudices against this man." The pencil, the button, the clothing were all red herrings, intended to distract and confuse. But the greatest bit of trickery, he said, was the imaginary evidence of Dr. Chase, the so-called "expert" on blood stains. Chase was asking them to believe he could reanimate dried blood and closely examine microscopic cells, hundreds of which would fit onto a pencil dot. To send a man to the gallows based on this unproven science was nothing less than murder, Tapley implied. "You would not let a verdict concerning your neighbor's farm turn upon such an investigation," he said, "and oh! Gentlemen! How much more important is this issue."

Moving to the evidence on Smuttynose Island, Tapley reminded jurors that Karen had cried out, "John scares me!" and then "John kills me!" Clearly Karen was mistaken, because John Hontvet was ten miles away in Portsmouth baiting trawls. But just as clearly, Tapley proposed, was the fact that the figure Karen saw in the darkness did not resemble Wagner, whom she knew. And if Karen could not recognize Wagner, then the men standing at that New Castle bridge might also have misidentified him. At first, Maren had not recognized the shape of Wagner either. And was it not equally possible that poor Anethe Christensen had mistakenly identified her attacker as Louis Wagner?

Who could prove, the defense argued, that Wagner was not sleeping on the lounge at Johnson's from three a.m. to five a.m. as he claimed? Only John Hontvet and George Lowd (the brother-in-law of Mrs. Johnson) claimed otherwise. But Lowd and Hontvet were among the leaders of the conspiracy against Wagner, so could their testimony be believed? Perhaps John had unfastened the back door on his way to the privy in the wee hours and accidentally left it undone when he returned. And if three policemen had not seen Wagner lying by the pump, did it prove he was not there? Did Wagner's trip to Boston and his purchase of new clothes prove he was a murderer? All of the prosecutor's "evidence" could be correct, Tapley claimed, and Wagner could still be innocent of murder.

With these questions and a dozen more hanging in the air, Rufus Tapley, in retrospect, would have been wise to sit down. But he could not resist another lengthy and tedious attempt to convince jurors Smuttynose Island might not lie within the jurisdiction of the County of York. The battle of the borderline between Maine and New Hampshire had begun over the valuable fishing rights. In the early 1600s, when Sir Ferdinando Gorges and Captain John Mason divided their claims in the New World, whatever riches might lie on the unexplored mainland were unknown. But both English entrepreneurs had heard the flat, rocky Isles of Shoals could become a profitable fishery. So the founders divided the valuable islands in half, splitting them up the middle like a fisherman slices a cod. But exactly where the middle was located along the Piscataqua River and at the Isles of Shoals became a source of controversy in colonial days. That border dispute between Mason's patent in New Hampshire and Gorges patent in Maine was still unsettled, Tapley told the jurors. And before Louis Wagner could be condemned, they must resolve that centuries-old dispute.

Exactly what Tapley said, we cannot know. His diatribe was so detailed and technical that J. D. Pulsifer, the court reporter, merely offered a brief summary in the trial transcript. But it was too much, too late, and Tapley knew it. He regretted openly that his powerful opponent, Mr. Plaisted, would have the last word. The prosecutor's appeals "will be more fresh on your ears when you retire, and more eloquent than mine," Tapley said. And with that, the defense attorney told the jury, "I cast the prisoner upon your hands, hoping for him a safe deliverance."

Chapter 29

THE VERDICT

It was the clash of titans in Maine as the former Civil War hero H. M. Plaisted rose to deliver the state's closing argument. Like Rufus Tapley, Plaisted was experienced at the bar and well respected by his peers. He, too, had been sitting back throughout the trial, allowing his second-in-command to carry the weight. Mr. Tapley's closing argument on Tuesday, the early newspaper reported, "was universally pronounced an able and convincing one." On Wednesday morning, June 18, at the stroke of nine o'clock, the attorney general congratulated the assembled jurymen for their yeoman service in "this protracted and painful investigation."

"How stands the case at this hour?" Plaisted asked rhetorically. In nearly six hours, his opponent, the "able and astute" Mr. Tapley, had not mentioned one of his own witnesses and was unable to disprove a single fact in the case against the defendant. Their defense hung entirely on the words of Louis Wagner, who had used his precious time at the bar to malign nearly every government witness. Tapley had painted Wagner as an innocent man, a victim of circumstances, and a working-class hero. Over the next few hours, Plaisted concluded the prisoner was nothing less than a "fiend in human shape."

This was a classic case of robbery gone wrong, the prosecutor said. John Hontvet was successful and had money. Wagner was destitute and jealous. His clothes were ragged, his boots torn, his rent overdue, and he could not afford a plug of tobacco. Wagner knew Smuttynose Island intimately and knew the women were alone. An opportunity presented itself, and he took it. He had motive, means, and opportunity.

"He is a man of pretty good memory," Plaisted said of Wagner. The defendant could flawlessly recall every penny he spent, every hook he baited, every beer he drank, every woman he charmed, every article of clothing he owned, and every word he spoke in conversation. But he could not recall a single detail during the eleven "missing" hours that could be corroborated by his attorneys or by the police. Based on Wagner's testimony, Plaisted implied, four dozen government witnesses, including Maren Hontvet, were all liars, all perjurers, and all bad people—and the killer was still at large. But if Wagner himself was the killer, and if he had fabricated his complex alibi, then all the circumstantial evidence fit together seamlessly. It was simple deduction, the attorney general said: "He used that boat to go to Smutty Nose."

Like an actor in a Shakespearean tragedy, Plaisted recounted the horrible murder scene in the Red House one final time. Driven by impulse, Wagner had brought no weapons. He was a thief in the night, desperately poor, drawn to "get money enough" hidden in a place he knew well. There were no men on guard. If the women did not wake up, the money was his. When Karen surprised him, rather than run, he struck her with a kitchen chair, the only object at hand. The thief, who had previously barred the bedroom door, now released the lock. Why? How had he known where the women were sleeping? Plaisted asked. How had the thief known there were no men in the house or others on the island? Why did he bring no weapon? How had he known the front door would be unlatched or that there was money hidden?

All signs pointed to Wagner and no one else, Plaisted repeated. He had hoped to knock the women unconscious and complete the robbery anonymously. But when Anethe leapt from the bedroom window and saw him clearly in the moonlight, when she screamed his name—that act changed everything. The game turned deadly and the ax was near at hand. And it was not until Anethe called out "Louis! Louis!" that Maren knew who the stranger was. Before that, Plaisted noted, the only name spoken was John, a confusing detail that Maren could easily have deleted from her testimony. Or Maren could have lied and testified her sister, Karen, also cried out "Louis!"

"If she had so much desired the conviction of this prisoner, as has been suggested," Plaisted said of his star witness, "would she not have kept back the name of her husband from this terrible crime? But no, she tells you the truth, the whole truth, keeping back nothing... Was ever [a] witness more truthful and honest?"

For Plaisted, this was the bottom line. One could believe either Maren Hontvet or Louis Wagner, not both. And it was only because Maren had escaped certain death that Wagner's name was known at all. It was the one name Maren repeated endlessly as old Mr. Ingebretsen rescued her from Smuttynose. And it was beyond human comprehension, the prosecution concluded, that this very same accused man on this very same night would suddenly disappear off the face of the Earth. The odds that another homicidal maniac who looked like Louis Wagner had wandered onto an otherwise deserted island ten miles out to sea on a winter's night at 1:07 a.m. was beyond calculation. Had Wagner baited trawls with John or slept in his bed or been seen by a single soul, then Maren's accusation would have been instantly proven false.

As Tapley had done the previous day, Plaisted ticked his way through the entire case. But where the defense saw only questions, conspiracies, and collusion, Plaisted saw only clarification. Wagner was the key to everything. His familiarity with the island explained why the killer could find the hidden fresh-water well in the darkness and why he knew where to stash his boat. It explained the size-eleven footprints in the snow where the killer tracked Maren from house to house. Because Karen's trunk had been in Wagner's room all summer, it explained why hers was the only trunk in the house left untouched at the murder scene. Plaisted theorized the killer planned to set fire to the house with all three dead women inside.

He abandoned that plan because "he knew the blaze would light his course away from the island and arouse the inhabitants of neighboring islands."

Wagner's guilt explained Burke's stolen boat, the identity of the stranger coming from New Castle, the shirt in the privy, his tearful farewell to Mary Johnson, his blisters, his scratches, his wet and bloody clothes and wind-burned face. It explained his escape to Boston, the haircut, his sudden spending spree, the contents of his pockets, and the weird confessional outbursts. It made sense that Wagner had not asked the Boston police why he was being arrested. He knew, as he told Mary Johnson, he had gotten himself into trouble and would soon be taken.

"Where is the reasonable doubt of guilt in this case?" Plaisted thundered. "Find it if you can."

The Attorney General did not waste a minute of his speech on the question of jurisdiction. He did not argue, as the defense had done at length, about whether Anethe had a middle name. He was not concerned with the publicity the case had received or the impact of public opinion. He mentioned the controversial blood analysis only briefly. He assured the jurors that "circumstantial evidence is legal evidence." If the body of evidence presented was enough to convince their understanding, satisfy their reason, and ease their conscience—then it was sufficient to convict Wagner. For without such evidence, there would be no protection under the law for victims and no punishment of the guilty.

"Men do not commit atrocious crimes of this sort in the day-light, and in the presence of witnesses," Plaisted warned. "They seek the security of darkness and secret places."

Prosecutor Plaisted concluded his argument at twelve-thirty p.m. and the court adjourned for lunch until two o'clock. His closing speech was dubbed "an able argument" by the *Chronicle*. With the verdict imminent, at least a hundred additional spectators were on hand for the afternoon session, but they were required to wait outside on the courthouse lawn. The "trial of the century," now in its ninth and final day, had all but swallowed up the tiny rural town. As the *Times* reporter noted, "the business of caring for the growing crops and the duties of housewives must have been sadly neglected by the people in the vicinity of Alfred during the progress of this trial. All were orderly and quiet, far superior in every respect to those usually seen at murder trials in large cities."

Finally, it was Judge William Griswold Barrows's turn. Directing his attention to the twelve men to his left, who were required to stand in his presence, he announced that "the time for eloquence, and fervor, and excitement" was over. Barrows's job in charging the jury, he said, was to define a few legal terms, guide their decision, and sum up the case. They should not make "a hasty or ill-considered conviction upon insufficient evidence," he said. But while Tapley had tried to make each juror feel personally responsible for hanging the prisoner, Barrows explained that, if they chose to convict, "it is not you, but the law, which condemns him."

The jurors should not trouble themselves with the question of jurisdiction, the judge said. That was out of their hands and up to him. Anethe Christensen had been killed with ten mortal blows. This was not manslaughter, but a crime of murder, that is, the act of killing with malice. If Anethe had been killed in an attempt to plunder the house, or if she was killed because she could identify the thief or if she was killed so that the perpetrator could make his escape—these all constituted "malice." Echoing attorney Plaisted, Judge Barrows made it clear that, with little "direct" evidence from witnesses to the crime, they must rely on "circumstantial" evidence, and this was the process by which most crimes were solved.

After an hour of detailed and complex instructions, Judge Barrows was only halfway through his charge. "As it is your attention I desire," he told his mostly middle-aged jurors, "if you feel that you can give it better in a sitting posture, you may sit."

There was an enormous body of information to ponder, drawn from roughly sixty witnesses and many days of speechmaking. So Judge Barrows plowed on, offering advice and guidance on every aspect of the testimony. The jurors, he said, must weigh each bit of evidence carefully, decide who to believe or not to believe, and calculate how each bit of information impacted every other fact in the case. Did Wagner tell four fishermen he knew where to get money at the Shoals? Did Anethe actually see Wagner? Did the men on the bridge see Wagner or someone else? Was Wagner or George Lowd sleeping on the sofa at Johnson's house? Was the bloodstain analysis convincing?

The most important question of the day, Judge Barrows implied at last, was whether Wagner's alibi was fact or fiction. Why was it, the judge asked the jury, that the biblical Cain lied to God Almighty after killing his brother, Abel? "What could it be," he said, "but to postpone the discovery of what he had done?"

Barrows did not have to elaborate. If Wagner was lying, especially on such a grand scale and with such colorful details, then he was most certainly guilty. If he had fabricated one part of his story, then all his testimony must be in doubt, including his many attacks on the character of witnesses. Did the prisoner sometimes bend the truth out of fear for his innocent life, Barrows asked, or did he have "a disposition to misstate"? In other words, was Wagner a chronic liar? And if he was not, what should be made of his "strange speeches" that sounded to the Victorian ear like veiled confessions? ("Out of the abundance of the heart, the mouth speaketh," Barrows told the jurors.) Wagner had denied making statements sworn to by his fellow fishermen, by the Hontvets, by the men on the Newcastle bridge, by every member of the Johnson family and his roommates Kenniston and Moore, by Mrs. Brown and her ward Emma Miller, by shoemaker Mr. Todtman, and by the police. Were all these people lying or misinformed? Only the jury could decide. The guiding unalienable truth, Barrows said, was that "no man can be in two places at the same time."

At four-thirty p.m. the jury retired to deliberate on the great weight of testimony before them. Fifty-five minutes later they were back. The clerk of court called out the name of each member in the *State of Maine v. L. H. F. Wagner*.

"Gentlemen of the Jury," the clerk said as the crowd fell into a "painful silence," according to the *Times*.

"We have agreed," the twelve men said at once.

"Who shall be your spokesman?" the clerk asked.

"The foreman," they replied, indicating John L. Perkins.

"Prisoner, stand up. Look upon the jury," the clerk said, and Wagner stood. "Gentlemen of the Jury, look upon the prisoner. What say you, Mr. Foreman? Is the prisoner at the bar guilty or not guilty?"

"Guilty," the foreman said.

"In what degree?" the clerk asked.

"First degree," the foreman replied, and the jurors all voiced their agreement.

Louis Wagner listened "without moving a muscle" as the verdict was read, according to the *New York Times*. But as the guard attached his handcuffs, his face took on "a solemn and hopeless look," the *Portsmouth Times* reported. As he was being led from the courtroom back to Alfred jail, one of the deputies turned and asked the condemned man how he felt. "A damn sight better than I did after dinner," Wagner told him.

The verdict, according to the *Portsmouth Chronicle*, was "an agreeable surprise" because, while few Portsmouth locals had any doubt of Wagner's guilt, "many did anticipate an acquittal or at least a disagreement on the jury." The guilty verdict confirmed, the newspaper added, that the prisoner's intricate alibi "was only a yarn and not a true statement of fact."

The *Chronicle* also offers us an enigmatic footnote. At the conclusion of the trial, Maren Hontvet handed a bundle to a gentleman and asked that it be delivered to Wagner. The package, she said, contained Wagner's "character," which he had left at her house. Inside the package was a "dirk," or long dagger used by sailors in close combat, and a handmade weapon called a "slungshot." Similar to a flail, a slungshot is a weight attached to a rope or strap, frequently used by criminals in the nineteenth century when sneaking up on a victim. Is the story true? Were these gifts symbolic tokens of victory, perhaps previously carried by a fisherman in the Portsmouth lynch mob? Had Wagner accidentally left these items when he moved out of the Hontvet house months before the murders? Or had Wagner carried them to the island for his use on March 5? If Wagner's, why were they not introduced as evidence in the trial? Again, questions persist.

Reporters were banned from interviewing Wagner in the days leading up to his official sentencing, so the media quickly abandoned Alfred, Maine. The circus was over. On Wednesday afternoon, June 24, as the prisoner made one final trip to the courthouse, the little village was quiet once more. George Lincoln Came, the local bachelor farmer who had followed the case religiously, was on hand for the brief concluding event. During a solemn reading by the judge, the prisoner was sentenced to be hanged by the neck until he was dead. "I was present," Came wrote in his journal that night. At the end of the formal sentencing, Came noted, Wagner turned and looked directly at the judge. "I thank you," was all he said.

Louis Wagner was returned to the modern Alfred jail in shackles. He was understandably feeling ill, he said, and retired early. The following morning, as the guards were making their rounds, the infamous prisoner was gone. He had unlocked the iron gate of his tiny jail cell and disappeared into the wide world.

V

DEATH ROW

"He felt very, very sorry for himself; so sorry he could cry—and sometimes did. Like most people who pity themselves overmuch, he had no pity left for others."

—Edmund Pearson on Louis Wagner, 1926

"It's easier to fool people, than to convince them they have been fooled."

—Mark Twain, American novelist

Chapter 30

CAPITAL DEBATE

Students of the Smuttynose murder case have often argued that Wagner's defense team failed him. They accuse Tapley and Fischacher of being unprepared or too timid in their cross-examination or not clever enough in their efforts to raise a reasonable doubt. However, these may have been tactics, rather than errors. Wagner's attorneys very likely came to believe that their client did indeed kill Karen and Anethe. If so, their defense can be seen primarily as a calculated effort to keep a guilty man from hanging.

Throughout his opening speech at trial, Max Fischacher repeatedly noted it was Wagner himself who "insisted that he was innocent." As to Wagner's alibi, Fischacher told the jury, "You will be able to discern whether his explanation is a mere fabrication." They knew that the more the prisoner spoke, the more impossible his story became. The defense team sat silently back while most of the jury members were selected. They rarely objected or cross-examined key witnesses for the prosecution, remaining as deferential as possible to the judge and jurors, because they were seeking leniency rather than an acquittal.

In his closing argument, Harris Plaisted even suggested the defense team rarely objected to his witnesses because his opponents themselves believed in Wagner's guilt. Tapley's refusal to dispute Maren Hontvet's critical testimony, according to Shoals historian Lyman Ruttledge, "suggests that he knew Wagner was guilty." Tapley was forced to construct Wagner's defense, Ruttledge wrote, "out of the rottenest timber he had ever tried to handle." With so little to work with, says true crime writer Edmund Pearson, the defense team was forced into quibbling over legal technicalities and running down every possible option the law allowed. The hours spent reading seventeenth-century York County documents and debating the jurisdiction of Smuttynose Island may have irritated the jurors and harmed Wagner's chances. "This does not indicate that they had a very high opinion of their case as touching the innocence of their client," Pearson noted.

Even if Wagner was guilty, Tapley wanted justice. He clearly believed John Hontvet and his fishing friends conspired to bend the truth. He did not trust the hard evidence provided by the police. He questioned the admissibility of Anethe's dying declaration. And, as Fischacher feared, the jury may have been biased against the penniless Prussian immigrant from the start and may also have resented his fancy lawyer from Boston. Despite his denials, Officer Entwistle may have attempted to bargain Wagner into a confession, a practice still common in police stations today. The media undoubtedly shaped public opinion against Wagner when the newspapers initially named him as the killer, but the favorable jailhouse interviews that followed also convinced many who never met him that Wagner was an innocent man.

An item discovered in the *Bangor Commercial* published three years after Wagner's death offers an exclusive glimpse behind the scenes. The article, titled "An Unpublished Incident of the Wagner Trial," might just wrap up the entire case. While on business in Bangor in 1878, Max Fischacher was asked by an enterprising reporter whether he thought Wagner had truly been guilty. Fischacher, of course, declined to comment directly. "But I will give you a little circumstance bearing on that question which did not come out in evidence," he told the reporter.

Besides Maren's testimony, the most damning evidence at trial had been the "battle on the bridge" at New Castle. If Wagner was there, as numerous witnesses claimed, then his alibi was undeniably false and he was certainly guilty. The Portsmouth police, Fischacher told the Maine reporter, had rounded up "every man, woman, and child who claimed to have seen him that morning," and brought them to identify the prisoner in his cell. Near the close of the trial in Alfred, Fischacher had learned that one man named John Lyons, on seeing Wagner in the Portsmouth jail, said aloud that Wagner was not the man he met along the road in New Castle on March 6. Yet Lyons had testified for the prosecution earlier that week, confirming he had seen Wagner just after he crossed the washed-out bridge. Had Lyons lied under oath? This might be the break they had been waiting for. So on Saturday, in the middle of Louis Wagner's testimony, Fischacher had begged Judge Barrows to pause the trial. The adjournment was granted. Fischacher rushed from Alfred to Portsmouth.

"I found the man," he told the reporter years later. Fischacher confronted Lyons and asked him why, while at Portsmouth jail, he had denied seeing Wagner on the New Castle road, but then reversed himself, and testified in court that he had seen Wagner. Lyons admitted he had pretended not to identify the prisoner at first, when Wagner was glaring at him threateningly through the bars, but he later told the police the truth. The defense attorney was skeptical. This might be proof the police were coercing witnesses into lying. He pressed Lyons harder. Had he really seen Wagner or not?

"Now I will tell you how you can satisfy yourself that Wagner was the man," John Lyons told Fischacher. Lyons explained that, although he had not known who Wagner was when he saw him by the bridge at New Castle, he noticed there was a white spot on the buckle strap of his blue overalls. It was just one of those odd details that stuck in his mind as Wagner passed him, wet and disheveled, and headed frantically toward Portsmouth. Lyons had remarked on it to a friend.

"So when I got back to Alfred," the attorney told the Bangor newsman, "I examined the buckle strap, and sure enough, there was the white spot just as Lyons had described it." The witness Fischacher had hoped would prove Wagner was not on the bridge had instead made a stunning identification. The smoking gun was in the wrong hands, and the defense attorney returned to Alfred alone to wrap up the trial. "I did not have Lyons recalled," he told the Bangor reporter, and the obvious was left unsaid. Fischacher knew Wagner had been on that bridge.

When this revealing article was reprinted in the *Portsmouth Daily Chronicle* on September 27, 1878, the editor could not resist jabbing at local people, particularly the editor of the *Times*, who "held to the belief that Louis Wagner was not guilty." Even Wagner's lawyer, the newspaper taunted, had known his client was "a brutal cowardly wretch who murdered two poor women from whom he had received only kindness."

Even with this knowledge, Tapley did his best to keep Wagner off the gallows by dutifully filing every post-trial motion the law allowed. He immediately submitted his "exceptions" based on seven objections Judge Barrows had overruled in court, including the nagging issues over jurisdiction, Anethe's dying declaration, and the introduction of the button and the pencil as evidence. For the next two years, Tapley searched for legal loopholes and grounds for appeal, delayed the execution date, and pushed the governor of Maine to reopen the case or commute Wagner's death sentence to life in prison.

This crusade coincided with a popular movement against capital punishment in New England that was especially active among Quakers and Unitarians in the state of Maine. Already the first "dry" state in the nation to prohibit the public sale of alcohol, Mainers were very close to abolishing capital murder as well. With only two exceptions, no one had been executed by the state of Maine for almost three decades. And despite a rise in capital crimes, by 1873 there were fourteen prisoners living out their lives on death row at Thomaston State Prison.

"The state occupies a false position," the *Daily Eastern Argus* editorialized way back in 1854. "Legally it professes to believe in a mode of punishment, which it has too much humanity to carry into practice."

Wagner's death sentence, though generally acceptable to the public, troubled those who had succumbed to his charisma or who were prone to distrust any case based largely on circumstantial evidence. "We see a very high degree of probability in the case made by the government," the *Boston Advertiser* reported after Wagner's sentencing, "but not that infallible and immutable certainty on which alone we should be content to see a man hanged." Charles Thayer at the *Portsmouth Evening Times*, considering Maine soft on execution, wrote, "It is therefore probable that Wagner may yet live to old age and die a natural death."

Opposition to capital punishment in Maine had been brewing since the largest state in New England gained its independence from Massachusetts in 1820. The harsh Puritan penal system created by the state's founders was deeply embedded in Maine history. In the seventeenth century, that punitive system could sentence its citizens to death for a host of crimes including idolatry, blasphemy, public rebellion, witchcraft, bestiality, buggery, bearing false witness, rape, "man stealing," and burning a house or ship. Technically, a child subject to early Puritan law could be executed for failing to obey his parents. By 1829, while creating its own more lenient laws, Maine legislators had reduced the number of capital crimes to treason, murder, and arson.

Then in 1834, Joseph Sager poisoned his wife, Phoebe. Or so the county prosecutor claimed at Sager's murder trial in the state capital at Augusta. His housekeeper testified that Mr. Sager had left the breakfast table to make an "egg pop," a mixture of wine and egg, and served it to his ailing wife. She also drank a cup of tea. Sager urged Phoebe to drink up, because "all the best of it, the sugar, was at the bottom." Phoebe and the housekeeper noticed a white powdery substance on the milk pitcher, and they threw the milk out. Phoebe became terribly ill and, while lying on her death bed with her neighbors gathered around, she chastised her husband. "You are the whole cause of this, now," Phoebe told Joseph. "Be an honest man and confess it."

Like Louis Wagner, Joseph Sager did not confess. Investigators found traces of arsenic on the milk pitcher, but an autopsy team could not absolutely confirm the poison had killed Sager's wife. Phoebe had been sickly for many years, and the defense argued that her autopsy indicated heart and gall bladder ailments, among others. A neighbor testified that the Sagers had marital problems and that Joseph, who was fifteen years younger than his wife, had licentious urges. "I have frequently heard him damn her using the most profane oaths," the neighbor testified. Sager's attorney said there was absolutely no proof his client had done anything wrong. The evidence was strictly circumstantial, he argued, and threw suspicion onto the house-keeper. The jury could make Sager an innocent man, the attorney declared, or "you may fix the fatal cord around his neck, and behold him swinging in the air, a blackened corpse."

The jury did exactly that. Sager was promptly executed outside the Augusta jail in January 1835. As many as five thousand spectators showed up despite a heavy winter snowstorm the day before. After waiting two hours for a governor's reprieve that never came, Joseph Sager was hanged before a festive crowd. His friends immediately took the body to a nearby town where they attempted, in what sounds like a scene from *Frankenstein*, to revive his corpse using unspecified "galvanic means."

Sager remained dead, but his execution reanimated the debate over capital punishment. That same year, an "anti-gallows" governor was elected in Maine. Some legislators wanted only to move the spectacle out of the public eye, putting an end to the drunkenness, revelry, and pick-pocket-ing that inevitably occurred at public hangings. Proponents of the death penalty, drawing from Puritan roots, offered the longstanding argument that such horrible displays were designed to chasten the audience and dis-courage similar behavior. They quoted the familiar biblical passage from the Book of Genesis—"whoever sheds man's blood, so shall his blood be shed." Opponents countered that Maine residents were not bound to the ancient tenants of the Old Testament, but observed the Christian principles of for-giveness, love, and mercy. If the public spectacle was a deterrent to crime, they pointed out, then why had there been four new murders in Maine during the months following Sager's hanging?

Unable to ban executions outright, abolitionists managed to chip away at the process. In 1837, Maine passed a law requiring a one-year grace period between the final sentencing and execution of the condemned criminal. Capital prisoners were required to reside in solitary confinement at the state prison and work at hard labor. After a year, the governor was required to review the prisoner's case and sign a death warrant. Most Maine governors balked at this added step, not wanting to act in a judicial capacity, especially with public sentiment running against hanging.

One governor did sign off on the execution of Valorous P. Coolidge, a Maine doctor who killed a man who owed him money, but Coolidge managed to commit suicide in his cell before he could be hanged. Two sailors, Abraham Cox and Peter Williams, were hanged publicly for murder and piracy in Auburn, Maine, in 1858. Theirs was a federal case, however, and did not impact Maine's thirty-year record as a state soft on capital punishment. But there was no leniency for Francis Couillard Spencer. While serving a five-year sentence for assault, Spencer inexplicably stabbed the Thomaston warden in the neck, puncturing his carotid artery. Spencer was hanged in the prison yard in 1864 on the exact spot where he had killed the warden.

By 1867, under Maine's post-war governor Joshua Chamberlain, one of the ten men then living on death row at Thomaston had been there for twenty years. A hero of the Battle of Gettysburg, Governor Chamberlain suggested the legislature either abolish the death penalty once and for all or repair the current law that he considered unconstitutional because it effectively made the governor the hangman.

And yet, Chamberlain himself signed off on one execution—a controversial one. Clifton Harris was convicted of killing two women in the town of West Auburn. The two women were white and Harris was black. Maine was then, and according to the most recent US Census, still remains, the "whitest" state in the nation. The newspapers clearly saw racial prejudice at work here. Harris's partner in the crime, and likely the real killer of the two women, was white, and yet he was freed on appeal. And while Gov. Chamberlin commuted the sentences of three other white inmates, he issued a death warrant for Harris, who was executed in 1869 as soon as his one-year mandated waiting period was over.

The son of African American parents who had been kidnapped, sold, tortured, and enslaved, Clifton Harris was hanged behind prison walls at Thomaston. Only fifty witnesses were present. The *Weekly Kennebec Journal* described the scene for its readers, and for history, in horrific detail. As Harris dropped through the trapdoor of the gallows, "the hands commenced to twitch convulsively and there was an effort [by Harris] to pull them from the cords which bound them. The knees were drawn up and the body spun around and around. It was evident that the man was dying of strangulation. The struggle continued some two minutes with the exception of an occasional mighty effort of the chest. The body hung there for twenty-five minutes."

The inhumanity of this method of killing prisoners could not be denied. The debate over capital punishment heated up once again. The state of Maine was losing its taste for blood revenge and no condemned man would be hanged at Thomaston State Prison until 1875, when Louis Wagner and John True Gordon mounted the wooden stairs of the scaffold. Wagner, some still believed, was an innocent man. Gordon, already half dead from a self-inflicted wound, had to be carried the last few steps and positioned over the trapdoor. The scene that followed came very close to ending capital punishment in Maine forever.

Chapter 31

THE ESCAPE ARTIST

But before the state of Maine could hang Wagner, they had to catch him. From his arrival at Alfred, he had been studying his new escape-proof facility and conditioning his captors. He sometimes hid in the darkness of his tiny cell, then burst out laughing when the guards appeared with the worried warden in tow. The man who had bragged to his fellow fishermen about robbery at the Shoals now boasted to the watchmen that he could break out of the secure, new, thirty-thousand-dollar jail any time he pleased.

His disappearance from the secure facility on Wednesday, June 25, was doubly embarrassing because the week before, while his trial was still in progress, Wagner had shocked the prison guards with a demonstration of his jail-breaking skills. On the eighth day of the trial, following Rufus Tapley's passionate closing argument, Wagner was escorted back to the new Alfred jail.

"You think you have me here all safe and sound," he taunted Deputies Durgin and Stillings from behind the bars of his cell, "but I have no desire to escape, for if I desired to do so, I could go out any time." The guards were amused, but he had tricked them once too often. "Even if I were convicted," Wagner continued, "I would not attempt to break jail, for if the people want my life, let them take it here in Alfred."

With the trial ending and the verdict imminent, Wagner probably wanted to appear innocent and cooperative. The deputies, according to the *Chronicle*, laughed and told Wagner they were sure the new jail built of stone, cement, steel, and brick could certainly hold him.

"Well you just step around the corner and I will meet you there in two minutes," Wagner told his jailers. The officers humored their prisoner and moved from the row of cells to a nearby passageway. "Wagner, in just about one minute, came out of his cell and around into the alley where they were standing!" the sheriff reported to an astonished press.

The story of the prisoner's non-escape hit the newspapers the next day as attorney Plaisted was wrapping up the prosecution's case. Clearly, Officer Durgin had to admit, Wagner could have gotten out at any time during his two-month stay at Alfred. The clever prisoner had figured out how to snap open the heavy metal lock on his cell from the inside within seconds. Since all the mechanical locks operated on the same principle, he could pick any lock in the prison "with a rye straw," Durgin reported. Rye straw was often used as mattress stuffing. The thin, sturdy stalk, the part left over when the edible rye seeds were removed, made good, cheap bedding because it was unpalatable to mice. Rye was a popular crop in Wagner's homeland of Prussia where the straw was used to weave hats.

For a week after he was found guilty, Wagner waited to learn his fate. He also used the time to refine his escape plan and enlist two confederates. He knew that, if given the death penalty, he would soon be transferred to the larger, more crowded state penitentiary at Thomaston to wait out the obligatory year before hanging. So on the very night his sentence was issued, he told the guards he was feeling ill and went to bed early.

Luck was on his side. The two night watchmen hired exclusively to guard Wagner were new to the job. Their shift began at nine p.m. and half an hour later they checked his cell. The infamous Smuttynose murderer was sleeping beneath a blanket on his cot—or so they thought. Wagner had fashioned a dummy dressed in his clothes from a broom and a stool and was hiding just out of sight.

"He is all quiet," one of the watchmen said.

"Not much, my friends," Wagner thought to himself as he hunkered in the dark corner of his cell. He revealed his inner thoughts in a later post-capture interview. Now he listened as the guards walked about twenty feet to the door of the jailhouse office. They unlocked their office and stepped inside. Using his rye straw or a stick fashioned from a wooden toothbrush, Wagner expertly picked the lock to his cell and stepped free.

He climbed onto the metal railing outside his door and pulled himself up to the next tier of cells above him. At this point, he probably collected inmates William McCarley and Charles Harrington. The three men managed to hoist themselves up through a metal "scuttle," a small hatch that led to the rooftop ventilation shaft. Wagner was apparently the last man up because he later said he could hear the watchmen coming as he squeezed through the tight hatch. Tall and muscular, he managed to wriggle through the scuttle and close it softly without notice. He lit a match and gazed around. The ventilator shaft was nearby and the men easily drew themselves up and onto the jailhouse roof.

It was a well-planned operation. Initially, the prisoners intended to lower themselves from the roof to the ground. They brought along a 150-foot length of rope handmade from four-inch-wide strips of prison blankets. But the long drop in the darkness was likely deemed too risky. They made their way, instead, to a skylight on the jailer's side of the building. The convicts moved very slowly because the tin roof made a loud noise with each step. After breaking a pane of glass, they unfastened the hasp inside the skylight and opened it. They climbed down the handmade rope into the attic on the other side of the prison, which contained the quarters for guards and the warden's office.

Once in the attic, Wagner lit another match and the trio stepped silently down the stairway and past the barracks of snoring daytime jailers. A heavy metal hatch built into the wall of the top floor office allowed the warden to peer into the three-tiers of cells below. The metal hatch can still be seen in the building today. Wagner later said he considered opening the hatch to bid the night watchmen farewell but thought better of it. The convicts slipped down the stairway to the prison pantry where they enjoyed a farewell feast and packed some supplies. Although legend says the three men strode boldly out the front door of the jail, according to Wagner, they escaped out the back way. The three men exited through the kitchen door and hurried on foot to follow the railroad tracks, passing by the Alfred courthouse on their way out of town.

When the watchmen made their rounds at three a.m., one of the guards, noticing Wagner had not changed position said, "It seems to me that man on the bed is lying very still." On closer examination, they discovered the broomstick dummy, but amazingly, they did not raise an alarm. Based on Wagner's previous breakout and his promise never to escape, the guards apparently thought he was still hiding somewhere inside the building, ready to pop out at any moment. The sheriff was out of town that night and no formal search for the missing prisoners was initiated until after eight o'clock that morning.

"A large force are scouring the surrounding country in pursuit," the local daily confirmed. But the early edition newspaper jumped to the conclusion that Wagner and his confederates had somehow cut their way through the iron bars of their cells and chopped their way into the pantry before departing.

"The report of Wagner's escape at Alfred caused much excitement and no little indignation" according to the *Portsmouth Evening Times* that, at first, blamed the incident on the "apparent imbecility and inefficiency" of the officers in charge. There was wild speculation that Wagner would head inland to Canada, or that, as a fisherman and sailor, "he would strike out to the sea." Residents of the Isles of Shoals offered "ridiculous speculations" Wagner would return there to murder Maren Hontvet and all those who had testified against him, the *Times* added. The Hontvets, of course, had by this time abandoned the Shoals for Portsmouth, where many fearful citizens suffered sleepless nights.

The announcement that a convicted ax murderer was on the loose could not have come at a worse time. The coming Fourth of July holiday was the kick-off to the lucrative summer tourist season along the Atlantic coast. John R. Poor, the wealthy Spice King of Boston, was only days away from opening his grand Oceanic Hotel on Star Island. The Appledore Hotel, where the brokenhearted Ivan Christensen now worked as a carpenter for Celia Thaxter, had already launched its twenty-fifth season.

Portsmouth, meanwhile, was gearing up for the biggest celebration in the city's history. The year 1873 marked the 250th anniversary of the arrival of the first English fisherman to the New Hampshire shores. A rousing publicity campaign was in progress to attract thousands of visitors to a thrilling homecoming event. Every entrance to the city was decorated with enormous wooden arches festooned with greenery and flowers and ready to welcome back the prodigal "sons and daughters" of Portsmouth. And now, as the *Chronicle* implied, a "cool villain" was at large. "Wagner possesses plausibility," the newspaper warned. "He is handsome, broad shouldered, and strong...Wagner is nothing if not sensational."

The enigmatic Prussian was headline news again. Over the next three days, as the killer remained at large, the story was telegraphed across the nation. But as the local reporters dug into the facts, the emphasis shifted. The "scandalous and disgraceful incompetency" was now laid at the door of York County Sherriff Bennett, who had been out of town on the night of the prison break.

The former jailer at Saco, Bennett seemed unconcerned with the crisis and was certain the escapees would soon be recaptured. The scandal expanded when Portland reporters discovered Bennett had spent the night running a private sting operation at nearby Biddeford. Bennett had hired an underage boy to purchase bottles of rum from six stores. Each "bust" earned the sheriff a $25 reward, and he had submitted a bill for $150 to the mayor of Biddeford. Worse yet, the sheriff then went on a nighttime frolic at Old Orchard Beach, the hot new tourist attraction. Bennett reportedly fell out of a carriage during his pleasure trip and broke his hip. He would be laid up recuperating in bed for the next few weeks.

The newspapers had a field day with Bennett, who apparently had taken Wagner at his word that he would not escape from the Alfred jail. Mr. Rice, the warden at Thomaston State Prison, lambasted his colleague in the press. Rice had warned Bennett "he would not keep Wagner a week unless he had him guarded more securely." Rather than keeping murderers off the streets, Rice said, Bennett apparently "has more important things, like keeping people from selling liquor." Rice visited Alfred after the escape and found the jail awash with infractions. A reporter from the *New York Times* also investigated the new facility and was amazed to learn that, due to a mechanical error, none of the locks in the three-tiered cells had been correctly installed. Prisoners roamed around the jail at their leisure.

"As I approached the building, prisoners could be heard laughing and singing inside," the New York investigator wrote. "I entered, and a dozen prisoners flocked about me. They are all at perfect liberty to roam about the corridors. They have no handcuffs and, seemingly, no restraint."

In the flaming light of Bennett's incompetence, Wagner's brilliant escape dimmed. "It was not a particularly sharp or shrewd piece of work on the part of Wagner," the *Portsmouth Times* commented. "Any clumsy lout could have walked out of the jail."

It was rumored that Alfred officials had allowed Wagner to wander off and did not want to see him caught. One New York scandal sheet invented the story that Wagner's guards had seen him sneaking out of his cell, but they were "frightened and offered no resistance." The same paper suggested Wagner's escape was "preconcocted" by the Alfred jailers and that Sherriff Bennett did not want to see Wagner hanged. "Was it a put up job?" the daily newspaper wondered.

These wild tales mingled with honest reporting as Wagner and his companions wandered the countryside. The slow response from Alfred, which had given the prisoners a twelve-hour head start, was grist for the rumor mill. It was fully thirty-six hours after the jailbreak that York County authorities finally got around to notifying Marshals Johnson and Entwistle of the Portsmouth police that their infamous inmate was missing.

A photograph of Wagner was circulated on a postcard with a five-hundred-dollar reward for his capture. Wagner was credited with stealing a boat in the port town of Kennebunk, Maine. He was known to have robbed a house in East Rochester, New Hampshire. One newspaper speculated he was en route, not to Canada, but to New York City, where he expected to clear his name and be set free.

The rumor mill ground to a halt early on the afternoon of Saturday, June 28, when a starving and disheveled stranger with a German accent knocked on the door of the Tanner family home in Farmington, New Hampshire. The stranger was "footsore and weary." He asked for directions to Canada, nearly three hundred miles away, and begged for food. While the stranger was eating his meal, Mr. Tanner rounded up a few neighbors to assist him in capturing what was obviously the escaped killer from Alfred. By the time Tanner returned home, Wagner had finished his meal and was back on the road. The men followed and he was taken with little resistance.

"I only went away to exercise my limbs," Wagner later told reporters from his jail cell in Farmington. "I did not know as I could use them after being confined so long, and had trouble in doing so."

In little more than three days, he had covered forty-five miles. His rambling explanation, part fantasy and part fact, was eagerly transcribed by the press. It offers one more glimpse inside the inscrutable mind of the Smuttynose murderer.

"I also wanted to see the pretty girls whom I flirted with at the trial," he said. "I like pretty girls. They like me. I did not see many. I should have come back Tuesday or Wednesday and got in the same as I got out. I was tired and wanted a little vacation. I am satisfied for the present. People don't think I am a murderer. If they did, they would not treat me so kindly. They know I am innocent."

Chapter 32

DEAD MAN TALKING

Wagner's not-so-thrilling getaway left observers scratching their heads. By his account, the three escapees had merely wandered aimlessly in the wilderness. Whatever they stole from the prison pantry was quickly consumed and they survived only on berries and plums foraged along the way. Wagner said he attempted to milk a cow into his hat, "but she would not stand." Deathly afraid of wild animals in the woods, he tried to sleep in the road at night and was nearly run over by a team of horses. The convicts walked into Rochester village in New Hampshire and spoke openly to people as they passed. How could the same man who had engineered the escape from Alfred jail be so clueless? The only conclusion, according to a Portland newspaper, was that Wagner was nothing more than "an idiot."

After intensely studying the Smuttynose case, crime writer Edmund Pearson rejected all rumors of Wagner's innocence. For Pearson, Wagner was part child, part beast. Although he craved male attention and female sympathy, Wagner was ultimately a loner who trusted no one and envied everyone. He was a man both frightened and frightening. "It must be remembered that although he could be sly, and at times seem almost clever," Pearson concluded in *Murder at Smutty Nose*, "he was really stupid, dull, brutal."

The pattern of Wagner's jailbreak bears an uncanny resemblance to his escape from Smuttynose. Just as he boasted to other fishermen that he knew where to get money at the Shoals, the prisoner boasted to the Alfred jailers that he could escape—but would not do so. Again he paused to eat a meal before leaving the scene. His actions at Smuttynose and Alfred were carefully plotted, daring, and required great physical strength. But when it came to escape, he was lost, weak, and dependent. He became suddenly helpless and needy. At first, after leaving Alfred, he traveled with fellow prisoners Harrington and McCarley. But there was a disagreement along the way and, when he woke up in the woods on Saturday morning, the two other men were gone. They had separated themselves from the murderer with the five-hundred-dollar bounty on his head.

One Maine historian has suggested that during his escape, Wagner bumped into a traveling peddler and Adventist elder named Elisha Johnson, who immediately recognized the prisoner. "I am innocent. I swear it!" Wagner told Elder Johnson and begged the old man with the long white beard not to turn him in. "If you are innocent, go back and give yourself up," Elder Johnson said. "God will protect you."

Instead, cast off and alone, Wagner resorted to the same behavior he had exhibited at the Isles of Shoals, in Portsmouth, and in Boston. Instead of keeping low and avoiding capture, he sought out a friendly face, knocked on the door, and begged for food.

In the North End of Boston, Wagner had given in to the police without even asking the reason for his arrest. In Farmington, Mr. Tanner and his three friends easily caught up with Wagner, who was resting on a large rock by the side of the road. They asked if he had escaped from Alfred jail. Wagner denied he was the missing convict. One of the men raised a pole and threatened to hit him, Wagner later reported.

"Don't you strike me," Wagner warned them. "If you do, you'll be sorry." By Wagner's exaggerated account, by this time twenty-five farmers surrounded him. "They were all frightened. They were all scared. I made no resistance," Wagner told reporters.

Newspaper accounts contradict Wagner's version and list only the four men in pursuit, including Mr. Cheney, Tanner's nearest neighbor. *Foster's,* a local daily that still covers news in the Farmington region, originally reported Wagner was wielding the stick. An updated report admitted that Mr. Tanner did shout "Kill him! Kill him!" as the posse approached Wagner on the road. Wagner told the men he would sit and wait passively for the local deputy to arrive. Then suddenly he began to "manifest some ugliness and a disposition to fight." Mr. Cheney took hold of Wagner first and the four men escorted him back to Tanner's house to wait for the village authorities. There, Wagner revealed his true identity and talked at great length about his adventures. He said he wanted to go back to Alfred and live out his final year, during which time he hoped some evidence would appear to prove he was innocent of the murders.

Deputy A. J. Scruton of Farmington picked up Wagner at Tanner's farm. An enterprising photographer snapped a picture of the two men sitting in a buckboard in Farmington. The photo was quickly issued as a souvenir card for popular Victorian stereoscopic viewers. As the newspaper reported, Wagner's hands are shackled in the picture and he looks understandably disheveled and discouraged. He had botched his second bid for freedom.

Once again, Wagner's mere presence disturbed the peace of a town. After serving his prisoner a hearty meal at Farmington village, Deputy Scruton locked Wagner inside a small wooden building and hired a man named Stephen Roberts to guard the prisoner. The next day was Sunday and curious townsfolk were buzzing with the big news of the captured ax murderer and rushing to the site. They peered in through the windows and the cracks in the door of Wagner's makeshift prison. Roberts continually ordered the crowd to move away but they soon swarmed back. During one such maneuver, a young spectator named James Nash stumbled and fell. The overzealous Roberts arrested Nash, cursed him out, and locked him in another "hot dead-air dungeon" for the next fourteen hours. At least sixty Farmington citizens signed a petition against Roberts who was then sued by Nash for "malicious imprisonment."

To Victorians, an attempted escape was tantamount to a confession of guilt. And again, the more the prisoner talked, the less sense he seemed to make. During his twenty-four-hour stay at Farmington, according to *Foster's*, "Wagner talked more or less incoherently, partly rational and partly demented." He appeared to the reporter like "a man broken down in mind, and if not insane now, bids fair to become a lunatic not long hence. This may be all feigned or it may not."

Among the spectators was an impressionable Farmington girl who heard Wagner's tale of woe and believed every word the handsome prisoner spoke. She listened with rapt attention as he explained how Maren Hontvet had killed her own sister and framed him for the deed. Half a century later, that woman would swear she had heard the truth from Wagner's own lips.

The press and the public, however, were growing weary of Wagner's antics and his lies. Even the editor of the formerly supportive *Portsmouth Times*, commenting on the Farmington arrest, wrote: "Now we have inflicted upon us another string of stories about Wagner...Let's hear more about the farmer [Mr. Tanner] and let Louis Wagner go serve his sentence, because we have heard enough about him."

On Monday, July 2, Deputy Scruton drove his prisoner to Rochester, where they proceeded by train to Saco, where "the locks cannot be picked with a stick." Wagner bid farewell to Deputy Scruton by announcing he would return and pay Farmington another visit in a few weeks. "He is evidently a strange bird," *Foster's* noted, "and whether he will now be kept caged is a question."

Wagner held another press conference in Saco, waxing on with what one Boston paper called "petty talk." Referring to his jailer at Alfred, Wagner said, "I like Bennett, he has treated me well...If Mr. Bennett would let me go out for an hour a day I would like it. I would not run away. I did not wish to."

But Sherriff Bennett was greatly chastened by the embarrassing escape and his own suspicious activities at Old Orchard Beach. Mistakes had been made. As hordes of Fourth of July tourists headed to the hotels and beaches that dotted the Atlantic coast, the Alfred jailers insisted they were sparing no expense to "Wagner-proof" Maine's newest prison. Fireplaces were being screened off. Wire netting was being installed over all open windows.

Fishing nets would now cover all hatches and ventilators wide enough for a man to fit through. And, of course, all the faulty locks had been sent off to the supplier in Boston for repair or replacement.

While waiting in Saco jail, Wagner confessed he and his two henchman had robbed a house in East Rochester, a village known locally as Gonic, New Hampshire. They made off with a small wooden trunk containing three thousand dollars in government bonds. The occupants of the house chased after the three thieves, who dropped the trunk and fled. Wagner was still in Saco when a scuffle arose in Farmington over who would collect the five-hundred-dollar reward for capturing him. Deputy Scruton offered to split the money five ways with the other captors, each to receive one hundred dollars. Mr. Tanner, however, insisted he was owed the entire amount. Wagner, incredibly, told reporters that Tanner had promised to give him the reward for his own capture so that the prisoner could finally pay his lawyers. "But I think they fool me," Wagner added. Again, he saw himself as the victim.

By August 2, after several weeks in the back-up jail at Saco, Wagner was quietly returned to the newly reinforced Alfred facility. His move rated only a single sentence in the *Portsmouth Journal*. Resettled this time at the upper corridor of the prison, Louis Wagner all but disappeared from the headlines during the busy tourist season. A rumor circulated he had escaped from Alfred a second time and voluntarily returned to his cell without being noticed. "We don't believe the story," the *Journal* noted, but they did not hesitate to pass it along.

On the Isles of Shoals, Wagner was not forgotten. Although deserted by its former Norwegian residents, Smuttynose was populated almost daily by "lovers of the horrible." A brief notice in the local newspapers offers ghoulish proof: "The old house on Smuttynose Island, Isles of Shoals, in which the Wagner murder was committed is rapidly being cut to pieces by relic hunters. The bedroom where there were so many spots of blood is completely honey-combed, and the woodwork around the window through which Mrs. Hontvet escaped has been entirely removed."

With Smuttynose now a household word, a banking firm tendered an offer of fifty thousand dollars to the Laighton brothers for the purchase of the infamous island. Oscar and Cedric turned the offer down.

In a continuing effort to keep his client alive, attorney Rufus Tapley had filed a complex series of exceptions at the close of the trial in June. Tapley argued that Judge Barrows had wronged the defendant on several occasions during the proceedings at Alfred. Barrows responded in great depth to Tapley's objections at the end of September. As the date of the Supreme Court decision approached, a writer from the *Portsmouth Journal* visited Wagner, who openly discussed his case with anyone who would listen.

"Wagner's latest dodge is to blame poor Mrs. Hontvet of the murders," the *Journal* writer said. These accusations, made by the killer from his prison cell, are the origin of the surviving conspiracy theory that claims Maren murdered her sister and sister-in-law. They are the seeds of what would become a bestselling novel and Hollywood film. Wagner also swore that John Hontvet had spent five hundred dollars paying off witnesses to testify against him. "What a precious villain," the *Journal* exclaimed. "The stories that he is looking very thin and is failing in health [are] untrue," the *Journal* added. "He never looked better, and is in fine spirits."

Thanks to the thorny issue of jurisdiction, the Smuttynose case had already become "a capital trial of unusual interest," according to one New York law journal. Tapley had argued that, because the crime had occurred in an "unincorporated" place, then the jurors and the judge in the County of York had no legal authority to find Wagner guilty or to sentence him to death. But Judge Barrows put the matter permanently to rest. While it was true there had been a brief scuffle over ownership of the Isles of Shoals in the late 1600s, Barrows agreed, that was old news. Prosecutors Yeaton and Plaisted had proven conclusively that Smuttynose had long been part of York County, while the defense team had not proven otherwise. To prevent future confusion, the court made it clear that all parts of Maine "are included within the body of one or another of the counties into which the state is divided." There was no question as to "the precise spot on the face of the earth" where the murders occurred, Barrows wrote. Wagner had not killed the women in a place where no laws applied.

The defense also failed to quash Anethe's cries of "Louis! Louis!" as mere hearsay. Her screams, as reported by her surviving sister-in-law, were considered a "dying declaration." Whether she was right or wrong, Anethe had believed she was being attacked by Louis Wagner, and her final words were admissible as evidence. Despite Tapley's efforts, the contents of Wagner's pockets, his clothes, the pencil, and the bloody shirt were all accepted into evidence. "We found no good case for a new trial," the court concluded, and all the prisoner's exceptions were overruled. The death sentence would stand. Unless the governor stepped in, the prisoner was condemned to die.

Tapley's legal maneuvers had failed, but he would not give up. He had managed to buy his client three additional months of life. On September 24, Wagner was taken into the custody of Warden Rice and transferred about one hundred miles north from Alfred to the State Prison in Thomaston, Maine. But hardly anyone noticed. Five days earlier, in what the papers dubbed "Black Friday," a major American bank, heavily overinvested in the burgeoning railroad industry, suddenly closed its doors. The ripple effect caused thousands of businesses to go bankrupt and millions of workers lost their jobs. The Panic of 1873 kicked off a depression that would linger until the end of the decade.

More bad news followed for Wagner. Maine governor Sidney Perham held all the cards. He could pardon the Smuttynose murderer, commute his sentence, or move forward with the execution. After consulting his governor's council, Perham scheduled the prisoner's hanging for January 29, 1875. Perham, in his final months in office, had kicked the ultimate decision to his successor. The prisoner's fate was soon in the hands of Nelson Dingley Jr., a Harvard graduate and former journalist, who became the next governor of Maine.

At Thomaston Prison, Louis Wagner sank into near obscurity for much of the coming year, abandoned by everyone except his loyal attorney Mr. Tapley, who soldiered on with his client's defense. In mid-November 1873, as the Smuttynose killer was settling into his new surroundings, another Maine ax murderer took center stage. So many spectators thronged to the compact brick courthouse at Belfast, Maine, that the trial of John True Gordon had to be moved to a larger building.

Gordon was accused of hacking to death his brother, his sister-in-law, and their seventeen-month-old daughter as they slept in the family bed in rural Thorndike, Maine. Gordon then poured kerosene on the bodies and set fire to the farmhouse to cover up the murders. Although Gordon swore he was innocent, his bloodied six-year-old nephew, Ira, who had been sleeping in a crib nearby, survived the massacre. Questioned by police, the little boy said, "Uncle John hit me with an ax. He struck papa too, and mamma." On January 20, 1874, John T. Gordon was sentenced to be "hanged by the neck until you are dead," and soon joined Wagner on death row at Thomaston. The two would share the gallows in an unforgettable exit.

Chapter 33

JOHN TRUE GORDON

The two ax murder cases were hauntingly similar. Both Louis Wagner and John True Gordon were twenty-eight years old when afflicted by what the newspapers called "homicidal mania." Both men knew their victims well, lived among them, and had intimate knowledge of the scene of the crime. Both men were large, muscular, and powerful, but considered lazy and shiftless by those who knew them. Both attacked their helpless victims as they slept in the darkness of early morning. Both were undone by a single surviving witness. And both appear to have had deep emotional connections to their mothers.

From the earliest reports, John True Gordon was named as the only likely suspect. He was angry and jealous of his younger brother, Almon, age twenty-six, who had been working the family farm for six years. John had assumed he would inherit the entire two-story home and farm from his elderly parents, but his father had recently decided to give half of the property to Almon, since the younger son was married, industrious, and had two children to feed. Worse yet, Almon's wife, Emma, just twenty-three years old, had secretly written to John Gordon's fiancé, warning her of John's defective character. Gordon had discovered the letters, adding revenge to his motive.

Just hours before the tragedy, John Gordon had complained to friends that his brother was a "damned whelp" and that "Almon's life or mine is short in this world." When the fire was discovered, Gordon made no attempt to rescue his brother's family from the burning bedroom. Instead he told one witness they were "all burned up" and to another he exclaimed "damn 'em, let 'em burn." As townspeople rushed in to help, Gordon turned his attention to removing furniture from the house. One neighbor heroically put out the flames and then dragged the charred corpses into the yard. Only then was the real horror revealed.

"The lower limbs of the dead were burned to a crisp, yet the wounded heads were scarcely singed," an eye witness reported at the trial. The ax, covered in blood and hair, was found lying across the threshold of the bedroom door. An empty bottle of kerosene lay nearby. Gordon's only outburst on seeing his brother's family bludgeoned and burned was, "What will my poor mother say?"

While Wagner, the mysterious foreigner, had charmed many with his handsome Arian looks and unctuous ways, Gordon was the local bad boy with a longstanding reputation as a thief and a thug. With his high forehead, square jaw, and small close-set eyes, Gordon more closely matched the Victorian image of a criminal. Even before his trial, Gordon was examined in his cell by an amateur phrenologist who measured the shape and size of the prisoner's head. Phrenology was a popular pseudoscience, heavy with racist and sexist overtones that proposed to define a person's character, thoughts, intelligence, morality, and emotions by mapping the size and shape of the human skull. The "expert" felt the bumps and depressions of the prisoner's skull in thirty-five key areas supposedly related to human traits.

Gordon's head, according to the *Phrenological Journal* of 1873, was twenty-two inches in circumference with a fifteen-and-a-half-inch neck. His physiognomy was "decidedly repulsive," with the enlarged animal portion of his brain above the ears tending toward destructive behavior, jealousy, and revenge. Gordon possessed "the head of a natural tyrant." A student of phrenology who examined Wagner's shapely head after his death, by contrast, concluded in the same journal the state had executed an innocent man.

"All that have known [Gordon] were impressed with his brutality," the *Kennebec Journal* reported soon after the Thorndike murders, "and considered him malicious and malignant enough for any foul deed which could be done in the dark without facing an opponent." Gordon told the press he was only stopping by the family farm that night because he was on his way to find work in Massachusetts. He was quickly arrested. There was not "a shadow of a doubt" in town he was the killer, and if not for their respect for the law, the citizens of Thorndike might have "torn him limb from limb or hung him to the nearest tree," the Kennebec newspaper stated.

Gordon's trial also mirrored Wagner's. Attorney General Harris M. Plaisted was again the lead prosecutor. He delivered another hailstorm of circumstantial evidence, calling more than fifty witnesses. Gordon's trial took place over eight days, compared to Wagner's nine. Although public opinion was not in his favor, the Thorndike Killer still managed to pack the courthouse gallery with female spectators. Gordon testified on his own behalf but was in the witness chair for only two hours, not two days like Wagner. He claimed the police and witnesses, including his six-year-old nephew, had conspired against him and he had no animosity toward his brother, Almon. His blood-stained clothes were introduced as evidence, the result of a bloody nose, the defendant claimed.

Gordon had been sleeping in another part of the house on the night of the murders, so there was no room for an elaborate alibi. Instead, he produced a lengthy handwritten letter found on the floor of the local jail after his arrest. The letter was signed by Charles Green, who confessed he was the killer. Gordon said he saw Mr. Green on the night of the murder, but the mysterious man was seen by no one else and never reappeared. The letter was generally assumed to be a hoax, written by Gordon or one of his friends. While Wagner's jury took only fifty-five minutes to reach a verdict, the twelve men from Belfast deliberated a full seventy minutes before declaring Gordon guilty of murder in the first degree and shipping him off to the Maine State Prison.

Like so many towns near the Atlantic coast, Thomaston, Maine, claims to be among the earliest sites where European explorers came ashore. A memorial cross at the town landing marks the imagined spot where Captain Weymouth anchored his ship ten miles up the St. Georges River in 1605. Once a key shipbuilding center, Thomaston became synonymous with the Maine State Prison, which dominated the village center along the Route 1 tourist highway heading north to Camden, Rockport, and other scenic vacation points. Thomaston was the inspiration for a fictional state prison in *The Shawshank Redemption*, a film based on the novella by Maine author Stephen King. The site of the prison today, however, is a flat ten-acre field awaiting development. After 178 years in operation, the buildings were razed in 2002 and the prisoners moved surreptitiously in the night by bus to a modern and often controversial new "Supermax" facility in the neighboring town of Warren. The seventy-six-million-dollar super-maximum security state prison can accommodate more than nine hundred inmates with a staff of roughly four hundred men and women.

Thomaston prison was established in 1823, soon after Maine became a state. The original prison was primitive by comparison and terrible by design. Its purpose, an early report stated, was to punish lawbreakers, not to reform them. Its earliest cells were "dark and comfortless abodes of guilt and wretchedness." The chosen site, not surprisingly, was owned by the first governor of Maine, who sold his property to the state for three thousand dollars. The ten-acre package included a limestone quarry that was no longer commercially profitable, but was ideal for criminals condemned to hard labor. Prisoners worked long days at the quarry, then were lowered into deep holes in the ground. Inmates in the fifty-six underground cells were given only a hammock, a box to sit on, and a copy of the New Testament they could read during fading daylight hours. One of the first prisoners was a thirteen-year-old boy. A model on display at the Thomaston Historical Society shows the grim below-ground accommodations in those harsh days.

Despite Wagner's initial fear of Thomaston and his hatred of Warden Rice, by 1873 the state prison turned out to be a kinder, gentler place than its reputation implied. New buildings with tiered cells like those at Alfred had long replaced the subterranean jail. Besides laboring in the quarry, prisoners raised their own food and acted as their own cooks, tailors, and shoemakers. Convicts built wagons, buckboards, wheelbarrows, sleighs, and buggies. Selling the objects made by prisoners reduced operational costs to a minimum and, during the Civil War, the prison even made a profit. Although the facility has moved to another town, the Maine State Prison Showroom in Thomaston still sells novelties, furniture, gifts, and crafts made by inmates.

The two ax murderers became model prisoners and made no attempt to escape as 1874 ticked by. Wagner worked in the harness shop and Gordon chose the blacksmith shop. Wagner reportedly remained upbeat and clutched his bible like a good luck charm, endlessly proclaiming that God would not kill an innocent man. Over time, he managed to charm a number of prison guards and even to attract the sympathy of Warden Rice.

How connected the two condemned men became, whether they shared stories or believed in one another's claims of innocence, we will never know. The walls surrounding Thomaston prison are gone and most of its secrets have been lost. With Thorndike, Maine, only forty miles away, Gordon's mother likely visited him. The two remained close. Lucilla Gordon was sixty-eight at the time of the murders. She sat in the chair beside her son, John, throughout his trial while his elder father is not mentioned in the press reports. The Maine newspapers noted that Mrs. Gordon had previously "come to his rescue" when young John Gordon was in trouble, intervened when he was caught stealing, and had "saved him from the measure of penalty which the law would have meted out." At trial, she testified her two boys had gotten along favorably, unable to accept one had killed the other.

Upon arriving at Thomaston, Wagner also reached out to his mother half a world away. He wrote her a letter in his native language and, after translating it, his jailers mailed it off to Prussia. A summary of its contents appeared in the *New York Times* and in newspapers nationally. Wagner's language, once again, was both confessional and guarded. The *Times* summarized the letter this way:

"He expressed the deepest sorrow that in leaving Prussia he did not leave his bad habits behind—that in exchanging countries he did not exchange his vices for virtues. He says he is filled with sorrow that his excesses and vices should lead people to suspect him of the great crime with which he had been charged; that he did not murder the women; and that if he had wanted their money he would have obtained it in a much easier way than that. He adds that, although the thought of death on the gallows is painful, yet it is preferable to a lingering lonesome life within prison walls. His letter closes with the hope that he shall meet his mother in a better world than this."

By late November 1874, with his execution set for the coming January, the *Portsmouth Journal* reported from Maine that Wagner "awaits calmly his fate." While finally accepting the end was near, according to the report, "he thinks that after he is gone the Almighty will cause the guilty individual to come forth from his hiding place and confess the dark deed."

Then in mid-January, with the execution looming, the Maine House of Representative voted 90 to 20 to ask Governor Nelson Dingley to grant Wagner a brief reprieve until March 26. Attorney Rufus Tapley had once again bought Wagner some time. He successfully argued the previous governor, whose term expired in 1873, did not have the legal right to schedule an execution in 1875. That task was up to the sitting governor.

Reform was in the air. A bill to abolish capital punishment in the state of Maine was again on the docket. If Tapley could stall long enough, the law might change in his client's favor. But the bill went down in flames in February 1875. Maine would not abolish the death penalty until 1876. Still, Wagner's reprieve convinced some, as the Portsmouth lynch mob had feared, that the man who slaughtered two innocent women would never meet the hangman in Maine. He might, instead, join the growing list of men who had long survived on Thomaston's death row.

At the Isles of Shoals, frustrated by Wagner's longevity, his continued attacks on Maren Hontvet, and rumors of his innocence, Celia Thaxter was finishing her powerful essay "A Memorable Murder." The newspaper accounts, she told her literary friends, James and Annie Fields, had revealed the "sickening details" but had not captured the pathos of the crime or the personality of the two Norwegian victims.

But the *Atlantic Monthly* did not publish true crime stories in 1875, especially works by women. Celia was breaking new ground and, before she turned the piece in to editor William Dean Howells, she wanted feedback. In March, Celia wrote to Annie Fields: "I am only waiting for Wagner to be hung or not (next Friday is the day appointed for his execution) to rush to your threshold with my manuscript and read it to you [and James] that you may tell me if I offend against good taste or the proprieties of existence. For it is a delicate subject to handle, so notorious, so ghastly and dreadful." Celia was right. Her story offended many *Atlantic* readers when it appeared. Twenty years after its publication, abolitionist Frank Preston Stearns still found it necessary to criticize Celia's essay as "a peculiar subject for a cultivated person to fasten on." Yet it remains, arguably, her greatest work.

John True Gordon, observers noted, grew listless and depressed in early March as workers began assembling the wooden scaffold inside the prison walls. Gordon was "extremely restless," the Maine papers said. He could not sleep and had "a bad sensation in his head." Fearing the worst, Gordon selected a passage from the New Testament to be used as the epitaph on his tombstone. He chose: "Come unto me, all ye that labor and are heavy laden, and I will give you rest" (Matthew 11:28). And he selected a popular Protestant hymn for his burial service that begins, "Jesus, Lover of my Soul, let me to thy bosom fly."

Wagner, by contrast, "never lost his cheerfulness." And despite his pious proclamations, he showed no interest in planning his epitaph or funeral hymns. He was pacing and puffing on his pipe, wrote the *Portland Press*, when the local sheriff entered his cell about two weeks before the scheduled execution in March.

"I have some news to tell you," the sheriff said.

"Ah, what is it?" asked Wagner.

"I have to tell you," replied the sheriff, "that your counsel, Mr. Tapley, had raised a legal point in your case and you are reprieved by the governor for four weeks."

"There!" Wagner replied in exultation. "Haven't I told you all along, Mr. Sheriff, that they wouldn't hang me? I tell you so now. That thing will never be done. Mark my word."

Tapley did not get his new trial, but he managed to convince the governor and his council to seriously reexamine Wagner's case. They patiently listened to the familiar Wagner alibi and, according to the *Portsmouth Journal*, even traveled to Portsmouth where they "examined the localities and interviewed the leading witnesses." It was another extraordinary accomplishment for the irrepressible attorney in a complex series of appeals, reprieves, injunctions, petitions, and motions for commutation. The harder Wagner's attorney fought, the more the public wondered about his client's guilt. But Tapley was running out of tricks and his client was running out of time.

The independent review of Wagner's case by the governor's council did not uncover new evidence. "They have neither heard nor seen anything calculated to create the impression that the verdict of 'guilty' was wrong," the *Journal* concluded. Wagner's fanciful story just did not match the facts already in evidence. Nevertheless, the man who held Wagner's life in his hand was also a former journalist whose brother, incidentally, owned a local newspaper. Gov. Nelson Dingley insisted on meeting the condemned man in person and made a special visit to the prisoner's cell at Thomaston. The governor, a man with an overgrown goatee, an imposing forehead, and penetrating eyes, looked the infamous prisoner up and down. Cranking up his charisma, Wagner asked politely, "Do I look like a man who would commit such a crime?" The governor, after a pause, summed up the entire case in a single sentence. "You look, to me, like a man that got himself into a corner and murdered his way out," he said.

The hearing that followed was a devastating blow. There would be another brief reprieve. But the hanging of the two ax murderers was firmly scheduled for June 25, 1875, exactly two years from the reading of Wagner's guilty verdict at Alfred.

By early June, Tapley was grasping at legal straws. His "writ of error" sent to Attorney General Plaisted was effectively a list of nine alleged typographical errors in the court paperwork. Wagner's death sentence, for example, did not specify the hanging should take place "within the walls" of Thomaston Prison, the attorney complained. The petition was quickly dismissed. On June 18, Warden Rice told the two men, each in his own cell, they had received their last reprieve. Their cases were hopeless, he told them, and "they must make up their minds to suffer death on the gallows."

As expected, Gordon received the news "with great emotion" and fell back into a state of numbed depression. "I was in hopes that they would let me live," he said through his sobs. For what reason, Gordon pleaded, could anyone believe he had murdered his infant niece, the girl whom he had bounced on his knee as if she were his own child?

The two men were removed from their work duties and required to spend their final days in solitary confinement in the upper corridor of the old part of the prison. Gordon, locked in Room 151 at the end of the hall, returned to his despondent state. Yet he was seen by some reporters, his face peering through the bars of his door, wearing "a pleasant smile for all."

Wagner, housed in Room 146, was located closer to the guard's station. Visitors who managed to get near the guardroom saw him puffing his pipe and heard him humming songs to comfort himself. But despite reports he was in high spirits, according to one keen observer, the prisoner let down his guard on hearing the warden's fatal news. "Oh, my God," Wagner said with tears in his eyes. "Can that be so?"

"Gordon looks like a bad man," the *Kennebec Journal* offered in a special report, "bearing a cowardly, craven countenance that impresses you with the guilt of the poor trembling creature that crouches before you with half-closed eyes. But Wagner impresses you favorably. Let him tell his story, while standing before you with his erect manly form, and handsome expressive face, and flashing eyes, *and should you forget the testimony at the trial,* you will be half inclined to believe him innocent, and that it would be wicked to hang such a man. He is evidently a smart villain."

The end was near. Following the warden's visit, every precaution was put into place, the newspapers reported, to prevent either man from committing suicide. Gordon confirmed the biblical passage to be inscribed on his tombstone and his family arranged to collect his remains after the execution. Gordon then received a message from his mother saying she was too sick to visit him one final time. With no loved ones to receive his body, it was agreed Wagner would be buried in the old prison cemetery. Then Wagner, too, received a farewell letter from home.

"My Dearest Son," Wagner's mother wrote from Germany. "When I received your letter I thought that you were free again, because there was a picture therein. But when I opened the letter and saw your picture and read the contents, I almost lost my mind. You can easily imagine the effect, for I am hardly able to carry a pail of water up stairs. Dear son, I am sick, and your trouble, in addition to it, is too much for me."

From his mother's letter, we learn that Wagner had a responsible, married brother named Augustus. His mother also mentioned a woman named Minnie "who cries and prays the dear God that he will not take you away." She was likely Wagner's sister, or sister-in-law, or former girlfriend, but the *Portsmouth Evening Times* suggested that Minnie was Wagner's wife. The entire Wagner family was planning a trip from Prussia to the United States, his mother wrote, but she was afraid of America, "so much so that my bones tremble when I think about it."

Wagner gave permission for his mother's letter to be translated and published, knowing it would boost his public image. Her closing lines offered one final plea: "I have always thought that some of the gentlemen would take pity on a poor sick mother, and not take away her dear child, and I hope they will fulfill my wish, for my poor child has never done any harm to any body in Germany, and the same I hope, also, in America."

Chapter 34

FINAL HOURS

Louis Wagner lived just long enough to read the essay that would define his place in history. Celia Thaxter's "A Memorable Murder," critics later claimed, is a powerful personal study of man's infinite capacity for evil. The prisoner managed to obtain a copy of the May issue of *Atlantic Monthly*. He was reading it in his death row cell on June 24, 1875, the day before his execution.

According to Celia, the former fisherman was a "Prussian devil" and "a creature accursed" and "a blot on the face of the day." Wagner had committed "one of the most monstrous tragedies ever enacted on this planet," she wrote. Seemingly unimpressed by one of the finest nonfiction essays in American literature, the Smuttynose murderer set the magazine aside. "Dat woman must tell such black false lies to make money," he told a reporter. "I sleep sound all de night, and shall tonight, and de next night, and de next."

Despite frequent newspaper notices that only prison guards, officials, and the prison chaplain were allowed to see the condemned men, at least one journalist slipped inside. Edward P. Mitchell was a twenty-three-year old, twenty-dollar-a-week reporter for the *Lewiston Journal* when he and Louis Wagner chatted amiably on death row the night before the hanging. Mitchell had been hired by Lewiston editor Frank L. Dingley, whose brother Nelson Dingley, Jr. was governor of Maine. Mitchell was also friendly with Attorney General Harris Plaisted, so Warden Rice had given the well-connected journalist a backstage pass.

To fill his newspaper column in Maine, Mitchell revealed in his memoir decades later, he was required to cover everything from haunted houses, poultry shows, and spelling bees to murder trials and hangings. He also reviewed books, stage plays, and music concerts and even constructed the paper's weekly puzzle. Mitchell interviewed celebrities who visited Maine, including gunfighter "Wild Bill" Hickok and cartoonist Thomas Nast, best known for his iconic images of Uncle Sam, Santa Claus, the Democratic donkey, and the Republican elephant. Mitchell later spent fifty years as editor of the *New York Sun* for which he was awarded a Pulitzer Prize. He is also remembered today as a founding father of modern science fiction; Mitchell wrote short stories about cyborgs, invisible men, time machines, and light-speed rocket ships, all before the famed novelist H. G. Wells, who gets most of the credit today.

Mitchell's exclusive face-to-face interview with Wagner and his account of the "appalling spectacle" the next morning was shared by newspapers across the country. Sitting in the cramped concrete cell late at night, the two men "slowly and deliberately" went through the details of the murders, the trial, the alibi, and Wagner's claims against the treacherous Hontvets. The young reporter felt himself being seduced by the prisoner's round face, mild eyes, and good-natured conversation. Although he would be dead within hours, Wagner displayed "no discernable wickedness." Mitchell had arrived, after studying the facts, convinced Wagner was a liar and a killer. "And yet, when I left that night," Mitchell reported to his readers, "after seeing how the condemned bore himself, and hearing his simple, forcible discussion of the case, there was doubt and not certainty in my mind."

Wagner's dogged optimism, his unshakable denial of guilt, and his complete lack of remorse for the victims, once his closest friends, still haunt students of the Smuttynose murder case. In twenty-seven months, no one had managed to extract a confession from the prisoner. Wagner had been cajoled by friends, threatened by lynch mobs, baited by lawyers, bargained with by police, and probed by journalists.

Now the prison chaplain, Reverend J. K. Mason, gave it one last try. An avid abolitionist and prison reformer, Mason lived in a charming Greek-revival home near the prison that served as the parsonage for the Congregational Church of Thomaston. (Built on the property of one Ezekiel Blood, strangely, Rev. Mason's home was known in Alfred as the "Blood House." Rev. Mason had taken a keen interest in prisoners who might be "wrongly incarcerated" and was especially drawn to Wagner's intractable stand on his own innocence. Besides the prison staff and sheriff's men, Mason was the only person allowed to visit him as the execution loomed.

Unanswerable questions about Wagner's faith only muddle the debate. For some observers, his religious zeal was "apparently genuine." For others, as the *Portsmouth Journal* implied, his pious facade was "an extraordinary piece of simulation." The *New York Times* labeled him "superstitious" and suggested that he was being "buoyed up by some sort of fatalism." Carrying a bible for two years, however, had not worked the magic Wagner anticipated. His newest good luck charm was a folded letter written in German he carried in his inside shirt pocket. It was not the message from his ailing mother, but rather an anonymous missive, reportedly sent by a Catholic priest in Boston. The letter predicted the prisoner would be "all right in the life to come." It also promised that, if he carried the letter close to his heart, "no mortal power could harm him." Wagner's spirituality, it seems, was little more than a rabbit's foot.

Rev. Mason was on a mission to save Wagner's soul. But to do so, he had to unseat the prisoner's final hope of a supernatural escape from death and, instead, turn him toward the redemptive power of confession. Wagner did ask the chaplain for help. It was a small favor, but hidden in this incident may lie the secret to his long-professed innocence. Wagner was not "bad enough at heart," he told Rev. Mason, to compose a farewell letter to his mother. He could not bear to break her heart with the details of his impending execution. The chaplain agreed to write the letter for him. This last request resonates with a brief conversation Wagner had with a death row deputy sheriff known as Mr. Grouse.

"It is a bad thing to die on the gallows," Wagner reportedly told Mr. Grouse.

"You can die easily if you are innocent, as you say you are," the deputy replied.

"Yes," said Wagner, bursting into tears, "but I have a mother!"

Ultimately, it was impossible for Louis Wagner to tell the world he had murdered two innocent women for the equivalent of a week's wages. He could never confess to anyone because he could not let his mother know the truth about her son. He could not bear the thought of her shame and disappointment. So his last hope was her last hope. If he could carry off a dignified and noble death, admitting nothing, then his mother could keep her false faith in him alive.

And so, after the reporter and the chaplain were gone, Wagner slept soundly from eight-thirty p.m. until six a.m. on the morning of his execution. "I tried to dream," he told a guard on June 25, 1873, "but I slept so soundly that I forgot all about it."

John True Gordon, however, would not be so lucky. Gordon was awake until after ten p.m. visiting with friends from Thorndike in his cell. He slept little if at all. His legacy would best be summed up in a well-known phrase from New Hampshire's famous orator, Daniel Webster: "There is no refuge from confession but suicide; and suicide is confession."

Wagner woke to a cloudy and misty dawn. He had six hours to live and was uncharacteristically nervous. "He has hitherto believed in the saving power of the charm which he wore next to his heart," the Associated Press telegraphed from Thomaston, "but at last, realizing its impotence, he seems [to be] breaking down." Gordon was weaker still and near collapse. Both men refused the traditional prison breakfast of bread and coffee. "They were the last men in the prison who would be selected by a stranger as the two who were to die on the scaffold today," said the *Portsmouth Times*.

By eight-thirty a.m., when Warden Rice arrived on death row, both men had been stripped of their clothing and searched for concealed weapons. The warden expressed his sincere condolences to both men and bid them farewell. Both reiterated their innocence to him. Wagner, having regained his composure, again said, "God will not let Louis Wagner be hung." Gordon, however, was judged to be too frail to attend a planned church service and the formal ceremony in the chapel was cancelled. A guard was posted in the corridor outside the cells.

At nine o'clock, Sherriff Torrey and his assistants arrived at Thomaston Prison to make the final arrangements for the hanging. They reported to the office of Warden Rice, who was just returning from consoling the inmates. A brief private worship ceremony, it was determined, would be held in the prisoner's cells. At around ten o'clock, the gates opened to members of the media, to the dozen witnesses required by law, and to a few specially invited guests, the Hontvets possibly among them. The spectators, all told, numbered between thirty and forty. Other than a few morbid curiosity seekers who gathered outside the gates, it was business as usual in Thomaston. As the spectators filed in, Sherriff Torrey and his deputies passed through the guard room, and down a hall of about twenty-six feet, where they served each prisoner with his death warrant.

Reports differ as to whether it was one of the sheriff's deputies or Rev. Mason who discovered John True Gordon curled in a widening puddle of blood on the floor of his room. At ten forty-five came the "startling announcement" that Gordon had attempted suicide. Warren Rice exhibited the weapon to the assembled press corps. The utility knife, a traditional cobbler's tool, had a two-and-a-half inch blade ground to a fine point. The short, wooden handle was wrapped in cloth. There was speculation someone had tossed the blade through Gordon's cell door from the corridor below. More likely it had been passed to the prisoner, perhaps during a farewell handshake, as he met with friends late the previous night. Gordon had probably squirreled it away until he found himself alone in his room for the very last time. He used the crude weapon to cut his femoral artery, a key supplier of blood on the inner thigh. He also managed to stab himself in the left breast just above the heart, inflicting a wound that "must have proved fatal within an hour or two at most."

As soon as the alarm was raised, three surgeons rushed into Gordon's cell to arrest the flow of blood. The warden and the sheriff were highly excited, according to eyewitness reporter Edward Mitchell. They had to decide, and quickly, whether to disregard the legal warrant and let Gordon bleed out, or whether to hang both men before noon as the law required, one of them insensible and almost dead. Only they could decide.

The other Thomaston convicts were all in their cells, their work suspended on the day of the execution. Yet somehow they all knew about Gordon. The news was telegraphed from inmate to inmate by an invisible communication system. Locked in isolation, only Wagner was out of the loop and knew nothing of Gordon's plight.

At eleven a.m., as the clock began to run down on Wagner's ultimate hour, the guards required that he put on his "grave clothes." Early Thomaston prisoners wore shirts with one red sleeve and one black. Those were replaced at some point by the traditional black and white striped suits, often called "cruel garb," because they made the inmates highly visible outside prison walls. Wagner groaned heavily as he stripped and pulled on the colorless shroud he would soon be wearing in the coffin waiting for him just below the scaffold in the prison yard. Again he faltered and began to cry as he protested his innocence. Twenty-five minutes later, the sheriff and his deputies entered Wagner's cell and pinioned his arms. Then they went to prepare the other prisoner.

At eleven forty-five, Wagner left his Thomaston cell for the last time. There would be no more tears. For his mother, he must show courage. Supported by two deputies, Wagner was marched resolutely down a passageway toward the prison yard. "His face kept an expression of perfect calmness without the slightest suggestion of bravado," an observer remembered.

The gallows was located in a deep, unused limestone quarry between the carriage shop and the repository. The deeper parts of the quarry were filled with water and, other than the dismal stone walls, nothing was visible except a small pond with a few ducks swimming. The spectators, including seventeen journalists, stood in silence, waiting for the condemned men to appear. No one outside the high stone walls could see what was going on inside and life on Main Street in Thomaston carried on as if nothing special was happening.

Wagner and the small procession exited the western door of the prison and crossed the prison yard. They entered the woodworking shop, passed down into the basement, and out. Suddenly the first prisoner appeared to the visitors. He walked firmly up the steep wooden steps of the platform. He was escorted to the central trap panel that would drop away at the appointed time. In moments, the hood would be placed over his head and the noose fixed around his neck. His face was still blank and Wagner exhibited no fear as he searched the crowd for familiar faces.

"Good morning, Mr. Rice," he said, spotting the prison warden. Then to the overseer of the harness shop where he had worked for the last year, he added, "Goodbye, Mr. Smith."

Wagner had not yet seen his death row companion who followed him to the scaffold, half-conscious from his bloody wounds, his face as white as a corpse. In the words of correspondent Mitchell, "The limp body of Gordon, half-naked and hideously red-stained, was borne to the gallows and held up, reeling and quivering, by the strength of four deputies while the noose was adjusted and the black cap drawn down over eyes that could see nothing."

"Poor Gordon! Poor Gordon!" Wagner called out as the Thorndike killer was placed beside him in a sitting position on a box over the trapdoor.

"Now Wagner," the sheriff announced, "if you have anything to say, or any confession to make, you can have a chance."

Chapter 35

UPON THE GALLOWS

Seven men convicted of murder were hanged on the gallows in Thomaston yard. Legend says they were all "launched into eternity" from the same tall platform, but according to the Associated Press, most of the wooden scaffolding was newly constructed for the June 25, 1875, event. Only the hinged trapdoor beneath Wagner and Gordon was recycled. Francis Spencer, the convict who stabbed the previous warden at Thomaston, had stood on the same spring-operated "drop" in 1864. It was used again in 1869 with Clifton Harris, the African American who may have been innocent of killing two white women. It would be used with the next three murderers executed at Thomaston in 1885 since, contrary to another popular legend, Wagner and Gordon were not the last men hanged in Maine.

Before these seven men fell, the same mechanical drop had been used in a double execution at Auburn, Maine, in 1858. Abraham Cox and Peter Williams are rarely listed among the men executed in Maine because they were sentenced by a federal court, but their final moments bear comparison to Wagner's dramatic exit. Cox and Williams were charged with mutiny and piracy on the high seas by the US government. The two sailors had killed the captain and three crewmen of the ship *Albion Cooper*, hacking them with an ax and razors before throwing their weighted bodies overboard and burning the ship. Thousands of Maine residents thronged to the town of Auburn to view the enormous gallows that stood twelve feet square and thirteen feet tall. From the *Boston Herald* we learn that the infamous trapdoor measured five-and-a-half feet long by four-and-a-half feet wide and sat about eighteen inches above the floor of the scaffold. The crowd, in a carnival mood, awaited the final words of the condemned men.

Cox, an elderly "negro cook" from Kennebunkport, approached the drop without fear. He had been terribly abused by his shipmates, "maddened to desperation," as he explained. He admitted to planning his revenge. "If this jail and courthouse were a lump of gold, and were mine," Cox said, "I would give it, could it deliver me from having done what I did."

His mate Williams, however, upon mounting the gallows, was overcome by a religious frenzy. He fell quivering to his knees on the trapdoor, praying for the Lord Jesus to appear from the sky and deliver him from death. The previous day, Williams had told reporters a baby girl, the sister of Mary Magdalene, had appeared to him in his cell and forgiven him his evil sins. Being thus forgiven, Williams reasoned, he was again an innocent man and could not be hanged. But in his final moments on the drop, to the astonishment of the audience, Williams made a full confession. "I have killed them all!" he cried. "I killed all four of them myself!"

Louis Wagner, it was hoped, would finally do the same to clear his conscience. And it was here, as the prisoner stood on the well-used trapdoor, that the sheriff asked for the final time, "If you have anything to say, or any confession to make, you can have a chance."

But the prisoner's face bore only the familiar "placid expression" he had carried since his arrest and trial. There would be no admission and no apology. Edward Mitchell, the young man from the *Lewiston Journal*, was among the seventeen reporters in attendance. He heard Wagner say, "Standing here to die, I proclaim my innocence before God." The Associated Press carried a longer, but puzzling farewell speech.

"No sir!" Wagner replied clearly and calmly. "I have nothing to say, except the same as I told the true story in open court. After my death the truth will come to light. I believe in the Bible, and I have always believed in

God. And though the virtuous people in the United States believed in God also, but this makes me think differently."

Interpreting Wagner's rambling last words to its readers, the Associated Press reporter added that, "He said he had been brought up to read his Bible, and he thought that those who did not read their Bible were better off."

Wagner was ultimately disappointed. His bible and other talismans had failed him. His charm and lies did not work. His two escape attempts were bungled. There would be no divine intervention or last-minute reprieve. But despite his disappointment in the Almighty and in everyone he knew, the Smuttynose murderer did not break down. He did not crack or cry or confess or take his own life. He gave his faithful mother a gift. He left her the hope her son had not killed two innocent women. And he successfully planted the seed of doubt about his guilt that would blossom for decades, perhaps for centuries to come.

There was no need to request any final words from John True Gordon. He was beyond speech, sitting limply on a wooden box on the drop supported by two deputies. His head drooped and his white burial shroud was filling visibly with crimson blood. Gordon groaned faintly as the deputies lifted him to a standing position. A noose was placed over each man's head and fixed snugly into the most deadly position around their necks. Gordon's face, when briefly lifted into view, was ghostly white and his eyes were shut. The rope used, the newspapers dutifully reported, was manila cordage, one-and-a-half inches in circumference. The special hanging rope had been stretched and waxed so that it was "as pliable as a silk cord."

Wagner exhibited "a pleasant look on his face as long as it was visible," Mitchell observed. He showed "courage and self-control to the last," the *Baltimore Whig and Courier* reported, but the final details of the execution were "too horrible to be paraded before the public." As the black hood was placed on his head, Wagner gave a final pitying glance at his companion on the drop. "Good and poor John, we're gone," he said.

Sheriff Torrey uncovered the spring that would release the trap. The pins that secured it were removed, and the sheriff solemnly said: "And now by the authority in me vested by the Governor of the State of Maine, I hereby hang you by the neck till you are dead, dead, dead. And may God have mercy on your souls."

There was nothing left but the fall. If the force of it did not break Wagner's neck, he knew, he could strangle at the end of the rope, his consciousness fading for up to six agonizing minutes. Clifton Harris had suffered in the "dance of death" for two minutes in this very prison yard just six years earlier. But the odds of a speedy delivery were in Wagner's favor. The distance from the trapdoor to the ground, according to various reports, was between five and seven feet. This system, known as "standard drop hanging" was typically used in America at the time. It was considerably more humane than the "short drop" method commonly used at public hangings prior to the Civil War in which a cart or horse or ladder or platform was pulled out from under the victim.

The system most frequently used in countries around the world today, the "long drop" method, required jailers to weigh the prisoner prior to execution and to perform a simple calculation. The heavier the prisoner, the shorter the fall required to break the neck with relative accuracy. The victim then died of asphyxia while unconscious. A drop too far might decapitate the prisoner. William Marwood, the official hangman of England, first demonstrated his long drop system in April 1872, the same month Wagner moved in with the Hontvet family on Smuttynose Island. Marwood's chart, or "drop table," told the executioner, to the nearest inch, the ideal length of rope required for each prisoner. Through experimentation, he also perfected the precise arrangement of the noose against the victim's neck. Marwood hanged 176 prisoners in his long career in London, but there is no evidence his scientific system was used with Wagner and Gordon.

At eleven minutes before noon, the newspapers reported, Sheriff Torrey placed his boot on the spring of the trapdoor. With a heavy thud, the drop fell open and "all that was mortal of Louis Wagner and John True Gordon was dangling in the air."

Neither of the fallen bodies moved a muscle, their necks evidently broken. Eight minutes later, Wagner's pulse "denoted 100" while Gordon had no pulse after seven minutes, the AP reported. According to the three surgeons on the scene, Wagner's neck "was very much discolored and a dark livid streak was visible." Gordon did not show the mark so plainly. The prisoner's were pronounced dead eighteen minutes after the trapdoor opened. Their bodies were cut down and placed in the waiting coffins.

A few photographs of the Thomaston gallows exist. Nineteenth-century images show the stark wooden scaffold rising against the bleak walls of the limestone quarry. All the images on record depict the scene before the trapdoor was sprung. Yet none of the historic photos uncovered to date show Wagner and Gordon on the gibbet. Considering the infamy of the prisoners, it is likely a professional photographer was present on execution day, but any record of the horrific scene was likely banned or suppressed due to Gordon's pitiable ending.

"The whole proceeding was but little better than hanging a corpse," L. C. Bateman reported to the *Phrenological Journal*, "and in my opinion one of the most outrageous acts of brutality ever committed in our state, a scene which I trust may never be witnessed again."

From a postmortem examination of Wagner, the amateur phrenologist was certain Maine had murdered an innocent man. Wagner's beautifully shaped skull and his noble bearing on the scaffold provided all the evidence Bateman needed. The "indelible disgrace" of Wagner's execution, he sermonized to fellow phrenologists, was the ultimate proof that capital punishment was "a relic of barbarism worthy only of the dark ages of superstition and ignorance."

The media response, overall, was that justice had been served. Although human judgment can be flawed, the *New York Times* observed, "there seems to be no reason to doubt that these two men were justly convicted and hanged." The *Boston Advertiser* reported that "the death of these assassins is a gain to the world which their crimes darkened." Back in Portsmouth, news that Wagner had finally "climbed the golden stairs" was greeted with surprise, according to the *Daily Chronicle*. "So much distrust had been generated by the obstacles thrown in the way of the legal punishment of crime in Maine that there were few who actually had faith that Wagner would ever hang."

Gordon's suicide attempt, by all accounts, confirmed he was guilty of slaughtering three members of his own family as they slept. Wagner's ability to stick to his story and to hold up his head in the face of death appeared even more impressive, even manly, by contrast. The two-year gap between the trial and the execution had also dulled the public memory of the island ax murders and its victims. It was inevitable, the *New York Times* suggested, that Wagner's "bravado and unblanching fortitude under very trying circumstances . . . seems to have succeeded in convincing many of his innocence." And while human beings are inclined to pity these men for dying on the gallows, the *Boston Advertiser* warned, that pity "has something unnatural and inhuman in it." Reporter Edward Mitchell also reminded his readers that Sheriff Torrey and his deputies had done the best job they could under circumstances that would "appall the stoutest heart."

Printed broadsides had long been a tradition of public executions in England and in the United States in the eighteenth and nineteenth centuries. Often called a "bloody murder," these cheap one-sided paper sheets were sold as souvenirs of the grisly event. They typically contained an illustration of the condemned man or woman with the prisoner's dying speech, often set to verse. Gordon and Wagner were no exception. A broadside with a woodblock image of both men, composed in their memory, was printed at Rockland, Maine. The crude poem of twenty-four stanzas offers the following sentiment:

Gordon and Wagner, these young men's names,
In innocent blood their hands are stained;
God's righteous laws they did defy,
And on the gallows they now must die.

God in his written book hath said,
"By the sweat of our brow we must earn our bread,"
But these two men they worshipped gold,
And for the love of money their lives they sold.

Parents and friends all over this state,
O, don't forget these young men's fate;
You that have children—dear loved ones,
Remember these criminals are somebody's sons.

Friends of John True Gordon collected his remains after the body was examined by the prison surgeons. Gordon was buried in his hometown of Thorndike, but with his grave placed at a significant distance from the three family members he had hacked and burned. Gordon's father passed away three months after his son's execution, while his doting mother survived until 1888.

Because he had no relatives or loved ones in America, the newspaper reported, the Medical School of Maine at Bowdoin College made application for Wagner's remains. Finding fresh corpses for research and student autopsies in the nineteenth century was an ongoing and controversial problem. Bodies might be obtained under shady circumstances and from great distances. They were sometimes shipped in whiskey barrels. In one recorded incident, a Bowdoin dean inquired about purchasing three human specimens from the University of Maryland at fifty dollars each, the price to include the cost of the whiskey. Corpses, in whole and in part, were stored floating in alcohol on the top floor of Bowdoin's Medical Hall. In a legendary campus prank, a cadaver borrowed from the surgery lab was placed in the office chair of a departing professor.

In 1869, the year Clifton Harris was hanged at Thomaston Prison, Maine enacted a law that would apply directly to Louis Wagner. "When any person convicted of crime dies or is executed in the State prison or any jail," it read, "the warden or keepers shall, on request, deliver his body

291

to instructors in medical schools established by law." The distance from Thomaston to the Bowdoin campus in Brunswick, Maine, is roughly fifty miles. And yet there is a small, relatively modern-looking memorial marker hidden in the grass of the old Thomaston Prison cemetery. It reads simply: "L.H.F. Wagner, Died June 25, 1875." Whether Wagner is buried there or whether his body ended up on a student's dissection table has not yet been confirmed.

In the romantic imagination of Celia Thaxter, Louis Wagner remains the "agonized ghost" of Smuttynose Island, watched over by the souls of Karen and Anethe Christensen. "He prowls eternally about the dilapidated houses at the beach's edge," Celia wrote in 1875, "close by the black, whispering water, seeking for the woman who has escaped him—escaped to bring upon him the death he deserves, whom he never, never, never can find, though his distracted spirit may search till man shall vanish from off the face of the earth, and time shall be no more."

VI

AFTERMATH

"Many things which are false are transmitted from book to book, and gain credit in the world."

—Dr. Samuel Johnson, English lexicographer

"It is not pleasant to think that the island has become more widely known through the medium of an atrocious murder committed here in March 1873.

—Samuel Adams Drake, New England travel writer, 1875

"Among the early settlements in America I know of but one that has so utterly disappeared that the only trace of it left is a little graveyard."

—Reverend Alfred Gooding speaking on Star Island, 1914

Chapter 36

THE OCEANIC BURNS

On the day Louis Wagner was hanged, an anonymous mourner left flowers on the graves of Karen and Anethe Christensen. The floral arrangement, in the shape of a cross and a crown, was set between their matching white tombstones at Harmony Grove in Portsmouth. The message was clear. With their murders avenged, the two restless souls could finally lay their burdens down and receive their heavenly reward. It was, the newspaper noted, "a touching memorial indeed."

The two Norwegian women had made a dangerous transatlantic crossing only to be killed in their safe island home by a man who had traveled much the same route from his native Prussia. It was the only immi-grant-on-immigrant murder then in the casebooks of Maine, but more would follow. And while the rest of the nation quickly forgot the tragedy at Smuttynose, as Celia Thaxter predicted, the memory of Louis Wagner's crime still inhabits the Isles of Shoals. No island visitor can escape the grim details. The story is told aboard every boat that ferries passengers from the mainland to the historic Oceanic Hotel that still stands on Star Island. But while the great white wooden hotel that dominates the island bears the same name, it is not the Oceanic that John Poor's men were building on the morning of March 6, 1873, when Maren Hontvet screamed for their help. The original Oceanic, the one that wiped out the ancient fishing village of

Gosport, met its fate only months after Wagner's execution. Its destruction was nothing less than a well-timed case of poetic justice.

A bright light at sea woke many coastal citizens at two-thirty a.m. on November 12, 1875. After only three seasons, the luxurious Oceanic Hotel had been struck by lightning and was ablaze. The guests had long departed and the expansive building, after receiving a fresh coat of paint, had been shut up for the winter. Due to a heavy gale and rough seas, the only damage report in the *New York Times* the next day came from observers peering at the island through telescopes from miles away.

Two watchmen who were sleeping in the hotel reading room had to leap for their lives out a second-story window, but were unable to fight the fire. Owner John Poor had been on the site just the day before with a crew of a dozen workmen, the *Portsmouth Chronicle* reported. The Oceanic's 147 guest rooms, grand dance hall and dining hall, its staff quarters, steam elevator, card-playing and billiard rooms, bowling alley, gift store, bar, and great piazza were all destroyed in the fire. "The scene of so much enjoyment…lies in ashes, from which it may or may not arise," the *Chronicle* commented.

John Poor had insured the hotel through more than a dozen separate policies totaling fifty thousand dollars with an additional seventy-five thousand dollars on its furniture and contents. A court battle broke out when it was discovered a key policy had been marked "cancelled" the day before the fire. The insurance company also argued that, according to Poor's policy, a "family" was supposed to be living in the hotel year-round.

While the legal fight dragged on, as Oscar Laighton recalled, Poor rebuilt before the ashes of the first hotel had cooled. The second Oceanic Hotel, however, was a different structure entirely. To cut down on construction costs, Poor recycled three of the old Caswell family buildings that had long stood on the island, connecting them to a new central lobby and dining hall. The odd-shaped building that survives today did not have all the modern Victorian conveniences or the same grand architectural design as its predecessor. The wealthy Mr. Poor, it seems, had lost his taste for the tourist business. A 1903 obituary for the prominent merchant of Stickney & Poor spoke highly of his extensive pear orchards and his service as alderman in Somerville, Massachusetts. No mention was made of his failed island hotel or the devastated town of Gosport.

In 1876, Poor sold Star Island, its buildings, his new dock, and a small fleet of boats to the Laighton brothers at Appledore for one hundred thousand dollars. It was only one-third of the capital Poor had invested, but it was still a huge sum for Oscar, Cedric, and their sickly mother, Eliza, to borrow. The two brothers managed to keep both hotels running for the next twenty-five years.

As their father had done with the Appledore, the Laighton brothers now shifted the promotion of their new hotel away from high tech and high society toward an emphasis on health, scenery, relaxation, and culture. "Star Island is by all means the most historical place in New England," their brochure now claimed. "There is no spot in the world where the overworked and tired brain, the exhausted, emaciated body, will so rapidly recuperate as upon Star Island."

The 1875 Oceanic fire almost drove the family of John B. Downs, the last true Shoalers, off the island for good, but again they clung to rocks like barnacles. Downs had frequently welcomed the charming Louis Wagner into his Gosport home. Wagner had cuddled their son in his muscular arms. Yet the day after the shocking murders were revealed, feeling betrayed, John Downs had joined the Portsmouth mob bent on lynching Wagner in the city streets. The Downs family escaped from their house next to the burning hotel in 1875 wearing their nightclothes. According to the newspaper, they salvaged only a featherbed, a gun, a cow, and a dog. But newspapers are frequently wrong. Miraculously, a sudden shift in the wind preserved their house and it suffered only "a severe scorching." The man who had refused to sell out to John Poor continued to live on his beloved island until his death at age seventy-seven in 1888.

The old stone chapel on the hill, still standing, also survived the hellish fire, but the town of Gosport, New Hampshire, was doomed. Former residents of the island fishing community gathered in March 1876 for what was intended to be the election of their representative to the New Hampshire state legislature. But a group of Oceanic Hotel employees, arriving on a steamer from Boston, also showed up to vote. The confrontation over who should represent Gosport was "disorderly and riotous to an extreme degree." John Downs's son was appointed to the New Hampshire legislature, but after the state discovered there were no year-round residents left in the town other than the Downs family, the lawmakers abolished the island town of Gosport. Star Island was officially annexed to the mainland town of Rye, once the site of New Hampshire's first fishing outpost in 1623. White Island, with its brick lighthouse, as well as Seavey and Lunging Islands, also became part of Rye, New Hampshire—but not a single voter was added to the town rolls.

Back on Smuttynose, enlivened by Wagner's hanging and Celia's *Atlantic Monthly* essay, the souvenir-hunters continued to strip off small pieces of the murder house. A photograph from that era clearly shows where the next occupants of the Red House replaced the wooden siding below Maren Hontvet's bedroom window after the tourists had carved out their keepsakes. A prized relic, the broken handle of the ax, had gone on display in the front window of William B. Lowd's store in Portsmouth within days of the hanging. It was the property of Calvin L. Hayes of Kittery, who had been a member of the original coroner's jury. Today the head of the murder ax lies in the collection of the Portsmouth Athenaeum, with the wooden heel and shoulder of the handle still loosely attached. The whereabouts of the longer piece of the handle that Hayes picked out of the snow on March 6—the belly, throat, grip, and knob portion—remains missing.

Shoaler John Downs, who lived in the "murder house" as a boy in the 1880s, recalled strangers knocking on the door. They asked for guided tours and for permission to cut out pieces of the woodwork. Lemuel Caswell, formerly of Star Island, was then the landlord at Smuttynose Island and he encouraged this practice—for a fee. Caswell could make more money off the tourists, he reminded his tenants, than from their meager rent.

In 1881, a guest visiting the murder house told the occupants he had once been Wagner's "keeper," although at which jail, the report in the *Portsmouth Journal* does not specify. The jailer said he sometimes disguised himself and stood by Wagner's cell, listening as the prisoner told his story to someone. The former guard "would assume a different disguise and hear a different story," he said. Wagner was, he concluded, a compulsive liar.

In August 1882, while Lemuel Caswell was managing the island for the Laighton brothers, a barn and outbuildings near the Mid-Ocean House burned. Caswell was able to save the oldest hotel on the island. The Hontvet House, barely sixty feet away, was unscathed, as was the Haley Cottage. It has been widely reported that the murder house burned in 1885. Not so. In 1892, summer visitors flocked to Smuttynose for a series of musical concerts. The island was "brilliantly illuminated" the *Sunday Boston Globe* reported. The hotel and all the island houses, including the old Haley Cottage and the "Wagner Cottage" next door, were occupied by tourists, the media reported. Finally in 1908, the infamous murder house disappeared in flames.

Three years later, under the management of Clarence Caswell of Portsmouth, the Mid-Ocean House followed suit. The dilapidated hotel burned for an hour on a frigid February night, then the embers continued to glow, creating an eerie light visible from the mainland. Incredibly, Sam Haley's Revolutionary War–era cottage, located only a few feet away from the buildings on either side, survived all these fires. It continues to serve as shelter to the summer stewards of the island.

Among the last to make the macabre pilgrimage was a Portland lawyer who had studied the Wagner case at school. Out of "morbid curiosity" while visiting the Oceanic Hotel, he borrowed a dory and rowed across Gosport Harbor to Smuttynose in the early twentieth century. He felt compelled, he wrote, to look out through the very bedroom window where Anethe had leapt to her death. Like countless visitors before, he approached the island as if it had been permanently cursed by the murders. The island was silent and foreboding. The roof of the Hontvet House sagged and its shingles were falling off. The doors were gone, the wallpaper was shredded, and the window sash was missing once again.

"I went into the house," the lawyer wrote, "through which the storms of years had likewise surged, drenching its silent floors with wet. And as I stood amid the broken shadows of its blanched walls, I had no difficulty in recalling the crime and its details with photographic distinctness."

Chapter 37

CELIA'S WORLD

It is beyond a reasonable doubt that our vivid shared image of the Hontvet House comes largely from Celia Thaxter. Her "A Memorable Murder" essay was something risky and powerful when it appeared in 1875. Laurence Hutton, a critic and literary editor of *Harper's Magazine* who spent ten years summering at Appledore with the Laightons, recalled Celia Thaxter reciting this famous work to her visitors: "I have seen her auditors literally moved to hysterics as she related the story...which I consider one of the strongest pieces of prose in the English language."

While such high praise as Hutton's usually fades with time, Celia's essay is enjoying increasing critical attention. She is now credited as a founder of true crime literature, the kind that rises above the seedy, gruesome, and exploitative murder accounts intended for "lowbrow" audiences. As a native Shoaler, Celia was already an expert at describing the island environment that became the scene of the crime. To further evoke pity for Karen and Anethe, Celia took her readers inside the minds, not only of the three female victims, but of the killer himself.

Her essay followed in the footsteps, scholars now suggest, of Thomas De Quincey, the early nineteenth-century essayist and self-confessed opium addict. The successful crime writer must evoke a "sympathy of comprehension" De Quincey wrote, that allows the reader to enter into the feelings of the person who is on the brink of death. It was not enough, he wrote, to merely recount the facts or describe the scene. Like a great poet, the crime writer must also replicate the tempest that rages inside the mind of the killer, tapping into his jealousy, vengeance, ambition, and hatred. The successful crime writer, De Quincey said, should recreate the murderer's inner hell, "and into this hell we are to look."

In *Blood & Ink*, a guide to "fact-based crime literature," scholar Albert Borowitz sees a direct line dating from these early writers to Truman Capote's so-called "non-fiction novel." Capote also used strong evocative settings and fictional elements in his 1966 bestseller *In Cold Blood*, the psychological study of a mass murder in Kansas. Hailed as a breakthrough genre, Capote's true crime classic, Borowitz suggests, is actually "a logical outgrowth of the pioneering nineteenth century crime studies of Thomas De Quincey and Celia Thaxter." Norman Mailer is also cited as a modern author who followed in the same track. Mailer's Pulitzer Prize–winning novel *The Executioner's Song*, about serial murderer Gary Gilmore who was executed by a firing squad in 1977, is another successful marriage of "highbrow" literature with the true crime genre.

Celia's murder narrative appearing in the prestigious *Atlantic* gave it enormous literary clout. For that, we can thank her husband, Levi Thaxter, educated at Harvard, and his Boston family connections. Levi was not only Celia's childhood tutor, but he also helped put the Isles of Shoals on the must-see list for vacationing New England artists and intellectuals.

The fact that the murders happened in Celia's own backyard, on an island her family owned, was also a critical factor in the success of her essay. Her descriptions ring true. Louis Wagner disturbed the peace of her tranquil isolated world. He shattered the dreams of her beloved Norwegians. So for Celia, seeing Wagner hanged was personal. But the murders also impacted Celia on a metaphorical level. Wagner came to represent an inescapable force of Nature. It was as if he could not be stopped. On her beautiful island, surrounded by predatory creatures, the dangerous ocean, and deadly storms, Wagner was one more evil element forever lurking on the horizon.

The quality and originality of "A Memorable Murder" was hers alone. "Celia Thaxter's life and personality were absolutely unique," critic Laurence Hutton reminds us. Raised on barren islands by the brilliant but iconoclastic Thomas Laighton, she grew up innocent and wild. She really was, as Nathaniel Hawthorne described her, the "pretty Miranda," who in Shakespeare's play *The Tempest* was banished to an island at the age of three with her magical father, Prospero.

Celia joined no religious group and had no social pedigree, and yet, to her adoring public, she represented the perfect example of Victorian womanhood. She was a handsome and charming hostess, "simply dressed always, but most effectively, in some Quakerish garb of grey stuff with soft veiling material about her own throat," Hutton wrote. "Her hair during the later years of her life was quite white and her manner was invariably cordial and cheerful." She was best known for harmless little poems about sea moss and sandpipers. And yet, when threatened by Louis Wagner, she became the literary equivalent of Annie Oakley, a sharpshooter of words.

As far as we know, Celia Thaxter never returned to Smuttynose Island after the murders. Wagner had destroyed her childhood love of the island, and it was overtaken by what one Victorian travel writer called "a melancholy celebrity." As her own celebrity grew in the decade following the trial, she suffered the death of her beloved mother, Eliza, her estranged husband, Levi, and her loyal editor, James T. Fields. In 1879, William Morris Hunt, one of the greatest artists of his era and Celia's lifelong confidant, was discovered drowned in a small pond behind the Appledore Hotel.

"I found him," Celia wrote to a close friend after Hunt's death. "It was reserved for me, who loved him truly, that bitterness…We took him in, put [him] in blankets, rubbed and rubbed. It was mockery. He had been dead for hours."

There were good times, too. Celia toured Europe, tended her famous island flower garden, and became an expert at painting ceramic cups, dishes, and vases she sold at a profit to tourists. Her sons John and Roland married and gave her grandchildren. She published many poems and stories for young people, often focused on nature and the environment. She painted and listened to musicians play Beethoven at her summer salons. With Louisa May Alcott, Sarah Orne Jewett, and Harriet Beecher Stowe, she was hailed as one of America's best female writers. Advertisers asked her to endorse products ranging from typewriters to cigars. She appeared in an educational card game called "Authors" alongside the likes of Shakespeare, Milton, and Dostoevsky.

In 1884, a half dozen survivors of the famous "Greely party" were discovered alive after years marooned in the Arctic. Upon arriving at the Portsmouth Naval Shipyard to recuperate, General Adolphus Greely made a special trip to the Isles of Shoals to thank Celia Thaxter for a book of her poetry he had carried on his journey. "It tided over many a weary hour of our solitude," Greely told her.

But the ripe years waned quickly. When her mentor, the Quaker poet and abolitionist John Greenleaf Whittier, passed away in 1892, she was among thousands of mourners who viewed his body as it lay in the parlor of his simple home in Amesbury, Massachusetts. Two years later, on August 26, 1894, Celia Thaxter said she was tired and went to bed early. She died the following morning at age fifty-nine. Two of her beloved Scandinavian girls named Mina and Nicolina Bernsten were with her at the end. According to her brother Oscar, Celia asked Mina to open the bedroom window in the morning. When Mina turned back to the bed, Celia's "spirit was gone." Her body lay in state on a bed of wildflowers in her parlor at Appledore. A few close friends and family carried her coffin to a low, rocky hill behind her cottage where her parents, Eliza and Thomas, were buried. Her friends then made a pilgrimage to Celia Thaxter's favorite childhood places and the source of her poetry; they traveled in a small sailboat one day to the lighthouse on White Island, to the stone chapel on Star Island, and to the graves of the lost Spanish sailors on Smuttynose Island.

With their famous sister gone, life was never the same for Oscar and Cedric. By 1897, when hundreds of Unitarians held the first of many summer conferences at the Oceanic, the Laighton brothers were in financial freefall. Cedric died in 1899 and the bank foreclosed on Oscar's mortgage. On September 14, 1914, the grand Appledore Hotel and most of its surrounding cottages burned. Two years later, the bank threatened to sell the Oceanic Hotel to a commercial resort company. The Star Island Corporation, a Boston-based group of Unitarians and Congregationalists, stepped up and purchased the islands. Now based in Portsmouth, the nonprofit group operates the "vintage" hotel for summer visitors. The island scenery has changed little since the second Oceanic opened its doors in 1875. "Uncle" Oscar Laighton, a bachelor to the end, was a fixture at the Star Island conferences until his death in 1939, three months shy of his hundredth birthday.

Appledore Island, its few ramshackle cottages overgrown with poison ivy, became a military base for spotting submarines in World War II. Appledore got a new lease on life in the 1960s when it was adapted into a summer marine biology school for undergraduates. It continues today, run cooperatively by Cornell University and the University of New Hampshire. The Shoals Marine Lab is a natural laboratory, an "island of learning" for the study of birds, fish, and other marine life. And each year, on a small plot of land where the grand hotel once stood, Marine Lab volunteers lovingly recreate the historic island garden of Celia Thaxter.

Celia's view of Appledore as heavenly and her rejection of Smuttynose as hellish was an irresistible symbol for at least one visiting minister in the mid-twentieth century. Reverend Carl Heath Kopf of Boston, known as the "teen minister," compared the two islands in a radio sermon on sexuality for his young listeners. Appledore, he said, represented the sweetness of reading good books and living a moral life. Smuttynose, by contrast, symbolized cheap, tawdry books and sinful habits. Like Dr. Jekyll and Mr. Hyde, goodness and evil are "set as close within us as Appledore and Smuttynose are at the Shoals," Kopf sermonized.

Chapter 38

THE HONTVET LEGACY

Maren Hontvet and Ivan Christensen never wanted to see Smuttynose Island again. With the bodies of Karen and Anethe still lying on the floor of the Red House, John Hontvet and his brother, Matthew, had managed to sift through the family's bloodied storage trunks to give the police a precise accounting of the money stolen. Later, the task of repacking those trunks and moving Maren's few household possessions to Portsmouth certainly fell to the brothers. Whether the two Hontvet men continued to use the weathered duplex, at least temporarily, as the base of their fishing operation is unknown.

In the summer of 1874, with Wagner still on death row at Thomaston, Ivan Christensen gave up on America. A broken man, he recuperated somewhat while working as a carpenter at the Appledore Hotel. He could not bear, at first, to leave the islands where he and his wife had found brief happiness and hope. But he could not bring himself to cross to the other side of Appledore Island, where the Ingebretsen family lived, and look across the ocean channel toward Smuttynose Island. Ivan returned to Norway, but he did come back. He was remarried in 1877 and, after living in New Brunswick, Ivan became a carpenter and cabinetmaker in Boston. Anethe's husband died there in 1921, survived by his second wife and three children.

"Maren and her husband still live blameless lives," Celia Thaxter wrote in 1875, "with the little dog Ringe, in a new home they have made for themselves in Portsmouth, not far from the river side; the merciful lapse of days and years takes them gently but surely away from the thought of that season of anguish; and though they can never forget it all, they have grown resigned and quiet again."

The Portsmouth City Directory of 1873 lists a Mary "Huntved" living on Water Street in a modest dwelling next door to Johnson's boarding house. Curiously, she is described as "the widow of John." The rental property was built in 1830 by a downtown merchant named Leonard Cotton who died in 1872, the year before the Hontvets arrived. The Cotton Tenant House is currently among the restored historic buildings on the campus of Strawbery Banke Museum.

Terrible and wonderful things occurred to Maren and John in the two years following Wagner's execution. First, John got his new boat. He would serve as ship's "master" to the small group of owners and investors who put up $6,500 to construct his modern new fishing vessel. In April 1876, the schooner *Mary S. Hontvet*, named for Maren, was launched into the Piscataqua River from Fernald's boatyard. Measuring 75 feet on the keel and at 116 tons, Captain Hontvet's sleek new craft was among the fastest in the region. John fitted out his schooner for serious trawl fishing at the Grand Banks off Newfoundland. With local fishing stocks depleted, John had been forced to expand his business or fail like so many smaller family operations. Now he was a key New England player in the high-risk, high-profit trawl fishing industry in the cold distant Canadian waters.

Before John's schooner had returned from its first successful journey on May 18, 1876, a "startling rumor" found its way by telegram into newspapers across the country. The report originated in a "special dispatch" to a Concord, New Hampshire, paper by an unknown writer. It stated an unnamed "Swedish" woman, formerly a resident of Smuttynose at the Isles of Shoals, had recently made "some startling disclosures" on her deathbed. The brief bulletin concluded: "This woman, as the report has it, confessed to her relatives in her dying moments that she killed Anethe and Karen Christensen, the two women who were so horribly murdered one April [sic] morning in 1873. Louis Wagner, Prussian fisherman, was arrested, tried, and convicted of the crime and last year he was executed in the prison yard at Thomaston, Maine."

The deathbed confession story, a cruel and obvious hoax, was a terrible blow to the Hontvets. Sympathetic local editors immediately published denials. *The Daily Kennebec Journal* retaliated with this headline: "A False Rumor Contradicted—Wagner Without Doubt the Murderer!" Mrs. Hontvet, the newspaper pointed out, was still alive in Portsmouth and "bears the marks of her suffering on that night." The *New York Times* reported the deathbed confession in a single sentence on May 18 and declared the rumor to be "without foundation" in a single sentence on May 19.

The source of the fake story, the *Kennebec Journal* suggested, may have come from supporters of an abused and deformed boy named Jesse Pomeroy. The so-called "Boston Boy Fiend" was the focus of the latest grisly murder coverage in penny dailies. Convicted of torturing, mutilating, and killing other children, young Pomeroy was scheduled to be executed. Many New Englanders were squeamish about the thought of a teenager being hanged. The Maren confession hoax may have been an attempt by death penalty opponents to create sympathy for the Pomeroy case. If Mrs. Hontvet had confessed to the Smuttynose killings, and if Louis Wagner was innocent as he had claimed, then the boy serial killer deserved leniency—or so the reasoning went. If that was the cause, then it worked, because Pomeroy was sentenced to life in prison in 1876. The young "fiend" remained in prison for fifty-six years.

It is equally probable the Maren hoax was perpetrated by abolitionists in Maine, where legislators were on the brink of ending capital punishment. Or it may have originated from an unsupervised reporter at one of the sleazier penny dailies who did not bother to double check the facts. Or it was simply a heinous practical joke. Whatever the cause, the false and malicious confession story stuck like glue. Thanks to Wagner's insistence that the real killer might someday appear, and despite immediate retractions of the hoax by reputable newspapers, the damage was done. It became the theme of a modern novel and film and is widely repeated to this day.

The next good news was the arrival of Maren and John's only child. Clara Eleanor Hontvet was born in Portsmouth on January 6, 1877. The couple had been married ten years and Maren was then forty-two years old. But tragic news soon followed. John's younger brother, Matthew, their strong and silent supporter during the Smuttynose tragedy, drowned at sea while fishing off the Grand Banks. Matthew "Huntwell," as the newspapers reported his name, had fallen from his dory while pulling his trawls in rough weather. Matthew was in his mid-twenties and unmarried.

Louis Wagner had been right about one thing; John Hontvet was "forehanded." All John's planning and saving and expertise paid off. The *Mary S. Hontvet* was among the most successful fishing schooners ever to sail out of Portsmouth Harbor. For the next few years, the shipping news trumpeted her success as she returned from journey after journey. In February 1877, for example, the new schooner arrived in Portland, Maine after a two-week trip, having caught 27,300 pounds in two intense fishing days, netting a profit of $1,600. In October, after delivering a boatload of apples to Prince Edward Island in Canada, the *Mary S. Hontvet* returned with a catch of 35,000 pounds. Capt. Hontvet and his crew caught 44,000 pounds in January of 1879 and 60,000 pounds two months later.

There was "considerable uneasiness in town" when the schooner was caught in a severe storm in the winter of 1880, but in early August she delivered a record 80,000 pounds of fish, while investors and crewmen lined up to cash in on her next voyage. Days later, heading to sea once more, Capt. Hontvet's fine schooner ran aground near the breakwater at New Castle. The *Mary S. Hontvet* slipped her anchor in the roiling Piscataqua currents and wrecked at a dangerous spit of land the locals called "Pull and Be Damned." At the next high tide, she broke free, but sank up to her bow with one hundred barrels of salt aboard. Abandoned, she drifted out to sea in a dense fog. Amazingly, a local steamer was able to lash onto the schooner floating on her side. After breaking off her masts, the steamer captain was able to right the ship and tow her to a nearby boatyard for repairs. Since the master and crew had abandoned their ship, it was subject to a hefty salvage fee that was hammered out during a libel case in the New Hampshire district court.

By 1881, John Hontvet was captain of another vessel that nearly lost two dory fishermen in a heavy storm off Nova Scotia. Miraculously, the two men were saved after drifting for sixty-two hours at sea. A year later, after serving aboard a ship out of Baltimore, John bought the schooner *Active* for six hundred dollars, coincidentally, the exact sum he told Louis Wagner he had saved up for a new boat a decade before. By the tenth anniversary of the murders, after coasting with various cargo from Baltimore to Bangor, the shipping news reported that Capt. Hontvet was in New Brunswick. His next delivery of coal was from Philadelphia to Walker's Wharf off Water Street at Portsmouth, right back to the spot where he and Wagner had talked on the night of the murders.

Life improved for Maren in Portsmouth. She was a mother at last, even a celebrity of sorts, respected by many for her bravery at Smuttynose and at the trial. Wagner was finally dead and she could visit the graves of her sister and sister-in-law with just a short walk up South Street. There was money enough to live comfortably, and yet Maren ached to revisit her homeland. John was often away for months at a time and in constant danger. There were also the incessant whispered rumors after the hoax article appeared.

Back on the Shoals, Maren's former neighbors were suffering too. In 1881, Annie Ingebretsen, who had been working at the Appledore Hotel since she was a child, died at age eighteen. What the papers called "brain fever" was most certainly a suicide. Annie's devoted sister, Ovidia, the paper reported, "became insane shortly before her sister died from ceaseless care and anxiety." Ovidia was delivered in a mad and agitated state to a sanitarium in Massachusetts. The following year, Waldemar Ingebretsen died mysteriously from a fall at a Massachusetts hospital while awaiting treatment for his crippled leg. His father, Jorges, the fisherman who had ferried Maren to safety on the morning of the murders, carried his son's body to Portsmouth for burial. Another son of Jorges Ingebretsen, who also worked for the Laightons at Appledore, drowned when his boat capsized at the Shoals. Celia Thaxter's idyllic Norwegian colony was in disarray.

It has been suggested that Maren returned to Norway as early as 1880 or 1881, but her departure date, so far, has been difficult to pin down. We know from the *Portsmouth Journal* that John Hontvet visited her at least once. In late March 1884, the paper reported he had returned "from a visit to his family in Norway where he had been for several months." Immigration records back this up. He came home alone, leaving Oslo, Norway, on March 6 aboard the *Thingvalla*. He would never see Maren again. Within days of arriving home in the United States, John was aboard his schooner *Active*. The restored schooner *Mary S. Hontvet,* meanwhile, was being captained by another Norwegian out of Gloucester, Massachusetts. John next appears in the local maritime records as captain and part-owner of another fishing vessel, the *Clara E. Simpson*. John was aboard his latest ship when he got the news of his wife's death.

Maren Sebeille Hontvet died in Norway on June 24, 1887, more than ten years after the fraudulent deathbed confession had appeared. The date is noted in the family bible and is confirmed in the church records in the rural Norwegian parish of Sandar. The cause of death is listed as kidney disease. Rumors that Maren left an actual deathbed confession in Norway are entirely false.

That is not quite the end of the Hontvet story. By 1890, after living briefly in the seaport of Salem, Massachusetts, John married a woman named Annie. They bought a parcel of land and moved back to the Portsmouth area. The couple had a child, also named John C. Hontvet, although in his will, Capt. Hontvet referred to the boy as his "adopted son."

Having survived thirty years of hurricanes, frozen rivers, lightning storms, and shipwrecks, John was sailing out of Long Island Sound toward Maine in December of 1894 when a British tramp steamer rammed into the *Clara E. Simpson*. In two minutes, John's schooner and its cargo were sunk. He and two sailors survived by scrambling up the rigging to the topmost point. They were quickly cast into rough seas, where they clung to floating wreckage until they were rescued. John's brother, Hans Hontvet, who had come to Portsmouth to find work with John, was killed in the crash along with two other crewmen. Hans left a widow and seven children in Norway.

There was one wreck to go. Amid a severe February gale in 1895, the *Mary S. Hontvet* met her fate. The fast Portsmouth-built schooner sank in waters off Georges Banks. Of the thirteen men aboard when the ship left Gloucester, nine were Scandinavian, two were Canadian, and one was from the Azores Islands. All were lost.

That same year, on the day after Christmas, Maren's daughter, Clara Hontvet, age nineteen, married Lauritz Lowe of Norway. The groom was twenty-nine and had been in America nine years. Their wedding was held at St. John's Episcopal Church in Portsmouth, the site of Karen and Anethe's funeral twenty-two years earlier.

John Christian Hontvet died at his farm on Greenland Road on the outskirts of Portsmouth on December 29, 1904. Once the leader of a Portsmouth lynch mob, John had become a respected businessman, a Mason, and a member of the Knights Templar. Although a mariner most of his days, farmer John bequeathed no boats, but left his land, buildings, horse, cows, fowl, carriages, and his farming tools to his wife and daughter.

Clara Hontvet Lowe survived only to age thirty-six. She died of bronchial pneumonia ten days after the birth of her fifth child. But the family name carried on. Clara's first daughter, Maren Sebeille Lowe, born at Portsmouth in 1897, was named in honor of her courageous grandmother.

Chapter 39

LAST MEN HANGED

History often erodes a mountain of data into a memorable, but inaccurate, nugget of information. So it is no surprise Louis Wagner continues to be cited as the last man hanged in Maine. The abolition of the death penalty was enacted there in 1876, the year following his execution. Wagner's final protest of innocence on the gallows combined with the repugnant hanging of the half-dead Mr. Gordon certainly influenced the landmark legislation. But it is not true, as has been claimed, that the law was changed because Wagner was innocent.

Maine had been moving toward abolition of the death penalty since it gained statehood in 1820. By adding a one-year waiting period for condemned killers and by making the governor the de facto hangman, abolitionists were able to slow down the execution process and keep the public debate alive. And with each gruesome hanging, thanks to the graphic media coverage, what had initially been an active minority of college professors and peacemaking Quakers grew into a popular movement against capital punishment.

But not all Mainers agreed. On the one hand, a group of liberal Protestants known as Universalists openly opposed the hanging of Wagner and Gordon. Even the worst of men, the Universalists believed, were capable of salvation under a benevolent God. On the other hand, members of the Congregational church held to the more traditional Puritan view that man's depravity and sinful nature demanded punishment. Each execution, they believed, stood as a stern warning to future transgressors of God's commandment that "thou shalt not kill."

The 1876 ban against executions stood until 1883, when Maine reinstituted the death penalty, but only in cases of murder. That same year, a thirty-seven-year-old escaped convict named David Wilkerson and two other men broke into a store in Bath, Maine. During their escape, Wilkerson shot a police officer in the head with his .32-caliber revolver before he was captured. Also in 1883, Raffaele Capone and Carmen Santore, two Italian railroad workers, were convicted of shooting a coworker named Pasquale Coscie and robbing him of thirty dollars. Capone, Santore, and Wilkerson were all found guilty, sentenced to be executed, and sent to Thomaston Prison.

Capone and Santore were hanged from the scaffold in the Thomaston quarry on a fair, but chilly April day in 1885, almost ten years after the execution of Wagner and Gordon. Santore went to his death "head high," the *Boston Daily Globe* reported. "Me no 'fraid. Ready to die," Santore announced. Capone, however, insisted the building of the scaffold and the entire hanging ceremony was being staged to frighten him into confessing. He was certain, he said, he would not really be hanged.

Upon reaching "the drop," the same trapdoor where Wagner and others had stood, both men broke down. Capone and Santore repented their sins and forgave all their enemies, without exception. The sheriff tapped the spring with his foot. Eight minutes later, both men had no pulse. In thirteen minutes, there was no perceptible heartbeat. In twenty-three minutes, they were declared dead and, if their families did not claim the bodies, they were given to the Maine Medical Institute.

Things did not go so smoothly with David Wilkerson in November. Due to a poorly tied noose, he strangled in a slow, twisting agony. Two years later, Maine reestablished its ban on capital punishment by a wide margin. Since 1887, there have been half a dozen attempts to restore the death penalty in Maine, but the lessons of history have been well learned.

A freakish sidebar to the state's death penalty law occurred in the winter of 1890 when the mutilated torso of Hiram Sawtell was discovered in a shallow grave in the woods of Berwick, Maine. The victim's head and arms had been hacked off with an ax. Medical examiners and witnesses were able to prove Isaac Sawtell had killed his brother over a property dispute. Both men were from Boston, but the murder had taken place in a barn in Rochester, New Hampshire. Isaac had transported his brother's body seven miles across the state line into the jurisdiction of Maine, possibly to avoid the death penalty if captured. His plan failed. Isaac was sentenced to be hanged in New Hampshire, but he died in jail the day before his execution. The "Modern Cain and Abel" murder gave rise to this couplet:

Two brothers in our town did dwell;
Hiram sought heaven, but Isaac Sawtell.

Most of the seven men executed at Thomaston were "outsiders" and not representative of the general population. Some were recent immigrants and one was black. A few suffered inhumane torture as they strangled slowly in front of witnesses and reporters. And at least one, according to persistent myth, was an innocent Prussian fisherman. Ironically, thanks to Wagner's one-man publicity campaign, his lies have acted, in part, as a bulwark against the return of the death penalty in Maine. But in response, the continued abolition of capital punishment in Maine has bolstered the false legend of Wagner's innocence. "It is a powerful argument," one Bowdoin College sociologist says of the Wagner legend, "whether it is true or not."

Although David Wilkerson may forever be the last man hanged in Maine, Louis Wagner remains the best known member of that infamous list. None of the other convicts executed at Thomaston has become a key character in a bestselling novel or portrayed in a Hollywood film. Yet a quick follow-up on the four lawyers in the Wagner trial proves there has been no shortage of nightmarish murders in the home state of Stephen King, America's preeminent horror writer.

Chapter 40

LEGAL EAGLES

Prosecutor George Yeaton is largely remembered, the *Portsmouth Herald* recalled, as the man "who won fame for his masterly prosecution of Louis Wagner." But state records show Yeaton was paid only $125 for his extensive work on that case. For most of his career, he was a respected and serviceable county lawyer who earned a solid living representing the wealthy owners of railroads, banks, and cotton mills.

But there was at least one equally grisly crime in Yeaton's record. He later defended a prominent businessman in his hometown of South Berwick, Maine. In 1900, the charred body of a pregnant woman was discovered inside a burning barn. After a six-month investigation, local police arrested forty-two-year old Edwin H. Knight. Police alleged that Knight had killed the victim, a housekeeper named Fannie Sprague, when she revealed to him she was carrying his child. A local business owner, churchgoer, and father of six, Knight was also a former South Berwick town selectman.

The case against Knight was solid, but circumstantial. He had been seen with Sprague around the time of the murder. His boots matched the plaster cast made of footprints at the scene. The victim had been bludgeoned by wood ripped from a cart that Knight owned. Sprague's three-year-old son had seen a man matching Knight's description entering the barn with his mother. Most damning was the revelation that Fannie Sprague, who was five-months pregnant at the time of her murder, had worked briefly as

Knight's housekeeper five months earlier. But Edwin Knight was not a foreigner, black, or poor, and his attorney was the former York County prosecutor. Despite compelling evidence, Knight was acquitted. Fannie Sprague's murderer was never found (or was he?) and, even in historic South Berwick, her mournful tale is rarely ever told.

During the 1901 trial, attorney George Yeaton built a beautiful home in the center of South Berwick village. The house later became a restaurant and is currently a bed-and-breakfast within easy walking distance to Berwick Academy, a private day school founded in 1791. George Yeaton lived to age eighty-one.

Even more bizarre was the "Mystery of the Headless Skeleton" that landed on the docket of Attorney General Harris M. Plaisted a few months after the Wagner case in 1873. James M. Lowell was accused of murdering his estranged twenty-eight-year-old wife, who had disappeared three years earlier. The decapitated skeleton of Marie Elizabeth Lowell, still wearing the black silk dress and laced serge boots she was last seen in, was discovered in a desolate Maine location. The defense argued the identity of the corpse could not be determined. Plaisted told the jury, with evident sarcasm, the defense planned to prove "that this woman never had a head."

The milliner who had worked on Mrs. Lowell's dress identified the skeleton's clothing down to the last stitch. The skeleton of the victim was exhibited in the courtroom, sending "a thrill of superstitious horror through the crowd," according to a nationally circulated report. The victim's skull was never recovered. Plaisted's circumstantial case proved Lowell, who was wildly jealous of his wife, had abused and threatened her so often she had moved out of their house. He was found guilty, sentenced to be hanged, and sent to Thomaston Prison, where he apparently lived out his days, cheating the hangman. Harris Plaisted, already a Civil War hero and a former judge, later served Maine as a congressman and then as governor.

One of the more colorful cases in the life of Rufus Tapley had occurred years before the Wagner trial when "Judge" Tapley was still on the Maine Superior Court bench. In 1866, Jane Swett of Kennebunk killed her husband after thirty-one years of marriage. Handsome Charles Swett was a self-appointed preacher and untrained country doctor who, one historian writes, "was addicted to alcohol, morphine, and women." When drunk, Swett was often violent. He beat his wife, attacked his daughter, contracted venereal disease from prostitutes, brought other women home, and squandered the family savings. Jane Swett confessed that she put morphine in her husband's whiskey bottle, but claimed that she had only tried to "reform" her husband by making him sick. Theirs had been an arranged teenage marriage, Swett said, and she had never loved her profligate husband.

At trial, the prosecutor painted Charles Swett as the victim of an abusive wife in a loveless marriage. Swett's bad behavior, the government claimed, was his wife's fault. Jane was "a woman of ungovernable temper and fiendish passions," the prosecutor said. She had destroyed her husband's "high hopes" and "holy purpose." His addiction to alcohol and his infidelity, the prosecutor added, was any man's natural response to an insufferable marriage. The jury found the fifty-one-year-old defendant guilty of manslaughter, but recommended mercy. Judge Tapley sentenced Jane Swett to six years in prison. She served out her term, moved back to Kennebunk, and died years later at the town poor farm. Hon. Rufus P. Tapley, who presided over the Swett case, died exactly two decades after the Wagner trial at age seventy, and is buried in Saco, Maine.

Max Fischacher's career is harder to track than that of his Victorian colleagues. The German-born attorney continued to represent the underclass of European immigrants who were streaming into Boston in the late nineteenth century. According to a Harvard alumni publication, he died at Roxbury in 1913. It appears Fischacher was dead right about Dr. Horace Chase, the self-proclaimed chemical expert from Boston who "proved" that Wagner's clothes were spotted with human blood. While the conclusion was correct, Chase's science was bogus. And years later, in a strange sidebar to the Wagner case, it was Dr. Chase himself who many suspected of murder in a scandalous Boston trial.

The curious case began when Dr. Chase, a widower, married a wealthy socialite and widow named Jennie Paul of Swampscott, Massachusetts.

Her fortune, however, was tied up in a legal trust that prevented her new husband from inheriting a million dollars. In an odd move, the new Mrs. Chase legally adopted the doctor's adult son, who was only nine years her junior. When Mrs. Chase mysteriously died in 1905, her adopted son and only direct heir stood to inherit her money. But the young man died suddenly of an apparent suicide by gas soon after. Dr. Chase argued that the million dollars now belonged to him.

It was hard not to believe that Dr. Chase had orchestrated two murders. During a probate hearing, a lawyer who had represented the late Mrs. Chase, produced a secret affidavit. Before her death, fearing that her husband might kill her, she had signed a document claiming Dr. Chase had forced her to adopt his son "under threat of abandonment" to get control of her money. Dr. Chase testified he had married his wife only for love, not money. Her unfounded fears, he said, stemmed from "a frenzied condition" that occasionally caused his late wife to become vindictive towards him. There were suggestions that Chase had poisoned his wife and killed his own son, but Chase was never indicted. When the court refused to accept the forced adoption as legal, Dr. Chase was denied the inheritance. Wagner's "blood expert" put up a fierce courtroom battle over the money, but lost.

One more bizarre footnote to the Wagner trial involves Nathum Tarbox, one of the twelve jurors who took just fifty-five minutes to find the defendant guilty of a hanging offense. An 1888 article in the *Lewiston Journal* titled "The Unhappy Husband," tells the sad tale. A thirty-eight-year-old Maine fisherman named John Curtis went out of his mind when his wife threatened divorce and left him. She moved into the home of a relative, taking her three children and removing more than one thousand dollars from the family bank account. Curtis was so distraught that he took some rope and hanged himself from a nearby tree. But "before he was extinct" a neighbor cut him down. Recovering consciousness, Curtis immediately went next door to the home of Nathum Tarbox, the Wagner juror. Curtis found another length of rope and was found hanging from a tree in the backyard of Mr. Tarbox.

But no follow-up to the Smuttynose murder case is more poignant than the rise and fall of Thomas Entwistle. The assistant marshal who twice shielded Louis Wagner from the vengeful Portsmouth mob became a legend in his own time. Born in England, Entwistle had arrived in Portsmouth as a boy of seven, worked in a nearby cotton mill, and served with distinction throughout the Civil War, where he was twice wounded. He moved up the ranks at the police department, then worked as a blacksmith and captain of the watch at the Portsmouth Naval Shipyard. By 1895, he was back in his old job as Portsmouth city marshal. Entwistle was a vestryman at the local church, a state senator, and a father of five. "His life career has been one of heroism and manly courage," the *Granite Monthly* reported in 1910. And yet, Thomas Entwistle is remembered today primarily as the corrupt enabler of the city's illicit sex trade.

Marshal Entwistle did not create the combat zone on Water Street but it appears to have thrived under his administration. By the turn of the twentieth century, there were a dozen brothels or "fancy houses," as they were euphemistically known. Mary Amazeen Baker, the most notorious of Portsmouth madams, opened the Gloucester House in 1897, two years after Entwistle took office. Located just a few yards from what had been Wagner's boarding house, the Gloucester House stood invitingly in a four-story brick building near the ferry landing where sailors from the Portsmouth Naval Shipyard first arrived in the city. The prostitutes who worked there, some as young as fourteen, were the city's worst kept secret. Mrs. Baker exhibited the new girls by touring them around town in her carriage. With her red beehive hairdo, her furs, and her diamond-capped teeth, Mary Baker was impossible to miss. Politicians, foreign dignitaries, local professionals, judges, and academy school students were also known to frequent Baker's glitzy establishment.

Police records indicate almost no arrests and fewer fines for owners of the Water Street brothels and their sex workers during Entwistle's fifteen-year administration. But the wheels came off the lucrative flesh trade in 1912. During the month of August, four marines were found dead along

Water Street. The first body was discovered propped against the wall of a Portsmouth whorehouse like a discarded puppet. His head, unsupported by a recently broken neck and a severed spinal cord, drooped to one side and both his legs were doubled up unnaturally beneath the body. Three more unsolved murders in the midst of a summer crime wave drew the media spotlight onto the city's smoldering South End, leaving Portsmouth in "a state of siege," the *Portsmouth Times* announced.

Police corruption on Water Street was well known, but now the officers seemed equally inept at protecting local citizens. Puddle Dock residents armed themselves against robbers and killers, hunkering in windows at night, guns in hand. Days later, in a rare acknowledgment of ongoing "white slavery," a woman was charged with drugging and abducting four-teen-year-old Ellen Duffy to a Portsmouth bordello.

"We were in a restaurant," Duffy told the newspaper, "and all the while the woman kept talking to me that if a man came to see us that night I should do what he asked me to."

The police, residents complained, were protecting the brothels and not the citizens of Water Street. Sheriff Entwistle, his thick mustache and hair now white, fanned the flames of public indignation when he refused to comply with the police commissioner's request to retire. When Mayor Daniel Badger reluctantly made the Water Street bordellos a campaign issue in the upcoming election, Portsmouth's dirty little secret finally became a public issue.

"As mayor of this city," Badger announced, "I call on you to close forthwith and permanently keep closed all houses of ill repute in this city, and to close forthwith and keep closed all places where intoxicating liquor is sold illegally."

Marshal Entwistle, then in his seventies, wrote a blistering attack on Mayor Badger. Was the city going to shut down all the tobacco shops, auto garages, newsstands, and drugstores too? His comparison of prostitution to tobacco and newspapers did not sit well with locals in an era of rising social reform and temperance. Mayor Badger easily won reelection, Thomas Entwistle quickly resigned and the bordellos were shut down.

David Ferland, a former Portsmouth police chief and scholar of local crime says Entwistle was not so much a villain as a scapegoat. For decades, city leaders had turned a blind eye toward the waterfront bordellos until public sentiment shifted and the mayor was running for reelection.

"It was political. The whole Water Street debauchery had run its course," Ferland says. "But up until that point, Entwistle was exactly the marshal the city wanted him to be. Everybody was looking the other way because they were making money. I think Entwistle was a remarkable police officer, probably our most famous."

Visitors who take the "underbelly" walking tour of historic Portsmouth today are often confused by the beautiful and extensive riverside park. What happened to the many whorehouses that once lined Water Street? The answer is weird, but true.

In the 1930s, two retired Portsmouth schoolteachers suddenly inherited three million dollars. Josie and Mary Prescott had grown up on the seedy and dangerous Water Street. Their father ran a store, possibly in the building where Louis Wagner had boarded with the Johnson family. Through their lawyer, the elderly Prescott sisters bought up most of the dingy commercial property along the waterfront. They decreed that the many sin-stained buildings should all be torn down, along with unsightly water towers, rotting wharves, and coal pockets. The Prescott sisters presented the open land as a gift to the city for public use. Today, Prescott Park is a family-friendly destination for outdoor theater, lush gardens, and celebrity concerts that draw thousands of summer visitors daily.

Chapter 41

PURE MURDER

For fifty years following Wagner's execution, the facts of the Smuttynose case reigned over the rumors and false statements, most of the latter having been invented by the killer himself. Local newspapers from Boston to Bangor retold the story fairly accurately at five- and ten-year intervals, usually recycling details directly from previously published accounts or from Celia Thaxter's popular essay. A twenty-fifth "anniversary" snippet in the *Portsmouth Journal*, for instance, noted that the graves of Karen and Anethe "who were admired by all" had become "a Mecca for visitors." A lengthy fortieth anniversary recap in the *Portsmouth Herald* listed all the witnesses and even chronicled the demise of all the Wagner jurors, including the fact that juror Benajah Hall committed suicide by drowning.

These articles inevitably repeated Wagner's denials and the caveat that not everyone at the time was convinced of his guilt. The quickie flashback articles did not mention the Victorian fascination with Wagner's Arian good looks or his hangdog charm and its seductive power over reporters of the era. The retrospective accounts kept the story alive for generations of new readers, but they also condensed the complex series of events recounted in these pages and the weight of evidence against Wagner into a few words. The subtleties of Wagner's devious personality and the catalog of his lies was lost along with the evidence presented at trial. They did not mention the popular distrust of circumstantial evidence, the biased and imaginative reporting of the competing penny-dailies, or the anti-death penalty movement sweeping over the state of Maine.

America, meanwhile, had changed radically. Visitors to the 1876 Centennial Exposition in Philadelphia, the year after Wagner's death, saw a brave new world taking shape. Designed by a twenty-seven-year-old German immigrant on a 285-acre tract, America's first "world's fair" drew more than nine million visitors. "The American invents as the Greek sculpted and the Italian painted—it is genius," the *Times of London* announced after touring the great American Machinery Hall exhibit. Only one hundred years old, the United States was on the brink of becoming the planet's greatest industrial power.

Had Wagner or his two victim's survived the next fifty years, they would have witnessed the wholesale use of electric lights, refrigeration, radios, telephones, moving pictures, automobiles, X-rays, airplanes, and other life-altering innovations. In hindsight, the faster the twentieth century moved, the more simple, mannered, and quaint the past appeared. The more often small boats were powered by motors, for example, the more incredible Wagner's feat of rowing seemed. The discovery of fingerprints and blood typing made the evidence at the Wagner trial seem even more circumstantial. The rise of detective fiction made the Smuttynose case more hauntingly mysterious. Classic unsolved homicides involving Jack the Ripper and Lizzie Borden turned Americans into amateur sleuths. Advances in police methods, legal rights for defendants, courtroom procedures, and prison reform made Wagner's treatment, exceptionally good for his era, look primitive by comparison.

By the time true crime writer Edmund Lester Pearson began digging into the Wagner case, World War I was a fading memory. Women had gained the vote, Prohibition was in force, and the Roaring Twenties were in full swing. Born in 1880 in Newburyport, Massachusetts, just over the border from coastal New Hampshire, Pearson was certainly familiar with the bloodiest event on the Isles of Shoals. Educated at Harvard, Pearson was no pulp murder groupie. He was, by contrast, a bibliophile, an egghead, an elitist, and the editor of publications at the prestigious New York Public Library.

Picking up where Thomas De Quincey left off a century before, Pearson became a connoisseur of what he called "the pure crime." The perfect murder, for Pearson, was not one where the clever killer got away scot-free. Ideally, the murderer should be discovered, captured, and executed. Pearson was looking, instead, to drag the study of murder up from the gutter and to examine it intelligently, even artistically. Pure crime, he noted, was the criminal equivalent of a beautiful painting or a sublime musical composition. His "pure murder" was an aesthetic ideal that could be held up to the light and examined critically in hopes of unlocking the secrets of human nature. Why do some people kill while others do not? But not all crimes were worth studying. De Quincey made that point clear, Pearson wrote, when he "disposed of the stupid notion that any murder is interesting if it is gory enough."

Like any scholarly discipline, there were rules to follow. Pure crime had to be "mellowed by time," Pearson decided, not freshly torn from the headlines. Crimes of passion were too dull and common to qualify for serious analysis. Gangsters and mobsters were simply mechanics and butchers, not artful murderers. Serial killers like Dr. H. H. Holmes, the mass murderer of the 1893 Chicago World's Fair, might be brilliant, but his crimes were merely habitual and repetitive. Pearson's pure crime was an isolated act. It must take place on the razor's edge of right and wrong. Why bother contemplating why an evil person does evil things? The iconic crimes sprang from the hearts of law-abiding well-mannered citizens who, one day, suddenly crossed over to the dark side. Think Adam and Eve. Think Cain and Abel.

"Beginning in the 1920s," writes crime historian David Schmid, "Edmund Pearson seemed to succeed, almost single-handedly in raising true crime narratives to the level of literary art... The philosophical and aesthetic questions raised by murder are of much more interest to Pearson than is a blow-by-blow account of the murders themselves."

Pearson's first foray into the dark realm focused on five vintage homicides, mostly unsolved and based on circumstantial evidence. *Studies in Murder* (1924) opened with the Lizzie Borden ax murder case, Pearson's all-time favorite crime mystery. The book became a surprise bestseller. He followed that with "the complete historical record" of fourteen stories "written to interest everyone." *Murder at Smutty Nose and Other Murders* (1926) featured a seventy-page overview of the Wagner case. It was important to Pearson that readers know his interests were scholarly, not prurient. He also knew that, to sell many copies and become profitable, his books had to be lively and readable, not didactic or preachy. Inspired by Celia Thaxter's "Memorable Murder," he located a rare copy of the Wagner trial transcript, combed through newspaper accounts, and visited the scene of the crime.

Pearson saw Louis Wagner as the quintessential social deviant. The poor, frustrated, and friendless fisherman was outwardly attractive, yet "as dangerous as a rattlesnake." Camouflaged by his social graces and good looks, Wagner appeared to be a friendly neighbor when, in fact, he was stalking his victims, Pearson wrote. He was "a wolf in sheep's clothing," according to Mollie Clifford, who had been a young girl living on Lunging Island when Wagner came begging for free meals. As Maren Hontvet told Celia, Wagner "was always lurking in corners, lingering, looking, listening." The more Pearson came to know Wagner, the more he despised him, and in turn, wanted to warn his readers of such monsters hiding in plain sight. The message was not whether Wagner had done the deed, but "how" and "why."

Methodical and practical, Pearson was frustrated by the willingness, even eagerness, of seacoast locals to spread rumors and repeat false statements, when, in fact, they knew very little about the case. Why did people insist it was impossible for a powerful dory fisherman to row eighteen miles, when it was blatantly obvious from the trial testimony, from common sense, and from simple observation that it was not a terribly difficult feat? Why would any sensible person, after examining the facts, doggedly insist Wagner was innocent simply because he said he was? This, for Pearson, was dangerous thinking. This was the true mystery of the Isles of Shoals.

"Out of 430 murderers observed by a prison doctor," Pearson wrote in 1926, "only three disclosed the slightest remorse for their crime. So we need not feel that Wagner's protestations of innocence have any power to remove the weight of proof against him."

Pearson was equally frustrated by the common misconception that circumstantial evidence is inherently weak or unfair. In an article written for *Scribner's Magazine,* he contested the fallacy, as prosecutor Plaisted had done in the Wagner case, that circumstantial evidence was a "chain" and that if one of its links could be broken, then the case must fall apart. Instead, Pearson argued, circumstantial cases are built upon a number of often unrelated elements—facts, objects, and incidents—that point in a certain direction and indicate the truth. It is the accumulation and interconnection of the elements that leads to a conclusion. If one or more of those elements proves to be false, but the weight of evidence still points toward the criminal, then a guilty verdict is fair and reasonable.

"Circumstantial evidence is conclusive proof only to intelligent persons," Pearson wrote bluntly. "To the stupid, it may mean little."

For Pearson, the aesthetic beauty of Wagner's crime, if such a thing is possible, could be found in his many contradictory choices. His bold and impulsive decision to row ten miles out to sea on a winter's night might well have yielded the perfect robbery. But he killed when he could have run away. He ran, but was unable to hide. He lied because he was incapable of confessing. And yet, despite all the evidence against him, Wagner continued to attract sympathizers and defenders, even into the 1920s, a phenomenon that Pearson hoped to destroy with his detailed analysis of the case.

Today, we know that the "Maren did it" theory was entirely a hoax, perpetrated and retracted as false in 1876, years before Maren Hontvet moved back to Norway where she died in 1887. Pearson, however, never located the origin of the hoax. In a letter to Judge Justin Henry Shaw of Kittery, Maine, in 1927, Pearson revealed his frustration at being unable to track down the source.

"Of course," Pearson wrote, "I heard the death-bed confession yarn, from a man on Star Island, who pointed out another man who said he had newspaper clippings about it. I tried hard in Portsmouth, at the newspaper office, and elsewhere…to find some reference to it in print—not to confirm or deny it, for I knew it was bosh—but simply to find out, if possible, when it started."

In *Murder at Smutty Nose*, unable to officially debunk the rumor, Pearson was only able to express his indignation. "As to Wagner's contention that the murders had been done by the Hontvets," he wrote, "this remained entirely in the realm of cheap gossip. Neither he nor his lawyers had the effrontery to suggest it in court. No one living at the time would have paid any attention to a charge at once so silly and so cruel."

And yet people did pay attention. Following his intense study, Pearson concluded that Wagner was brutish, stupid, cowardly, egocentric, and without an ounce of compassion or pity for anyone except himself. But to the author's dismay, the "Maren theory" seemed to be gaining converts as the case moved out of living memory and into the realm of legend. The more people told the story, the more the facts waned and the mystery expanded.

Instead of silencing the skeptics with the truth, *Murder at Smutty Nose* seemed to summon a coven of conspiracy theorists. A new wave of pro-Wagnerites, many of whom knew only the bare bones of the story, announced that the "real" killer of Karen and Anethe Christensen had escaped justice. Such blind faith in the face of so much evidence, for Pearson, was criminal behavior. "To seek to clear Louis Wagner at the expense of Maren Hontvet is to engage in a second hunting of that wretched woman," he wrote. "It is only a little less despicable than the pursuit which took place over the rocks of the island on that winter night." People who blamed Maren, to Pearson, were almost as guilty as the killer himself.

From Plymouth Rock to Paul Revere, Americans love their legends. By insisting on Wagner's guilt, Pearson was robbing the region of a time-honored myth. He might just as well have insisted that George Washington had lied when he chopped down the cherry tree.

"Interest and discussion in the [Wagner] case has again been aroused by the recent publication of an unusual book by Edmund Lester Pearson," an editor of the *Portsmouth Herald* wrote on March 5, 1927, the fifty-fourth anniversary of the tragedy. Pearson's definitive work immediately drew fire, often from anonymous letter writers who thought they knew better. When a letter to a Boston newspaper regurgitated the Maren deathbed confession as fact, Judge Shaw of Kittery fired back a written rebuttal. He had been in contact with Mr. Pearson, Shaw wrote, and owned a copy of the complete trial transcript. Shaw called the Maren story "a very stupid fake." Wagner "did not have a ghost of an alibi," Shaw argued.

Contacted for his opinion on the Boston article, Celia Thaxter's son, John Thaxter, who owned a home in Kittery Point, called it "a cock-and-bull yarn from start to finish." After summarizing the murder story and reporting on the controversy, the *Herald* editor concluded that "in many respects the Smuttynose case is the most remarkable of all stories in criminal history."

There is undoubtedly a taint of intellectual snobbery and conservative bias in Pearson's analysis of Wagner. Pearson was, after all, a law-and-order man. In his time, Pearson personally favored the death penalty and opposed the insanity defense for capital crimes. But he succeeded in presenting the facts of the Smuttynose case to the public like no one, not even Celia Thaxter, had done. So we can allow him the exaggerated conclusion that: "No person competent to judge, who has dealt with fact rather than rumor, has ever doubted the justice of the verdict."

In 1927, after the success of the Smuttynose book, Pearson was able to quit his library job and devote himself to writing full time. His later books returned twice more to the Lizzie Borden case and his many essays appeared in respected periodicals such as *Vanity Fair* and the *New Yorker*. Film trivia buffs often note he was also the unnamed scriptwriter for the film *Bride of Frankenstein*. Edmund Pearson died at age fifty-six of bronchial pneumonia. The *New York Times* eulogized him as "America's greatest fact-crime writer," and he is widely referred to as the "father of true crime."

But the legends Wagner planted continued to grow. In 1936, for example, the year before Pearson's death, an elderly Farmington, New Hampshire, woman (she signed her name "A.S.B.") sent a letter to the *Rochester Courier*. As a young girl, she had seen Wagner in person after his capture, she wrote. She heard him tell his story. Wagner had told her that Maren Hontvet was the real murderer. Wagner's claim was proven, ASB believed, when it became known that Mrs. Hontvet had confessed. Maren had killed her sister "in order to get some property that was owned by them jointly," the Farmington woman explained. (Neither woman owned any property.) When the state of Maine "learned the truth," and realized that they had hanged an innocent man, they abolished capital punishment, ASB wrote. "I don't understand why anyone continues to say that Wagner was the criminal," she concluded, although she had all the facts wrong. "I think this is a true story."

Intrigued by the Farmington woman's letter, a *Rochester Courier* reporter named Francis Goodall decided to "get at the actual truth." As a boy of twelve, he too had seen Wagner in person and remained curiously sympathetic to the sad-faced prisoner. Goodall made an in-depth study in Maine newspaper archives and read Pearson's book. Goodall's lengthy report appeared in the *Courier* the following year.

"If ever a case were proved up to the hilt in a court of law," he concluded, "it was that of Louis Wagner." Maren's testimony was "unimpeachable," the reporter said, and it was "preposterous" to think dozens of witnesses had banded together to perjure themselves. Wagner's alibi, meanwhile, was "absurd." At the risk of losing a longtime newspaper subscriber, Goodall laid it on the line. Mrs. ASB, he concluded, had been taken in by "one of the coldest-blooded and brutal killers in New England's entire criminal history."

Former Portsmouth Police Chief David Ferland has studied the Wagner case from every angle. Asked point blank who killed Karen and Anethe, he does not hesitate.

"It was Wagner," Ferland says with certainty. "It was a state-of-the-art investigation for the time. He was represented by good counsel in a pretty transparent trial. A lot of people with integrity were involved in the case or testified, and if there was any cover-up or impropriety, it would have come out."

Chapter 42

WEIGHT OF WATER

Historians agree there is no immutable single version of the past. History is forever being revised, reinterpreted, and repackaged to fit our shifting needs and views. We all see Louis Wagner through twenty-first-century eyes. But professional historians are careful to avoid interpreting our ancestors as if they lived in present times, knew what we know, thought like we think.

The police, for example, cannot be faulted for failing to "read him his rights" when arresting Wagner, since the Miranda warning was not established in the United States until 1966. Wagner's lawyers had no idea whether the blood evidence introduced by Dr. Horace Chase was scientifically accurate. The twelve jurors at the Alfred trial were all white males from rural Maine, and their opinions about justice, women, race, religion, foreigners, science, and everything else were products of their time and their region. Every person in this story lived in a world where bathtubs, oil lamps, and outhouses were the norm, while fast-acting aspirin tablets, minty toothpaste, hot showers, and endless rolls of fluffy, white toilet paper were still years into the future.

Thinking people from the past thought and acted exactly like us is sometimes called "presentism" and is a critical fallacy historians try to avoid. Writers of novels, however, are not bound by such rules, even when the novel draws heavily from historical facts. In a brief introductory note to her popular novel *The Weight of Water* (1996), Anita Shreve alerts readers that passages are "taken verbatim" from the Wagner trial transcript. Her characters, she says, "are either the product of the author's imagination *or, if real, are used fictitiously.*" In other words, even the so-called "historical" characters in the novel might say and do things they never did in real life.

The novel also borrows heavily from Celia Thaxter and other Shoals sources, so much so, that a *New York Times* review of her book suggested that "you might well take it along on your next cruise as the definitive guide to the islands." Besides a near-complete retelling of the actual murders, Shreve's novel recycles stories of Blackbeard the Pirate, the shipwrecked Spanish sailors, Sam Haley's silver bars, Celia Thaxter's literary salon, colonial fish drying, Indian raids, and more.

"History can't belong to anybody," Anita Shreve told a documentary filmmaker after the publication of *The Weight of Water*. "I use history in the service of fiction. It is the story and the language that come first." Her book, she said, is just the opposite of what is traditionally known as historical fiction, although it is often described as "half" historical fiction.

The author tumbled fact and myth together to create the background for a contemporary parallel plot about a magazine photographer named Jean James who is assigned to take pictures of Smuttynose Island. Jean arrives aboard a forty-one-foot sailboat with her brother-in-law and his sexy girlfriend. Jean's husband, a somber alcoholic poet, and their lively five-year-old daughter are also aboard. Shreve's protagonist becomes obsessed with the island murders.

"I have to let this story go," Jean declares as the novel opens. "It is with me all the time now, a terrible weight." Later, as if channeling Thomas De Quincey and Edward Pearson, Jean James thinks, "Sometimes I imagine the murders to have been a thing of subtle grace and beauty, with slim arms raised in white nightgowns against the fright, the rocks sharp and the gale billowing the thin linen like sheets on a line."

Shreve "discovered" the islands while sailing off coastal New England in the 1970s. "We were lost in the fog," she recalls, "and in that dramatic way that fog lifts, all of a sudden there they were." She wrote a six-page short story at the time, she says, but set it aside until 1995 when athlete and actor O. J. Simpson was acquitted of killing his ex-wife, Nicole, and her friend Ronald Goldman. Simpson's eight-month "trial of the century," like the Wagner trial, was a media circus. The sense of injustice Shreve felt in the Simpson case convinced the novelist "how necessary it was for me to write the book."

The injustice as seen in *The Weight of Water*, however, is not to the surviving victim Maren Hontvet, but to Louis Wagner. Both Shreve and her imaginary character Jean did much of their research on the murders at the Portsmouth Athenaeum, an actual archival library where the real murder ax is now housed. In the fictional Athenaeum, as depicted in Shreve's novel, Jean discovers a long confessional letter written by Maren Hontvet (spelled "Hontvedt" in the book). In the imaginary letter, translated from Norwegian, Maren hates her older sister, Karen, and tolerates her "estranged" husband, John, a detail possibly borrowed from the estranged relationship between Celia and Levi Thaxter. The fictional Maren has an incestuous love affair with her little brother, Evan Christensen (who in reality was Maren's half-brother and ten years her junior). Things go downhill from there. Maren confesses all, and in the stormy conclusion of the novel, Louis Wagner becomes the victim and is hanged as an innocent man.

Some critics found the parallel plots, separated by more than one hundred years, difficult to follow. Others found Maren's lengthy confessional letter and the steamy, sexual subplot too modern and contrived to swallow. Professor C. Lawrence Robertson at the University of New Hampshire wondered whether Shreve had overstepped the bounds of good taste and human respect when using historical figures in the service of fiction.

"Does an author have the right to malign the lives of real people, at one time very much alive, to support a fictional account of a modern story?" Robertson wrote in the *Portsmouth Herald* in March 2000. Does a simple disclaimer at the front of a novel, Robertson argued, give the author license to create an "untrue, unfair, and impossible account" that attacks the memory of people who are not alive to defend themselves and smear their descendants as well? Apparently so. Fiction writers have been murdering facts since Shakespeare wrote his often inaccurate historical plays based on the British monarchy.

Professor Robertson's complaint was about breaching the boundaries of good taste and human respect rather than good writing. The problem, in fact, is that Shreve's novel blends reality and fantasy so dramatically and seamlessly that readers who are unfamiliar with the Wagner case come away convinced that Maren was the actual killer. Because the novel cleverly ignores incriminating evidence against Wagner while inventing clues that point to Maren, the reader cannot possibly find the historical truth within the novel. Too many of the facts are missing or have been altered.

Shreve's research into the case was driven, she says, by her frustration at not knowing whether Wagner was truly guilty, a frustration that Wagner orchestrated and exploited to save his own life. The murders, the novelist concluded from what she read, were crimes of passion. "It's very hard for me to work up a scenario in which Louis Wagner felt passionately enough about this," Shreve says.

Through Jean James, the reader participates in what appears to be the same historical search for truth, even examining some of the same historical clues, but ultimately the characters in *The Weight of Water* are not authentic, nor are they intended to be. Shreve's version of Maren is no more historical than the depiction of "Honest Abe" in the novel *Abraham Lincoln Vampire Hunter*. Shreve's novel is not really about an ax murder, but is an exploration of the destructive power of jealousy. Both Maren and Jean James were living claustrophobic lives, trapped in what Shreve called a "tight caldron."

Anita Shreve did her homework, nonetheless, even traveling to Larvik, Norway, to tour Maren Hontvet's homeland. And not only does the novel fabricate details that make Maren a believable murderer, but it subtly chips away at the historical case presented at Alfred, making Wagner more sympathetic. For example, in the novel, Wagner is accused of rowing a twenty-five- or thirty-mile round trip to Smuttynose (actually about eighteen miles). Shreve then adds an hour to the average time it takes to row from the South End of Portsmouth to the open sea in a fair tide. This moves the clock from a trip that takes three-quarters of an hour to an hour and three-quarters for the first leg of the journey. The test trip made as part of this research took only thirty minutes. When members of a Portsmouth book club asked Shreve why she did not dig deeper into the case, she responded candidly as a novelist, not as an historian. "I didn't want to know any more," she said. "That would interfere with a work of fiction."

The problem for the maligned Maren Hontvet may come less from the novelization of her life than from the modern reader's hunger for plot twists, duplicitous characters, and trick endings. A narrative about a criminal, even an ax murderer, who is quickly caught, justly tried, and summarily punished no longer satisfies. Anita Shreve dramatized and repackaged the Maren conspiracy theory for countless thousands of twenty-first-century readers—but she did not invent it. With the exception of Thaxter and Pearson, and the trial transcript, the rumors continued to fly.

Besides Edmund Pearson's book, the only significant study of the murders available to tourists in the twentieth century was a forty-eight-page booklet titled *Moonlight Murder at Smuttynose* (1958). And it has been available for five dollars almost exclusively at the summer gift shop inside the Oceanic Hotel on Star Island. Its author, Lyman Ruttledge, was a long-time Shoals historian with a flair for the romantic. Shreve lists his booklet among her sources for *The Weight of Water*.

Like Pearson before him, Ruttledge never located the source of the Maren hoax and was forever troubled by the rumors. He dealt with "the ghost of Maren's confession" in a footnote to his little volume. Ruttledge knew a woman, he wrote, who insisted her grandmother had seen the deathbed confession document. As the story goes, a well-known, but unnamed, Portsmouth-area attorney was summoned to the bedside of a dying woman in the 1880s who revealed herself to be Maren Hontvet. The mystery woman signed a statement admitting she had killed Karen and Anethe with an ax. That deposition somehow made its way into the hands of the grandmother of Ruttledge's friend. Of course, the grandmother lost the document over the years and never showed it to anyone before she too passed away.

"If anyone who reads this wishes to create a new sensation," Ruttledge wrote in a footnote, "he may employ some elderly person to write out a deposition, forge Maren's name, age it with heat and stains, and come to me for the name of the attorney who took it down." Ruttledge was kidding, of course. He assumed the deathbed confession a hoax. But that is essentially what Anita Shreve did. Like the perpetrator of the 1876 hoax, the novelist brought Wagner's desperate lie to life, but on a grander scale and in a more convincing manner than he could have dreamed possible.

Skeptics continue to opine that Maren could not possibly have survived six hours outdoors in her nightclothes. But Maren was a sturdy woman from the frozen land of Norway. She had slept seven winters on Smuttynose in an uninsulated wooden house buffeted by sea winds and snow. The main source of heat was a woodstove in the kitchen. We can safely assume Maren was not wearing the flimsy sexy sleepwear often depicted in pulp detective magazines. Instead, she was wearing the warmest, most practical, possibly homespun sleepwear available, probably a traditional ankle-length gown with long sleeves and a high button-up collar. She also grabbed an extra skirt, she testified at trial, as she leapt from the window, eventually curling herself among the protective rocks while cuddling her little dog, Ringe, for warmth.

Newspapers and travel brochures regularly noted that temperatures at the Isles of Shoals could be twenty degrees cooler in the summer than on the mainland. The reverse was true in the winter with warmer-than-usual weather at the Shoals. An 1840 item in the *Portsmouth Journal*, for example, noted that during a record low of twelve degrees below zero the previous winter on the mainland, the Shoals never dropped below four degrees Fahrenheit. "The general average in the morning there in winter is from 28 to 32 [degrees]," the *Journal* commented. Records also indicate the spring-like weather was mild on the night of the murder.

By comparison, consider those poor sailors of the *Nottingham Galley* who were wrecked on nearby Boon Island in December 1710. Captain John Deane and his small crew were marooned on an exposed slab of frigid rock. They endured soaking wet conditions without warm clothes, shelter, or the ability to make a fire. They had almost no food beyond seaweed and mussels for twenty-four days and were reduced, in the end, to eating the flesh of the deceased ship's carpenter. Surely Maren's few hours of winter terror, as horrible as it was, cannot match three weeks exposed on Boon Island—and yet 10 out of 14 of the *Nottingham Galley* men survived.

The suggestion by a Portsmouth ferryboat captain that Celia's mentally and physically challenged son, Karl Thaxter, was somehow involved in the tragedy is beyond ridiculous and unworthy of comment. Karl, who remained close to his mother until her death, became an accomplished amateur photographer and captured some beautiful portraits of the Scandinavian residents of Appledore Island.

The theory of the "mystery schooner" that occasionally surfaces after too many drinks in a barroom debate has its origin, once again, with the killer. According to Wagner, someone had told John Hontvet there was another fishing boat tied up at Gosport Harbor on the night of the murder. It was rumored that a man in a dory had hailed the schooner as he passed and asked to buy some fish. Wagner implied in court that the unidentified man in the dory was the real killer. John and Ivan said the man was Wagner. There is nothing here we can cling to, however, just more mist and gossip, and none of it overturns the facts or raises a reasonable doubt.

One final attack on Maren Hontvet must here be blown to shreds. In March 1980, years before Shreve began her research in earnest, the widely-circulated *Yankee Magazine* published a clear and accurate account of the case called "Horror on Smuttynose." It was illustrated with bright red splatters of blood and the editor advised those who were squeamish not to read further. The article drew a "pretty shocking response" from an associate professor at a university in Maine, which *Yankee* published the following year. The letter writer denounced the "accepted story" of the murders as utterly false. The professor's single scrap of evidence, he believed, was indisputable—Maren had blood on her nightclothes when she was rescued. A careful reading of the trial transcript, he argued, indicated that Anethe's wounds had likely spurted blood when she was struck repeatedly by the ax. Since Maren had suffered only "contusions and cold feet," the professor concluded from the record, that to get blood on her clothes, she must have been the killer, or at least an accomplice.

For the *Yankee* skeptic and others, the "smoking gun" may come down to a turn of phrase in a Victorian stenographer's notebook. Or the evidence is a lost document that someone's grandmother swears she saw long ago. Or it could just be a hunch, a tingling sense of imbalance or injustice. That's all it takes. One seemingly loose thread, to some minds, and the entire tapestry of facts comes unraveled.

Forget the hailstorm of evidence presented at the trial. Forget that Maren Hontvet hid among the deserted buildings of Smuttynose and ran down among the rocks and broken shells to Haley's Cove, or that she stumbled and fell in the icy darkness before hiding all night among jagged granite slabs, some as sharp as razors. And forget that, after tending Maren's wounds on Appledore, Celia Thaxter wrote: "Upon her cheek is yet the blood-stain from the blow he struck her with a chair, and she shows me two more upon her shoulder, and her torn feet." The blood was certainly Maren's own. For too many of us these days, being contradictory is more important than being right.

A dozen novels later, Anita Shreve still cherishes the Isles of Shoals. "The place itself was such a profound character in the novel," she recently said en route to a literary conference at the Oceanic Hotel. "I can't just take from the place. I have to give back. Whenever I'm asked, I will come."

"The place spoke to me and haunted me for really quite a while," Shreve says today. Her next novel, *The Pilot's Wife* (1999), was also set in the Portsmouth area. That same year, Oprah Winfrey featured Shreve's novel as a selection in her famous millions-selling book club. A former school teacher and journalist from the Boston area, Shreve was suddenly an internationally known author. *The Pilot's Wife* would soon be adapted into a made-for-television movie, but there was an even bigger offer on the table that year. *The Weight of Water* was about to become a Hollywood blockbuster.

Chapter 43

LOUIS IN HOLLYWOOD

Academy Award–winning director Kathryn Bigelow is best known for visu-ally exciting ultra-action films like *Point Break, Strange Days*, and *The Hurt Locker*. Her fans and critics were not sure what to make of the *Weight of Water* with its dueling plots and slow pacing. Was it an art film, an historical or psychological drama, a thriller or an action film?

After a lackluster response at the Toronto Film Festival in 2000, the movie circulated around Europe in search of a distributor. It was finally released at a handful of American theaters in 2002 and sank like a stone. Not even the presence of actor Sean Penn or a half-naked Elizabeth Hurley could save the *Weight of Water* movie. The estimated sixteen-million-dollar budget returned only a few hundred thousand dollars at the box office, according to published reports. In a bizarre coincidence, actress Katrin Cartlidge, who portrays the despondent Karen Christensen, died suddenly the same year at age forty-one.

Every movie gets a second chance on video and many online reviews have given the film "thumbs up." For students of the Wagner case, Bigelow's film is a rare opportunity to see the 1873 story brought to life in living color and Dolby digital sound. A host of talented film professionals were employed to recreate authentic period clothing, props, hairstyles, and even speech patterns and dialect. Studio carpenters built a full-sized replica of the two-story Hontvet House on Taylor Island in Nova Scotia where scenes from *The Weight of Water* were filmed. The barren rocky site, not far from Halifax, looks similar to Smuttynose, but because it is connected to the mainland by a causeway, the island was more convenient for filming. When shooting was over, the duplicate Red House was dismantled and trucked away.

The film opens dramatically in the streets of Portsmouth as Louis Wagner shouts "I'm innocent!" amid the din of the howling lynch mob. John Hontvet and Ivan Christensen, both played by Danish actors, usher Maren into the Portsmouth jail. Wagner, played by Irish-born Ciaran Hinds, is wild-eyed and frenzied. Unlike the smooth-shaven, charming, and well-dressed historical Wagner, the fictional character wears a ragged beard, long disheveled hair, and a coarse fisherman's outfit. He is supposed to look guilty in service to the twisted plot. Maren Hontvet is played brilliantly, critics agreed, by the highly respected and expressive Canadian actor Sarah Polley.

The tag line on the movie poster—"Hell hath no fury . . ."—pretty much gives away the plot. By one-quarter of the way into the movie, the modern-day photojournalist Jean James (played by English actress Catherine McCormack) has begun to suspect Maren was the killer. Anita Shreve's elaborate alternate reality is even more striking on the silver screen. In one fictional scene, Wagner kisses Maren and she reveals his indiscretion to the jury in her trial testimony. While actor Hinds was considerably older in the film than the twenty-eight-year-old Wagner, Polley was much younger and more attractive than the historical Maren.

Cinematically, many of the invented details work and Maren inches toward her breaking point on the desolate island. We see her ominously gutting fish with a sharp knife as Wagner flirts with her sister, Karen. In the movie, John Hontvet is a cold and distant husband. Karen grows increasingly intolerable. When her beloved brother, Ivan, (also her incestuous childhood lover in the film version) arrives from Norway, to Maren's horror, he has brought along a new bride. Maren seethes with jealousy over beautiful Anethe. In the end, she snaps, attacking her only two female companions on the lonely island. In the modern-day plot, photographer Jean James spots her husband flirting with his brother's girlfriend. Jean snaps too. The parallel endings are both pure fabrication.

Louis Wagner would be thrilled with *The Weight of Water*. The dark and vindictive conspiracy theory he concocted alone in a tiny Maine jail cell has now been spread across the globe. It has been translated into foreign tongues and projected larger-than-life onto motion picture screens. It is, at this moment, being downloaded onto television sets and portable media players. In the creative and skillful hands of Anita Shreve and Kathryn Bigelow, the false "Maren theory" reached its high water mark. But even as we are being seduced by great actors, and even when those actors are reciting, line-for-line, the exact words spoken by the historical characters they represent, we need to pinch ourselves and remember—it's only a movie.

We cannot, in good conscience, ignore Wagner's cries of innocence. But those cries were carefully and justly examined by a jury in 1873, in Rufus Tapley's appeals to Judge Barrows, again by the Maine governor's review team in 1875, by scholars like Pearson and Ruttledge, and in these pages. In Shreve's novel, after stealing documents from the Portsmouth Athenaeum, Jean James tries to rationalize the theft. "I want to know what it was," she tells herself, "to find the one underlying detail that will make it all sensible. I want to understand the random act, the consequences of a second's brief abandonment."

So do we all. And so the story never dies.

Kathryn Bigelow was not the first important filmmaker to consider adapting the Smuttynose event. Academy Award–winning producer Louis de Rochemont, best known for his *March of Time* movie newsreels, began dropping hints to reporters soon after World War II that he was developing a script based on the tragedy. Fiercely independent, de Rochemont created early "noir" crime films with the help of the FBI and J. Edgar Hoover. De Rochemont experimented in widescreen cinemascope and produced *Lost Boundaries*, one of America's first "race films" to tackle Civil Rights issues and employ black actors. The maverick producer worked secretly with the

CIA on an animated propaganda version of George Orwell's political fable *Animal Farm*. His work defies classification.

From his home and headquarters near Portsmouth, de Rochemont claimed there was an "almost inexhaustible wealth" of motion picture material to be found in his backyard along the Maine and New Hampshire seacoast. The irascible filmmaker was drawn to the Wagner case, he noted, not for the murders, but for the outrageous celebrity trial that followed. He saw the story as an early example of journalism run amok, with reporters more interested in Wagner's lies and conspiracy theories than in the facts of the case. Louis de Rochemont intended to modernize the story and to shoot the scenes locally (and cheaply) at the Isles of Shoals. It would have been an indictment of the "Maren theory." But after decades of hype, his project never got the green light.

Poet John Perrault composed "The Ballad of Louis Wagner" to ease his troubled mind. Filmmakers Gary Samson and Dorothy Ahlgren at the University of New Hampshire made a short black-and-white movie of Perrault's ballad in the early 1980s. Laurence Robertson was so shocked by *The Weight of Water* that he produced a video documentary about the murders. Robertson, a professor of dance, also choreographed an entire ballet to honor the lives of Karen and Anethe Christensen and to counter what he calls "Maren's character assassination" in the novel. Local artists have been inspired to illustrate the story and playwrights have adapted the tragedy onto the regional stage.

In the film *The Weight of Water*, Sean Penn plays Thomas James, the hard-drinking Pulitzer Prize–winning poet with the acid tongue. Whenever Penn speaks, a sultry jazz clarinet moans in the background. As the Smuttynose murder "mystery" deepens, Shreve's fictional characters debate the classic conspiracy theories so well-known in the seacoast region. Rich James (played by Josh Lucas) and his doubting brother, Thomas, are skeptical of Jean's growing belief that Maren is guilty.

"I'm working on the Oswald single-ax theory myself," Sean Penn jokes, comparing photographer Jean's obsession with the Smuttynose murders to the conspiracy theories that still cling to the assassination of President John F. Kennedy.

Over cocktails at a waterfront restaurant, the foursome struggle to understand why a woman would bludgeon and strangle her closest family members. When actor Josh Lucas raises the most obvious and important question of all, Sean Penn gets the best line in the film.

"It is remotely possible," Rich points out, "that they hanged the right guy."

"Oh, come on Rich," Thomas says with a drunken sneer. "What's the fun in that?"

Chapter 44

VICTORIAN PSYCHO

In 1904, workmen tearing down what may have been the former Johnson boarding house found an eight-inch dagger lying beneath the floorboards in one of the rooms. Of all the crimes committed on Water Street and all the mariners and fishermen who had lived there, Louis Wagner and his thirty-year-old crime immediately came to mind. "The blade is stained with what looks like blood," the *Portsmouth Herald* gushed in an exclusive report, "and while there is no certainty that Wagner used the knife, in all probability it belonged to him. The story of [his] crime is one of the most revolting in the history of this vicinity."

By the next day, relic collectors were clamoring to purchase the rusty stiletto. Had Wagner stashed it after the murders? Not likely. Even the dumbest of killers would have dropped the weapon into the deep ocean during the long row back to the mainland, not carried the evidence home. It turned out to be part of a knife-and-cane set. Blades embedded in walking sticks were commonly sold for defense and as souvenirs, but not as tools carried by fishermen. Interviewed for the 1904 article about the dagger, Thomas Entwistle, the corrupt city marshal, remembered the capture of Wagner as "the most strenuous time he has ever seen during his service in the police department."

Another more intriguing relic has gone missing. The Empire-design sofa that both Wagner and fisherman George Lowd claimed to have occupied during the night of the murder was apparently an antique of note. Embellished with claw feet and "profuse carving," it had reportedly arrived in Portsmouth in 1810, a gift of Admiral Lord Nelson to his niece upon her marriage to a parson named Johnson. By 1873, it had found its way into Matthew Johnson's little bar room next to the work area where John Hontvet's crew baited their trawls. It was salvaged and restored by a prominent Portsmouth family but, at this writing, has disappeared.

A few years ago, an online auction advertised a rare pocket diary dated 1873 with handwritten entries related to the Smuttynose murders. A collector snapped it up, but found the pages almost empty except for a brief daily weather report and the occasional memo scrawled in pencil. A note dated March 7 reads: "Weather fair, have a severe headache, horrid murder at the Isle of Shoals, a man kills 2 women."

On March 12, the diarist, likely a teenaged boy, bought a new pair of rubbers and noted that Louis Wagner was arraigned for murder in South Berwick. And on March 14, we find this curious memo: "Weather fair and warm, reported that Mrs. Hontvet is dead." Although it turned out to have no major historical significance, the otherwise sparse diary proves that, for this writer, the most memorable events of 1873 were the attack, arrest, trial, escape, and recapture of Louis Wagner.

By 1883, the murder ax was still in the hands of the York County clerk of court along with the articles taken from Wagner's pockets at his arrest. Through a local judge, an antique dealer, and two generous local women, the ax with the broken handle resides today in the collection of the Portsmouth Athenaeum. What happened to Wagner's other possessions, including a plug of tobacco "as large as the end of one's thumb," is a mystery. The 1883 inventory, according to the *Portsmouth Journal*, also included the killer's wallet, a silver watch chain, shirt and coat buttons, a three-cent piece, a gold ring, a half dime, and a hunting case silver watch, the final item possibly recovered from the Boston shopkeeper to whom Wagner traded it.

More mementoes from the case may lie, even now, hidden in someone's attic trunk or in a library vault. We know Wagner wrote to a young woman he met in Alfred, for example, and those letters have not turned up. But we can safely guess that such letters, probably composed with the help of a kindly prison guard or chaplain, contain no smoking gun or incriminating confession. We have seen all the evidence, uncovered all the lies, and learned all we need to know about Louis Wagner.

"I hope you will find the right man who done it," Wagner told John Hontvet from his cell in the Portsmouth jail on the day after the murders.

"I got him," John replied. And so do we. Case closed?

To defend Louis Wagner still, when even his attorney knew he was guilty, requires us to believe in miracles. Maren Hontvet accused one person. From ten miles at sea, she named a man who, by incalculable odds, had vanished from Portsmouth during the precise hours the murder occurred.

To defend Wagner, we must believe another killer with size-eleven boots knew there was money stashed in the only occupied house on Smuttynose Island, knew where to hide his boat, knew the only door was unlocked and the house was unguarded, knew the women were alone, and knew where to find the island well in the darkness where the bloody towels were found. We must accept the dory, belonging to fishermen with whom Wagner worked, was taken by other hands, coincidentally disappeared off Water Street around eight p.m. on March 5, and reappeared near Devil's Den in New Castle early the next morning. And we have to believe every witness who saw the same man dressed like Wagner hurrying from New Castle to Portsmouth was either mistaken or lying. We must assume, despite the Johnsons' sworn testimony, Wagner found the boarding house door unlocked, he slept on a lounge where another man slept in the very room that John Hontvet walked in and out of when baiting trawls all night. Indeed, if we are to believe Wagner's alibi with all its invisible and nameless characters, we must also discount his myriad lies. We must accept, for example, that he escaped Alfred jail to exercise his limbs and to "see the pretty girls" whom he had flirted with at the trial.

Even if there was collusion among the fishermen or police corruption or tampering with evidence, how do we explain Wagner's strange appearance on the morning of the murders and his sudden departure to Boston? Although he claimed to be sick from drinking, vomiting, and passing out in the frozen street, he chose that very morning to leave town. With barely two hours of sleep the night before, he suddenly elected to go job hunting and visit friends. We must assume it was sheer coincidence he left Portsmouth on the train just before John Hontvet arrived aboard the *Clara Bella* with news of the murders.

If his story is true, then Wagner had purposely withheld his overdue rent from Mrs. Johnson, saving the exact amount of money in the precise denominations as that was stolen at Smuttynose. How curious, after saving so prudently, he chose that very morning to splurge, using all his money to shave and buy new clothes, leaving himself not even enough cash to pay for a night's lodging in Boston or to purchase a return train ticket home. And how odd that, when arrested, his hands were freshly blistered. How strange that, upon learning two of his only friends were savagely killed, Wagner expressed no surprise or sorrow, then accused his surviving best friends of murdering their own family. Even without the white button, the blood stains, the shirt in the privy, Anethe's dying declaration, and Maren's testimony—Wagner's own actions and words make a compelling circumstantial case. His motive, means, and opportunity all remain intact. His lies are a matter of record.

Not every piece fits. Maren's confusion over the color and shape of the killer's hat is a prime example. In the dark and under the duress of seeing her family attacked and killed, she may have gotten a detail wrong. Or perhaps Wagner swapped hats. We will never know. The goal of the prosecution in any court case is not to dispel all doubt. There may always be "the shadow of a doubt." The job of Yeaton and Plaisted in 1873 was to convince Wagner's jury he was guilty beyond a "reasonable doubt" in the mind of a "reasonable person."

Yet reasonable people sometimes reach crazy conclusions. "You're always going to find people who are incredibly gullible," says retired police officer and counter terrorism expert Terry M. Kalil. A frequent visitor to Smuttynose Island, Kalil now conducts college classes in criminal law and crime scene investigation. He routinely uses the 1873 murders as a teaching tool with his students who compare the circumstantial evidence, Wagner's alibi, and the various alternative theories.

"The best predictor of belief in a conspiracy theory is belief in other conspiracy theories," according to Viren Swami, a psychology professor at Westminster University in England. Swami, an expert in conspiracy belief, was quoted in the *New York Times* following a bombing incident in Boston in 2013. His research indicates that people with low self-esteem or who feel powerless and uncertain are attracted to one conspiracy theory after another. A person drawn to alternate theories about the Kennedy or Lincoln assassinations, for example, is more open to theories about alien astronauts or may believe that the US government faked the moon landing.

In a frightening and changeable world, a strong belief that flies in the face of accepted facts may make a person feel more comfortable, wiser, and in control. This form of extreme cynicism, it has been suggested, may be the natural reaction of our brain when attempting to solve unsolvable problems, especially in a crisis or natural disaster. What looks like a wild belief may actually be a rational, but highly oversimplified explanation of the facts. The intelligent brain recycles and reassesses a complex pile of data until it creates a functional narrative that, while possibly untrue, still "makes sense" to the individual at the time. If that tendency was true among Victorians in the rapidly changing Industrial Age, it is equally true today in our world of global terrorism, natural disasters, political upheaval, and financial instability.

"It seems as if every tragedy these days comes with a round of yarn-spinning," a *New York Times* reporter commented after the "Boston Massacre" spawned a wild burst of speculation about two young terrorist bombers. Within days, the same theories had evolved from discussions into a "completely alternate version of reality." The rise of the Internet has made it possible for conspiracy believers to easily and quickly find one another and then, in solidarity, to reinforce one another's alternative views.

It is easy to question Wagner's guilt if you do not know the facts, and until now, those facts have been hard to come by. Others may simply object to the Wagner verdict on principle, as did his lawyer Rufus Tapley, because they oppose the death penalty. For them, America has scarcely progressed since the days of the scaffold at Thomaston Prison. A reform movement at the turn of the twentieth century led to the abolition of the death penalty in nine more states. But the Progressive Period was short-lived, and many of those states later reversed their decision. With the assistance of Thomas Edison's engineers, New York introduced execution by electric chair in 1890. The more "humane" gas chamber was established in 1924, but later discontinued as "inhumane." The nation's last public hanging drew twenty thousand spectators to a Kentucky "carnival" at 5:45 a.m. on August 14, 1936. Death by lethal injection became the popular substitute for all other methods in 1982.

Opponents continue to chip away at death penalty law. The Supreme Court has banned executions in cases of rape and for prisoners who are insane, suffer from mental illness, or were under eighteen years old at the time of the crime. Anti-death penalty advocates, using DNA evidence, continue to prove innocent prisoners are repeatedly convicted and even executed. At this writing, only eighteen states have banned the death penalty, six of them in the twenty-first century. That leaves thirty-two states where executions are legal, with Texas as "ground zero" for executions in America. By comparison to the nine men hanged in the history of the state of Maine, George W. Bush presided over the execution of 152 death row inmates during his tenure as governor of Texas. The raging debate continues, state by state.

In the decades since the murders, Louis Wagner has become a kind of human Rorschach test. People have seen him as either cunning or foolish, pious or devilish, charming or creepy, gallant or cowardly, misunderstood or misanthropic. Indeed, it was his changeable nature that made Wagner so paradoxical to Victorians who found him terrifying, fascinating, and yet strangely comical. Through the lens of modern psychology, we may see something more.

Sigmund Freud was only nineteen years old in 1875 when the *New York Times* prophetically noted the Wagner case "may hereafter be quoted by students in psychology endeavoring to unravel the mystery of human crime." Those first college classes in the budding new field of psychology had not yet opened, and Freud's work in psychoanalysis was still two decades away. The contemporary concept of antisocial personality disorders did not take shape until the twentieth century.

You might say Wagner was ahead of his time, which is why he could fool so many of his contemporaries. His alibi was so packed with inventive details that it felt like truth. Wagner wept, joked, blustered, prayed, and flirted like an ordinary man, but he was only aping the emotions he observed in others. The mannered Victorians, with their elaborate social rules, didn't know what to make of a handsome character who could kill in cold blood, eat a meal with a body lying nearby, then calmly lie about his actions. But we do. We see him every day. Our cinemas, books, televisions, and newspapers are overcrowded with psychopaths, fictional and factual, from the flesh-eating serial killer Hannibal Lecter to the latest school shooter. Like Wagner, they draw massive media attention, while their victims too often fade into obscurity.

"[We] are not some kind of inherent monsters," serial murderer Ted Bundy said in a taped interview before his execution in 1989. "We are your sons and your husbands. We grew up in regular families."

Convicted of thirty-six unthinkable homicides and suspected of many more, Bundy is an extreme example of the handsome and alluring killer with no moral conscience. While true crime writers increasingly include Louis Wagner among the rapidly expanding canon of infamous American psychopaths, we cannot know if he committed heinous crimes in his past or would have done so again. He was no grinning Charles Manson, no "Son of Sam" the sniper, nor a necrophiliac Jeffrey Dahmer. Wagner has been compared to Albert DeSalvo, the "Boston Strangler" of thirty women, for his half-hearted escape attempt, but they have little in common.

Not all psychopaths are killers and vice versa. And while the terms *psychopath* and *sociopath* are often used interchangeably, the latter usually denotes a slightly lesser monster, shaped by childhood or social pressures into a potential villain who may or may not break the law. Downgrading Wagner to *sociopath* better suits his crime. He was a petty burglar who, considering the rigid social pressures of his time, found it easier to kill than to reveal himself as a thief. As Maine Governor Nelson Dingley told Wagner, "You look, to me, like a man that got himself into a corner and murdered his way out."

Even setting aside the murders for a moment, we know enough about Wagner to place him among an estimated 4 percent of Americans who exhibit antisocial tendencies. So much of his behavior, if he were alive today, would set off the alarms that warn us there is a sociopath lurking in the room. If we know how to spot these dangerous people who surround us, we are less likely to fall under their spell or to be hurt by them. And in that context, understanding the Smuttynose killer may be a valuable exercise.

Any of a dozen popular books by psychologists and health professionals now offer advice for avoiding an army of charming antisocial predators. The Internet is rife with self-help articles with titles like "How to Spot a Sociopath" or "10 Signs Your Boyfriend is a Psychopath." Be aware of braggarts, the experts warn us, and stay away from people who crave pity, feign illness, pretend to be your soul mate, and blurt out strange confessional statements and then deny they said them. Shun those, we are told, who never accept responsibility and who blame everyone else for their problems. Avoid anyone who attaches to you like a parasite, even a loving parasite, since sociopaths do not really experience love. They may suddenly disappear for days. These people are inveterate liars, incapable of shame or guilt. But they can also be clever and some have an uncanny ability to twist facts into a bizarre alternate reality. They never confess or apologize because, within their private delusional world, everything they say becomes true—so true, in fact, that some can pass a lie detector test.

You cannot reason with a sociopath, the experts say. If you try to get rid of him, as John Hontvet did with Wagner, he may stalk you and question you to worm his way back into your confidence. Wagner was loitering, as he often did, on the Water Street docks on March 5 when the men on the *Clara Bella* arrived. He interrogated his former boss about his fishing profits and asked three times about the women on the island. He overheard that John, Matthew, and Ivan would be stranded all night in Portsmouth and had left their wallets behind on Smuttynose. He promised to bait trawls with them, but did not return. Sociopaths are impulsive and grandiose by nature. They are also risk takers. Any abandoned boat would do for Wagner, but Burke's dory was familiar and crossing to Smuttynose was something he knew he could do.

More than anything, worse even than having his duplicity exposed, the sociopath cannot bear to be wrong. He is egomaniacal, narcissistic, a superior creature living without sin among us weak and sentimental fools. "I know I'm wrong," Maren heard Wagner mutter to himself during an argument among fishermen at Smuttynose, "but I'll never give in!"

"The sociopathic mind makes excuses for everything," says criminal law instructor Terry Kalil, "because they cannot admit that another person is right."

From within his parallel world, as Wagner told the judge at his arraignment, he was innocent because he could easily have robbed the women "if they were asleep." The sociopath's lies are convincing because he truly believes them. Wagner had no need to confess, because, as he repeated on his way to the gallows, "God will not let Louis Wagner be hung,"

Celia Thaxter and others saw through the mask. Wagner's persona "was a wonderful piece of acting," she wrote. The Johnsons on Water Street and the Browns in Boston were immediately wary of their boarder's suspicious actions. And while Wagner seduced his share of reporters one-on-one, the more time a newsman spent with the blank expressionless prisoner, the more artificial he became. Wagner "has made up his mind to play a game of bluff," the *Portsmouth Chronicle* noted soon after the murders. The

Portsmouth Journal referred to his alibi as "an extraordinary piece of simulation." Even the supportive *Portsmouth Times* had to admit that "Wagner *acts and talks* like an honest, intelligent man." On hearing Wagner's wild story after his escape from Alfred jail, the local reporter threw up his hands in confusion. "It may be all feigned or it may not," he wrote.

We all have our bad days. One or two creepy characteristics does not make us sociopaths. But by every measure, Wagner earns a perfect score on the sociopathic checklist. Anyone matching his personality profile today is well worth avoiding. That lesson is clear.

But what of his surviving victim? Driven from Smuttynose Island by an ax-wielding maniac, Maren was then driven from America and back to Norway by those who accepted Wagner's lies. Even in death, even today, her reputation continues to erode against an endless repeating tide of popular fiction and false rumors. As we run screaming from dangerous men like Louis Wagner, we must, in all conscience, rush to the rescue of the historical Maren Hontvet. At the very least, we owe her battered soul a reprieve.

Epilogue

BACK ON THE ISLAND

There are no ghosts here for me, only gulls. I am writing these final words on the picnic table outside Captain Haley's ancient cottage with the cove and Malaga in front of me. While every building around the cottage has burned or collapsed, the oldest of them all still stands. At some point, for reasons yet unknown, the two-story cottage was lifted and moved about thirty feet to the crest of the sloping lawn. There are no ghosts here, but many secrets.

The tumbled stones that once supported the old Hontvet House are to my left. A gull couple have made their nest in the thick grass there and it holds three gray dappled eggs. The large stone foundation of the Mid-Ocean House, glistening with poison ivy, is to my right behind Rozzie Thaxter's one-room shelter. From the front lawn, I can see seven of the other eight islands at the Isles of Shoals. I have been watching a storm migrate south from Maine, across the entire New Hampshire coast, and into Massachusetts. Lightning crackles from dark clouds above the mainland, while here on Smuttynose Island the sun still shines.

Although we can see the rest of the world from here, we are not part of it. These islands have their own climate, their own history, even their own air. A city family visiting for the first time in the nineteenth century found the Isles of Shoals so small and fragile, they feared the next tide might wash them away. And yet they possess a reality so unique and strong that when Shoalers return to the mainland, we call it "going back to America."

There are no ghosts on Smuttynose, but there is darkness, plenty of it. On nights when no moon shines, the hundred-yard journey across the path from the cottage to the outhouse will test the courage of any visitor. You must walk like Frankenstein's monster, lurching around the damp rocks with arms outstretched, navigating by touch. A flashlight provides some security, but only within the range of its narrow beam, calling everything beyond into question. Halfway to the privy, something furry skitters by. Waving the light left and right, you are suddenly aware of the utter darkness at your back and what sounds like heavy breathing. You turn sharply, ducking to avoid the imaginary ax blade. Someone leaps as your light plays against the tall swirling grass. An empty T-shirt and a ragged towel flutter on a clothesline suspended between two cast-off wooden oars. As you turn back, the damp petal of a drooping lily kisses your cheek. Who needs ghosts when we have imagination?

Did I mention the gulls? They were scarce in days gone by. Colonial fishermen shot them for food. Oscar Laighton shot them for sport. Legend says the gulls came to Smuttynose when their previous home on Duck Island was used as a target for bombing practice during World War II. Now thousands of herring gulls and blackbacks battle for the uninhabited portion of the island, which is pretty much the entire twenty-seven-acres.

In the daylight in the air, gulls are majestic as they soar in the breeze that blows perpetually across the Shoals. But in the darkness on the ground, gulls are ventriloquists. They can sound like crying babies and laughing children, like braying mules, clucking hens, moaning ghosts, howling cats, bleating lambs. They make sounds like dogs, owls, parrots, and monkeys, like rusty door hinges and screeching brakes, like trains and cows, people praying, people singing, crowds murmuring at cocktail parties. They sound like boats arriving and boats departing, like clocks ticking, like a woman in the throes of childbirth or screaming bloody murder.

Had the gulls been on guard here in 1873, Karen and Anethe might have survived. They would have warned the women of Wagner's approach. When tourists walk the island today, I can track them by the angry gulls that swirl overhead like the spout of a tornado. Someone, I can see even now, has slipped onto Smuttynose from Gosport Harbor, distressing the gulls at what we now call Wagner's Cove. It is probably just a weekend sailor ferrying his dog from a sleek yacht to relieve itself on the rocks and sea moss.

There has never been another murder here on Smuttynose, to my knowledge, yet the dying goes on. A muskrat trapped in the old stone well squeaks as he drowns, his tremors breaking the skin of the pungent black water. Norway rats kill baby chicks and suck the gull eggs dry. The rocks are strewn with empty crab and mussel shells, dropped from the sky by hungry birds.

Although Smuttynose has always been the most verdant spot on the Shoals, until the seagulls came, much of this land was barren. The further one wanders toward the back of the island today, the more primitive it gets, especially in the breeding season in late spring and early summer. That's when I clear the three-quarter-mile trail to the spot that Nathaniel Hawthorne called the most desolate spot on Earth.

Each year, I dedicate a week to reclaiming this narrow, overgrown path for humankind. The gulls are never pleased. They protect their gray eggs and peeping gray chicks with Hitchcockian passion. Visitors are advised to carry sticks above their heads, not as a weapon, but as a decoy. Seagulls like to attack from the back, screeching as they dive in a fearsome war whoop. They attack the highest point of their enemy, even hitting the stick with their sharp beaks. The gull wingspan can reach five feet and they can inflict a nasty head gash at forty miles per hour. They carry a fishhook-shaped barb in the middle of each webbed foot that they use like a tiny dagger. They fire their guano from the air or upchuck a foul semi-digested bile of raw seafood that hits like a ball of hot pus and does not clean up easily. Trust me, I know.

Past the last stone wall, as you approach the rock cairn, the island turns into a killing field, strewn with bones and feathers and streaked in rancid sun-baked guano. This is ground zero of Gull City, the heart of the island population. The eight-foot high cairn, built by hands unknown, is their Temple of the Sun. Here, epic battles are fought and great orgies are held. Here, the weak and the elderly are eaten alive. Beyond the cairn, waves crash against dark granite boulders. From here to Europe it is nothing but open sea. Although this spot is scarcely ten miles as the gull flies from my house in Portsmouth, it is the most primal place I know. Hundreds of years ago, Smuttynose Island was crawling with human beings. Today we are nearly extinct.

I am honored to be among the few humans to witness the ritual sunrise ceremony here. Each morning, as a vague dawn evolves, the natives grow restless. Then, at the first hint of a small orange circle, a thousand silent birds chant in unison. It is unearthly. Or perhaps, we are the unearthly creatures, and this is how life was meant to be. Soon the pulsing chant of the flying dinosaurs fills the prehistoric terrain. It rises in volume and intensity until the entire population of Gull City joins in. Together, by the sheer force of their collective will, they convince the Sun God—one more time—to release its mighty heat and precious light.

I come to this desolate tip of the universe as often as possible, usually alone. I have made my peace with the flying creatures here. I know I will be reviled and attacked when I arrive. But when I squat down and sit still, I know I will be ignored. If I drop dead here, my bird neighbors will pluck out my eyes to feed their young. Those are the rules. The violence is predictable and sensible here.

It is only upon returning to the civilized side of Smuttynose, to the site of the Hontvet House, that I must come to terms again and again with Louis Wagner. Making sense of Wagner's senseless frenzy was the genesis of this book. And now I know. Evil truly does live among us. It hides in plain sight. It will take whatever is in your wallet when you sleep, and then, without the wisdom God gave a seagull, Evil will take your life in the bargain.

AUTHOR'S NOTES

1. Wagner's Dory

It was Kittery Point, Maine, lobster fisherman David Kaselauskas, when I told him I was working on this book, who talked his friend Dan O'Reilly into rowing to Smuttynose early one morning in May 2013. I went along for the ride on David's boat. Both men were seventy-five years old at the time. "We're both ancient," Dave told me. "Why, Dan and I can remember when rainbows were black and white and the Dead Sea was only sick." I asked him why he continued to fish for a living at his age. "Because the worst day on the water still beats the best day on dry land," Dave replied. While the notion that Louis Wagner could not row eighteen miles in eleven hours is 100 percent false, critics still offer this as "proof" of Wagner's innocence.

2. Our Founding Fishermen

Our best guess is that the native word "Piscataqua" translates to "where the swift river branches." One of the fastest navigable rivers in North America, the Piscataqua region includes the fragile salt-water ecosystem of Great Bay and Little Bay, the inner dimensions of which, it has been suggested, make up New Hampshire's "second sea-coast." The tributaries of the mighty Piscataqua include the Salmon Falls, Winnicut, Squamscott, Lamprey, Oyster, Bellamy, and Cocheco Rivers. Your best introduction to the history and environment of this region is *Cross-Grained & Wily Waters* (2002) edited by W. Jeffrey Bolster. The book includes a water-resistant map for exploring this amazing tidal region. Northern New Englanders like to refer to the claim that America was founded primarily as a haven for religious freedom as "the Pilgrim myth." Economics, politics, and the search for wealth and power were equally important motivators. Much of the material for this brief background comes from research I did for my book *Under the Isles of Shoals: Archaeology & Discovery on Smuttynose Island* (2012) which I see as a companion volume to this study of the Wagner case. That book includes almost 200 illustrations related to Prof. Nate Hamilton's ongoing archaeological dig sponsored by the Shoals Marine Laboratory on Appledore Island. In addition to Brian Fagan's *Fish on Friday*, see Mark Kurlansky's *Cod: A Biography of the Fish that Changed the World* (1997). I was also influenced by the theories of W. Jeffrey Bolster, a sailor, friend, and author of the award-winning book *The Mortal Sea* (2012). Bolster offers an alarming historical perspective on the declining fishing industry in the Gulf of Maine. It should be noted here that Maine has another Smutty Nose Island further north that lies alongside Monhegan and Manana Islands in Lincoln County. There is also a second Malaga Island in Casco Bay, where a mixed-race population was evicted by the state of Maine early in the twentieth century. The fact that New Hampshire patent owner John Mason and Maine patent owner Sir Ferdinando Gorges divided the Isles of Shoals between them in the early 1600s indicates their enormous value as fishing outposts. The battle over the border between the two states was still in play when New Hampshire claimed jurisdiction of the Portsmouth Naval Shipyard (established 1800) in 1992. At stake were millions of dollars that the state of Maine collects annually from Granite State citizens who work at the shipyard. The Supreme Court ruled that the shipyard, located on an island on the Kittery side of the Piscataqua River, is officially in Maine. It was this same fuzzy borderline that played a role in the Wagner case.

3. The Wild Wild East

Archaeology Professor Emerson "Tad" Baker teaches history in Massachusetts, but lives in coastal Maine, so he knows the region well. He is always my key source on seventeenth century seacoast history. His book *The Devil of Great Island* (2007) is a brilliant historical study of politics and superstition on nearby Great Island (now New Castle, NH). For a solid history of the founding of this region, the classic source is *The Eastern Frontier* (1970) by Charles E. Clark. It is coincidental that the two seminal books about Shoals history by Celia Thaxter and John Scribner Jenness came out in 1873, the same year as the murders, also the year tourism boomed on the seacoast, and the year that the Oceanic Hotel replaced the ancient fishing village of Gosport. While *Among the Isles of Shoals* is romantic and anecdotal, Celia Thaxter was no historian or scholar, and her book tends toward legend and lore. Those readers seeking facts are better off beginning with *The Isles of Shoals: An Historical Sketch* by John Scribner Jenness. Both are available for free on Google Books. Because the Shoals were divided between Maine and New Hampshire, this early fishing history was dredged up in the Wagner case. Ironically, thanks to the Oceanic Hotel and the murders, the 250 year history of fishing at the Shoals largely died in 1873. Again *Under the Isles of Shoals* (2012) will reference many of the quotations and sources in this chapter. Anyone fascinated with early Gosport can search for the town records online as published serially in the *New England Genealogical Register* (1913–14). It is from the imaginary story of Blackbeard's abandoned wife that Shoalers draw their most popular catch phrase. Each time visitors leave Star Island, the young hotel workers known as "pelicans" call out to the departing ferry, "You will come back! You will come back!" While treasure hunter publications continue to advertise the myths, only a single pirate tale has been documented and those men were captured with their booty on Star Island in 1703. See *Quelch's Gold* (2007) by Clifford Beal or search online for my article "The Brief Career of Pirate John Quelch."

4. The First Tourists

Besides Celia Laighton Thaxter's own works, the three key sources on the "Island Poet" and her family on Appledore are: *Sandpiper* (1963) by her granddaughter Rosamond Thaxter (who built the only other cabin standing on Smuttynose Island); *Beyond the Garden Gate* (2004) by Norma Mandel: and *One Woman's Work* (2000) edited by Sharon Stephan. I have included a solid list of the best books about the Isles of Shoals in a separate bibliography following these notes. But be careful. The history of these islands can be a seductive topic. Again see my *Under the Isles of Shoals* (2012) and the handy sourcebook *Gosport Remembered* (1997) edited by Peter E. Randall and Maryellen Burke. I also always rely on the Star Island Collection of documents and photographs that is housed at the Portsmouth Athenaeum. In *American Small Sailing Craft* (1951) famed maritime historian Howard I. Chapelle referenced a small boat design known as the "Isles of Shoals" boat or "shay." This design, Chapelle wrote, was an "enlarged copy" of the original New Hampshire fishing boats or "shallops" that appeared after the islands were taken over by hotels. With the fishing industry in decline, these boats were used by former fishermen to ferry tourists and take them on fishing trips. We see this economic adaptation continuing today with traditional fiberglass lobster and fishing boats now being used to take tourists on whale watches, deep sea fishing parties, and tours demonstrating how lobster fisherman pulled their traps from the sea.

5. The Norwegians

For years I carried on a rousing debate about the Wagner case with historian Robert "Bob" Tuttle whose wife Dorothy was forever working on a book about the murders. When they died their research went to the Portsmouth Athenaeum and was kindly directed to my use. It has been a key source for this book. Dot's study led her to Norway and her work inspired C. Laurence Robertson at the University of New Hampshire to create his teacher study guide, an excellent documentary video, and a ballet—all on the murders. (The ballet includes a score drawn from traditional Norwegian music by University of New Hampshire music Professor Christopher Kies.) This chapter includes information on Norwegian immigration and marital systems borrowed from Robertson's teacher guide by Julia Celebi at the Magnolia Midlands Science Center. For research concluding that Maren and John arrived separately from Norway, Robertson credits genealogy studies by Dorothy Tuttle and Gloria Echarte (who is descended from a Shoals family) and by genealogist Blaine Hedberg. Besides Celia Thaxter's kindly portrayal of Norwegians in *Among the Isles of Shoals* (1873) and "A Memorable Murder" (1875), we have her brother Cedric Laighton's wonderfully readable *Letters to Celia* (1972) edited by "Old Shoaler" Fred McGill. See also "New England Interest in Scandinavian Culture and the Norsemen" by Oscar J. Falnes in the *New England Quarterly (1937)*. Of the many books available on violinist Ole Bull, I chose *Oleana* (2002) by Paul W. Heimel.

6. Poor Karen and Mr. Poor

There is precious little available on the Stickney & Poor Spice Company and its founders, so I cobbled together bits about John R. Poor from his obituaries and various newspaper and magazine accounts. There is a brief history of the company in *Ideas that Became Big Business* (1959) by Clinton Woods. Although he is not always the most reliable source, Oscar Laighton tells his version of Poor's arrival in *Ninety Years at the Isles of Shoals* (1930). Oscar lived just shy of his 100th birthday and liked to spin a good yarn. After buying out the Gosport residents for John Poor in 1872, Nathan Mathes was at it again the following year. In 1873 Mathes began buying up property near the Little Harbor inlet in New Castle, New Hampshire. This time Mathes was acting as "front man" for a wealthy liquor distiller named Daniel E. Chase who also wanted to get into the hotel business. Chase was a primary investor in the Wentworth Hotel that opened the year after the Oceanic under the management of Charles and Sarah Campbell, who were also witnesses at the Wagner trial. Curiously, Daniel Chase and John Poor were both from Somerville, Massachusetts and both served at this time as city alderman. It is very likely that Chase, who had been summering in the region with the Campbells, told his fellow alderman Mr. Poor about the growing tourism business at the Shoals. Within three years both Massachusetts investors had sold off their costly properties and pulled out of the seacoast hotel business. Celia Thaxter wrote three poems about Norwegians named Karen, Thora, and Lars. All three appear in *The Poems of Celia Thaxter (1896).* For a literary analysis of Celia Thaxter's poetry read *Poet on Demand* (updated 1994) by Jane Vallier. A Quaker group from Philadelphia on a summer outing to Appledore Island met young Waldemar Ingebretsen (they called him "Vladimir") and his many siblings the year before the murders. The tourists visited the rustic Norwegian family's garden bursting with flowers and gave religious books to the children. (See *Friend's Review*, June 21, 1873.) The following year Waldemar was a key witness at the Wagner trial and he would die in a tragic accident ten years later. To be totally accurate, another Shoals historian tells me, I should mention that another fisherman named William Robinson also briefly resisted Mr. Poor's offer to buy up his property on Star Island.

7. With an Ax

I borrowed the chapter title "With an Ax" from a paperback of the same name (Pinnacle Books, 2000) by historian H. Paul Jeffers who contacted me many years ago during his research for a chapter on the Smuttynose murders, one of 16 ax murder cases covered in his book. As a longtime proprietor of the Portsmouth Athenaeum, I know the murder ax all too well and have even appeared holding it in a television show called "Mysteries at the Museum" on the Travel Channel. The Ursula Cutt story appears in the first volume of Charles Brewster's *Rambles about Portsmouth* (1869). One of Brewster's ancestors, he believed, was killed in an Indian attack during King Williams War. I read way too much about the Lizzie Borden case for this book, but decided to keep the comparisons here to a minimum. *Parallel Lives* (2011) by two historians at the Fall River Historical Society is packed with previously unseen details about both the Borden family and the city where they lived and died. For their permanent impact on a small community, the Villisca, Iowa. ax murders seem more akin to the Smuttynose case. For much more detail, see the excellent DVD documentary *Villisca: Living with a Memory* (2006) based on a lifetime of research by Dr. Edgar V. Epperly .

8. Best of Friends

The locally published *Sprays of Salt* (1944) by John W. Downs has many other insights about the final days of life at the Shoals, although John Downs occasionally got names and dates wrong. I first heard about the Mary J. "Mollie" Lehee Clifford (1865–1918) memoir from Portland playwright Carolyn Gage while we were attending an event at the Shoals Marine Lab on Appledore Island. The manuscript comes from the Maine Women Writer's Collection in Westbrook, Maine. Again we are dealing with questionable childhood memories and most of Clifford's memoir seems to come right out of her later reading of Celia Thaxter, but there are original passages too. Clifford was born on Lunging Island (formerly Londoner's Island) which still has only one house on it. The tides swoop in and divide the island in half twice daily. I spent a day there with a History Channel film crew years ago shooting what was supposed to be an episode on pirate gold. I went along as an unpaid "history consultant" and noted on-camera that there was absolutely no way that Blackbeard had buried his "treasure" there in an imaginary cave hidden under solid rock. Actors dressed in Pirates of Penzance-style costumes wandered around the island all day toting plastic guns and a plastic chest of plastic coins. A costly drill rig floated to the island uncovered nothing and my interview ended up on the cutting room floor.

9. On Water Street

Details here come largely from the 1875 trial transcript. For a full history of the Portsmouth waterfront through four hundred years, see my book *Strawbery Banke: A Maritime Museum 400 Years in the Making* (2007) that has extensive footnotes and four hundred pictures. The local expert on the Red Light district is Kimberly Crisp, whose research into the bordellos on Water Street has been invaluable and recently appeared, in part, as an essay in *Portsmouth Women* (2013) edited by Laura Pope. From a beautiful summer in his spacious room on Smuttynose, attended by Maren Hontvet, Wagner suddenly found himself living with two male roommates near the rotting docks of Water Street. His possessions had been lost in the wreck of the *Addison Gilbert* and he was penniless, while John Hontvet was thriving. This reversal of fortune, I believe, is crucial to understanding why Wagner took a desperate impulsive risk. Again, the source for the evolution of the fishing industry comes from *The Mortal Sea* (2013) by W. Jeffrey Bolster, a game-changing award-winning volume that tracks a thousand years of man's devastating, very possibly irreversible, impact on the sea and the creatures that live in it. The Wagner murders and the simultaneous disappearance of Gosport Village are directly tied to the declining fish stocks due to overfishing and to the rise of successful "high-tech" fishermen like John Hontvet. Bolster points out that New England fishermen were the first to raise the alarm. By the 1850s they were already petitioning their legislators to take action to protect fishing stocks, while scientists of the era claimed that the sea was boundless. Today the roles in the debate have reversed with scientists now raising the red flag against the protests of the dying fishing industry. Meanwhile, the problem worsens with each passing year. The Hontvet and Gosport events can be read as early tragedies arising from the frustration of small independent fishermen whose livelihood continues to falter as the sea's bounty declines. Fishing in small boats was—and remains—an extremely dangerous job. The year 1871 was among the most deadly: 145 men and 19 vessels from New England fisheries were lost.

10. Rowing

The working title of this book was "Death Rowing," which did not make the final cut. For years I rowed my Alden Ocean shell, a fiberglass sliding-seat model, on the rivers of the Piscataqua. I often traveled miles and miles without having a single thought, and I imagine Wagner was simply hypnotized by the activity. Today I find the same thing happens on my stationary rowing machine. While I managed to invent no dialogue in this volume, following Celia Thaxter, I admittedly slipped into the killer's mind in an effort to reconstruct his actions and motivations. While critics point out that Celia often referred to Wagner's "blackness," when he was decidedly Caucasian, I did not pursue this topic. Black has been forever equated with evil intent in European and American literature, but it is also clear from her other writings that, like most New Englanders of her time, Celia did not believe in full racial equality. Despite her connection to white abolitionists like John Greenleaf Whittier, Thomas Wentworth Higginson, and Harriet Beecher Stowe, she had almost no contact with African Americans in her life. Her poem "The Connoisseurs" (1879) all but blames the "dusky children" of the South for the Civil War. In describing Wagner's journey past three historic lighthouses in 1873 I relied on "Lighthouse Guy" Jeremy D'Entremont, but readers will find an enormous documentation of White, Whaleback, and Portsmouth Harbor Light in the five-hundred-plus page book *Friendly Edifices* (2006), by Jane M. Porter. As to whether Wagner knew Karen was then living on Smuttynose Island, I believe he did not, and that her sudden cry in the darkness triggered his deadly response. Celia's suggestion that Wagner muttered to himself that Karen would be dead in exactly three months is certainly exaggerated or entirely false.

11. Louis! Louis!

As much as possible, I wanted the narrative to simply flow in these dramatic chapters that are extrapolated entirely from the testimony of Maren Hontvet, Celia's reportage, and the recollection of those who visited the island after the murders. Maren's memory of her frantic final conversation with Karen and Anethe is always subject to question since she was not fluent in English. While researching this book, I slowly transcribed the trial transcript which has been largely unavailable and I plan to make it available in digital form for readers who, like me, suffer from "Smuttynose fever" and want to explore the entire document.

12. Hunting Maren

Visitors to the island today must remember that the empty cove area was crowded with dilapidated wooden buildings at the time. The long fish house that stood atop

Sam Haley's stone pier has since been moved to Cedar Island and recycled. The Mid-Ocean House was a large two-story building that could support over twenty guests, so there were many hiding places for Maren. Checking each one would have taken Wagner a good deal of time.

13. Escape

I have always been skeptical about the local belief that Maren hid inside a cluster of huge boulders now called "Maren's Rock." I suspect this spot quickly became part of the legend because the formation juts up at the far end of the island, is easily visible across the harbor to tourists at the Oceanic Hotel on Star Island, and is distinctive looking in early photographs. I have struggled my way out to Maren's Rock a few times and it is a formidable spot, even in summer, with steep slippery rocks lashed by the waves. One slip could be deadly. On the morning after the murders Maren managed to get the attention of the Ingebretsen children when she signaled them from the side of Malaga Island that faces Appledore. Malaga is scarcely a separate island at all. Just three hundred by five hundred feet of jagged rock and only eighteen feet above sea level, historians assume the island got its name from early Basque fishermen, but that is pure speculation. Incredibly, one of the earliest known houses built at the Isles of Shoals was located here on Malaga in the 1640s, but was long gone in Maren's day. The fact that Maren had blood on her nightgown has fueled one conspiracy theory that is dealt with in the final section of this book. The information here comes mostly from Celia's "Memorable Murder" essay. To her credit, while the romantic writer did have a tendency for "coloring in" details, she also had an excellent memory. A few years ago I found a descriptive letter written by Celia to a friend when she was twelve years old in 1847. Discovered in an online auction, the letter remains her earliest known correspondence, and yet, she remembered many of the childhood details accurately in her memoir of the Shoals written twenty-five years later.

14. The American Killer

By heading toward the inlet at Little Harbor instead of returning the boat to Pickering's Wharf, Wagner saved about two miles of rowing. He also reduced his chance of being spotted from houses on the New Castle and Portsmouth shore, by soldiers at a series of coastal defense camps including Fort Stark and Fort Constitution in New Castle, by fishermen heading to sea, by the lighthouse keeper's at Fort Point and Whaleback, and by the watchmen at the Portsmouth Naval Shipyard. But after abandoning the dory, he then had to walk past a series of witnesses to get back to Portsmouth. For much more on the evolution of American horror see *Murder Most Foul: The Killer and the American Gothic Imagination* (1998) by Karen Halttunen, especially chapter 3 on "The Pornography of Violence." A key source on the Jewett-Robinson case and the rise of the penny post is the shockingly-titled *Froth and Scum: Truth, Beauty, Goodness, and the Ax Murder in America's First Mass Medium* (1994) by Andie Tucher. See also chapter 5 of *Sensationalism and the New York Press (1991)* by John D. Stevens or an in-depth scholarly approach in *The Murder of Helen Jewett* (1998) by Patricia Cline Cohen.

15. The Stranger

You can learn a lot about Charles and Sarah Campbell and see photos of them in my book *Wentworth by the Sea: The Life and Times of a Grand Hotel* (2004). I had no idea when I wrote that history that the Campbells were witnesses at the Wagner trial. They opened their hotel on the New Castle bluff in 1874. As noted, their key financial backer was Daniel E. Chase of Somerville, Massachusetts who was an associate of John R. Poor, also of Somerville, who was then building the Oceanic Hotel on Star Island. The Campbells quickly went bankrupt and the hotel was purchased by Portsmouth ale tycoon Frank Jones who greatly improved and expanded it. Charles Campbell stayed on for years as the hotel night watchman. The hotel was temporarily home to the delegates of the famous Treaty of Portsmouth that ended the Russo-Japanese War in 1905 under the direction of President Theodore Roosevelt. Wentworth by the Sea was abandoned for two decades in the late twentieth century, then revamped for twenty-six million dollars and reopened in 2003. From the hotel today you can catch the same view Wagner had looking seaward, toward Little Harbor, and off toward Portsmouth. Despite an explosion of new homes nearby, you can also trace Wagner's walk from the cemetery and across the bridges to the Portsmouth South End. The rest of the material in this chapter comes directly from the trial transcript and, I believe, exposes a wealth of revealing behind-the-scenes dialogue related to Wagner's character that is rarely covered. Those who pose alternate murder theories must explain away ten witnesses who followed the progress of the stranger from New Castle to Water Street on the morning of March 6. If only one of those people saw Wagner and testified truthfully, his alibi collapses.

16. The Arrest

It is a challenge, due to his duplicity, to integrate what Wagner said with other testimony, but I have done my best to represent his actual words where possible and invent nothing. It is important to note that he was among the last witnesses for the defense to appear at the trial in June. Wagner had by then heard all the testimony from dozens of prosecution witnesses, so he was able to recast his version of the events to what is presented here. Wagner's conflicted attitude toward alcohol is curious. He made it clear to his roommate Frederick Moore, to Mary Johnson, and to deputy Entwistle that he was not drunk. But his alibi depended on convincing a jury that, while he was not known to be a drinker, he chose the night of the murder to visit two saloons and imbibe enough beer to fall down, vomit, and pass out in the street as he claimed. I'm fishing here, but he seems to relate drinking to being out of control, and while he is willing to admit he was sick, he will not be perceived as lacking in judgment. Every action he takes, for Wagner, has purpose. Whether we are tapping into Wagner's earlier misadventures while under the influence, or perhaps into his relationship with an absentee father in Prussia, I leave to the armchair therapists.

17. Lynch Mob

Here the extensive media coverage and the trial transcript begin to overlap. For more on the Portsmouth Stamp Act Riot of 1760 and the Newspaper Riot of 1865 see my articles on SeacoastNH.com. As often as possible I reference specific newspapers, but the same content often appeared in many publications. Roughly two hundred clippings, large and small, are contained in the Tuttle Collection at the Portsmouth Athenaeum.

18. Evidence and Alibi

My analysis of the two competing Portsmouth dailies and their editors was informed by a discussion with Steven Fowle who carries on the tradition of "America's Oldest

Newspaper" by publishing the free fortnightly *NH Gazette* (establish 1756) from his home. He is the reigning expert on the history of Portsmouth media. See also "The New Hampshire Gazette" by Frank W. Miller in the *New England Historical and Genealogical Record* (1872, pages 132–40). For added details on attorney Charles Yeaton I relied on Wendy Pirsig of the Old Berwick Historical Society in South Berwick, Maine.

19. The Funeral

The usual sources apply here. I recommend anyone to take a tour of the historic St. John's Episcopal Church in Portsmouth with its above-ground cemetery and historic artifacts. Those who follow the path of the lynch mob will find much of the street names unchanged, although the city has grown significantly in recent years. I resisted requests to publish specific directions to the graves of Karen and Anethe. Those readers who feel compelled to seek them out will do so. Celia's letter about the murder to her friend Elizabeth D. Pierce was published in *Letters of Celia Thaxter* (1895) edited by her friends Annie Fields and Sarah Orne Jewett.

20. Opening Ceremonies

There is precious little data about the first three seasons of the original 1873 Oceanic Hotel that burned flat in 1875, but we have a few dramatic photographs. The deep connection between Celia Thaxter's Appledore Hotel artistic salon and the *Atlantic Monthly* is wonderfully documented in *Republic of Words* (2011) by Susan Goodman. See also *One Woman's Work* (2001) edited by Sharon Paiva Stephan. On Celia's laugh and character see "Reminiscences of Literary Boston" by Elizabeth Stuart Phelps in *McClure's Magazine* (August 1896). Although I gathered most of the sources on the Oceanic Hotel here separately, it turns out that many key quotes also appear in *Gosport Remembered* (1997) in a chapter titled "A First Class Watering Place" (pages 89–99). That valuable book includes the material from *The Isles of Shoals in Summer Time* (1875) by William Leonard Gage. The insightful comment by Samuel Adams Drake about Gosport being "improved out of existence" comes from *The Pine-tree Coast* (1891) and largely inspired a secondary theme of this book on the fishing village that vanished.

370

21. The Examination

The three months between the murders and the trial is a period mostly ignored by briefer accounts of the Wagner case, yet it is important to the development of his public image as presented by the media in an era unfamiliar with the concept of sociopaths. While preparing this chapter I was introduced to Dr. Martha Stout's *The Sociopath Next Door* (2006) and Dr. Robert Hare's *Without Conscience* (1999). Although Wagner appears to be a textbook psychopath, like Edmund Pearson, I prefer to let readers draw their own conclusion from Wagner's words and actions. I first "discovered" the story of ax murderer James Cullen in a news clipping and, digging further, was surprised to find he has his own Facebook page, based on a recent theatrical production of his life. The chapter "They Lynched Jim Cullen" by Dena Lynn Winslow in *Lynching Beyond Dixie* (2013) is a good overview. For more on the Saco murder see Elizabeth De Wolfe's *The Murder of Mary Bean and Other Stories* (2007) that includes both factual and fictional accounts. Heritage tourists may want to visit the Saco Museum in Saco, Maine, and the Counting House Museum in South Berwick. I was speaking to the Piscataqua Pioneers in Maine near press time for this book when Sarah Dennett, a descendant of Justice Alexander Dennett, gave me a copy of the two handwritten arrest warrants issued prior to Wagner's hearing on March 12, 1873. They state that Wagner did "with force and arms . . . kill and murder" his two victims with an ax. The last page is a tally of costs for the warrants totaling $13.10.

22. Dream Team

Local gossip has long suggested that Wagner's lawyers were less than aggressive in his behalf. But, again, few critics have read the trial transcript, and fewer understand how the transcript was made by the court stenographer in 1873, leaving out a great amount of detail that we will never see. Tapley and Fischacher were faced with defending an indigent immigrant whose every word contradicted the evidence, and yet they attempted every legal option to save his life. My profiles of the two defense attorneys were cobbled together from a dozen minor online sources and I've included a few more details on their later cases in the chapter titled "Legal Eagles." For much more on the execution of Ruth Blay on Gallows

Hill see Carolyn Marvin's *Hanging Ruth Blay* (2010). It is a good example of how far New England jurisprudence had advanced in the century leading up to the Wagner trial. The bulk of the material here and in the coming chapters is a comparison of the official trial transcript with a variety of newspaper accounts.

23. Alfred

I strongly recommend a daytrip to rural Alfred, Maine, for anyone interested in the Wagner case. The highlight is certainly the Alfred jail where, if you can convince the local store owner, you can still view the original prison cells slowly decaying at the center of the building. What was once the oldest and largest Shaker society in Maine with hundreds of members is gone. It survived from the late 1700s until 1931 and is memorialized today at the Alfred Shaker Museum built in a restored carriage house. My research on court stenographer J. D. Pulsifer went down many blind alleys and narrow streets. His instructions to students to "Give all the evidence, but not all the words" and other tidbits come from his article "Preparing a Record" in the *Shorthand Review*, (January 1891). An article in the *Lewiston Evening Journal* (January 4, 1896) honored Pulsifer, one of its frequent contributors, who was then dying from "softening of the brain." He was remembered as a lover of classical literature, a great storyteller and lover of jokes, and a man who read the Congressional Record every day. "He was a great stickler for fine points," the *Journal* noted. A lengthy memorial tribute to Judge Barrows appeared in the 1887 (Volume 78) issue of *Maine Reports: Cases Argued and Determined in the Supreme Judicial Court of Maine*, available on Google Books. I was directed to a transcript of the George Lincoln Came journal while visiting the Alfred Historical Society. See also *Alfred, Maine: The Shakers and The Village* (1986) by Harland H. Eastman.

24. A Hailstorm of Evidence

From here through the next five chapters we are solidly into the trial transcript published in a small thick leather-bound version in 1874. Despite its length and detail, we know from stenographer J. D. Pulsifer that it is not a word-for-word transcript of everything that was said. I worked from a Xerox of the copy at the

Portsmouth Athenaeum and typed the entire thing by hand in order to analyze it closely. Remember that Wagner was tried only for the death of Anethe, not Karen. The immediate impression one draws is how expertly the prosecution used the first two dozen witnesses to lay out the chronology of the events.

25. Four Women

Without delving into amateur psychology, I wanted to show that Wagner had a complex relationship with women by giving readers a good look at the testimony of his two mature landladies and their nineteen-year old assistants, never forgetting that Maren and Anethe had also served in the same capacity as his caretaker on Smuttynose. All four were strong independent women who lived in the seedier parts of Boston and Portsmouth. All four had clearly felt some sympathy for Wagner, if not a physical attraction, before they learned of his capacity for murder. Despite attempts by the defense attorney to sully their character, they all turned in powerful independent presentations at Alfred. Later we will learn much more about Wagner and women in a letter he wrote to his mother and in her reply.

26. Cops and Blood

Despite Fischacher's desperate defense, I was unable to uncover any hint of impropriety on the part of the police either in Boston or Portsmouth, and we should not use twenty-first century stereotypes to assume these were anything but likeable cops doing their duty. While it is certainly possible that the bloody shirt found in the privy was planted by someone to bolster the evidence against Wagner, it is entirely logical that Wagner tore it up, smuggled it out of the house, and tossed it in the privy. His claim that he left the shirt on his bed and told his landlady to tear it into rags is certainly another of his clever lies. Wagner could not have anticipated the inordinate effort the police and prosecution would make to have the stain scientifically analyzed. Court reporter Pulsifer did an extraordinary job of documenting the long and dull medical testimony of blood expert Dr. Horace Chase. Max Fischacher, in turn, showed his true skill at the bar when he adroitly disputed the science behind Chase's conclusions. And while Chase very likely believed that his tests were accurate, they were not. Yet his false science does not in any way indicate that Wagner was innocent or that the prosecutor's case was flawed. Dr. Chase will reappear in the "Aftermath" section of this book in another case that implies that the good doctor may have been a murderer himself. For more on the history of blood analysis Colin Wilson's *Written in Blood* (1989) and chapter 3 of *Sourcebook in Forensic Serology, Immunology, and Biochemistry* (R. E. Gaensslen, 1983) titled "History and Development of Medic-Legal Examination of Blood." The quote about the three types of liars comes from *Transactions of the New Hampshire Medical Society* (May 24 & 25, 1897). From the wealth of information on the Parkman murder I selected *Dead Certainties* (1991) by Simon Schama, but I suggest starting with the PBS special *Murder at Harvard* (2005) from the American Experiences series.

27. Wagner's Last Stand

Max Fischacher's defense certainly pales in comparison to the prosecutor's well constructed case, but his slips and gaffs read to me like a man nervously sinking into the quicksand of the clever lies and contradictions created by his talkative client. Once on the witness stand, Wagner could not prevent himself from attacking the character of everyone who had testified against him in what was certainly his own attempt to cast a reasonable doubt on the veracity of their statements. He had always been able to charm and inveigle his victims. Like the classic sociopath, he could never admit to being wrong about anything and now believed he could sway the jury despite his inability to back up his tall tales. His testimony is a truly remarkable performance and his sheer bravado convinced many in the audience, some reporters, his attorneys (at least initially), and later his jailers and the warden of the Maine State Prison.

28. Circling the Wagons

Within Tapley's failed five-hour effort to depict Wagner as a heroic victim of mistaken identity, one point continues to needle me. Was Wagner dumb enough to openly reveal his desire to rob someone at the Shoals? Yes, I think he was, and he may have been referring to robbing a house at Lunging, Star, or Appledore, rather than Smuttynose. But his reported threat to commit a robbery within three months is hard to swallow and leads me to think that John Hontvet had a strong hand in coloring the testimony of his fisherman friends, especially when we consider that John wanted to see Wagner shot or hanged by the lynch mob. Tapley and Fischacher's suspicion that the police and the prosecution were overly influenced by John Hontvet may indeed be true, but that does not change the facts of the case as some critics have suggested.

29. The Verdict

Yeaton's cross examination of Wagner demonstrates the prisoner's genius at impromptu fabrication. At the eleventh hour, Fischacher delicately tried to introduce the theory that, if Wagner was innocent, then Maren was the most likely alternative killer. But he was thwarted by the testimony of Dr. Parsons. The "Maren theory" got most of its publicity from Wagner's later discussions with newspaper reporters. Fischacher's secret search for the man who claimed Wagner was not at the New Castle bridge is revealed in the next chapter.

30. Capital Debate

Again, what is so often missed in discussions of the case is how close Maine was at this precise moment to overturning the death penalty and how many abolitionists would use Wagner's claim of innocence and Gordon's attempted suicide to further their cause. Had I not sifted slowly and methodically through every page in the expansive Tuttle file, I might have missed the revealing clipping in which Fischacher confronted witness John Lyons. This never-before-discussed detail confirms what the jury and every serious student of the case has concluded, that Wagner was on the bridge at New Castle. A good overview of the death penalty in Maine can be found in Edward Shriver's 1990 article "Reluctant Hangman" in *The New England Quarterly* and John Galliher's *America without the Death Penalty* (2002). See also "Capital Punishment" in www.maineanencyclopedia.com. For more on the death of Phoebe Sager see the *Trial of [Joseph] Sager for the Murder of his Wife* (1834). You can Google the "Last Words of Peter Williams and Abraham Cox" and also download "Seventy-Five Years Have Passed Since Last Hanging in Auburn," *Lewiston Evening Journal*, March 16, 1932. See also "A Double Execution" in the *New York Times*, September 2, 1858.

31. The Escape Artist

The day-to-day details of Wagner's escape and recapture have received almost no public coverage since they occurred. His careful planning, including slowly constructing a rope from scraps of bed sheets, certainly shows he was capable of premeditation in the Smuttynose robbery. His ability to use humor and feigned honesty to befriend and then to distract the prison guards from his secret escape plan should also be noted. Wagner's own picture of himself hiding in the shadows of his cell as the watchmen pass is all too similar to Maren's report to Celia that he was "always lurking in corners." Among the most thrilling moments in this research was "discovering" that the three-tier prison cells still survive at the heart of the old jail building at 5 Court Street in Alfred, Maine. See also Sharon Cummings article "Old Alfred jailhouse saw inmates come and go" in the online version of the *Portsmouth Herald* (August 2, 2012).

32. Dead Man Talking

My apologies for the punning chapter title, but it was impossible not to reference one of actor Sean Penn's best movie roles (*Dead Man Walking*) in comparison to his walk-through performance in the film version of *The Weight of Water*. With the recapture, once again, I prefer to point out patterns rather than attempt psychoanalysis for which I am unqualified. Attempts to classify Wagner as either shrewd or foolish, evil or innocent, inevitably miss the point that his behavior is complex, impulsive, and sometimes self-destructive. Yet even these characteristics become predictable the more we come to know him, and that was a guiding principal of this volume.

33. John True Gordon

The timely appearance of Gordon also factors in to the legend of Wagner's innocence. While the two men were amazingly similar, the media tendency to present complex things in stark black and white favored Wagner. Besides looking and talking less like a criminal to Victorians, he had not murdered a child, killed his own brother, or set their bodies on fire. To some, Gordon made Wagner appear, by comparison, incrementally less evil and potentially his polar opposite. Emeric

Spooner reprinted important newspaper accounts of "The Thorndike Slayer" in *Return to Smuttynose Island*. There is also a published transcript titled: *Trial of John T. Gordon: for the murder of Emma A. Gordon at Thorndike, June 16th, 1873*. Curiously, the last man hanged for murder in Rhode Island in 1845 (and pardoned posthumously in 2011) was also named John Gordon. For a condensed history of Thomaston Prison see Jeffrey D. Merrill's introduction to *Maine State Prison, 1824–2002* (2009) and also a brief history in *Maine Mothers Who Murdered, 1875–1925* by Annette K Dorey (2012). See also "An Abstract of the History of Maine State Prison 1822–1886" in *Maine Historical Magazine* (Vol. VI, No. 12, 1891).

34. Final Hours

How odd that Wagner would spend his final hours on death row with a future Pulitzer Prize winner. For the best of Edward Page Mitchell (1852–1927) see his *Memoirs of an Editor* (1924). Although Wagner told the Boston police he could not read the English newspaper, he either read, or someone read to him, Celia Thaxter's much-anthologized essay. His comment after reading the lengthy article comes from the July 5, 1875 *Portsmouth Journal*. I assume that Wagner's Christian faith, like his rheumatism, was play acting, but that is not to discount the importance of superstitious beliefs and good luck charms among the fishermen of his era. The relationship between the two killers and their mothers (and probably their fathers) might have filled its own chapter, but we simply do not have enough data to draw conclusions. I stretched my views to the limit in the next chapter with my theory that Wagner's refusal to confess, besides being key to his sociopathic nature, may stem from an effort to shield his aging mother from the truth about her bad boy.

35. Upon the Gallows

Two newspaper references hinted that Wagner's body went to Bowdoin for dissection, and while it seems a strong possibility, no evidence, at this writing, has been found. A quick call to archive assistant Kathy Petersen of the George J. Mitchell Department of Special Collections & Archives at Bowdoin College Library turned up no record of a cadaver delivered to the medical school there in 1875. That is no surprise, but I'll bet an enterprising grad student will someday prove my theory. The use of cadavers for surgical practice and anatomy lessons is frequently mentioned in Bowdoin college course summaries of the era. There are other references to cadaver pranks as well. For a brief anecdote about a floating head in a whiskey barrel see *Tales of Bowdoin* (1901) by Bowdoin Men. Maine passed an anti-grave robbing statute in 1820, the same year Maine attained statehood and Bowdoin instituted its college of medicine. Body snatching became a lucrative "underground" business. For a time, being found in the possession of a body intended for the purpose of dissection was considered a felony. For mention of Bowdoin Medical seeking cadavers from other colleges, see *Body Snatching* (1992) by Suzanne M. Shultz. While I assume it is coincidental, within two weeks of Wagner's hanging, Thomaston Prison chaplain Rev. J.K. Mason was on his way to Bowdoin College to receive an honorary degree. In *The Invention of Murder* (2011), author Judith Flanders notes that in early nineteenth-century England, the dissection of felons was reserved for members of the faculty.

36. The Oceanic Burns

For more on the 1875 Oceanic Hotel fire see articles reprinted in *Gosport Remembered* (1997). The full report on John Poor versus his fire insurance company is available on Google Books. For more on the demise and annexation of Gosport see Langdon Brown Parsons' *History of the Town of Rye, NH* (1905). The lawyer who visited the Hontvet House was Herbert Milton Sylvester from his book *Old York* (1905) published three years before the house burned. Those wishing to visit or stay at the Oceanic Hotel or attend classes at the Shoals Marine Lab will find travel and contact information at the end of this book.

37. Celia's World

Of Celia Thaxter's murder essay English-born biographer James Parton wrote in 1883 that "a more haunting tale of horror was never produced by Poe or De Quincey." Speaking of Celia and other Victorian women in the arts, Parton added: "Women in our day have attained the first rank, and have made the first rank higher." Thomas De Quincey's satirical essays including "Murder, Considered as One of the Fine Arts" are also available online. Professor Elizabeth Hewitt of Ohio State University kindly sent me a copy of her recent scholarly paper that proves

Celia Thaxter's 1875 murder essay is still being read and analyzed. See "Criminal Minds: Literary Tourism and True Crime in the Gilded-Age Periodical" (2012). "A Memorable Murder" is available from many sources online. I listed all the classic sources on Celia Thaxter and the Isles of Shoals separately in my bibliography.

38. The Hontvet Legacy

The genealogical material comes from a variety of sources mentioned in the acknowledgements including people who communicated with my website and especially from the yeoman work done by Bob and Dot Tuttle and their friends. The Tuttles also tirelessly combed local newspapers for reports on the life and death of the schooner *Mary S. Hontvet* and the later ships owned or operated by John Hontvet. The reference to Ivan Christensen's life after Smuttynose comes from *Norwegian Sailors in American Waters* (1933). Maine researcher Emeric Spooner tracked down the long lost source of the deathbed confession hoax in *Return to Smuttynose Island*. True crime writer Harold Schechter has an entire book on Jesse Pomeroy titled *Fiend: The Shocking True Story of America's Youngest Serial Killer* (2012).

39. Last Men Hanged

The notes on capital punishment continue mostly from the sources referenced in chapter 30, especially Shriver's "Reluctant Hangman" and chapter Four in *America Without the Death Penalty*. See also the front page of the *Boston Daily Globe* (April 17, 1885) for the article "Double Execution In Maine: Santore and Capone, the Two Italian Murderers, Die on the Scaffold at Thomaston." For more on the Sawtell murder a good place to start online is "The Disappearance of Hiram Sawtell" in the *Boston Evening Transcript* (February 13, 1890) and a vivid forensic description in *A Text-book of Legal Medicine* (1905) by Frank Winthrop Draper. The couplet about the Sawtell brothers comes from the book *Bloody Verses* (1993) by Jonathan Goodman.

40. Legal Eagles

Details on the unsolved murder of housekeeper Fannie Sprague comes from my own research courtesy of a news clipping file of the 1901 trial archived at the

Old Berwick Historical Society in South Berwick, Maine, and can be seen on SeacoastNH.com. George Yeaton apparently got the killer acquitted. The story of the "headless corpse" is described in the 1875 transcript of the *Trial of James M. Lowell* by attorney Harris Plaisted. Jane Swett's sad case, judged by Rufus Tapley, is briefly considered in *Women Who Kill* (1980) by Ann Jones. My summary of the case involving Dr. Horace Chase is drawn from a variety of newspaper accounts found online. It appears that Wagner's "blood expert" got away with murder, but was unable to collect on his dead wife's fortune.

The final years of Marshal Thomas Entwistle are adapted from a chapter in my book on *Strawbery Banke* (2007). Again, for a good summary of the last madams of the Red Light district on Water Street see the essay by Kimberly Crisp in *Portsmouth Women* (2013). A number of modern high schools and colleges use the Wagner case as a teaching tool. Excerpts from arguments by the defense and prosecution appeared for students of public speaking as early as 1922 in *The Art of Debate* by Prof. Warren Choate Shaw, now available online.

41. Pure Murder

It was Edmund Pearson's out-of-print essay in *Murder at Smutty Nose* that inspired this book. Pearson has yet to receive his deserved recognition, or even a major biography. Yet he has been the unwavering voice of reason here in the seacoast against the growing tide of treacle and blather related to the 1873 tragedy. His research on the Smuttynose story was so impeccable, and his prose style so crisp, that it still holds up ninety years later. His seventy-page analysis, abridged and heavily illustrated, also ran in the October 1931 issue of *True Detective Mysteries* under the title "The Moonlight Murders of the Isles of Shoals." Pearson's essay in *Scribner's Magazine* (December 1937) that is referenced here is titled "What is Evidence?" His magazine essays, his scholarly work on old books, particularly his book-length study of "dime novels," are still worth digging into, while his work on the Lizzie Borden case is required reading for devotees of the 1892 Fall River tragedy. Lizzie Borden died in 1927 and it is worth wondering whether her notoriety had an impact on the Wagner legend hoax. Although acquitted of killing her father and stepmother, Borden planted the image of a hatchet-wielding New England woman firmly in the psyche of the American public. If Lizzie got away with murder, might Maren have done the same? Our brains quickly connect the two disconnected dots. The association is strong, as strong as O. J. Simpson selling orange juice on television commercials, but superficial and meaningless all the same.

42. Weight of Water

When questioned about her use of historical figures in a fictional work, Anita Shreve told *Foster's Daily Democrat* (January 22, 1998), "It's important for a writer to put thoughts of other people out of their mind. It's too easy to be intimidated, and if that happened, books like *The Weight of Water* would never be written." Pressed on whether it was acceptable to portray an historical figure as a killer, Shreve replied, "I did have some pause. No one wants to accuse someone of murder, but others have, and I felt that opened the door."

There was a creeping fear among the stewards of Smuttynose Island that Shreve's novel and the subsequent movie might turn the island back to the days when tourists swarmed there after the murders seeking bloody souvenirs. That never happened, partly because the island is privately owned and largely inaccessible, and partly because the movie quickly died at the box office. Yet countless island visitors, including local tour guides, and even a few historians continue to declare that the novel "proves" Maren was the killer when the "evidence" is fictional. Or it arouses their suspicion about the case. "I can't believe people still take that seriously," Anita Shreve told me one evening more than a decade after the release of the book. She was signing her latest novel in the green room of The Music Hall of Portsmouth prior to an appearance to a packed house of primarily female fans. Well, dear reader, people still do take it seriously. The two *Yankee* essays on the murders were reprinted in 1985 as part of a *Best of Yankee Magazine* coffee table book and may also appear online. The key article, "Horror on Smuttynose," is by Mark Bastoni and first appeared in March 1980. The conspiracy theory rebuttal by L. Morrill Burke appeared in the August 1981 issue of the magazine. *Yankee* editor-in-chief Judson D. Hale mentions the murders in his book *Inside New England* in a chapter called "The Dark Side." See *Boon Island: A True Story of Mutiny, Shipwreck, and Cannibalism* (2012) by Andrew Vietze and Stephen Erickson for a thrilling retelling of an old tale.

43. Louis in Hollywood

Foster's Sunday Citizen announced on November 9, 1997, that conspiracy-theory filmmaker Oliver Stone had optioned the rights to the novel, *The Weight of Water*. New Hampshire and Maine would be "Left Out Again" according to the headline, since the movie was to be shot in Nova Scotia, Canada, where production costs were 40 percent cheaper than in the United States. None of the money from the location shooting would find its way into the local economy. "The book is a work of fiction," Shreve told *Foster's* "I don't know any more than anyone else about what happened." Shreve initially feared that the people of Portsmouth would think "an outsider had trespassed on their territory," but Portsmouth welcomed her. The author told the *Longmeadow News* of Westfield, MA (March 23, 2000), that Kathryn Bigelow, whom she called "a very gutsy female director," brought her novel to Oliver Stone's attention even before it was published. The film languished without a distributor and was not shown in the seacoast region until The Music Hall of Portsmouth arranged a special two-day screening to an overflow audience.

44. Victorian Psycho

The story of the dagger found in the floorboards appeared in the February 4, 1904, *Portsmouth Herald* with the headline "Was It Wagner's?" I now own the leatherette pocket diary from 1873 with the scrawled pencil messages. The name of the young diarist appears to be Charles Stackpole of Lowell, MA, but there are other names listed too. Someone used the diary for years to record petty cash expenses. Inside is a tintype of an anonymous and sad-looking woman with a bird's nest wig. As I was writing these notes the state of New Hampshire was once again debating whether to end capital punishment, but legislators voted, once more, to maintain the death penalty. Again I recommend the introductory books on modern sociopaths by Dr. Martha Stout and Dr. Robert Hare, but there are many to select from. The *New York Times* article referenced here (May 21, 2013) by Maggie Koerth-Baker is titled "Why Rational People Buy into Conspiracy Theories." It is uncanny how precisely the characteristics currently used to describe a sociopath match the behavior of Louis Wagner. My goal in this book has been to describe what we know about Wagner as fully as possible from documents about the case in order to allow readers to make the comparison.

SELECT BIBLIOGRAPHY

Part I. Sources on the Smuttynose Murders and Related Crimes

Altick, Richard D. 1970. *Victorian Studies in Scarlet*. New York: Norton.

Axelrod-Contrada, Joan. 2000. *The Lizzie Borden "Axe Murder" Trial: A Headline Court Case*. Berkeley Heights, NJ: Enslow Publishers.

Bryan, Patricia L., and Thomas Wolf. 2005. *Midnight Assassin: A Murder in America's Heartland*. Chapel Hill, NC: Algonquin Books of Chapel Hill.

Clifford, Nathan, Hon. and United States, *Reports of Cases Determined in the Circuit Court of the United States for the First Circuit (1858–1861, Vol. 1.* Boston: Little, Brown & Company, 1869.

Cohen, Patricia Cline. 1998. *The Murder of Helen Jewett: The Life and Death of a Prostitute in Nineteenth-Century New York*. New York: Alfred A. Knopf.

Dempewolff, Richard F. 1942. *Famous Old New England Murders and some that are Infamous*. Brattleboro, Vt: Stephen Daye Press. (Chapter 1: Murders on the Isles of Shoals).

De Quincey, Thomas. 1889. *Murder Considered as One of the Fine Arts; Three Memorable Murders; The Spanish Nun*. New York: Putnam.

De Wolfe, Elizabeth A. 2007. *The Murder of Mary Bean and Other Stories*. Kent, Ohio: Kent State University Press.

Dorey, Annette K. Vance. 2012. *Maine Mothers Who Murdered, 1875–1925: Doing Time in State Prison*. Lewiston, ME: Van Horn Vintage Press.

Draper, Frank Winthrop. 1905. *A Text-Book of Legal Medicine*. Philadelphia: W.B. Saunders.

Eastman, Harland H. 1986. *Alfred, Maine: The Shakers and The Village*. Sanford, ME: Wilson.

Faxon, David. 2009. *Cold Water Crossing: An Account of the Murders at the Isles of Shoals*. CreateSpace Independent Publishing.

Ferland, David. 2014. "Historic Crimes & Justice in Portsmouth, New Hampshire."

Foster, William, L. 1897. "Medical Expert Testimony: Transactions of the New Hampshire Medical Society at the 106th Anniversary held at Concord, May 24 and 25, 1897." *JAMA: The Journal of the American Medical Association*. XXIX (23): 1182.

Gaensslen, R. E. 1983. *Sourcebook in Forensic Serology, Immunology, and Biochemistry*. Washington, DC: U.S. Dept. of Justice, National Institute of Justice.

Galliher, John F. 2002. *America Without the Death Penalty: States Leading the Way*. Boston: Northeastern University Press.

Hale, Judson D. 1985. *The Best of Yankee Magazine: 50 years of New England*. Dublin, NH: Yankee Books. (See "Horror on Smuttynose," Mark Bastoni, March, 1980 and "The Real Horror on Smuttynose," L. Morrill Burke, August, 1981).

Halttunen, Karen. 1998. *Murder Most Foul: The Killer and The American Gothic Imagination*. Cambridge, MA: Harvard University Press.

Hare, Robert D. 1999. *Without Conscience: The Disturbing World of the Psychopaths Among Us*. New York: Guilford Press.

Hartwell, Edward Mussey. 1881. *The Study of Anatomy, Historically and Legally Considered*. Boston: Tolman & White.

Hewitt, Elizabeth. "Criminal Minds: Literary Tourism and True Crime in the Gilded-Age Periodical" *Paper presented at the annual meeting of the American Studies Association Annual Meeting, Hilton Baltimore, Baltimore, MD, 2012*.

Jeffers, H. Paul. 2000. *With an axe*. New York: Pinnacle Books, Kensington Pub. Corp.

Jones, Ann. 1980. *Women Who Kill*. New York: Holt, Rinehart, and Winston.

Kopf, Carl Heath. 1941. *Windows on Life*. New York: The Macmillan Company.

Maine, State of. *Records of the Supreme Judicial Court of Maine*, Vol. 61; *Journal of the Executive Council 1874–75*; *Records of the Secretary of State*, Vol. 4.

Marvin, Carolyn. 2010. *Hanging Ruth Blay: An Eighteenth-Century New Hampshire Tragedy*. Charleston, SC: History Press.

Merrill, Jeffrey D. 2009. *Maine State Prison, 1824–2002*. Charleston, SC: Arcadia Publishing.

Mitchell, Edward Page. 1924. *Memoirs of an Editor; Fifty Years of American Journalism*. New York: C. Scribner's Sons.

Morley, Jackson (editor). 1974. "Tragedy on the Isles of Shoals," *Crimes and Punishment*. USA: BPC Publishing Ltd. Vol. 20.

Newspaper accounts from the *Boston Daily, Portsmouth Daily Evening Times, Portsmouth Chronicle, Portsmouth Journal, New York Times, Portland Press, Portland Argus*, and others. Smuttynose Murder Collection, Portsmouth Athenaeum, Portsmouth, NH

Pearson, Edmund Lester. 1926. *Murder at Smutty Nose: and Other Murders*. Garden City, NY: Doubleday, Page & Company.

Pfeifer, Michael J. 2013. *Lynching Beyond Dixie: American Mob Violence Outside the South*. University of Illinois Press.

Perrault, John, 2003. *The Ballad of Louis Wagner: and Other New England Stories in Verse*. Portsmouth, NH: Peter E. Randall.

Plaisted, Harris M. 1875. *Report of the Trial of James M. Lowell indicted for the Murder of his Wife, Mary Elizabeth Lowell: Before the Supreme Judicial Court of Maine, for Androscoggin County* Portland, ME: Dresser, McLellan & Co.

Porter, Joseph W. (editor) 1891. "An Abstract of the History of Maine State Prison 1822–1886." *The Maine Historical Magazine*. Bangor, ME: B. A. Burr, VI (12).

Potter, L. F. 1873. *The Murder of Granville Hayden*. Aroostook County, Maine.

Ramsland, Katherine M. 2007. *Beating the Devil's Game: A History of Forensic Science and Criminal Investigation*. New York: Berkley Books.

Rundle, Kelly, Tammy Rundle, and Edgar V. Epperly. 2006. *Villisca Living with a Mystery*. Los Angeles, CA: Fourth Wall Films.

Robertson, C. Laurence, Stuart Williams, Eric J. Gleske, and Christopher R. Kies. 2001. *Murder on Smuttynose*. Durham: University of New Hampshire (VHS video).

Robertson, C. Laurence. 2002. *Murder on Smuttynose: A Teacher Study Guide*, self-published, Portsmouth Athenaeum.

Robinson, J. Dennis. 1997 to present. Various articles on the Smuttynose murders published in *Portsmouth Herald, New Hampshire Gazette, Foster's Sunday Citizen* and archived on SeacoastNH.com.

Rutledge, Lyman. 1970. *Moonlight Murder at Smuttynose*. Boston: Star Island Corp. (booklet)

Sager, Joseph J. 1834. *Trial of Sager, for the Murder of his Wife. State of Maine vs. Joseph J. Sager. In Supreme Judicial Court, at Augusta, October term,1834.* Augusta, ME: Luther Severance.

Schama, Simon. 1991. *Dead Certainties: Unwarranted Speculations*. New York: Knopf.

Schechter, Harold. 2012. *Psycho USA: Famous American Killers You Never Heard of*. New York: Ballantine Books.

Schmid, David. 2005. *Natural Born Celebrities: Serial Killers in American Culture*. Chicago: University of Chicago Press.

Schriver, Edward. 1990. "Reluctant Hangman: The State of Maine and Capital Punishment, 1820-1887." *The New England Quarterly.* 63 (2): 271–287.

Shreve, Anita. 1997. *The Weight of Water*. Boston: Little, Brown.

Shultz, Suzanne M. 1992. *Body Snatching: The Robbing of Graves for the Education of Physicians in Early Nineteenth Century America*. Jefferson, NC: McFarland & Co.

Snow, Edward Rowe. 1949. *Strange Tales from Nova Scotia to Cape Hatteras*. New York: Dodd, Mead.

Songini, Marc L. 1995. *New England's Most Sensational Murders*. North Attleboro, MA: Covered Bridge Press.

Spooner, Emeric. 2009. *Return to Smuttynose Island: and Other Maine Axe Murders*. Maine: E. Spooner.

Stevens, John D. 1991. *Sensationalism and the New York Press*. New York: Columbia University Press.

Stevens, Robert, and Julia Celebi, 1992. *Murder at Smuttynose: An Integrated Critical Thinking Activity*. Unpublished: Portsmouth Athenaeum Collection.

Stout, Martha. 2005. *The Sociopath Next Door: The Ruthless Versus the Rest of Us*. New York: Broadway Books.

Stange, Eric, Melissa Banta, and Simon Schama. 2003. *Murder at Harvard*: PBS Home Video.

Taylor, Alfred Swaine. 1858. *Medical Jurisprudence*. Philadelphia: Lea & Blanchard.

Thaxter, Celia. May, 1875. "A Memorable Murder." *Atlantic Monthly*

Tucher, Andie. 1994. *Froth & Scum: Truth, Beauty, Goodness, and the Ax Murder in America's First Mass Medium*. Chapel Hill London: University of North Carolina Press.

Tuttle, Robert and Dorothy Tuttle. 2010. *Smuttynose Murder News Clipping Files and Research Collection*, Portsmouth Athenaeum.

Wagner, Louis H. F. 1874. *Report of the Trial and Conviction of Louis H.F. Wagner for the Murder of Anethe M. Christenson, at a special setting of the Supreme Judicial Court, held at Alfred, Me., June 9, 1873*. Maine: W.S. Noyes.

Wilson, Colin. 2003. *Written in Blood: A History of Forensic Detection*. New York: Carroll & Graf.

Yang, Janet, Alice Arlen, Christopher Kyle, Kathryn Bigelow, Anders W. Berthelsen, Katrin Cartlidge, Ciarán Hinds, et al. 2003. *The Weight of Water*. United States: Studio Home Entertainment.

Part II. Sources on the Isles of Shoals, Portsmouth Area, and The Sea

Baker, Emerson W. 2007. *The Devil of Great Island: Witchcraft and Conflict in Early New England*. New York: Palgrave Macmillan.

Bardwell, John D. 1989. *The Isles of Shoals: A Visual History*. Portsmouth, NH: Published for the Portsmouth Marine Society by P.E. Randall, Publisher.

Benjamin, S. G. W. 1878. *The Atlantic Islands as Resorts of Health and Pleasure*. New York: Harper & Bros.

Bigelow, E. Victor. 1923. *Brief history of the Isles of Shoals, off Portsmouth, New Hampshire*. Lowell, MA: Published by the Congregational summer conference, Star Island.

Bolster, W. Jeffrey. 2012. *The Mortal Sea: Fishing the Atlantic in the Age of Sail*. Cambridge, MA: Belknap Press of Harvard University Press.

Bolster, W. Jeffrey. 2002. *Cross-grained & Wily Waters: A Guide to the Piscataqua Maritime Region*. Portsmouth, NH: Peter E. Randall.

Borror, Arthur C. 1980. *Breeding birds of the Isles of Shoals: With Special Reference to Appledore Island*. Ithaca, NY: Shoals Marine Laboratory, Cornell University.

Brewster, Charles W. 1873. *Rambles about Portsmouth*. Portsmouth, NH: L. H. Brewster.

Brighton, Ray. 1973. *They Came to Fish; a Brief Look at Portsmouth's 350 years of History, its Local And World-Wide Involvements and the People Concerned, through the Eyes of a Reporter*. Portsmouth, NH: Peter E. Randall.

Cann, Donald, John Galluzzo, and Gayle Kadlik. 2007. *Isles of Shoals*. Charleston, SC: Arcadia Pub.

Chadwick, John White. October, 1874. "The Isles of Shoals," *Harper's Magazine*.

Clifford-Flanders family, Mollie Lee Clifford, Margaret Clifford Flanders, and Marion Lee Flanders. 1852. *Clifford-Flanders Family Papers*, Westbrook, ME: Maine Women Writer's Collection.

DeCosta, B. F. 1869. *Sketches of the Coast of Maine and Isles of Shoals, with Historical Notes*. New York.

Downs, John William. 1944. *Sprays of Salt*. Reprinted 1997, Portsmouth, NH: Peter E. Randall.

Drake, Samuel Adams. 1891. *The Pine-Tree Coast*. Boston: Estes & Lauriat.

Fagan, Brian M. 2006. *Fish on Friday: Feasting, Fasting, and the Discovery of the New World*. New York: Basic Books.

Falnes, Oscar J. 1937. "New England Interest in Scandinavian Culture and the Norsemen." *The New England Quarterly*. 10 (2): 211–242.

Faxon, Susan C., Alice Downey, and Peter Bermingham. 1978. *A stern and lovely scene: a visual history of the Isles of Shoals :* Durham, NH: University of New Hampshire.

Fowler-Billings, Katharine. 1959. *Geology of the Isles of Shoals*. Concord, NH: New Hampshire State Planning and Development Commission.

Gage, William Leonard. 1875. *The Isles of Shoals in Summer Time*. Hartford: Case, Lockwood & Brainard Co.

Gjerset, Knut. 1933. *Norwegian Sailors in American Waters; A Study in the History of Maritime Activity on the Eastern Seaboard*. Northfield, MN: Norwegian-American historical Association.

Goodman, Susan. 2011. *Republic of Words the Atlantic Monthly and its Writers, 1857-1925*. Hanover, NH: University Press of New England.

Heimel, Paul. 2002. *Oleana: the Ole Bull colony*. Coudersport, PA: Knox Books.

Hutton, Laurence, and Isabel Moore. 1905. *Talks in a Library with Laurence Hutton*. New York: G.P. Putnam's Sons.

Jenness, John Scribner. 1873. *The Isles of Shoals an Historical Sketch*. New York: Hurd and Houghton.

Kingsbury, John Merriam. 1991. *Here's How We'll do it: An Informal History of the Construction of the Shoals Marine Laboratory, Appledore Island, Maine*. Ithaca, NY: Bullbrier Press.

Kurlansky, Mark. 1997. *Cod: A Biography of the Fish that Changed the World*. New York: Walker and Co.

Laighton, Cedric, Celia Thaxter, and Frederick T. McGill. 1972. *Letters to Celia: Written During the years 1860–1875 to Celia Laighton Thaxter by her Brother Cedric Laighton*. Boston: Star Island Corp.

Laighton, Oscar. 1930. *Ninety Years at the Isles of Shoals*. Boston: Beacon Press.

Mandel, Norma H. 2004. *Beyond the garden gate: the life of Celia Laighton Thaxter*. Hanover, NH: University Press of New England.

McGill, Frederick T., Jr, and Virginia F. McGill. 1989. *Something Like a Star: A Rather Personal View of the Star Island Conference Center*. Boston: Star Island Corp.

Melville, Andrea. 2008. *An Island Kingdom a Documentary Featuring the 400 year History of the Isles of Shoals*. Vermont: Barking Spider Productions.

Metcalf, H.H. August 1914. "The Story of the Isles of Shoals" *Granite Monthly*.

Næss, Harald S., Faith Ingwersen, and Mary Kay Norseng. 1993. *Fin(s) De Siècle in Scandinavian Perspective: Studies in Honor of Harald S. Naess*. Columbia, SC: Camden House.

Openo, Woodard D. 1992. *Tugboats on the Piscataqua: A Brief History of Towing on one of America's Toughest Rivers*. Portsmouth, NH: Published for the Portsmouth Marine Society by Peter E. Randall.

Parsons, Langdon Brown. 1905. *History of the Town of Rye, New Hampshire from its Discovery and Settlement to December 31, 1903*. Concord, NH: Rumford Press.

Parton, James. 1883. *Noted Women of Europe and America... from the Most Recent and Authentic Sources*. Hartford: Phoenix Publishing Co.

Pope, Laura (editor). 2013. *Portsmouth Women: Madams & Matriarchs Who Shaped New Hampshire's Port City*. Charleston, SC: History Press.

Porter, Jane Molloy. 2006. *Friendly Edifices: Piscataqua Lighthouses and Other Aids to Navigation 1771–1939*. Portsmouth, NH: Published for the Portsmouth Marine Society by Peter E. Randall.

Randall, Peter. 1995. *Out on the Shoals: Twenty Years of Photography on the Isles of Shoals*. Portsmouth, NH: Peter E. Randall.

Randall, Peter, and Maryellen Burke. 1997. *Gosport Remembered: The Last Village at the Isles of Shoals*. Portsmouth, NH: Published for the Portsmouth Marine Society by Peter E. Randall.

Robinson, J. Dennis. 2004. *Wentworth by the Sea: The Life and Times of a Grand Hotel*. Portsmouth, NH: Peter E. Randall.

Robinson, J. Dennis. 2007. *Strawbery Banke: A Seaport Museum 400 years in the Making*. Portsmouth, NH: Published for Strawbery Banke Museum by Peter E. Randall.

Robinson, J. Dennis. 2012. *Under the Isles of Shoals: Archaeology & Discovery on Smuttynose Island*. Portsmouth, NH: Portsmouth Marine Society Press.

Rutledge, Lyman. 1972. *Ten Miles Out; Guide Book to the Isles of Shoals, Portsmouth, New Hampshire*. Boston: Isles of Shoals Association

Rutledge, Lyman. 1965. *The Isles of Shoals in Lore and Legend*. Barre, MA: Barre Publishers.

Scott, Jack Denton, and Ozzie Sweet. 1977. *The Gulls of Smuttynose Island*. New York: Putnam.

Stearns, Frank Preston. 1895. *Sketches from Concord and Appledore*. New York: G. P. Putnam's Sons.

Stephan, Sharon Paiva (editor). 2001. *One Woman's Work: The Visual Art of Celia Laighton Thaxter*. Portsmouth, NH: Peter E. Randall.

Stone, Nathaniel. 2002. *On the Water: Discovering America in a Rowboat*. New York: Broadway Books.

Sylvester, Herbert Milton. 1909. *Old York*. Boston: W.B. Clarke Co.

Thaxter, Celia, and Oscar Laighton. 1935. *The Heavenly Guest, with other Unpublished Writings*. Andover, MA: Smith & Coutts Co.

Thaxter, Celia. 1873. *Among the Isles of Shoals*. Boston: J.R. Osgood and Co.

Thaxter, Celia. 1896. *The Poems of Celia Thaxter*. Boston: Houghton, Mifflin and Company.

Thaxter, Celia, Annie Fields, and Rose Lamb. 1895. *Letters of Celia Thaxter.* Boston: Houghton Mifflin.

Thaxter, Celia. 1988. *An Island Garden.* Boston: Houghton Mifflin.

Thaxter, Rosamond. 1962. *Sandpiper; the Life of Celia Thaxter.* Sanbornville, NH: Wake-Brook House.

Tolles, Bryant Franklin. 2008. *Summer by the Seaside: The Architecture of New England Coastal Resort Hotels, 1820–1950.* Hanover: University Press of New England.

Vallier, Jane E. 1994. *Poet on Demand: The Life, Letters, and Works of Celia Thaxter.* Portsmouth, NH: Peter E. Randall.

Williams, Lois. 2006. *Religion at the Isles of Shoals: Anglicans, Puritans, Missionaries, UUs (Unitarian Universalists), and UCCs (United Church of Christ).* Portsmouth, NH: Star Island Corporation.

VISITING THE ISLES OF SHOALS

"Among the rocks, artists sketch, children play, and lovers whisper."

—James Parton, 1883

Seven of the nine Isles of Shoals are privately owned while White Island, site of the nineteenth-century lighthouse, and the attached Seavey Island are owned by the state of New Hampshire. Most first-time visitors take one of the ferries for a narrated tour around the islands. A great many return for a walkabout history tour of Star, the only island directly accessible to the public in season. Those who desire the full experience usually sign on to one of the many summer conferences and stay in the 1875 Oceanic Hotel or one of the other rustic island accommodations. Others opt for a private retreat. There are also summer educational programs in marine biology at the Shoals Marine Lab on Appledore Island. There are no public accommodations, ferries, or programmed tours of Smuttynose Island. Visitors are welcomed during daylight hours in season and usually arrive in the tiny cove via small private boats. There are no long-term public docking facilities at the Isles of Shoals, but temporary moorings in Gosport Harbor are sometimes available.

For more information contact:

- Star Island Corporation (StarIsland.org)
- Shoals Marine Lab (sml.cornell.edu)
- Isles of Shoals Steamship Company (IslesofShoals.com)
- Island Cruises aboard the MV Uncle Oscar (UncleOscar.com)
- Portsmouth Harbor Cruises (PortsmouthHarbor.com)
- Discover Portsmouth (PortsmouthHistoy.org)
- Portsmouth Athenaeum (PortsmouthAthenaeum.org)
- Isles of Shoals Historical and Research Association (ISHRA.org)
- SeacoastNH.com
- SmuttynoseMurders.com

ABOUT THE AUTHOR

J. Dennis Robinson is the author of a dozen books about American history for young readers and for adults. He writes frequently about the history of Seacoast, New Hampshire. Robinson is a popular lecturer, a steward of Smuttynose Island, and the owner of the website SeacoastNH.com. He works from a small converted garage near the swirling Piscataqua River, within sight of the state of Maine.

INDEX